Fulham

A CENTURY OF MEMORABLE MATCHES

To my wife Pauline,
whose patience and forebearance have been above and beyond.

First published in Great Britain in 2011 by The Derby Books Publishing Company Limited, Derby, DE21 4SZ.

This paperback edition published in Great Britain in 2013 by DB Publishing, an imprint of JMD Media Ltd.

ISBN 978-1-78091-295-0

Printed and bound in the UK by Copytech (UK) Ltd Peterborough

100

Fulham

A CENTURY OF MEMORABLE MATCHES

Dennis Turner

contents

6		Introduction			
8	Match 1	Fulham 0 v Tottenham Hotspur 0	58	Match 26	Fulham 2 v Millwall 1
10	Match 2	Aston Villa 5 v Fulham 0	60	Match 27	Fulham 6 v Bury 0
12	Match 3	Fulham 0 v Portsmouth 0	62	Match 28	Everton 0 v Fulham 1
14	Match 4	Bristol Rovers 0 v Fulham 1	64	Match 29	West Bromwich Albion 1 v Fulham 2
16	Match 5	Fulham 3 v Southampton 0	66	Match 30	Fulham 2 v West Ham United 0
18	Match 6	Fulham 0 v Hull City 1	68	Match 31	Fulham 1 v Wolverhampton Wanderers 2
20	Match 7	Fulham 2 v Manchester United 1	70	Match 32	Fulham 3 v Chelsea 0
22	Match 8	Fulham 0 v Newcastle United 6	72	Match 33	Fulham 3 v Manchester United 3
24	Match 9	Fulham 5 v Stockport County 1	74	Match 34	Fulham 1 v Southampton 1
26	Match 10	Fulham 1 v Chelsea 0	76	Match 35	Grimsby 5 v Fulham 5
28	Match 11	Fulham 3 v Liverpool 0	78	Match 36	Fulham 5 v Hull City 0
30	Match 12	Fulham 6 v Arsenal 1	80	Match 37	Fulham 4 v Newcastle United 5
32	Match 13	Fulham 5 v Birmingham 0	82	Match 38	West Ham United 2 v Fulham 3
34	Match 14	South Shields 1 v Fulham 0	84	Match 39	Doncaster Rovers 1 v Fulham 6
36	Match 15	Fulham 1 v Everton 0	86	Match 40	Manchester United 2 v Fulham 2
38	Match 16	Fulham 1 v Manchester United 2	88	Match 41	Manchester United 5 v Fulham 3
40	Match 17	Blackpool 4 v Fulham 0	90	Match 42	Fulham 5 v Leyton Orient 2
42	Match 18	Fulham 10 v Torquay United 2	92	Match 43	Fulham 6 v Sheffield Wednesday 2
44	Match 19	Fulham 3 v Bristol Rovers 2	94	Match 44	Wolverhampton Wanderers 9 v Fulham 0
46	Match 20	Fulham 2 v Tottenham Hotspur 2	96	Match 45	Fulham 1 v Tottenham Hotspur 1
48	Match 21	Fulham 3 v Southampton 3	98	Match 46	Bristol Rovers 2 Fulham 1
50	Match 22	Fulham 3 v Chelsea 2	100	Match 47	Fulham 5 v Sheffield United 2
52	Match 23	Fulham 3 v Derby County 0	102	Match 48	Fulham 1 v Burnley 1
54	Match 24	Fulham 1 v Sheffield United 2	104	Match 49	Fulham 1 v Burnley 2
56	Match 25	Fulham 8 v Swansea Town 1	106	Match 50	Fulham 4 v Sheffield Wednesday 1

108 Match 51 **Fulham 10 v Ipswich Town 1**

110 Match 52 **Fulham 2 v Liverpool 0**

112 Match 53 **Northampton Town 2 v Fulham 4**

114 Match 54 **Fulham 4 v Stoke City 1**

116 Match 55 **Fulham 2 v Manchester United 2**

118 Match 56 **Fulham 4 v Huddersfield Town 3**

120 Match 57 **Halifax Town 0 v Fulham 8**

122 Match 58 **Bradford City 2 Fulham 3**

124 Match 59 **Everton 1 v Fulham 2**

126 Match 60 **Birmingham City 1 v Fulham 1**

128 Match 61 **Birmingham City 0 v Fulham 1**

130 Match 62 **West Ham United 2 v Fulham 0**

132 Match 63 **Fulham 4 v Hereford United 1**

134 Match 64 **Birmingham City 3 v Fulham 4**

136 Match 65 **Fulham 1 v Lincoln City 1**

138 Match 66 **Newcastle United 1 v Fulham 4**

140 Match 67 **Derby County 1 v Fulham 0**

142 Match 68 **Fulham 1 v Liverpool 1**

144 Match 69 **Portsmouth 4 v Fulham 4**

146 Match 70 **Fulham 0 v Chelsea 1**

148 Match 71 **Liverpool 10 v Fulham 0**

150 Match 72 **Fulham 2 v Walsall 2**

152 Match 73 **Wolverhampton Wanderers 5 v Fulham 2**

154 Match 74 **Swansea City 2 v Fulham 1**

156 Match 75 **Fulham 7 v Swansea City 0**

158 Match 76 **Torquay United 2 v Fulham 1**

160 Match 77 **Fulham 3 v Doncaster Rovers 1**

162 Match 78 **Carlisle United 1 v Fulham 2**

164 Match 79 **Aston Villa 0 v Fulham 2**

166 Match 80 **Fulham 3 v Preston North End 0**

168 Match 81 **Fulham 3 v Tottenham Hotspur 1**

170 Match 82 **Leicester City 3 v Fulham 3**

172 Match 83 **Fulham 5 v Barnsley 1**

174 Match 84 **Blackburn Rovers 1 v Fulham 2**

176 Match 85 **Manchester United 3 v Fulham 2**

178 Match 86 **Chelsea 1 v Fulham 0**

180 Match 87 **Fulham 3 v Bologna 1**

182 Match 88 **Fulham 3 v Tottenham Hotspur 2**

184 Match 89 **Fulham 3 v West Bromwich Albion 0**

186 Match 90 **Manchester United 1 v Fulham 3**

188 Match 91 **Fulham 1 v Chelsea 0**

190 Match 92 **Fulham 2 v Arsenal 1**

192 Match 93 **Fulham 1 v Liverpool 0**

194 Match 94 **Manchester City 2 v Fulham 3**

196 Match 95 **Portsmouth 0 v Fulham 1**

198 Match 96 **Fulham 2 v Manchester United 0**

200 Match 97 **FC Basel 1893 2 v Fulham 3**

202 Match 98 **Fulham 4 v Juventus 1**

204 Match 99 **Fulham 2 v Hamburg SV 1**

206 Match 100 **Fulham 1 v Athletico Madrid 2**

Introduction

Newspapers and football

It may be an exaggeration to claim that newspapers are the first draft of history but they are certainly a treasure trove of contemporary life, thought and events. And in the UK, we are lucky. The range of papers available to the public has covered the entire spectrum of opinion and income, particularly since the emergence of the tabloid press at the turn of the 20th century. And the efficiency of the British Library has ensured that these papers have been preserved and are accessible today.

And, fortunately, unlike politics, crimes and other general news stories, the details of sporting events cannot be revised as more information becomes available. The results never change and so the first draft is also the last draft. The match reports from the Edwardian era can be read today as though they were written last week. Allowances have to be made, of course, for differences in language and pace but the essence of the story is all the same. And since sport was a major diversion for so many working class households, football became a staple of the tabloid press long before the quality broadsheets gave it serious consideration.

There has, nevertheless, been a major change in the way matches have been reported over the years, a change that is probably attributable to television (and very recently the internet) more than any other single factor. Today, almost everyone will not only know the result of a game but will also have had the opportunity to have seen the highlights before the paper is printed. Right up until the early 1960s, newspapers were probably still the major source of information for most football supporters. Where previously reporters often adopted a languid, even florid, style in their reports, today they tend to focus on a single event in the game or the contribution from a single player, something to give their account an edge. Charles Buchan's report on the 1936 semi-final against Sheffield United and Geoffrey Green's account of the 1958 semi-final clash with Manchester United in 1958 are journalistic masterpieces, well written, concise, informative and detailed, a style many modern reporters could never emulate.

Fulham through the eyes of the press

Allowing for the changes in the way media has covered football, the history of Fulham Football Club can be told through the stories of the major matches, which is what this book is attempting to do. The size and quality of the reports usually reflects the Cottagers' standing in football's hierarchy, and the bigger the game in a general context (FA Cup semi-final, promotion/relegation decider, European match), the better the report. But a story develops which charts the path of a club with humble beginnings that rose and fell several times over the last 100 years. In fact, the recent depths were lower and current highs higher than any that preceded them. And all the important figures in the club's history all emerge from the stories.

As well as the contemporary newspaper account, the match details, the programme cover and a brief commentary explaining the context of the game are included on each double-page spread. Reading them chronologically, the history of Fulham Football Club unfolds. And not just the good news. The big defeats as well as the record victories, the relegations alongside the promotions, are all essential milestones in the story. In virtually every case, the matches picked themselves and quite naturally are spread relatively evenly across the last 100 years or so.

Chronological spread

Taking the year the Cottagers became a first-class club, 1903, as the start point and the Final of the Europa League in 2010 as the end date, the years in-between divide easily into five distinct periods, as follows:

1 1903–15 12 seasons and 12 matches

In these initial eventful games, Fulham made their debut as a first-class club, clinched successive Southern League titles and joined the Football League. There was also the unveiling of the redeveloped Craven Cottage which was sandwiched between two exciting runs in the FA Cup. Rounding off this period were a landmark personal achievement by a striker, the first competitive fixture against Chelsea and a memorable victory over Arsenal. In these 12 matches, Fulham grew from local club with its roots in the church to one with a national reputation.

2 1919–39 20 seasons and 15 matches

The self-contained inter-war period ended for Fulham where it started, in the old Second Division, but it was a roller coaster ride in between. A major scandal, a sensational FA Cup run and then the club's first relegation followed the initial excitement of the years immediately after World War One. The Cottagers came back within four years and in the 1930s, an era of high scores and impressive personal performances, they came close to winning a second promotion, this time to the top flight, they reached a second FA Cup semi-final and recorded the all-time record attendance at the Cottage.

3   1946–75   **29 seasons and 35 matches**

For many older supporters, these were the Cottagers' halcyon years, of legendary players and great matches, which defined Fulham Football Club for subsequent generations. The bookends of the period were the first promotion to the top flight as Second Division champions and the first appearance in an FA Cup Final after so many near misses. In between were two other promotions, three relegations and two losing Cup semi-finals all involving some of the greatest names in the club's history. An era of big games, big names and big crowds ended at Wembley in 1975 and few would have predicted the long slow decline which was to follow.

4   1975–97   **22 seasons and 16 matches**

These were the darkest ages, as Fulham slipped slowly towards oblivion. Just 20 years after the Wembley appearance, the Cottagers were in 91st place in the League and contemplating life in the Conference. Virtually bankrupt, they had been threatened with a merger with QPR and looked on the brink of losing their historic home. There were three relegations and no Cup run worthy of the name in these years. The one brief interlude of hope and excitement, a promotion in 1982, promised much but was never given the chance to develop.

5   1997–2010   **14 seasons and 22 matches**

And then the tide turned, and after the darkest ages came the brightest. An unlikely promotion under a manager in his first full season tempted Mohamed Al Fayed to buy the club and what was a small, ramshackle corner shop was transformed into a west London superstore. Big transfers, stellar names and a careful rebuilding of the club's infrastructure were rewarded with two record-breaking promotions, another FA Cup semi-final and, most remarkably of all, an appearance in the Final of a major European competition. Today, only seven clubs have been in the Premier League continuously for longer than Fulham and the club is currently in its longest-ever spell in the top flight.

The competitions

This simple book tells the story in the way those at the time saw it, in the words of contemporary reporters, rather than by those with the benefit of hindsight's perfect vision. The spread of stories by competition is also a fair reflection of the club's overall history and is as follows:

FOOTBALL LEAGUE	**59 matches**
Top tier	(21 matches)
Second tier	(26 matches)
Third tier	(9 matches)
Fourth tier	(3 matches)
FA CUP	**26 matches**
FOOTBALL LEAGUE CUP	**6 matches**
EUROPEAN COMPETITIONS	**5 matches**
SOUTHERN LEAGUE	**4 matches**

The opponents

Although 73 different clubs have been involved in the 100 matches, several names appear with predictable frequency. The big names today were the big names of previous generations and matches against them brought out the best in Fulham and were the games the supporters most wanted to see.

Not surprisingly, Manchester United top the list with nine appearances. The first was a sensational FA Cup tie way back in 1908, which drew the first 40,000 crowd to the Cottage and put the Cottagers on the national football map, and the most recent in December 2009 when Fulham scored a comprehensive win over the League leaders. At both the start and end of the period covered by this book, United were the dominant force in English football and a victory over them was to be celebrated.

In second place, equally predictably, are the neighbours, Chelsea. Throughout the last 100 years, the Stamford Bridge club has always had a swagger and brashness which has rather put the Cottagers in the shade. But the six matches included in this series start and end with Fulham victories and include two other wins for the smaller club. Sadly, one of the two Chelsea wins was in the semi-final of the FA Cup in 2002.

The fact that there are five games against both Liverpool and Spurs indicates that matches against these two clubs generally involve an above-average share of drama and excitement. On two memorable occasions, in 1966 and 2007, Fulham secured season-defining victories over the Reds which helped preserve the Cottagers' top-flight status. There were, on the other hand, two League Cup defeats, one heroic and one rather less so. Spurs were Fulham's first-ever first class opponents in a match, like two other of the five, that was drawn. More than any other opponent, the matches against Spurs are included because of the quality of the game rather than the significance of the outcome.

Although a quarter of the games are against just four big clubs, smaller clubs have played as big a part in Fulham's history. Birmingham appear four times, Bristol Rovers, Portsmouth, Southampton and Swansea three times each and there are two games against both Doncaster and Hull. The series ends against Athletico Madrid, a match which highlights the remarkable road the Cottagers have taken over 100 years.

Fulham 0 v Tottenham Hotspur 0

Saturday 5 September 1903
Southern League Division One
Attendance: 14,000

FULHAM		TOTTENHAM H
Jack Fryer	1	Charlie Williams
Bill Orr	2	Harry Erentz
Ted Turner	3	Sandy Tait
Ellis Green	4	Ted Hughes
Jock Hamilton	5	Tom Morris
Harry Robotham	6	John (Leonard) Jones
Harry Fletcher	7	John Walton
Hugh May	8	John Jones
Alex Davidson	9	John Brearley
James Fisher	10	David Copeland
Everard Lawrence	11	Johnny Kirwan

Founded in 1879, Fulham progressed through a series of local competitions, and from home to home, until the pace accelerated in the mid-1890s. The Craven Cottage site was secured in 1894, and the first game played there in 1896, the same year as Fulham made their FA Cup debut. Professionalism was adopted in 1898, when the club joined the Second Division of the Southern League. These were the days when the Football League comprised just two divisions (of 18 clubs) and the Southern League was widely regarded as the Edwardian equivalent of the Third Division.

The year 1903 was pivotal in Fulham's history. Despite twice winning the Second Division and finishing runners-up once, the club missed out on promotion to the First Division of the Southern League through losing Test Matches (Play-offs). But when in 1903 Fulham became a limited liability company, the ground was revamped and 14 new players were signed, the chairman, local businessman John Dean, was able persuade the authorities that the club was ready for the top flight. Election rather than promotion was the route upwards.

Spurs were Fulham's first opponents as a first class club. Founded in 1882, the North London club had been members of the Southern League since 1896, and were champions in 1900. They had also won the FA Cup in 1901, the last non-League side to do so, and six of that Cup-winning side were in the line up against Fulham two years later. In goalkeeper Jack Fryer, however, the Cottagers had their own FA Cup star. He had played in three (losing) Finals for Derby and was the biggest name among the 14 new signings. A big man in every sense, Fryer was an outstanding goalkeeper who became club captain, a fans' favourite and an influential figure behind the scenes for the next decade. In those early days before a manager was appointed, club affairs were in the hands of Herbert (Bert) Jackson, a former player and then secretary.

SOUTHERN LEAGUE DIVISION ONE
FULHAM V TOTTENHAM HOTSPUR
A bright opening day at the new Craven Cottage

Never before in the history of football has such a large and enthusiastic crowd been seen at Craven Cottage as that which assembled to witness Fulham's first Southern League encounter since the club's promotion to the First Division. Long before the time fixed for kick-off, dense crowds had been surging around the entrance, and before four o'clock there were 14,000 spectators on the field. Curiosity as to the prowess of the new club added to the well-known record of the Spurs, brought about this brilliant 'housewarming' of the renovated ground. During the last few months, the Craven Cottage enclosure has undergone a complete metamorphosis, and undoubtedly can now rank as one of the very best football grounds in the country.

The side nearest the river and the ends adjoining and facing Bishop's Park have been banked up to afford standing accommodation for thousands of spectators, who will now be able to get an uninterrupted view of the play. Facing the river, four huge stands, each seating 300 people, have been erected by Messrs, Robert Iles Ltd of Waltham Green in a manner reflecting credit on the firm. These stands, we understand, are to be added to by the erection of a further one, which is to be completed within a few weeks. The Fulham executive showed their up-to-dateness by engaging the Borough Band to play selections both before the match and at half-time, a provision that was greatly appreciated.

As the Fulham team, headed by their famous goalkeeper, Fryer, entered the enclosure, a tremendous cheer greeted them, which was repeated for the Spurs, an indication that North country enthusiasm is spreading to the South.

Fulham lost the toss and played towards the park end and Davidson at once sent a swinging pass out to his right wing. This was a smart and clever move, and Fletcher received the ball with ready promptitude, but his middle lacked the power, and Williams had no trouble in saving. Then Spurs got clean away, and a centre by Walton was headed away when all the forwards looked dangerous.

The footwork was good and, considering the heavy rains overnight, the going was remarkably good. In the opening exchanges little of note occurred but play became fast and furious, both teams putting in all they knew. The crowd was roused to the highest pitch of excitement as May, Davidson and Fisher came charging down in a body with the ball in control and the visitors' goal was in imminent danger. The Spurs' backs, however, were all there, and after a severe tussle, the defence got the better of the deal and the ball was despatched to the other end.

Now followed some effective work by the Hotspur half-backs but the forwards hardly took advantage of their chances and Brearley, Copeland and Walton each lost fair opportunities. A nice burst to the other end saw Fletcher rouse the enthusiasm with a brilliant sprint down the touchline but just as hearts were beating with expectation, he kicked the ball too hard and the chance was lost. Some desperate work took place round the Spurs goal and but for a wonderful clearance by Williams, Fulham must have scored. Returning again to the attack, Erentz proved a little too clever for Davidson and later on Walton, with a long kick, saved the situation from a shot by Hamilton. Tottenham were prevented just in time by Orr and Turner, and the ball subsequently did a good deal of journeying, half-time arriving without either side having scored.

The second half was characterised by very fast play which occasioned many stoppages, the men being all too anxious to get every ounce out of themselves. About 20 minutes after the re-start, the visitors lost Morris, who got badly kicked on the kneecap and had to be carried off, Walton subsequently playing half.

Fulham played throughout with much dash and determination, proving that the hopes of their supporters are not groundless and though they were unable to score and the whistle sounded a pointless draw, their general play gives high promise.

Aston Villa 5 v Fulham 0

Saturday 4 March 1905
FA Cup Third Round
Attendance: 47,000

ASTON VILLA		FULHAM
Billy George	1	Jack Fryer
Howard Spencer	2	Harry Ross
Freddie Miles	3	Harry Thorpe
Joe Pearson	4	Robert Haworth
Alex Leake	5	Billy Morrison
Joe Windmill	6	Billy Goldie
Billy Brawn	7	Albert Soar
Billy Garraty	8	Bobby Graham
Harry Hampton	9	Alex Fraser
Joe Bache	10	Willie Wardrope
Albert Hall	11	William Lennie

In March 1904, Fulham made a hugely significant acquisition, persuading the highly-rated Arsenal manager Harry Bradshaw to become the Cottagers' first manager. A pioneering football administrator, Bradshaw (described as the best Arsenal manager before Herbert Chapman) was probably the most significant figure in the Cottagers' pre-1939 development. In five years at the helm, he guided teams to two divisional Championships, into the Football League, and then to the verge of the First Division and the FA Cup Final. On top of that, he also oversaw a major rebuilding of the ground, which included the iconic Stevenage Road stand and Craven Cottage, pretty much as they are today.

Although the club spent most of its first two Southern League campaigns in the comfort of mid-table, Bradshaw's team made a splash in his first season in the FA Cup. After beating Luton in the sixth qualifying round, Fulham claimed their first-ever Football League scalp when they beat Manchester United, then in the Second Division. It took three games to go through, Bobby Graham getting the winner on a Monday afternoon at Villa Park. It took another three games to dispose of Reading but Nottingham Forest, a First Division club and previous FA Cup winners, fell to a Willie Wardrope goal at the first attempt at the Cottage. Non-League Fulham were in round three, or the last eight of the FA Cup.

It was back to Villa Park for the second time that season, but to meet the mighty Aston Villa in front of a 47,000 crowd, at the time the biggest for any match involving Fulham. In the 1890s, Villa had been League champions five times and FA Cup finalists three times and were the last winners of the double before Spurs in 1961. With just three players who did not win full caps, the Villa stars were full-back Howard Spencer, defender Alex Leake and forwards Joe Bache and Harry Hampton, all England internationals. It was hard to think of tougher test for Bradshaw's team. Sadly, it was too high a hurdle for them to jump.

FULHAM'S WATERLOO

Fulham's display at Birmingham did not fulfil expectations. The Cottagers were decidedly unfortunate to catch Aston Villa at the very top of their game. From the start, Fulham seemed to crumble to pieces against Villa's most brilliant and masterful attack as well as their defence. The Cottagers' display, to say the least, was of the weakest description and extremely disappointing to the five or six thousand spectators who journeyed to the Midland town hoping to see a close and even game. In view of Fulham's remarkable record up to Saturday, it was hoped another drawn game would be placed to their credit. Five goals to nil. Fulham's great defence has been lauded throughout the season and the question that suggested itself to the minds of all was whether it would triumph over the attack of Villa. How miserably it failed is now a matter of common knowledge.

There are contributory causes no doubt, but one will have to think hard before they are discovered. It has been stated the Villa have played few games this season like that which enabled them to pass into the semi-final. Twenty minutes from the start, during which time Fulham were entirely on the defensive, Pearson made the best possible use of a free kick to open the home team's scoring account. Five minutes later, Hampton scored, receiving a deft pass from Bache. One minute from the interval, Hall scored a third. In the second half, Hampton headed the fourth goal from an overhead kick by Leake, and the fifth came from Bache. Thus were the goals scored.

The second half was chiefly notable for some really remarkable goalkeeping by Fryer. Time and again he effected some sensational clearances. He received a great ovation at the close of the game, and his display was the one redeeming feature of a game which will be long remembered as one in which Fulham were totally outclassed and hopelessly beaten.

Expertus writes: 'If I were asked to specify a worse exhibition of football than that served up by Fulham against Aston Villa, it would be difficult to do so. Under any circumstances, a 5–0 defeat wants explaining away but it was even worse than the actual result made it out to be, for had it not been for an International display of goalkeeping on the part of the lengthy Fryer, double the number of goals would have been to the credit of the Villa side at the close of 90 minutes. For Fryer, I felt the utmost sympathy. To play such a magnificent game and be on the beaten side was indeed the hardest of luck. Ross played a fairly good game, but he did not play as we know Ross can play. The defensive work thrown upon him proved too much and then, alas, he lost his temper. Thorpe was easily outwitted by the clever tactics of the Villa right wing and the halves were in poor form, not one of them playing within 50% of his proper form. As to the forwards, it is very difficult to write calmly of their display. I verily believe that had the match been prolonged for a week, a goal would not have been scored. They were slow, wanting in combination, quite afraid to go for the ball and utterly lacking in resource. Of the Villa team, I have nothing but praise. They appear to be a fine side, dexterous and wonderfully quick on the ball. The thousands of Fulhamites who took the journey had very little on which to congratulate themselves. They saw football, but not from the side they desire. Perhaps this defeat, severe as it was, will be a blessing in disguise for it will enable the Club to direct all its energies on improving its position in the Southern and Western Leagues.'

Fulham 0 v Portsmouth 0

Saturday 2 September 1905
Southern League First Division
Referee: J. Lewis
Attendance: 20,000

FULHAM		PORTSMOUTH
Jack Fryer	1	George Harris
Harry Ross	2	Roderick Walker
Harry Thorpe	3	George Molyneax
Robert Haworth	4	Thomas Bowman
Billy Morrison	5	Albert Buick
Billy Goldie	6	Edward McDonald
Albert Soar	7	Joe Warrington
Willie Wood	8	John Hunter
Frank Edgley	9	William Smith
Willie Wardrope	10	Stephen Smith
Fred Threlfall	11	Fred Cook

Few football clubs are as closely identified with their ground as Fulham and Craven Cottage. This is partly to do with location (on the banks of the Thames) and partly structure, the key elements of which date back to 1905. A court challenge to the legality of the license for the old 'Rabbit Hutch' and the opening of Gus Mears' Stamford Bridge a mile or two down the road, persuaded the board that Fulham needed to upgrade the ground if they were going to achieve their ambition of Football League status. An unknown Scottish engineer,

Archibald Leitch, was commissioned to turn the club's primitive Southern League home ground into an arena worthy of top-class football.

The work was undertaken after the closing game of 1904–05 against Brentford and the first of 1905–06, against Portsmouth, a period of just four months. The work was expensive (£15,000) but the results spectacular. The centrepiece was the Stevenage Road stand and Craven Cottage, while the other three sides of the ground were extended, properly terraced and fitted with crush barriers. Widely acclaimed at the time, the new Craven Cottage was the making of Leitch and helped define the character of Fulham FC for the next hundred years. It was a ground good enough to be used for the international between England against Wales in 1907.

For the opening game, Portsmouth, a Southern League side since 1899 and champions in 1902, were the opponents. The ground was officially opened by local MP (and club president) W. Hayes Fisher, a representative of the London Council and 'several celebrities of the football world', after a lunch in the Cottage. The match, however, did not live up to the billing, ending in a goalless draw, but these two teams, together with Southampton, were to be the strongest challengers for the Southern League title that season. It was a fortnight later, against Millwall, that the first goal was scored on the new ground, an honour that went to Fulham's mercurial winger, Fred Threlfall.

Herry Ross.

SATURDAY'S GREAT MATCH
Cottagers Draw with Pompey by 'Expertus'

Fulham's opening match was a huge success, not from the special point of view of goalscoring but in a general sense. About 20,000 paid for admission to the transformed Craven Cottage ground, and the sight of such a vast concourse must have been encouraging to the club Directors, under whose instructions during the past summer, the ground has been converted into one of the finest football arenas in the country. Amongst the spectators in the reserved part of the grandstand were Mr W. Hayes Fisher MP and Mr Timothy Davies, his political opponent. As was said in the private luncheon in the club pavilion, Fulham Football Club has progressed in a way that a few years ago would never have been dreamed of.

When the Cottagers appeared in the familiar black and white, a mighty cheer went up and the spectators devoted their attention to the preliminary movements of the players rather than the excellent music of the Fulham Borough Prize Band. Then Pompey appeared in salmon pink and white and there was another roar of applause as the cheering was taken up from one end of the ground to the other. No less hearty was the reception given to Mr John Lewis, the veteran referee, although later the crowd manifested very significantly their disagreement with some of his decisions. These exhibitions, I suppose, will always occur, but they are very undesirable.

Pompey won the toss and elected to play towards the 'Bishops'. Edgley had hardly released the ball when Portsmouth seized it. They were determined to go for all they were worth and they succeeded in the first half hour in making the pace particularly hot. They were sharp on the ball and their passing tactics did one good to behold them. The forward quintet decidedly 'took the eye' and when they sent a warning shot over the net, they were heartily cheered. They evidently meant going for all they were worth and the question was how long they would stay. Two or three corners fell to them but when Lee got in a shot, Thorpe was ready for him and sent him to the rightabouts. The Fulham backs soon showed their real form, and the tackling and clean kicking of Ross and Thorpe were only equalled by the cool, studied tactics of Fryer in goal.

Half an hour at high pressure was enough for Portsmouth. They slacked off considerably with the result that Fulham, who had plenty of reserve energy, became dangerous. Let it not be thought that Portsmouth were not alive to all possibilities. W. Smith, one of their best men, dodged the Cottagers with wonderful success but Thorpe baulked him and Fryer cleared with celerity. When Fulham forwards had any chances, they were not slow at this stage in securing them, and were well backed up by Morrison and his comrades. Soar justified his selection at outside right. His speed was a great advantage to him, and it was not long before he was sending in a few of those smart centres of which he is so capable. If his work did not bring goals, it was not his fault. After delivering a good swinging well-judged centre, his duty for the moment was over.

In the second half, Fulham showed decidedly better form and there was real hope they would pull off the two points. Threlfall's clever wing work compelled admiration but Wardrope laid himself open to criticism for missing what appeared to the crowd one of the very few chances of the day. The forward attack was stopped for a time when Warrington at the other end got perilously near and struck the Fulham goalpost, but Threlfall took up the fun again by sending in a fine shot at short distance which struck the top corner of the goal.

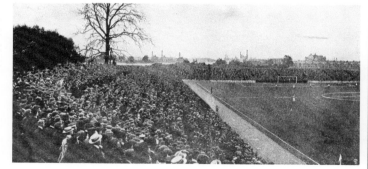

When these two were hotly attacking, the ball shot into the goal and there were loud cheers but the referee ruled no goal and the crowd were not slow in showing their disappointment at that decision. Soar had centred and Harris had partly saved when Wardrope and Threlfall ran in to head the ball through. But the goalkeeper missed it and the ball fell to Wardrope. The referee decided that the goalkeeper had been impeded. Soar and Threlfall continued to put in smart work. Edgley deserved to score when he twisted the ball round cleverly towards the net.

Just at the end, Portsmouth warmed up for a final effort and a cross by S. Smith was dangerous. Fryer ran out and stumbled and then had to go further in his endeavour to clear. Things looked highly dangerous and it was surprising that the Portsmouth forwards were not able to take advantage of an almost deserted goal get through. However, the danger passed and the game ended with neither team having scored a goal.

Bristol Rovers 0 v Fulham 1

Saturday 21 April 1906
Southern League First Division
Attendance: 6,000

BRISTOL ROVERS		FULHAM
Arthur Cartlidge	1	Jack Fryer
Hugh Dunn	2	Harry Ross
Richard Pudan	3	Harry Thorpe
Tom Tait	4	Pat Collins
Ben Appleby	5	Billy Morrison
Billy Hales	6	Billy Goldie
Billy Clark	7	Mark Bell
John Lewis	8	Walter Freeman
William Beats	9	Alex Fraser
Billy Gerrish	10	Willie Wardrope
Gavan Jarvie	11	Fred Threlfall

Despite the expenditure on the new Cottage facilities, there was still enough money to strengthen the playing squad. Bradshaw's most important acquisition was a 23-year-old right-half from Leicester Fosse, Arthur Collins, known to the supporters as Pat or 'Prince Arthur'. A dapper Edwardian dandy, Collins formed an outstanding half-back line with Scotsmen Billy Morrison and Billy Goldie, which was the backbone of the side for several seasons. Another key recruit was winger Fred Threlfall (right), a wonderfully extravagant but erratic ball player who had been Billy Meredith's deputy at Manchester City. Willie Wood, the scorer of one of Bury's six goals against Jack Fryer in the 1903 Cup Final, and Frank Edgley from Sheffield United were also signed.

Bradshaw's team came good virtually from the start of the season. It was not until November and the 10th game that they were beaten and at the halfway stage at Christmas, Fulham headed the table, three points clear of Southampton. There was, inevitably, a bit of a wobble. At the turn of the year, a defeat at Portsmouth and two draws checked the Cottagers' progress but then just one defeat in the final 14 games brought the Championship to SW6. The visit to Bristol clinched the title with a game to spare. Fulham finished five points clear of second place Southampton and seven ahead of Portsmouth in third.

It was a remarkable campaign. Only three games (out of 34) were lost and just 15 goals conceded. Only once was more than one goal scored against Fulham in a game and Wardrope was top scorer with 13 goals. Although Bradshaw used 23 players that season, eight of them played in at least 30 of the matches (Fryer, Ross, Thorpe, Collins, Morrison, Goldie, Wardrope and Threlfall). Crowds flocked to the Cottage and the 25,000 attendance for the visit of Spurs was bettered anywhere in the country that day only by the Merseyside derby. Fulham FC had arrived.

Fred Threlfall.

FULHAM THE CHAMPIONS
Holders of the Shield Defeated
By 'Expertus'

After being held by provincial clubs for the past five seasons, the Southern League shield will soon repose at Craven Cottage. The win over Bristol Rovers on their own ground made the Championship certain. That the shield has not been won by the forwards, I think, we all admit. The defence have been the sole cause of victory. The winning game at Bristol was a record in as much as never before have the Cottagers beaten the Rovers on their own ground. It is a notable fact that Fulham's position in the table has advanced by a double leap in two seasons. In 1903–04, their position was 11th. In 1904–05, they rose five places to sixth and this year the same increase of five places has given them the Championship. There will be 'sounds of the revelry by night' tomorrow at the Holborn Restaurant, with both the Southern and London League shields on view. And the Directors richly deserve their success. They spent a large sum of money in improving the ground and erecting stands worthy of the name, and the public have appreciated it. The Directors have catered for the football-loving public and have had their reward.

The referee was a dapper little man, reminiscent of a jockey. As he shook hands with Fryer, he looked up and Fryer looked down, and the contrast in sizes was so amusing that laughter as contagious as a Cork accent seized on the crowd, and we all had a hearty good laugh, the only laugh of the afternoon.

The game with the Rovers was a good one and although a high wind was blowing across the ground and a veritable dust storm swept across the enclosure, yet the game was worth watching. The Fulham team was only different from the previous week by the inclusion of Freeman in the place of Mr Wheatcroft at inside-right. The Rovers started with great dash and determination but the Fulham defence was more than sufficient to keep them out of the net. In the first few minutes, the home team forced three corners but it was a pleasing sight to see the excellent defence put up by the Cottagers. Collins was in his best form and the neat footwork he is so fond of was again prominent. Morrison, too, was a tower of strength, and his head popped up in the most unexpected places. After the visitors' defence had been extended by the pushful Rovers, the Cottagers found their feet, so to speak, and made tracks for the vicinity of Cartilidge. About a quarter of an hour had passed when Freeman helped with his head a free kick from Threlfall into the net. It was a simple goal, but both teams found themselves unable to repeat the performance.

After Freeman's goal, the Rovers monopolised play for the greater part of the time, but Fryer gave one of the best exhibitions he has given on 'foreign' soil', and proved himself a past master of resource. After the interval, Fulham's forward line put more vim into their work and pressed hard. Fraser hung on to the ball a little too much and should have passed out to Freeman more often but the game was on the whole a good one. It did become furious, so did the mob who howled like Furies, barracking Threlfall, Collins and Morrison and the unlucky referee. Three times did the Rovers crew demand penalties but the referee was obdurate. Once only was one possibly due, when Goldie handled. The sun was so bright, the wind so fierce and eddying that the referee evidently decided – and rightly so – that the handling was accidental.

Bell was the best forward with Wardrope with a close second. Freeman worried the Rovers very much and was really centre-forward. Fraser lay back too far. He was sometimes yards behind Freeman and Wardrope. Threlfall was irritatingly variable spoiling much sincious thrusting work by spells of inertness. Goldie was the glory of the half-back line. Morrison shone with fierce light in defence. Collins was excellent, not perhaps up to his highest excellency. Thorpe showed fine nervy strength, tackling cleanly and well and footing the ball with judgement. Ross was a tough and dour defender.

So the Championship of the Southern League in 1905–06 has been won by Fulham's persistent efforts. It is a splendid success, gained at the third time of asking. Nor can envious rivals cavil at the mode of winning since the club has fairly out-distanced all other pretenders to the proud position. Thus after six years, the Shield returns to London. Right well you have done Fulhamites, and the warmest and most sincere congratulations are hereby tendered to all concerned, Directors, Manager Harry Bradshaw and all their merry men.

A. COLLINS

Fulham 3 v Southampton 0

Saturday 20 April 1907
Southern League First Division
Attendance: 16,000

FULHAM		SOUTHAMPTON
Jack Fryer	1	George Clawley
Harry Ross	2	Jack Eastham
Harry Thorpe	3	Joe Hoare
Pat Collins	4	John Robertson
Billy Morrison	5	Frank Thorpe
Billy Goldie	6	James Bowden
Bert Kingaby	7	Edward Bell
Walter Freeman	8	Frank Jefferis
Bobby Hamilton	9	Walter Radford
Jimmy Hogan	10	Sam Jepp
Fred Threlfall	11	Fred Mouncher

Far from being complacent following the title success, Bradshaw was again active in the transfer market in the 1906 close season. He signed skilful Scottish international inside-forward Bobby Graham from Glasgow Rangers (later a Lord Provost of Elgin), full-back Ted 'Taffa' Charlton, who was still playing for Fulham after World War One, and Bert 'Rabbit' Kingaby, a winger from Aston Villa, the subject of a later landmark legal battle with the football authorities over transfers.

Although the title race was closer than the previous year, Fulham again emerged as champions. The margin this time was just two points, and the Championship was confirmed at home to Southampton in the penultimate game, which clashed with the FA Cup Final at Crystal Palace. But with just five defeats in 38 games, few could deny the Cottagers' claim to top spot. They were more adventurous in 1906–07 than in the previous season, scoring and conceding more goals – an extra 31, although there were four more matches. It was the home record which again provided the foundation of the success. At the Cottage, Fulham were beaten just once and collected 31 from a possible 38 points.

The team virtually picked itself, with 12 of the 21 players used by Bradshaw appearing in more than half the games, and 10 (Fryer, Ross, Collins, Morrison, Goldie, Kingaby, Fraser, Hamilton, Freeman and Threlfall) featuring in two thirds. Of the 10, only the injured Fraser missed the decisive game against the Saints. The visitors were without their leading scorer, Fred Harrison, but outside-left Fred Mouncher was in good form. Both would be Fulham players within nine months.

This second title success was celebrated by another bash at the Holborn Restaurant and brought to an end the non-League phase of Fulham's history. The final game, at West Ham, was lost, 4–1, the second time that season the Hammers had put four past Jack Fryer. The only negative about the title-clinching victory over Southampton was an injury to the great goalkeeper and captain, which effectively ended his first-team career.

Billy Morrison: the Cottagers' rugged but effective, centre-half.

CHAMPION COTTAGERS
Southampton Routed At The Cottage

Fulham made absolutely certain of the Southern League Championship by their fine victory over Southampton on Saturday. Had Fulham lost and Portsmouth won their two outstanding matches, it would have been necessary to decide the Championship on goal average. Such an unsatisfactory task has been avoided and, come what may, Fulham will enjoy a lead of two points over their great rivals. The Cottagers well deserve this honour, as not only have they played consistently throughout the entire season but they have wound up the campaign in brilliant style, and have not lost a League match since 26 January, and no less than 14 goals have been scored in the last half dozen matches. Now, only one match remains to be decided, the fixture with West Ham at Boleyn Castle, and bearing in mind the fact that the Hammers have twice defeated Fulham this season, it is as well that the Cottagers do not depend in any way on that match, especially now that Fryer has been incapacitated.

The big counter attraction at the Crystal Palace had an effect on the attendance at the Cottage on Saturday. The homesters played the same team which has performed so well in recent matches while the Hampshire men had to utilise the services of five reserves.

It was somewhat of a coincidence that the captains of Fulham and Southampton should both be custodians, and Clawley received a hearty handshake from Fryer. The famous Southampton goalie is always a favourite at Fulham. The homesters took matters into their own hands quite early in the game and soon demonstrated their superiority, Hogan almost doing the trick within a minute of the commencement. The home forwards played in good form, and were almost always in the vicinity of Clawley, but they failed to successfully steer the ball past the goalie, who defended in a style worthy of his great name. Just before the interval, Hamilton came within an ace of doing the needful from a centre by Kingaby following a free kick. Unfortunately for Fulham, his shot struck the cross bar and the chance was lost, the first half being drawn.

The second half saw a change come over the game. Fulham still continued to have all the best of the game but whereas all their efforts before the interval were unproductive, now the home forwards suddenly developed goal-scoring tendencies. Hamilton led off with a goal from a centre by Kingaby. It was a really fine shot and Clawley had no chance with it. Threlfall nearly did ditto a moment later, and then a clever individual burst by Freeman was crowned with success, taking the ball right up to Crawley and easily netting. A third soon followed from a penalty kick which Harry Ross converted. There was every probability of the score being increased so frequently did the Fulham men attack, and Hogan worked terribly hard to score his usual goal, but the fates were against him and Fulham had to be content to complete their home League engagements with a victory of 3–0.

Fulham 0 v Hull City 1

Tuesday 3 September 1907
Football League Division Two
Attendance: 14,000

The Cottagers' Journal.
OFFICIAL JOURNAL OF THE FULHAM FOOTBALL CLUB.
Edited by "MERULA."

PRESIDENT ... W. HAYES FISHER, ESQ.

Directors: Messrs. W. G. ALLEN, J. DEAN, E. D. EVANS, A. F. FOULDS, W. HALL, H. G. NORRIS (Chairman), and J. C. WATTS. Secretary-Manager: H. BRADSHAW.

No. 1, Vol. I.   SATURDAY, AUGUST 31, 1907.   One Penny.

FULHAM		HULL C
Leslie Skene	1	Martin Spendiff
Harry Ross	2	George 'Tot' Hedley
Archie Lindsay	3	John McQuillan
Pat Collins	4	George Browell
Billy Morrison	5	William Robinson
Billy Goldie	6	David Gordon
Bob Dalrymple	7	Joe Smith
Walter Freeman	8	Jack Smith
Fred Bevan	9	Joe Shaw
Archie Hubbard	10	Arthur Temple
Fred Threlfall	11	Edwin Neve

From the Board Room.

In presenting our official Programme in its new and enlarged form, under the more dignified title of the "Cottagers' Journal," we venture to express the hope that it will be welcomed as an improvement upon that of last season.

We could have wished that it had been possible to dispense with any advertising matter, but the cost of production is so heavy that to make it pay (and we frankly admit that we have sufficient of that much-abused commercial instinct as to desire that it should pay), advertisements are, at any rate for the current season, an absolute necessity. If, however, the sales during the season should be such as to warrant it, the space devoted to reading matter will be materially increased next season, and still further improvements added, it being our desire to make this Journal as necessary to the Fulham public as are the actual matches.

Even in its present form it challenges comparison with that issued by any other London club.

It is with more than ordinary pleasure that we are able to announce that the services of "Merula" have again been retained as Editor for the season, and in this connection it may be stated that this brilliant writer has an entirely free hand. In other words, he does not write "to order," nor are his weekly notes submitted to anyone connected with the club prior to their publication in this Journal.

Before we leave the matter of the Journal, may we mention that we have made arrangements whereby a copy will be posted to any address in England each Friday night for an inclusive sum of 4s. for the full season, or any single copy for 1½d. It is thought that this innovation will be an advantage to those who cannot attend every week and yet desire to keep themselves acquainted with the current topics of Fulham in particular and the League in general. Instructions for such copies must be made to Mr. Bradshaw at Craven Cottage.

Since the close of last season the Club has withdrawn from the Southern League on its election to the Second Division of the English League, a step which we believe has met with the almost unanimous approval of the club's supporters. The change has entailed an enormous cost in the matter of transfer fees, but we are hopeful that compensation will be forthcoming in the increased attractiveness of the matches.

Having regard to the long distances the players will be called upon to travel during the season, we have thought it desirable to withdraw from the Western League, a loss in revenue which we hope will be made up by larger attendances at the Saturday matches.

The Reserves will take part in the South-Eastern League and Premier Division of the London League, and having regard to the calibre of the players who will be taking part in these matches, we earnestly appeal for a large measure of your support.

We are especially grateful for the gratifying financial success which attended the playing of our practice matches. The new Putney Hospital and other local charities will benefit largely in consequence. It is another illustration of the old proverb, "Many can help one, where one cannot help many." Mention of this proverb reminds us that it can again be brought into practice by responding to the invitation appearing on the front cover of this Journal. We shall hope to hear from many friends during the week.

Craven Cottage will next Saturday be visited by Queen's Park Rangers. Kick-off, 3.30 p.m.

THE DIRECTORS.

Fulham's reward for two Southern League title wins was election to the Second Division of the Football League in 1907, in place of Burton United. Despite the objections of Chelsea, Chairman Henry Norris garnered 28 votes at the League's AGM, enough to ensure the Cottagers became the fourth London club (after Arsenal, Chelsea and Clapton Orient) to play in the growing national competition.

Rather bizarrely, it all began for Fulham at 5.00pm on a Tuesday evening and the opening match was against Hull City at the Cottage. Manager Harry Bradshaw, an inveterate dabbler in the transfer market, signed half a dozen new players, most of whom had top class experience. But he kept faith with his captain Harry Ross, the superb half-back line of Collins, Morrison and Goldie, and with popular winger Fred Threlfall. Bradshaw brought in Scottish international goalkeeper Leslie Skene since Jack Fryer was still injured, he strengthened the defence with the signing of full-back Archie Lindsay from Reading and among the forwards, Bob Dalrymple, once of Portsmouth and Glasgow Rangers, was the most significant acquisition. He continued his transfer activities as the season progressed.

Although the Hull result was not the debut the club had hoped for, it did not take the Cottagers long to find their League feet. The first win came four days later, at Derby, and against Chesterfield in October they rattled in five goals and six against Gainsborough the next month. The signings of centre-forward Fred Harrison and left-winger Fred Mouncher from Southampton in November added extra firepower to the attack and by Christmas the team had a more settled look.

By early spring, Fulham were among the promotion contenders, but a late stumble meant they had to settle for fourth place. At the same time, they were the season's FA Cup giant killers, falling in the penultimate round. It was exactly 50 years before they were to do as well in both competitions in the same season again – a very impressive debut.

DASH BEATS SKILL

Dash beat skill in the first Second League match played at Craven Cottage and Fulham open the season in the gloom of a maiden defeat. Just eight minutes after the start of a match destined to produce the abortive industry of the cleverer side, one John Smith, a nimble footed, quick brained inside-right of Hull City, profited by a mistake on the part of the new Fulham left-back, Lindsay, worked through into a position and won two points with a pretty shot that left Skene helpless. There were 82 minutes left for play but the mathematics of football is a law unto itself, and what was done in eight minutes could not be equalled in 10 times as long.

Hull City deserved a victory, if any victory is deserved which depends on the failure of the cleverer side to substantiate its skill. It may be said of the losers that some of the players are new, but the play is still Fulham's. For long portions of this game, the ex-Southern Leaguers overwhelmed the Northerners in what is commonly known as the science of the game. That branch of the sciences does not matter. In the science of goal-making, Fulham were left derelict. They repeatedly suffered 'hard lines': there were groans of dismay culminating in despair, but there were no goals.

The visitors were good winners. Though the superior value of their dash over Fulham's finesse was no doubt founded on the moral stimulus of the lead, the fact remains that they scored a good goal and by good defence prevented an equaliser. Luck, of course, was on their side. So much is almost tacitly understood in reference to a victory for a visiting side. However sound may be a defence that is often subjected to severe pressure, its success must to a certain extent be influenced by that form of luck which comes with the failure of the other side to consummate its good work. Much of the work of Fulham was good and would generally have been recognised as such had the accident of scoring operated in its favour.

On the other hand, much was, if not bad, certainly not good. Before Fulham become a thoroughly practical side, Bevan must be planed down into a square. This Bevan, who has played for Manchester City, Reading, Queen's Park Rangers and most recently for Bury, is a clever footballer but his cleverness is of that circumlocutory character which is generally regarded as a Scottish fault. Bevan is not Scottish, but his football is. And it is the worse for being so.

It would be unkind, not to say unfair, to saddle any one man in the Fulham team with the blame for yesterday's defeat – if, indeed, defeat be an offence, but I cannot help thinking that the kind of football played by Bevan communicated wrong ideas to the other forwards. The best of the forwards were Freeman and Dalrymple on the right wing. The latter is as good a right winger as Fulham want, and it is conceivable that if Fulham are to get goals, most of these will originate on the wing. Hubbard did not do as well as, to judge by his methods, he is capable of doing, while Threlfall retains all his old merits and all his old faults. If Threlfall could finish as he begins, he would be a very fine footballer. Unfortunately for him, finishing is more important than beginning.

For the rest, there is no cause for pessimism. Skene lacks inches but he is a goalkeeper throughout and the back and halves will no doubt settle down into that harmonious organisation which was the secret of Fulham's Southern League success. If Lindsay did not play up to his Reading form, those credentials are re-assuring and, in any case, the club has, in Charlton, a reserve right-back of at least equal merit.

In the long run, skill beats dash, but yesterday was only the second day of the football season, and Hull pluck beat Fulham science. It will not always be so, and one of these early days when science wins, dash will be held up to opprobrium and denounced as 'wildness'.

Fulham 2 v Manchester United 1

Saturday 7 March 1908
FA Cup Fourth Round
Referee: T. Kirkham
Attendance: 41,000

FULHAM		MANCHESTER U
Leslie Skene	1	Harry Moger
Harry Ross	2	George Stacey
Archie Lindsay	3	Herbert Burgess
Pat Collins	4	Dick Duckworth
Billy Morrison	5	Charlie Roberts
Billy Goldie	6	Alex Bell
Charlie Millington	7	Billy Meredith
Bob Dalrymple	8	Jimmy Bannister
Fred Harrison	9	Jimmy Turnbull
Alex Fraser	10	Sandy Turnbull
Fred Mouncher	11	George Wall

The Cottagers' Journal.

OFFICIAL JOURNAL OF THE FULHAM FOOTBALL CLUB.

Edited by "MERULA."

PRESIDENT ... W. HAYES FISHER, ESQ.

Directors: Messrs. W. G. ALLEN, J. DEAN, E. D. EVANS, A. F. FOULDS, W. HALL, H. G. NORRIS (Chairman), and J. C. WATTS. Secretary-Manager : H. BRADSHAW.

No. 27, Vol. I. SATURDAY, MARCH 7, 1908. One Penny.

From the Board Room.

FULHAM, 1; LEEDS CITY, 0. One more rung of the ladder has been ascended, and we have now but five matches to play away from home, namely, Gainsboro', Glossop, Hull, Blackpool, and West Bromwich. Our matches at home are against what would generally be considered stronger opponents. Let us name them : Clapton Orient, Wolverhampton, Leicester Fosse, Stockport, Stoke, and Bradford City.

Promotion will necessarily depend, not only on the successes we ourselves may gain, but on the failures of our competitors. Assuming a fair measure of success attends us in the near future, the match at Craven Cottage on the afternoon of Good Friday promises a record League attendance. Our match at Leeds was not altogether a pleasant one, for once again the climatic conditions were all against accurate football. It is very singular that so many of our away matches have had to be played, not only in a high wind, but upon muddy and sloppy grounds. It is true that the victory was a narrow one; that is, on paper, for on the actual play we were good value for a much more decisive win than is indicated by the actual score. The accident to Threlfall was most regrettable. We use the word "accident" advisedly, for we have no complaint to make on the score of rough play, or anything of that sort. It is a pity that the forward line which has done duty for so many weeks must undergo a change, and that at a time when every effort is necessary both in the League and Cup. However, we can only accept the conditions as they are, and hope for the best.

At the time of writing these notes we cannot with any degree of certainty state the formation of the front line, but the probability is that Millington will be given a trial at outside right, with Fraser at inside left. We do not like the idea of transferring such a good shot as Millington has proved himself to be over to the wing, but Fraser is essentially an inside forward, and is unable to do either himself or his team justice in any other position.

Our Reserves had a big victory over Hitchin in the South-Eastern League on Saturday last, and were also successful on Monday against Tottenham Hotspur, although by the narrow margin of a goal to nil.

Next Saturday our Reserves will be playing at home to Hastings and St. Leonards, also in the South-Eastern League, and on the same day the League team will be away at Gainsboro'.

Early dates will doubtless be found for the return matches at Craven Cottage against Clapton Orient and Wolverhampton Wanderers, the latter being strongly fancied as

If one match can be said to have put Fulham on the national football map, it was this sensational victory over Manchester United, even then one of the dominant sides in the country. This was the second of nine FA Cup ties between the clubs from 1905 to 2009, and was the last which Fulham won. It was by some distance the Cottagers' most famous victory in the period up to 1915.

At the time, United led the First Division (and eventually won the title) and were strongly tipped for the double. Their team contained a magnificent all-international half-back line (of Duckworth, Roberts and Bell), the legendary Billy Meredith on the wing and the prolific Sandy Turnbull up front. Fulham, Second Division newcomers that season and underdogs, had disposed of the

highly fancied Manchester City of the top flight in the previous round to reach the last eight for the second time in three years. Such was the interest in the game and the attraction of seeing United in London, that the tie drew the first-ever 40,000 Cottage crowd to the Cottage, an attendance record which stood for nearly 20 years. The report ignored the goals, which were scored by Harrison (12th and 65th minutes) for Fulham and Jimmy Turnbull (55th minute) for United.

After the game, the two teams, plus the players' wives, and directors and officials of both clubs, went to the Alhambra in Leicester Square. There, they were fed and watered, listened to several speeches, watched highlights of the game courtesy of the Alhambra's 'elaborate bioscope' (still a novelty) and enjoyed 'a smoking concert' of song and verse. The large audience viewing the film apparently 'gave vent constantly to its pleasure by rapturous applause and was thrilled by the incidents so truthfully and clearly set forth'.

In his speech, manager Bradshaw (who was said to be 'in a happy and optimistic mood') confessed that 'these Cup ties cause me a great deal of anxiety and worry' but none of the players 'suffered from anything more serious than could be removed by the agency of a good hot bath'.

FULHAM'S FIGHT ON THE ROAD TO THE PALACE

In a way that has won the praise of all London, and amid scenes of enthusiasm without parallel in the history of local football, Fulham on Saturday beat Manchester United, the talented leaders of the First League. The victory, which astonished the football world, was witnessed by 40,000 people and was obtained under circumstances as exciting as any which marked past Cup fights. By tactics, Fulham overthrew the artistic Mancunians. It was a match that thrilled, a victory that gave to London the pleasure of the knowledge that the Metropolis has doughty candidates for honours in the Final of the FA Cup. In pursuance of their win, Fulham meet Newcastle in the semi-final in view of which struggle special preparation will be undergone by the clever players under Ross at Southport. All Fulham is endeavouring to believe that Craven Cottage will have its representatives at the Crystal Palace.

Following out the advice I gave my readers, I turned up at Craven Cottage at 2.45pm, expecting to find a good number of people on the ground three quarters of an hour before the kick-off. The term 'a good number' seems rather funny now for there must have been about 25,000 present. And still they came rolling in their thousands. And what a crowd it was too! It was seething with excitement – that tense, strained excitement which grips the nerves and makes the blood gallop through the veins.

In strong contrast to the general demeanour of the crowd was the bearing of the Fulham lads when they tripped into the playing arena. Every one of them was self-possessed and quietly confident. In addition to this they were all in the pink of condition and prepared for a most strenuous, exhausting game. The most robust man in the team on all occasions is Harrison. His conduct on Saturday was most noteworthy and valuable, for he took advantage of many of the openings presented to him, some of which he utilised to deadly effect.

As to the game itself, it was won not so much by what the Fulham forward line did as by what the Fulham defence prevented the Manchester front line from accomplishing. Fulham went on to the field with a perfectly matured plan of campaign. Every man in the half-back and back lines and Skene in goal knew exactly what they had to do in order to spoil the Manchester attack and he did it for all he was worth. The Fulham forwards did the rest.

Let it be said at once that the front line of Manchester showed itself to be all that has been said during the past season but it ran up against a stronger defence than it has yet encountered. Both Wall, the clever and dashing international outside left, and Turnbull were made to look quite ordinary by Arthur Collins. And that 'giant' Meredith was made to appear quite harmless by tenacious Billy Goldie and Lindsay. In fact the 'bottling up' of Willy Meredith was one of the features of the match. Manchester United is still 'the team of all the talents' but in Fulham they met an inspired team – a clever team, a dashing go-ahead side and on the run of the afternoon's play they were beaten, deservedly so.

When Harrison came to the Cottage from Southampton he opened rather weakly and his play was not very convincing. However he has improved out of all knowledge and has shown magnificent form. On Saturday he plied his wings with well-judged passes, always placed himself in an advantageous position to receive the ball and worked like a Trojan. He has a very clever trick of catching the ball on the bounce, neatly lifting it over the head of an opponent and then dashing off for goal at full speed. This ruse came off quite a number of times.

Dalrymple and Mouncher both played capital games, Millington was nothing like the same 'gent' at outside right as he is at inside-left and Fraser was not a great success. Ross and Lindsay both acquitted themselves well and Morrison simply revelled in hard work. Morrison is a fine fellow and should be a joy to any club. I have praised Skene on so many occasions that I have exhausted my stock of adjectives.

When the final whistle went the huge crowd sent up a deafening roar of pent up joy and delirious enthusiasm. Hundreds of people rushed across the playing pitch and most players took prudence by the hand and ran off into the dressing room. Ross and Harrison were caught and despite the efforts of several burly policemen, the enthusiasts insisted on shouldering these players from the field to the dressing room.

Fulham 0 v Newcastle United 6

Saturday 28 March 1908
FA Cup Semi-final (at Anfield)
Referee: J.T. Howcroft
Attendance: 50,000

FULHAM		NEWCASTLE U
Leslie Skene	1	Jimmy Lawrence
Harry Ross	2	Bill McCracken
Archie Lindsay	3	Dick Pudan
Pat Collins	4	Alex Gardner
Billy Morrison	5	Colin Veitch
Billy Goldie	6	Tom Willis
Jimmy Hogan	7	Jock Rutherford
Bob Dalrymple	8	James Howie
Fred Harrison	9	Bill Appleyard
Charlie Millington	10	Finlay Speedie
Fred Mouncher	11	George Wilson

Beating Manchester United in the fourth round was as good as it got for Bradshaw's men. The draw for the semi-final was the hardest Fulham could have had. While Second Division Wolves (a team the Cottagers beat in the League four days after the semi-final) and non-League Southampton met in the other tie at Stamford Bridge, Fulham were paired with Newcastle United, the true aristocrats of Edwardian football. The Magpies were League champions three times in five years and FA Cup finalists on five occasions in seven seasons between 1904 and 1911. On the day at Anfield, the Cottagers were outclassed and did well to finish second. The 6–0 scoreline remains to this day the biggest winning / losing margin in the semi-final in the history of the FA Cup.

English Cup Semi-Final, 1908.
Newcastle United (6) v Fulham (0)
Appleyard opens the scoring.

Despite their comfortable semi-final win, Newcastle, the hot favourites, were beaten 3–1 by Wolves in the Final at Crystal Palace.

The Newcastle side was the most star-studded of the era. In virtually every position was a player of international quality, although the majestic wing-half Peter McWilliam was missing through injury. Goalkeeper Jimmy Lawrence, still holder of the Magpies appearances record, colourful full-back Bill McCracken, the cultured centre-half and captain Colin Veitch and the gifted 'Gentleman' James Howie at inside-forward were the biggest names on the United side and far more illustrious than any in the Cottagers line up.

For Fulham, the exciting but unpredictable winger Fred Threlfall was missing through injury. His deputy was Jimmy Hogan, a future Fulham manager (1934–35) who was to become a pioneering coach across much of Europe. This was his final appearance as a player for the Cottagers. This result started a semi-final jinx on Fulham that lasted nearly 70 years. Following further defeats at this stage in 1936, 1958 and 1962, the club held the unwanted record of most semi-final appearances without reaching a Final until John Mitchell's late, late goal at Maine Road in 1975 ended the sequence.

English Cup Semi-Final, 1908.
Newcastle United (6) v Fulham (0)
"just saved."

FULHAM'S LAST CUP-TIE
INGLORIOUS DISPLAY AT LIVERPOOL

Fulham mourned on Saturday. The Cottagers' cup of sorrow was full to the brim at Liverpool. All hopes of Fulham sending representatives to the Crystal Palace to compete in the Final for the possession of the FA Cup were dissipated. Never before had Fulham gone so far in the great national competition, and so well had Mr Bradshaw's lads performed against opponents of presumed superiority, that there were ardent Fulham people unwilling to entertain thoughts of defeat. To them, to all Fulham, Saturday's result at Liverpool came as a rude shock.

Fulham's distress

Reproducing their best form, Newcastle United toyed with the much-vaunted Fulham defence, and got Ross and his men in such difficulties that the Cottagers were well beaten at the interval and humbled at the end of 90 minutes play. It was not pretty football with which Fulham sought to meet the masterly United artists. It was not the well-planned, smooth-working game that the Cottagers have so frequently presented at their riverside ground. Fulham were painfully effete, their combination ragged, their attacks came with snatches. That was Fulham on Saturday, the Fulham that had its eyes on the Cup, the Fulham whose interesting policy was to capture the Cup and promotion in the same year.

Pace, dash and skill wanted

Disappointing in every way, with the exception of Skene, who often earned the applause of the unbiased crowd, Fulham were completely outplayed. They lacked pace, dash and skill, never combined effectively, and were really outclassed. The absence of Threlfall, for whom Hogan appeared at outside right, could not be regarded as any excuse for their failure and Newcastle also had to make a change in their side, an injury preventing M'William from playing, Willis completing the half-back line.

Considering to what extent Newcastle monopolised the play, they were never quite satisfactory but an obvious cause for the poor football was the state of the ground. Rain had fallen more or less throughout the week until Saturday morning, when hot sunshine and a fresh breeze was not sufficient to dry the turf which, heavy as it was, handicapped the players less than might have been expected. The mud did not cling and the conditions improved as the afternoon advanced, but were always adverse to a good exposition of the game.

Newcastle were mainly indebted for their victory to the excellence of their halves and the grand work of M'Cracken who, with the useful help of Pudan, made such an able defence that the Fulham forwards seldom looked dangerous. With the game going their way, the Newcastle forwards had constant opportunities, but never showed much cleverness in dribbling or passing. Appleyard and Rutherford were the most conspicuous so long as Fulham made a fight and in the later stages all five men worried an enfeebled defence but the United attack did not make a great impression as a winning combination.

Newcastle's goals

The game opened quietly and, after Lawrence had handled in the first few minutes, a series of attacks on Fulham's goal took place. Newcastle, though facing the sun in a fresh breeze, set the pace and held the upper hand. Speedie and Appleyard soon brought Skene's cleverness into evidence, but the centre-forward missed one clear opening right in front of goal. A mistake by Ross in the goalmouth was rectified and then the football became extremely dull until the Fulham forwards enlivened matters. Then, with the improvement of their opponents, the Newcastle men roused themselves. Speedie and Rutherford each dropped the ball into goal and, from a free kick, Appleyard headed through.

For the remainder of the first half the Fulham defence was severely tried. Goldie cleared a centre by Rutherford, but Howie racing up shot very hard, Skene getting the ball but failing to keep it out of the net. Appleyard should have increased the score before the interval, but with two goals to the good, Newcastle could feel quite confident on resuming. Their third point came from a free kick, Ross stepping aside at the last moment and the ball going direct into the net off a post when Skene obviously expected his colleague to clear. With the game as good as over, Rutherford scored again with a long shot, a low left foot free kick by Howie took effect, and just on time, Rutherford ran down the centre and brought the score up to half a dozen.

Excuses

Fulham could urge excuses if ever a beaten side could. It must be remembered that brilliant Leslie Skene, almost the only man to play up to the occasion, was beaten four times when badly injured. It was a particularly offensive foul that Appleyard committed and Skene, after receiving an ugly dig at the ankle, was in terrible pain. Ross had spent two days in bed nursing a cold during the week, Collins was not his usual great self whilst Hogan was but a shadow compared to Threlfall. Millington of all the forwards was the most progressive.

Few had anticipated a display so wholly unpalatable to the South, and the result was a crushing disappointment to the many followers of the Riversiders. The defeat was startling in its decisiveness. Yes, Fulham was sad – very sad – on Saturday night.

Fulham 5 v Stockport County 1

Saturday 5 September 1908
Football League Division Two
Referee: J.G.A. Sharpe
Attendance: 25,000

FULHAM		STOCKPORT C
Leslie Skene	1	Jimmy Molyneux
Ted Charlton	2	Bert Elkin
Archie Lindsay	3	Arthur Waters
Pat Collins	4	Peter Proudfoot
George Parsonage	5	Fred Burden
Bob Suart	6	Tom Galloway
Fred Threlfall	7	Tommy Green
Bob Dalrymple	8	James Hodgkinson
Fred Harrison	9	Billy Martin
Harry Brown	10	Jimmy Settle
Bert Lipsham	11	John Horrocks

After the excitement of the previous three seasons, life at the Cottage settled down in 1908–09, in what was to prove manager Harry Bradshaw's final season. In the League, 37 points from 38 games earned Fulham 10th place out of 20 clubs, and in the FA Cup, the club went out in the second stage to Spurs at White Hart Lane. In the close season, he declined the offer of a new contract preferring to become Secretary of the Southern League.

But there was something special that year, and it occurred in the second game, at home to Stockport. Fred Harrison, the 28-year-old centre-forward, had made an immediate impact when he was signed the previous November for £1,000. He scored 12 goals in 24 League appearances, as well six FA Cup goals in six games, including both in the famous win over Manchester United. Born in Winchester, Harrison (or 'Buzzy' as he was nicknamed) began with Southern League Southampton, and scored 87 goals in 160 outings for the Saints. He played for the South against the North in an international trial in 1904, but out of position and never won a full cap.

Several clubs were interested in this fast, robust forward with the fearsome shot, but Bradshaw got there first. At the Cottage, Harrison formed an effective striking partnership with Bob Dalrymple, the two scoring 98 goals between them in the four seasons they played together. Harrison was the first Fulham player to get to 50 first class goals. He managed five of them against Stockport in September 1908, a club League record that has been equalled (by Beddy Jezzard, Jimmy Hill and Steve Earle) but never beaten. The achievement drew no special mention in the next Fulham programme.

In April 1911, Harrison moved to West Ham and then Bristol City before ill-health forced his retirement. He, nevertheless, signed up in World War One, and was badly gassed. He recovered, however, to run a plumbing business in Southampton and was 89 when he died in 1969.

FULHAM'S FIVE
Plethora Of Goals At The Cottage

Scoring five goals, whilst their opponents answered only once, Fulham on Saturday played a game none-too-full of the scientific before 25,000 spectators. They were Harrison's goals, all five. The ex-Southampton lad who has, it goes without saying, never done anything like it before, was in rare scoring form, and clever indeed would have been the custodian to save any of the stinging little shots which he directed with such effect on Saturday. Apart from this record-breaking feat, the game had little else that was interesting and exciting. The score, although officially 5–1, was properly 5–2. We have to blame the referee there. That Mr Sharp ruled according to his firm belief is a proposition negatived by the fact that he had to consult his linesman before he gave his verdict after little Hodgkinson's marvellous effort.

* * * * * *

It was this movement by the small Stockport forward – who last year beat the Fulham goalkeeper – that formed one of the cited incidents of the play. Skene was undoubtedly beaten by Hodgkinson's shot, which followed a clever run by his irrepressible opponent. 'A yard over the line' was the judgement readily, and I believe unerringly, given by the judges near the goal. They screamed their just objections when the referee gave a decision adverse to the visitors.

* * * * * *

Generally the play was fast, but the work of the home lot was not the convincing action of a team with pretensions to true Championship form. I liked Threlfall, I liked Lipsham, we all liked Harrison and his style. Of the rest, Dalrymple was only clever on occasions and Brown rarely pleased his most prejudiced admirers. At half, all was different. The line was from left to right the trio of men who smash up powerful attacks and get on with forward work instantly that one associates with the history of the Cottage. Charlton was the better – a distinct first – of the backs, and of Skene, little can be written except in praise.

* * * * * *

Fulham have had to utilise 16 players to win two points. There were five men in the team against Stockport County who did not play against Glossop three days previously. The names of the five were Lindsay, Parsonage, Suart, Threlfall and Brown, and every man of them distinguished himself. Parsonage might fairly be regarded as the best man on the field, and this despite the remarkable performance of Harrison. The latter was in his best form. He was always in his place when wanted, and to this fact is due three of the goals he scored, for accurate centres from Lipsham and Threlfall only required his intelligent application of the necessary force.

* * * * * *

Fulham's first goal was decidedly lucky. Dalrymple took a shot from twenty yards, the ball struck Harrison's head and was deflected into the net. Three minutes from the finish a penalty was given against Parsonage for a technical offence, and Proudfoot hit the post with the kick. Two minutes later, Martin scored a smart goal for Stockport. The score was flattering to Fulham, but at the same time the home side was undoubtedly strong. Charlton played a fine game, while the wings had splendid support on either side. The Fuham right wing was a little stronger than the left. Elkin, an ex-Fulham man, played well at left-back for Stockport, and Proudfoot was the best half. The forwards formed the most promising portion of the team, with Hodgkinson and Martin the most enterprising.

Fulham 1 v Chelsea 0

Saturday 3 December 1910
Football League Division Two
Referee: H.S. Bamlett
Attendance: 30,000

FULHAM		CHELSEA
Arthur Reynolds	1	Jimmy Molyneux
Ted Charlton	2	Walter Bettridge
Jimmy Sharp	3	John Cameron
Pat Collins	4	Fred Taylor
Fred Maven	5	English McConnell
Bob Suart	6	Ben Warren
James Smith	7	Billy Brawn
Wattie White	8	Robert Wittingham
Bob Dalrymple	9	Evan Jones
Arthur Brown	10	Vivian Woodward
Willie Walker	11	Marshall McEwan

Edited by WILKINS MICAWBER.

PRESIDENT—W. HAYES FISHER, Esq., M.P.
DIRECTORS—Messrs. W. G. ALLEN, E. D. EVANS, A. F. FOULDS, W. HALL (Chairman), and H. G. NORRIS.
SECRETARY-MANAGER—P. KELSO.

No. 18. Vol. IV   December 3rd,   One Penny.

CASUAL NOTES
From the Board Room.

It was not a cheerful result which came across the wires last Saturday afternoon—a defeat by five goals to one requires a deal of explaining away, and we are not at all sure that the task—if it can be so called—is not beyond us. The fact of the matter is, Wolverhampton won because they played football the better suited to the conditions—6 in. at least of snow covered the ground, and short passing never looked like spelling goals. At the same time, the score exaggerated the play the last two goals being scored during the last few minutes, when Smith, our outside-right, was lying unconscious in the dressing room.

To-day we meet our neighbours—Chelsea—for the first time in League warfare, and whatever the result, feel assured the game will be a good one, strenuous, earnest, but played in that spirit of comradeship which

should always distinguish good players. Only one side can win, and in that event, one must lose. We hope we shall not lose.

Next week we shall be playing away, so far as the first team is concerned, Clapton Orient being our opponents and Homerton our destination. This will be another very hard match, and we hope as many as possible will travel across London to give that vocal encouragement which means so much.

On Monday, we meet Tottenham Hotspurs at Stamford Bridge in the Final of the London Cup. Kick-off, 2.30 p.m. This should be another attractive match. We hope to retain the Cup for another year.

To-day we are making our annual collection on behalf of the Fulham Soup Kitchen. Year by year, the amount collected has been increased, but this year, all records should be broken. Remember, that every penny means more than a meal to our less fortunate brothers and sisters. We thank you all in anticipation.

THE DIRECTORS.

The first of Fulham's most local of derbies did not take place until 1910. Over the next 100 years it was an irregular feature of the two clubs' fixture lists since they have spent more time in different divisions than the same one. In addition to the four FA Cup and two League Cup meetings, the Cottagers and the Pensioners/Blues have met in 32 League campaigns. In every other season, at least one division separated the clubs, and only once, in 1962–63, were the Cottagers in a higher division than their neighbours. While West London bragging rights over the series as a whole belong at the Stamford Bridge end of the Fulham Road, at least Fulham managed to open the exchanges with a win.

'Today we meet our neighbours for the first time in League warfare, and whatever the result, feel assured the game will be a good one, strenuous, earnest, but played in that spirit of comradeship which should always distinguish good players.' This was the understated

message in the Fulham programme for the game, omitting completely the background which gave some added spice to the occasion.

In 1905, when Fulham were still in the Southern League, entrepreneurial builder Gus Mears offered his new ground, Stamford Bridge, as a home to Fulham, for an annual rent of £1,500. When Fulham indicated they would prefer to stay at the Cottage but give their home a substantial facelift, Mears responded by starting his own team. Unsurprisingly, it was a little irritating to the senior club in the locale when the young upstarts by-passed the Southern League and gained entry to the Football League the year they were formed. Chelsea's first-ever competitive match was in Division Two of the Football League, and by the time Fulham joined, Stamford Bridge was hosting top-flight football.

Relegation meant the two clubs met in 1910–11, with the opening exchange at the Cottage, a match watched by a crowd of 30,000. An even bigger crowd (45,000) saw Chelsea win the return 2–0 in April and the season's honours were shared.

Fulham's international full-back Jimmy Sharp who later played for Chelsea.

SATURDAY'S HOMERIC CONTEST
By 'Ghee Whiz'

Candidates for Parliamentary elections don't always keep their appointments, but when the fulfilment of a promise comes immediately before the election, it stands a good chance of being made good. Thus both Mr Hayes Fisher, the Unionist, and Dr Sylvain Mayer, the Liberal, were as good as their word in the matter of attending the match on Saturday. Mr Hayes Fisher took up a good position in front of the press box but so far is sport removed from political circles, that not more than half a dozen seemed to recognise Fulham's sitting member. Dr Mayer replied in the affirmative to a question by a sporting elector as to whether he would, if asked, 'kick-off in the Fulham versus Chelsea match'. Needless to say, however, the spectators were not vouchsafed the pleasure of seeing Dr Mayer in the forward line of either team. He occupied a seat in the stand some little distance behind his political opponent who is, of course, President of Fulham FC.

The game was fought out with keenness which made it almost appear like a Cup tie. Although the Fulham turf was in really good condition considering the weather, the light was bad at the start and got considerably worse. When the game was yet young and the light good, Chelsea led strongly, and it seemed that the game was going well their way, and Reynolds was called on once or twice to meet the famous Chelsea forwards face to face. In fact, Fulham were really fortunate in not to have one goal scratched up against them in the first 15 minutes.

Smith Scores For Fulham

Within 20 minutes of the start, however, Fulham put up the first goal through the perseverance of Smith – easily one of the most useful men on the ground – who shot well but not very hard into Molyneux's charge. The Chelsea custodian got almost behind the shot, but not quite, and it bounced away from him. The Fulham winger, following up his shot, charged in and easily drove the ball into the net to the great delight of a large portion of the crowd. After this, the Cottagers began to repair their ranks somewhat. The defence gained greatly in reliability, and the check which the Chelsea forward line experienced was very noticeable. To see the Woodward-McEwan combination well held by Charlton, Collins and Co was indeed a sight worth noting.

Molyneux's Marvellous Save

If Molyneux was slightly faulty in his treatment of his first really trying shot – that from Smith – he made ample atonement for it by his treatment of an attack which came from Harrison. Mavin originated the movement by a long pass out to White, who sent the ball on to Harrison. The centre took it on up the field and drove it splendidly a little wide of the Chelsea goalkeeper. By a wonderful effort, however, Molyneux got down to the shot and stopped it by some means or other. This ended the first half and the second was not very eventful. There was a good deal of scrambling on Chelsea's part, for the team, hampered by the failing light yet consumed by the flame of rivalry, could accomplish very little by concerted movement. Fulham, apparently well content with their 1–0 lead, played cannily, their defence never giving the aggressors a ghost of a chance.

A Strange Closing Incident

Of the Chelsea forwards, Jones, who again acted as the pivot man, and Brawn on the right wing, were the only men who were really effective, and for them even, the half-backs made the effect of the bad light worse by passing the ball forward in the air in a rather disconcerting manner. Whittingham was occasionally brilliant in an individual way, and it was on one of those rare occasions – about 10 minutes from the call of time – that a rather strange and totally unexpected incident occurred. Whittingham was swiftly working his way into the Fulham province when in collision with Brown, he was seen to fall forward with considerable force. The referee, Mr Bamlett, rightly or wrongly, awarded a penalty kick and Whittingham, who took it, put the ball straight into the net, while the crowd roared approval. But then the whistle blew, and amid a mystified silence, Mr Bamlett indicated the position for the kick to be re-taken, but Whittingham, who again officiated, was not so lucky a second time. He drove over the crossbar and howls of triumph and disappointment arose from the crowd. The referee's reasons for his judgement were, I am told, that Brawn had encroached too soon on the penalty line.

The Result

It is in no way detracting from Fulham's victory to say that Chelsea had the luck of the day against them. Molyneux's slip was largely luck, as was Whittingham's shot in the first half which struck the crossbar. But the worst turn of luck was the accident which befell Taylor, that the sturdy half. Chelsea certainly have some scrap of consolation and explanation for the result, but it must be admitted that Fulham are a team of solid worth and merit.

Fulham 3 v Liverpool 0

Saturday 3 February 1912
FA Cup Second Round
Attendance: 30,000

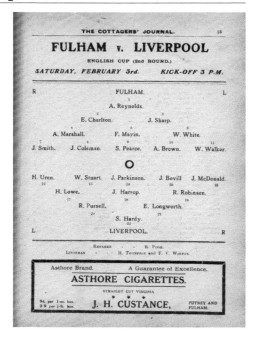

FULHAM		LIVERPOOL
Arthur Reynolds	1	Sam Hardy
Ted Charlton	2	Eph Longworth
Jimmy Sharp	3	Bob Pursell
Alf Marshall	4	Harry Lowe
Fred Maven	5	Jimmy Harrop
Wattie White	6	Robbie Robinson
James Smith	7	Jack Parkinson
Tim Coleman	8	Harold Uren
Bert Pearce	9	John McDonald
Arthur Brown	10	John Bovill
Willie Walker	11	Jimmy Munro Stewart

After the epic run to the semi-finals in 1908, the FA Cup generated little excitement at the Cottage, for several years the club failing to get beyond the last 32. But, in 1912, there was a promising run which was ended in the quarter-finals by an emphatic defeat by West Brom, who were to be beaten in the Final by Barnsley. Despite losing heavily twice in the League that season to Burnley, Fulham managed to overcome the Clarets in the first round of the Cup to set up their first-ever meeting with Liverpool.

League champions in 1906 and runners-up in 1910, Liverpool were an established top-flight club and with the likes of goalkeeper Sam Hardy, full-back Eph Longworth and centre-half Jimmy Harrop in their line up, had some of the outstanding figures in English football of their day. At Fulham, manager Phil Kelso, who had succeeded Bradshaw in 1909, was gradually re-fashioning the team. Arthur Reynolds had taken over the goalkeeping role, a position he made his own for 15 years, full-back Jimmy Sharp was re-signed, Fred Maven took over the centre-half berth and in local discovery Bert Pearce and the nomadic Tim Coleman, Kelso had found a potent strike pairing. He also signed England international inside-forward Arthur Brown whose move from Sheffield United to Sunderland in 1908 was for a world record fee of £1,600.

In his six full seasons before World War One, however, Kelso's sides flattered to deceive, and were regular occupants of a mid-table position. The FA Cup offered little more. In the whole of his long tenure (he retired in 1924), this run to the last eight was the best, and this win over Liverpool one of only two victories over a First Division side. This result remains Fulham's best against the red side of Liverpool. In next round, non-League Northampton were beaten 2–1 at Cottage before the Cottagers fell to the Throstles at the Hawthorns.

Goalkeeper Arthur Reynolds, first choice from 1910 to 1925 and for 420 games.

LIVERPOOL IN THE DOLDRUMS
(By Invicta)

The first meeting of Fulham and Liverpool will not be remembered with any feelings of joy by the followers of the latter club. Except for a period midway in the first half, when the Liverpool men's somewhat unwieldy methods met with a measure of success, there was never any real doubt as to Fulham's superiority.

With the exceptions made in favour of Longworth, M'Donald and Parkinson, not a player in the team showed the zest in the game and fire and continuity of effort which makes up what is known as real Cup-tie football. Bovill and Harrop did some effective work, but hardly in the Cup-tie spirit – to judge by external evidence. Where the difference was most notable, however, was in the respective forward lines.

The Fulham forwards had not only more dash and purpose, but individually they were cleverer than their visitors, and on the wings their superiority was most pronounced. It took the players some time to get at home on the iron-hard surface. M'Donald led a few attacks upon the Fulham goal, but the luck of the game was illustrated in the movement which produced Fulham's first goal.

Walker made a sort of speculative drive into the middle and midway between the goal and the centre line. The ball went straight to Pearce, who drew Purcell and tipped the ball obliquely forward for COLEMAN to take it on the run. The inside-right was splendidly placed. He shot as Hardy ran to meet him – the only hope – and the ball just touched the goalkeeper's hand in its progress to the net.

Liverpool's erratic marksmen

This goal was scored after 15 minutes of play, and it seemed to spur the visitors but their shooting was too bad for words. M'Donald had a glorious chance, and kicked the ball wildly to the corner flag. Bovill shot wide twice but he got in one lovely drive from 20 yards out, which had the ill-luck to be aimed straight at Reynolds. The first corner of the match fell to Liverpool just after the interval. It was splendidly taken by M'Donald, and, with Reynolds misjudging the flight of the ball, the ball lay for some seconds at the mercy of the assaulting party – but in vain.

Then Fulham had a corner and, as Walker swung the ball in, PEARCE threw himself forward and headed into the net, tumbling head over heels after it. Liverpool made another spurt, but there was not much heart in it and after COLEMAN had missed one chance, he made amends by meeting a centre from Walker and driving it obliquely across Hardy into the side of the network.

Except from a partisan standpoint, the game was not of a high standard of interest. There is always something unreal about a match played on a frost-bound ground. Liverpool have been described as a team of ups and downs. They must have had one of their worst fits of the 'downs' on Saturday and, for the sake of their supporters, it is to be hoped their form was too bad to be true.

Longworth stands alone

Longworth's display was one of the redeeming features. His kicking was true and he was usually to be found where the fight was the thickest. Criticism of the Fulham defenders must be modified by a recollection of the shortcomings of the opposition. James Sharp, however, opposed to Liverpool's better wing, gave a splendid display. Of the three effective half-backs, Mavin deserves special mention, though Marshall also did good work as a spoiler.

Although Coleman scored two goals, the forward honours go to Pearce, who was always a bit too fast and clever for the men opposed to him – Longworth excepted. Walker, nicely nursed by White and Brown, did a lot of good work, and it should not be forgotten that he was directly concerned in each of the three goals scored.

Fulham 6 v Arsenal 1

Saturday 8 November 1913
Football League Division Two
Referee: J.F. Pearson
Attendance: 30,000

FULHAM		ARSENAL
Hugh McDonald	1	Joe Lievesley
Ernie Coquet	2	Joe Shaw
Jack Houghton	3	Joe Fidler
Pat Collins	4	Matthew Thompson
Harry Russell	5	George Jobey
Wattie White	6	Angus McKinnon
James Smith	7	Jock Rutherford
Tim Coleman	8	Jack Flanagan
Bert Pearce	9	Stephen Stonley
Will Taylor	10	Wally Hardinge
Willie Walker	11	Thomas Winship

Centre-forward Bert Pearce, a local boy, who formed an effective striking partnership with Tim Coleman.

Over the last century or so, Fulham's links with Arsenal have been closer than with any of the other London clubs. The Cottagers' first manager, Harry Bradshaw, for example, was recruited from the Gunners and his successor at the Cottage, Phil Kelso, had also succeeded him at Plumstead. After them, another seven Fulham managers up to and including Malcolm Macdonald could include spells at both clubs on their CVs. In addition, the traffic of players in both directions was heavier than with almost any other club.

And it might have been even closer if Fulham director and briefly chairman Henry Norris had had his way. Norris, a local builder and sometime Mayor of Fulham and Conservative MP for Fulham East, was one of the key movers when the club became a company in 1903 and joined the Southern League. Although remaining on the Cottagers' board, his interest moved in the direction of south London and a near-bankrupt Woolwich Arsenal, then playing at Plumstead. He took over the ailing Gunners and proposed a merger between the two clubs, which was rejected by Fulham and the authorities. Thereafter, his focus was on Arsenal. He moved the club to Highbury and his appointment after World War One of Herbert Chapman as manager ushered in the Gunners' first era of success. By then, Norris had been banned from football for financial irregularities.

Bizarrely, Norris remained on the Fulham board while chairman of Arsenal. He therefore had a foot in both camps when the clubs first met in a League game in 1913 following the Gunners' relegation the previous April. (They had met in the FA Cup in 1904.) The Cottagers' key men in this comprehensive victory were the strike pair of Tim Coleman, a much-travelled England international and ex-Gunner, and local boy Bert Pearce. In the three seasons they played together, the two accounted for 96 of Fulham's 170 goals. They got four of them in that afternoon against Arsenal.

ARSENAL OVERWHELMED AT FULHAM
Sensational scoring in the second half: seven goals in half an hour

Lovers of sensational football had the treat of their lives at Craven Cottage on Saturday, for seldom are seven goals scored within half an hour as they were in the Second League match between those keen London rivals, Fulham and the Arsenal. The high position of both clubs in the table, coupled with the dual interest possessed by Messrs HG Norris and W Hall as directors of both clubs, led many to anticipate a draw, but although the match was of a very friendly nature and fought with good feeling on either side, there was nothing in the nature of a family party about it. It was a genuine sportsmanlike exhibition, with well-matched teams striving their utmost for mastery, but when after a barren hour of keen but not very exciting football, the luck changed. Fulham showed no mercy to their North London 'relations', but absolutely revelled in piling on the agony.

* * * * * *

The Cottagers are capable of great things, but they are a team of moods, and it happened to be the Gunners misfortune to find them right bang on top of their form in the last half hour. It was the smart opportunism of Coleman, himself an ex-Arsenal man, who turned the visitors' mistakes into good account for Fulham. Then came the mishap to McKinnon who, after hobbling about for a few minutes in great pain, retired to the dressing room. While the injured man was being attended to, the spectators and players witnessed the evolutions to two aeroplanes returning from the race to Brighton. Whether Fulham obtained special inspiration from that upward vision or not, they certainly played like a team inspired subsequently and with the Arsenal defence demoralised, carried all before them.

* * * * * *

The first half was as strenuously fought as anyone could wish. The Arsenal, although their attack was somewhat disjointed, were more dangerous in the early stages and, had they scored, it might have made a vast difference to the result. One or two centres were fraught with considerable danger to Fulham and served to demonstrate what a fine custodian Fulham have found in McDonald, another old Arsenal man, to take the place of the injured Reynolds. It was as well for Fulham that they had such sturdy defenders as Collins, who was making his first appearance in the first team after an injury in August practice, Coquet and Russell.

* * * * * *

Even before the interval, the shooting of the home forwards was the more dangerous, and Lievesley did well to save shots from Coleman, Pearce and Taylor, but neither of his saves equalled that of McDonald when he prevented Rutherford from scoring, or again when he was on his hands and knees trying to frustrate the efforts of Flanagan and Stanley. The former did in fact backheel the ball in front of an empty goal but no Arsenal man was ready to take advantage of a gilt-edged chance. Just prior to the interval, Walker all but scored for Fulham, but the blank score at half-time was a fair reflex of a closely fought half.

* * * * * *

The second half was full of sensations, as within a minute of the restart, Pearce shot wide when right in front of goal and Taylor struck a post with a rasping shot. Then the scene changed with kaleidoscopic rapidity, for Fulham attacked with such fury that they were irresistible and a perfect avalanche of goals followed in almost bewildering succession, so fast that one's powers of mental arithmetic were severely tested. The change began when Fidler missed his kick and let in Coleman who darted to the right like a flash of lightning and, shooting with equal rapidity, had the ball in the net before Lievesley suspected what was happening. Another Arsenal defender blundered trying to prevent Pearce from getting to a centre from Walker three minutes later, and the Fulham centre promptly put the ball over for Coleman to find the net for a second time.

* * * * * *

The basis of Fulham's success was thus laid before further misfortune befell the Arsenal in the injury which compelled McKinnon to withdraw from the arena, and against the depleted defence, the Cottagers were all-powerful and literally overwhelmed their opponents. After Pearce had almost shattered the bar with a terrific shot, Taylor netted with a fine shot. Goal followed goal with a frequency that left the spectators gasping, for hardly had Walker headed in a delightful centre from Smith, than Pearce did ditto to a centre from Walker and Fulham enjoyed the surprising lead of five goals. By and by, the Arsenal forwards tried to redeem their reputation and eventually some smart play by Winship and Hardinge culminated in Stonley beating McDonald. However, Fulham replied once more, and Pearce brought the scoring up to half-a-dozen before the whistle sounded for the finale.

Fulham 5 v Birmingham 0

Friday 25 March 1921
Football League Division Two
Referee: J.W.D. Fowler
Attendance: 40,000

FULHAM		BIRMINGHAM
Arthur Reynolds	1	Stanley Hauser
Ted Worrall	2	Billy Ball
Alec Chaplin	3	Jack Jones
Harry Walker	4	Joe Roulson
Jimmy Torrance	5	Alex McClure
Joe Edelston	6	Percy Barton
Billy McDonald	7	Lawrence Burkinshaw
Danny Shea	8	Johnny Crosbie
Barney Travers	9	Joe Lane
Donald Cock	10	Harry Hampton
Frank Penn	11	Edward Linley

The 1920s was a lost decade for Fulham. Tainted by scandal and marked by managerial instability, most of the time was spent in an ultimately unsuccessful fight against relegation. The best of those years came immediately after World War One when manager Phil Kelso put together a side that was attractive to watch and which looked as though it could mount a serious promotion challenge. His team contained some pre-war veterans, such as goalkeeper Arthur Reynolds and half-back Jimmy Torrance, and some wartime discoveries like full-backs Ted Worrall and Alec Chaplin, striker Donald Cock and winger Frank Penn (who was to spend 50 years at the Cottage as a player and trainer).

Into the mix, Kelso added some very shrewd signings. From West Ham for a nominal fee, he signed the 33-year-old inside-forward Danny Shea, an England international who had commanded the world's first £2,000 transfer fee when he moved from West Ham to

Blackburn in 1913. Despite his veteran status, Shea was still an exciting and individual talent who became a crowd favourite. After captaining Aston Villa's 1920 FA Cup winning side, double international Andy Ducat joined Fulham when he refused the club's demand to move to Birmingham. From Manchester City, Kelso recruited wing-half Joe Edelston, who remained at the Cottage for most of the interwar period. Finally, he paid a club record £3,000 for centre-forward Barney Travers in February 1921, the scorer of 19 First Division goals for Sunderland the previous season.

The 1920–21 campaign started badly for the Cottagers, with just three wins in the first 15 games. But a run of six wins in seven games following Travers' signing (he scored eight of Fulham's 14 goals in that sequence) took the club into mid-table. On Good Friday, divisional leaders (and eventual champions) Birmingham were the visitors to the Cottage and the huge crowd was treated to as good a display as Fulham were to put on in Kelso's final five seasons after World War One. It held out the prospect of much more the next year but it all unravelled in a most unexpected way.

Wartime discovery Frank Penn, who spent 50 years at Fulham as a player and trainer.

The Fulham team for the visit of Birmingham. Left to right, back row: Walker, P. Kelso (manager), J. Dean (director), Worrall, Reynolds, Torrance, Kinnear (trainer), Edelston, Bagge, T. Walker. Front row: McDonald, Shea, Travers, Cock, Penn, Chaplin

FULHAM'S BEST WIN
Birmingham endure record defeat
By Corinthian

Good football, blessed with fortune which was not bad when the ball was near to goal, gave Fulham a victory which was seemingly overwhelming against Birmingham. The winners deserved to get the two points but of course they were not five goals the better side.

Quite early in the game, Travers, the home centre-forward, sent in a splendid low shot which Hauser could have been forgiven for missing, and right away those who have watched Fulham's good midfield play and rather indifferent efforts around goal thought something might happen in the way of a surprise.

Then Torrance tripped Lane when the latter looked like getting through and from the penalty kick which was correctly awarded, Jones failed to score. The kick was a very hard one, but not so well placed as it might have been, and Reynolds distinguished himself by saving another penalty. By the way, Birmingham have missed seven penalties out of nine this season.

When The Scoring Started

Fulham had the reward of fine play 35 minutes after the start, when Cock, from a perfect pass by Travers, ran through. Jones could do nothing more than 'niggle' at Cock with slight shoulder flips in the back as the inside-left raced towards goal. Cock's shot sent the ball upwards into the net.

Within three minutes after that, Penn sent across a nicely judged centre which went to Travers but the latter, realising that Shea was better placed for shooting, allowed the ball to go on to the inside-right. Shea gauged the ball to an inch and putting all his kicking force behind it, gave Hauser no chance to save – a cool effort which was greatly appreciated by the spectators.

Then McDonald took a corner which sent the ball to Travers' head from whence it went into the net, leaving the Birmingham goalkeeper unsighted by the sun. Thus Fulham led by three goals at half-time.

In the second half, Birmingham did better, but lost two more goals. Travers made a good pass to the wing and McDonald promptly centred, which enabled Fulham's good centre-forward to race straight on to the ball and bang it into the net. After that, Shea snapped another opportunity and sent a shot which was so well placed that Hauser could only get his fingers to the ball – but could not stop it.

Fulham At Their Best

This defeat does not blight Birmingham's chances of promotion, for the result merely means that the Midlanders caught Fulham at their best, and any Second Division club which is in that unfortunate position must expect defeat. Fulham were thorough in their methods, and no one did better than Reynolds. This goalkeeper never made anything like a mistake and it is due to the losers to write that they were clever enough to compel some of the very best of goalkeeping in order to avoid a score.

Travers has made a great difference to the Fulham team. He has instilled a spirit of virility into the attack which has been lacking and his feet (I am told he can do something like 10.5 seconds for the 100-yard dash), dashes and robust charging, always fair, had the effect of putting the Birmingham defence off their game.

It was a victory well won but Birmingham can do better. This was, however, the biggest defeat Birmingham have experienced this season.

South Shields 1 v Fulham 0

Saturday 18 March 1922
Football League Division Two
Attendance: 12,000

SOUTH SHIELDS		FULHAM
Willis Walker	1	Arthur Reynolds
Mickey Ridley	2	Tom Fleming
Alf Maitland	3	Alec Chaplin
Jimmy Metcalfe	4	Andy Ducat
John Hardy	5	Jimmy Torrance
Dave Hutchinson	6	George Martin
Andrew Gray	7	Scotty Kingsley
Jackie Smith	8	Danny Shea
Ernie Simms	9	Barney Travers
Jos Hetherington	10	Jimmy Croal
George Keenlyside	11	Harvey Darvill

Behind this very small report is a very big story. With 10 games of the 1921–22 season left, Fulham were in fifth place, four points behind Stoke in the second of the two promotion spots, and serious contenders. Next on the agenda was a trip to the north east, to meet South Shields (later Gateshead) at Horsley Hill. It was a crucial game, which the Cottagers lost 1–0. Almost immediately afterwards, however, stories began to circulate that an attempt had been made by a Fulham player to fix the match. The next day, the FA had set up a joint commission of enquiry with the Football League which met for just 90 minutes in London on the Monday after the game. The commission, whose deliberations were in camera, included the former referee, John Lewis, the man in charge of Fulham's first game at the rebuilt Craven Cottage in 1905.

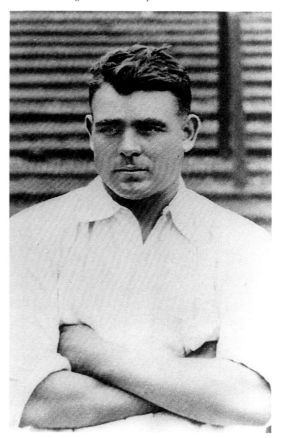

It was three weeks before the result was announced, on 8 April, the morning of the England–Scotland international. The verdict was a lifetime suspension for Fulham's star centre-forward, Barney Travers. Signed from Sunderland for a club record fee of £3,000 just 13 months earlier, Travers had been an effective and popular striker. He had travelled to the north east the previous day, so his teammates thought, to visit relatives in his old home area. But the commission believed he had offered £20 to South Shields left-back Alf Maitland (who gave evidence under oath) to ensure a Fulham win.

Over 60 years later, the Fulham captain that day, Alec Chaplin, remained convinced that Travers was acting under instruction, probably from manager Phil Kelso. None of his teammates believed that Barney had acted on his own but was made the scapegoat. No action was taken against the club or anyone else connected with the club. The commission thought Travers' motive was gambling-related and by the time the ban was lifted in 1945, his playing days were long gone.

Barney Travers.

INFLUENCE OF SIMMS
Fulham find South Shields a new side

It was a rare tussle for points at South Shields. The vastly improved form of the home side was chiefly due to the presence of Simms, acquired last week from Luton. His leadership bore the hallmark of intelligence, and it is a long time since the forward line has shown the same thrustfulness.

The goal which beat Fulham was obtained by Gray six minutes after the start and was just reward for a long-sustained attack with which they opened the game. The ball was swung in by Keenlyside in delightful fashion, and a first-time shot by the scorer gave Reynolds no earthly chance.

A feature of the Fulham game was the solid defence the backs put up, particularly during the first portion. Chaplin played wonderfully well, tackling and kicking with the soundest possible style, and he had a reliable partner in Fleming. The pick of the first-rate half-back line was Torrance, one of the most useful men on the field. Reynolds came through a Herculean task with credit. He saved all sorts of shots, and many that seemed certain to score.

It was exactly a month, on 17 April, before the Fulham programme made any official comment on the scandal. In 'Notes From The Boardroom', the club said:

'We regret that Bernard Travers, our centre-forward, whom we obtained from Sunderland last season, has been permanently suspended by the FA on a charge of attempted bribery in connection with our game at South Shields.

There was no charge against us as a club, and we would like to take this opportunity of assuring our patrons that whatever happened in connection with the game in question we had no knowledge of, nor should we countenance same in the slightest degree. At no time have we had any other thought or desire but to play the right game in the League.

We are sorry for Travers because we had faith in him, though any wrong doing cannot be tolerated in any form. It is a serious matter to us, for we lose the services of a player who cost us a lot of money to secure, and for this there is no recompense. Apart from this, however, we would wish that the incident had never occurred and are exceedingly sorry.'

Despite the official club denials, the incident cast a shadow over the remainder of manager Phil Kelso's career. He chose to retire after two more seasons at the helm, still aged only 53. Even in his final game, at home to Stockport in April 1924, there was a reminder of the South Shields match, for the visitors centre-forward that day was the same Ernie Simms who had played so well at Horsley Hill. After leaving the Cottage, Kelso never worked in football again and became instead a publican, first the landlord of The Grove in Hammersmith and then The Rising Sun in the Fulham Road. Although there were obituaries in the national newspapers when he died in February 1935, at the age of 64, there was no reference to the passing of the club's long-serving manager in the Fulham programme.

Phil Kelso.

Fulham 1 v Everton 0

Thursday 14 January 1926
FA Cup Third Round Replay
Referee: F.W. Warriss
Attendance: 20,116

FULHAM		EVERTON
Ernie Beecham	1	Sam Hardy
Reg Dyer	2	David Raitt
Alec Chaplin	3	John McDonald
Len Oliver	4	Joe Peacock
David McNabb	5	David Bain
Bert Barrett	6	Albert Virr
Jack Harris	7	Sam Chedgzoy
Teddy Craig	8	Bobby Irvine
George Edmonds	9	Bill 'Dixie' Dean
Bert White	10	Jack O'Donnell
Frank Penn	11	Alec Troup

In any list of Fulham's best FA Cup victories, three ties against Everton spread over 50 years would feature very near the top. Although the Cottagers have never won a League game at Goodison, they are unbeaten after four FA Cup visits, a sequence which started with this remarkable result in the winter of 1926. This was the second season of manager Andy Ducat's brief tenure. A traditional Victorian sportsman, Ducat, who had played for England at football and cricket, was temperamentally unsuited to the hurly burly of club management and this Cup run was the highpoint of his term in office.

When Fulham were drawn to play at First Division Goodison Park in round three of the FA Cup, there was little in the League form of either club to suggest that anything but a home win was the likely. Struggling in the bottom half of the Second Division, Fulham had won just two of their 10 games prior to the trip to Merseyside. And injuries meant Ducat had to play third choice teenager Ernie Beecham in goal. Everton, on the other hand, were handily placed in the top flight and had been beaten just three times in the previous 14 games. And in Bill 'Dixie' Dean, they had the most prolific striker in English football at the top of his game.

The 46,000 crowd was stunned when Fulham deservedly came away with a draw, which could so easily have been a win. Dean's opening goal five minutes before the interval was cancelled out by Teddy Craig's equaliser 23 minutes into the second half following a free-kick. Bill Prouse, who missed the replay, was Fulham's best player although young Beecham distinguished himself with a series of fine saves, none more so than in the last minute when Dean was clean through. There was much more of the same in the replay. Because of replays at Arsenal and Crystal Palace on the Wednesday, Fulham's replay was scheduled for 2.15pm on the following Thursday.

The snow-bound pitch just before kick-off.

GOALKEER DEFIES EVERTON

Big Cup Upset At Craven Cottage

By beating Everton at Craven Cottage, Fulham were the fifth London club to qualify at home in the Fourth Round of the FA Cup. Their opponents will be Liverpool on 30 January.

Even snow, which fell heavily throughout the greater part of the match, and darkness, which for a time made the ball invisible to spectators, could not spoil the game. Before the kick off, the ground was nearly an inch deep in snow and the touchlines and all other lines had been obliterated. A slipping, sliding, scrambling match seemed certain. Instead there was one of the most interesting games of the Third Round.

Fulham won, but were lucky. Their only goal, which was scored by White 17 minutes into the second half, had an element of fluke. Time after time, Everton had the home defence hopelessly beaten, only for a goal shot to fail by inches. But against this, Fulham were a man short throughout the second half. Chaplin, the left back, was injured soon after the interval and, although he remained on the field for some time, he limped painfully and was moved up to outside left. This made necessary a reconstruction of the side with its inevitable handicap to Fulham. A quarter of an hour before the end, Chaplin retired and Fulham finished with ten men.

Nevertheless, fortune proved a good 12th man for Fulham. Next in order of merit came goalkeeper Beecham and centre forward Edmonds, who owed his place to an injury to Pape. Edmonds kept his feet on a slippery surface in an astonishing way. He turned and side-stepped as though the conditions were perfect. He was the master of the Everton defence in the last half hour.

But the real salvation of Fulham was Beecham. He is not yet 19 years of age, but he showed both a coolness and a judgement that many a man of twice his experience might be proud to possess. He was here, there and everywhere. He leaped high to save, he dived wide and low to save. One of his best clearances came in the last minute. A number of spectators rushed over the ground and carried him to the entrance of the dressing room. He deserved it.

Everton played the cleverer football: they showed better combination, but even when they surrounded the Fulham goal, they could not find the net. When direction was good, Beecham contrived to get some part of his anatomy in front of the ball. On such a day, however, it was surprising that the players shot with any degree of accuracy.

Fulham's hero, teenage goalkeeper Ernie Beecham.

FULHAM THROUGH
How Pluck and Perseverance met its reward

In beating Everton by the only goal scored in this replayed Cup tie at Craven Cottage, Fulham reaped the reward of pluck and perseverance. They were by no means the better side. Still Everton have only themselves to blame for not having gained a substantial victory. They had five-sixths of the play in the second half when Fulham were a man short, Chaplin, who was hurt in the first half having to retire after a short spell at outside left.

Good football was out of the question but Fulham infused any amount of dash into their work and several times the Everton goal escaped narrowly before McNabb fired in a rocket shot that hit the upright.

Everton found their form just before the interval and by keeping the ball swinging about they were able to trouble Beecham quite a lot. The Fulham goalkeeper played a great game and although fortunate on possession, he always inspired confidence. At the end of the match, he was carried from the field shoulder high. He deserved the tribute he received.

Only once was he really beaten. That was just before the interval when Chedgzoy drove in a terrific shot that hit the upright as McNabb's effort had done at the other end. But then, luck was with him. The ball hit the post squarely and rebounded into play.

Deprived of Chaplin's help, and with a re-arranged defence, Fulham were largely outplayed in the second half and it was against the run of the game that they scored. After their goal had survived in extraordinary fashion from a number of attacks, a solo effort by Edmonds took play into Everton's territory by a lightening stroke. From a throw in, the ball was put in front of the Everton goal and McDonald delayed while attempting to clear. He was punished in the scramble that ensued, the ball was netted. It was too dark to see from the stand who specifically touched the ball last but the home side shook hands with White who presumably had the finishing touch.

The men from Goodison made strenuous efforts to make up the leeway but Fulham fought desperately in defence of their lead and succeeded in retaining it. They will next meet Liverpool at home. The attendance was 20,116.

Fulham 1 v Manchester United 2

Saturday 6 March 1926
FA Cup Sixth Round
Referee: T. Crew
Attendance: 28,699

FULHAM		MANCHESTER U
Ernie Beecham	1	John Mew
Reg Dyer	2	Charles Moore
Alec Chaplin	3	John Silcock
Len Oliver	4	Jimmy McCrea
David McNabb	5	Frank Barson
Frank Penn	6	Frank Mann
Jack Harris	7	Joe Spence
Teddy Craig	8	Thomas Smith
Albert Pape	9	Frank McPherson
George Edmunds	10	Charlie Rennox
Robert Ferguson	11	Charlie Hannaford

In the run up to their fourth FA Cup quarter-final, the club managed to upset the supporters. The prospect of a visit from one of the leading First Division clubs, persuaded the directors to double admission prices (10p to stand) but it backfired, and the crowd was a disappointing 28,699. But, having beaten three other top-flight clubs en route (Liverpool at home and Notts County away after the Everton victory), the Cottagers were hopeful of making it through to a second semi-final despite their poor League form.

As in 1908, Fulham's opponents for the quarter-final tie were Manchester United and it was the same 2–1 scoreline as 18 years earlier, but this time to the visitors. The Cup run had lifted the Cottagers' League form and they went into the match with four wins and a draw in their previous seven games, and unbeaten at home for over four months. Unfortunately, left-half Bert Barrett was unfit, and winger Frank Penn dropped back in his slot, and there were doubts about the fitness of skipper Alec Chaplin, for whom this was the first game back since getting a knock in the Everton replay. Fulham's centre-forward Albert Pape had started the season a United player. The visitors, with three straight League wins coming into this match, were also below strength. Their most notable omissions were long-serving goalkeeper Alf Steward (for whom the 37-year-old John Mew deputised) and the dependable wing-half (and briefly player-manager the next season) Clarrie Hilditch. His place was taken by Jimmy McCrae.

The result was a huge disappointment and virtually the end of Ducat's managerial career. Although Fulham survived in Division Two, he left that summer, ushering in a period of managerial instability. After just two managers (Bradshaw and Kelso) in 20 years (1904–24), Fulham had five managers (Ducat, Joe Bradshaw, Ned Liddell, James McIntyre and Jimmy Hogan) and one caretaker boss (Joe Edelston) in the next 11. After leaving the Cottage, Ducat reclaimed his amateur status and continued his county cricket career with Surrey. He died while batting at Lords in 1942.

A shot from Albert Pape beats Mew in the United goal.

FULHAM'S EXIT

Lucky Winning Goal for United
Fine Display By Mann

By Corinthian

Not only did Fulham display the pluck to recover from the loss of a goal scored by the visitors to Craven Cottage in the first minute of their Cup-tie game, but they went on for the remainder of the first half to show us the only true football that the game produced.

This was by no means a game for the over-excitable. In the first few minutes, McPherson injured himself by running on to Dyer's foot just as the latter had kicked the ball, but that did not prevent him from scoring a few seconds later. Spence got in a centre which McPherson met on the half volley and sent the ball, with a screw kick, twisting and swerving to where Beecham had gone on one knee to save. The ball went to the goalkeeper's hands and a goal seemed improbable. Beecham, before making sure that he had the ball, looked up to see what danger threatened in the way of a rush, and then found that the ball had dropped from his grasp and gone over the line. That was the first kick at either goal.

Goalkeeper Mew clears from Pape.

Another 90 seconds of Fulham superiority, and the home team had equalised. Craig made one of his many fine passes to Harris whose centre was cleverly trapped by Pape. The home centre-forward had the ball steadied in a trice, and his shot almost sent the ball through the roof of the net.

How many times Fulham, aided by a very strong wind, got near to scoring before the interval would be tedious to tell. Anyhow, Ferguson lobbed a most cunning shot towards the top corner of the net, and this would have scored but for the great alertness of Mew. Then Pape, with a hard low cross shot, was foiled by the goalkeeper, who made a full-length dive that was remarkable for one of his age and shape.

Extraordinary decisions by the referee just after the resumption must have irritated the home players. Rennox trod on Dyer's foot, and a free kick was given just outside the Fulham penalty area. Dyer was badly hurt and the feelings of the whole team must have been hurt also when they found that the free kick had been given to Manchester United, who almost scored.

Then, from about 12 yards out, Rennox tried to kick a breast-high ball into the net. McNabb could get no nearer to his opponent than attempt to put him off his kick. The Manchester player kicked hard over the crossbar and the referee gave a corner!

It was from that alleged corner that the winning goal was 'got'. After Hannaford's kick, Smith hooked the ball high into the net. That was but four minutes after half-time. From that point, there was little football good to watch. Spoiling was the keynote of the Lancashire side and, with the strong wind helping them to kick clear, they seldom allowed Fulham to look dangerous. In all this defensive play, the great player was Mann, who beat Harris for the ball continually, so that next to nothing was seen of the home outside right in the second half.

Fulham's chief fault was shown in the second half when, by failing to keep the ball low, they gave the wind every chance of beating them. Craig was the most subtle of their forwards, Penn was an ever-working half-back, which remark applies to McNabb, who had none-the-worse of his tussles with that most elusive centre-forward, McPherson, and both Dyer and Chaplin tackled and kicked with judgement and accuracy.

Blackpool 4 v Fulham 0

Saturday 5 May 1928
Football League Division Two
Attendance: 14,466

BLACKPOOL		FULHAM
Arthur Purdy	1	Ernie Beecham
Percy Thorpe	2	Jack Hedden
Laurie Barnett	3	Bert Barrett
Albert Watson	4	Len Oliver
William Grant	5	David McNabb
Billy Tremelling	6	Frank Penn
Mark Crook	7	Jimmy Temple
Johnny Oxberry	8	Fred Avey
Jimmy Hampson	9	Sid Elliott
Tom Browell	10	Teddy Craig
Richard Neal	11	Bob Ferguson

The past caught up with Fulham with a vengeance in 1928. After several seasons of flirting with relegation, the trapdoor to the Third Division South finally opened, and the visit to Bloomfield Road sealed the Cottagers' fate. It had been a most unusual season and escape from the drop seemed possible until the final game against Blackpool. But, when the occasion called for a big performance, the players came up short and Fulham dropped out of the Second Division for the first time since joining in 1907.

In many ways this was not the club's worst season. They lost just twice at home (only champions Manchester City had a better home record) and the goal tally of 68 was the highest since Fulham became a League club. Leading scorer Sid Elliott, moreover, set a new club record of 26 goals in 42 games, but crucially had failed to find the net in any of the last 12. And there were some remarkable scorelines. The week after losing 8–4 at Barnsley, Fulham beat Wolves 7–0 at home. In five matches they conceded five or more goals and there was not a single goalless draw all season.

The problem was the away form. The first 20 games were all lost and if the defeats in the final two away games of the previous season and the FA Cup exit at Southport in January 1928 are included, the losing sequence stretched to 23 consecutive games. A 1–0 win in the penultimate away game at Notts County and a 1–0 home win the following week over Reading meant the Cottagers travelled to the seaside knowing that a draw would be enough to keep them up and send Blackpool down. But, with only wing-half Alex Steele missing from the first-choice line up, Joe Bradshaw's men were beaten by half-time. It took four years and two changes of manager to get back, and only four of that team (Beecham, Barrett, Oliver and Penn) were to play for Fulham again in the Second Division.

Bert Barrett, one of the four Fulham players to survive relegation and play again when the club returned to Division Two.

WHY FULHAM FAILED
By Spartan

Fulham are precipitated into the Third Division as a result of their defeat at Blackpool. Only a point was needed for safety, and against a side which had conceded an average of nearly three goals a match, there seemed a good chance of getting it. But Fulham never looked like doing so.

They were run off their legs early on, when the home team established a two goals lead and never had a moment's anxiety afterwards. I must say that Fulham were unfortunate in having to play over half the game without Hebden, who was twice injured and retired for good a minute after the interval. All through, however, the attack was so ragged that it was hard to imagine how they were going to save the game. Little was seen of Elliott who has been so proficient for the Londoners this season.

Fulham's goal had many escapes before Hampson kicked the ball out of Beecham's hands into the net six minutes from the start. This was the culmination of a free kick conceded by Barrett for handling. Barrett did a lot of fine work after this, but could not atone for his act of folly. Oxberry scored the second goal and Hampson added two after the interval.

Fulham's failings were fundamental and they never looked like scoring. Beecham, who had twice the work of Purdy, made a number of thrilling saves. On the basis of this one match, Blackpool deserve to survive in the Second Division, but for Fulham after 20 years at this level, it will be a long haul back.

LUCKLESS FULHAM TO GO DOWN
Two defenders injured at Blackpool

The Second Division League relegation tangle was unravelled much according to expectations on Saturday, Fulham being the unfortunate club to accompany South Shields into the Third Division. Clapton Orient, though failing to score against the Wolves at the Lea Bridge ground, kept a clean sheet thus saving a point and finishing ahead of the Craven Cottage side.

The duel between Fulham and Blackpool at Bloomfield Road was a most desperate affair, for Blackpool had to win to escape relegation, while Fulham, away from home, were faced with the necessity of effecting a draw to save themselves from reduction to the lower class. Blackpool won the game by four goals to none but Fulham were severely handicapped by injuries to players.

Hebden, the full back, displaced a cartilage and was carried off the field and took no part in the game after the interval, while when Hampson scored the first goal for Blackpool, Beecham, the Fulham goalkeeper, was accidentally kicked on the head. Beecham was suffering from concussion for the rest of the game and afterwards had to be taken to an hotel and put to bed.

Hampson, the Blackpool centre forward, achieved a personal triumph by scoring three goals, while Oxberry also netted.

The relegated team: Left to right, back row: Oliver, Dyer, Moreton, Beecham, Barrett, Steele. Front row: Devan, McKenna, Elliott, Craig, Penn, McNabb.

Fulham 10 v Torquay United 2

Monday 7 September 1931
Football League Division Three South
Referee: L. Gibbs
Attendance: 9,706

FULHAM		**TORQUAY U**
Ernie Beecham	1	Joe Wright
Sonny Gibbon	2	Wally Webster
Bill Hickie	3	Jack Fowler
Len Oliver	4	Billy Clayson
Syd Gibbons	5	Don Hewitt
Bert Barrett	6	Bob Smith
Joe Proud	7	Ralph Birkett
Jim Hammond	8	Jimmy Trotter
Frank Newton	9	Jack Cooper
Johnny Price	10	Albert Hutchinson
Jack Finch	11	George Stabb

For three seasons, Fulham toiled in the Third Division South, gradually slipping lower down the table, from fifth, to seventh to ninth. Manager Joe Bradshaw departed in 1929 after failing to win promotion at the first attempt and his successor, Ned Liddell, looked even less likely to take the Cottagers back up. Then, in April 1931, James McIntyre arrived, the club's fourth manager in seven years, a man with a proven record at this level, having taken Southampton to the divisional title in 1922. In between the Dell and the Cottage, he had been in charge at Coventry.

Aged 50, McIntyre, unencumbered by self-doubt, liked to claim his managerial style was based on that of the great Herbert Chapman. He realised the value of good press relations, kept supporters informed of developments and was a shrewd operator in the transfer market. Although the nucleus of the side that brought him success in his first season was already in place, his first two signings made the critical difference. He went back to his former club Coventry for outside-right Bill Richards and paid Stockport £575 for centre-forward Frank 'Bonzo' Newton. A goalscoring sensation and a huge favourite with the Cottage faithful, Newton set a club record of 43 goals in 1931–32 (plus four in the FA Cup) as the team took the Third Division South Championship, scoring 111 goals, a record that remains today.

Jim Hammond, four goals against Torquay.

Fulham got off to a flying start, winning six of the first seven matches. The visit of Torquay was the fourth fixture, 48 hours after a defeat at Gillingham. The Cottagers had managed eight goals in their opening games whereas in their three previous games, Torquay had drawn once but been beaten 7–0 at Crystal Palace and 6–3 at home to Watford. A goalless draw was the least likely result but surpassing the Cottagers' previous best League win (7–0 at home to Wolves in 1928) was totally unexpected. Sharing the scoring honours that day, and the rest of the season, were Jim Hammond and Newton, and over the course of the season, the two claimed 74 of the club's 111 goals.

FULHAM'S 10 GOALS HIGHEST OF THE SEASON

DRAMATIC ROUT OF TORQUAY
Spate of goals after Webster's injury – four for Hammond

Some considerable time will probably elapse before we shall witness a more one-sided game than that which occurred last evening at Craven Cottage. In many respects, it was a howling farce.

Against a side which, even at its best, was sadly ill-equipped for the task in hand, Fulham did much as they liked. Hammond, the Sussex cricketer, scored four of the 10 goals, the last three in succession, and the officials tell me that the total number of 10 obtained yesterday stands as a record for the club since it joined the Football League. Torquay, who began the season with a declaration of rigid economy in reference to the number and, shall we say, the class of their players, have now lost 24 goals in their four games.

Mishap at full-back

The rout of Torquay was hastened by an accident to their back Webster, who hurt his head so badly in a collision after Fulham had scored the first of their 10 goals that he had to leave the field. Webster came back, heavily bandaged, just before the interval, and from that period he remained a dazed passenger at outside left. This was a heavy blow to Torquay, again without Butler, but, even before the compulsory re-arrangement of the team, never showed much likelihood of putting up any serious resistance.

Clayton, originally deputed for the third line in the absence of Meacock, had to go to full-back and Trotter played right-half. They were desperate measures that proved to no avail and Wright, though making a number of fine saves during the final stages, was never at his best prior to the interval.

Some good shooting

The ball was kept well on the floor and, during the first half, Finch, who was taking the place of Penn, created an excellent impression. In Price, he had a good partner and Newton made an intelligent and forceful leader, The defence, which now included Oliver at right-half, did all that was asked of them against a poor attack and Beecham for long periods might have sat in an armchair.

It says much, however, for the courage of Torquay that the Fulham goalkeeper was twice beaten during the closing stages. It was Hutchinson who reduced the long lead, and then Stabb, a young local amateur who has played for Paignton and though starting at outside left, led the forwards after the re-arrangement.

Order of the boot

Fulham scored six of their goals without reply in the opening half, the order being Newton, Finch, Proud, Hammond, Newton and Price, and the last five came in the course of 18 minutes. In the second half, the order of the boot was Hammond (three in succession) and Price. In this way, the Craven Cottage side put up the highest score of any Football League club during the present season.

Many years ago, and also at Craven Cottage, Fulham beat Wellingborough in a Southern League match 12–0 and in the April of 1930, their reserves overwhelmed the reserves of Brentford by 16–1, Avey scoring six.

The Fulham programme commented: 'The success really did not have much in the form of luck attached to it. The team won on their merits and as the game ran, they might easily have been credited with an even larger margin in their favour. They overwhelmed United in every department and there was no suggestion of weakness in any section of the team.

A couple of changes were made in our attack, the two young reserve wing players, Proud and Finch, having been deemed worthy of inclusion in the places of Richards and Penn, and it was their lively football that was a material factor in the sparkling display of our front line. We were pleased that our skipper, Len Oliver, was able to lead the team after being absent from a couple of games in consequence of an injury he met against Coventry. He gave a sound display in which he was admirably supported by Gibbons and Barrett. The Cottagers defence generally was a powerful combination though it is true that Beecham had a sinecure in goal. And I suspect that the two goals secured by Torquay were a long way removed from the gilt-edged variety.

It must be mentioned, of course, that Torquay had an early misfortune which, though I am of the opinion it did not affect the result, must have been disheartening to them. We did not escape Scot free in the matter of injuries, for we had both Newton and Hickie crocked. Newton pulled a leg muscle soon after scoring his first goal and thereafter his shooting was rather subdued. This will explain why he appeared to slow up as the game progressed. It always looked as if the Cottagers would gain an easy victory and Newton was justified in not taking undue risks.

Fulham 3 v Bristol Rovers 2

Saturday 30 April 1932
Football League Division Three South
Referee: W. Phipps
Attendance: 20,454

FULHAM		BRISTOL R
Jake Iceton	1	Joe Calvert
Arthur Tilford	2	George Russell
Joe Birch	3	Bill Pickering
Len Oliver	4	William Stoddart
Syd Gibbons	5	Herbert Blake
Bert Barrett	6	Jack Townrow
Bill Richards	7	William Routledge
Frank Wrightson	8	Morris Dando
Frank Newton	9	Tom Cook
Jim Hammond	10	Ronnie Dix
Jack Finch	11	Eric Oakton

The four-year sojourn in the Third Division ended on this spring afternoon in 1932, four years after the ignominious defeat at Blackpool had sent them down. Only wing-halves Len Oliver, the captain, and Bert Barrett played in both games. Among the pace-setters from the off, Fulham were in third place at the end of November and second at the turn of the year. By the end of February, they topped the table and remained there for the rest of the season. This was at a time when only the champions were promoted. Reading were the nearest challengers but in the last month of the season never got within four points of the Cottagers (only two for a win in those days) and a win over Bristol Rovers would bring the title to SW6 with a game to spare.

Chairman John Dean receives the Third Division South trophy the week after the Bristol Rovers match.

There had been a bit of a wobble early in the spring, which coincided with the loss of scheming inside-forward Johnny Price to injury with 12 games to go. But McIntyre opened the cheque book and signed Frank Wrightson from Manchester City. Beating Thames 8–0 at home on Easter Monday restored confidence, with Hammond and Newton back on the goal standard in a big way. And, Price apart, it was the strongest team that took on Rovers for this decisive match, with eight of the team playing in at least 30 games that season.

Remarkably for a Third Division game, the crowd at the Cottage of 21,572 was bettered only at Highbury and Goodison (where Everton were chasing the League title) anywhere in England that day. And they got what they wanted. Just as the Pirates had been the opposition when Fulham clinched their first piece of silverware 26 years earlier, so they again obliged (unwillingly) when promotion was clinched with a game to spare. After the final match the following week, at home to Exeter, the Championship trophy was presented to club chairman John Dean and four years in the wilderness came to an end.

Team picture. Left to right, back row: Oliver, Gibbon, Iceton, Birch, Penn. Front row: Richards, Hammond, Newton, Price, Finch, Gibbons.

FULHAM BACK TO DIV II
But they nearly made a mess of it

Fulham gave their supporters a fright, for the Rovers were the better side until injury upset them, and it was not until they got the lead midway through the second half that Fulham showed anything like the form that has put them at the head of the table. Over-anxiety was the cause of their poor efforts, some of the players being obviously too excited to do themselves justice. However, they won in the end and are now booked for Division II.

The Rovers had the better of the game in the first half when Oakton and Dando proved too fast and clever for the home defensive right flank, and Iceton was kept busy. His goal escaped luckily when Routledge just failed to hook in a centre by Oakton, but it fell to Cook in the 22nd minute following a corner.

Up to then, and for some time after, little was seen of the home forwards, and it was not until an injury to Pickering, the visitors left-back, sent him to limp at outside right with a consequent re-arrangement of the side, that they became really dangerous. Then Newton shot over and Calvert beat the ball away as Finch seemed to have the goal at his mercy.

With the wind behind them, Fulham showed more determination and skill in the second half, but they were greatly helped by the fact that Pickering was still limping on the Rovers right wing. Calvert made several smart saves before being beaten by a drive from Finch following a corner. The goalkeeper was completely unsighted or he might have got to the ball. Able to use one wing only in attack, the Rovers were not often dangerous, though Dix was given one glorious chance but shot over.

Fulham then had an inspired period and made certain by scoring two goals in two minutes, the first through Barrett who headed in a corner, and the second through Hammond who headed in a free kick. Pickering, who could hardly raise a gallop, caught Iceton napping when the Rovers made a sudden raid, his hard low drive curling out of the goalkeeper's arms and over the line, but Fulham by this time had the game well in hand.

The management had certainly anticipated a win, because at the close of the game a flag bearing the inscription 'Fulham champions of Div III 1931–32' was hoisted. Len Oliver (the captain) said after the match, 'Wonderful team spirit, the excellent work of our new manager (Mr J A McIntyre) and the unbounded optimism of Mr J Dean, our genial chairman, have been the secrets of our success.'

Of the hundreds of telegrams received by Fulham, none was more appreciated than that received from their nearest rivals – Reading. It read, 'Heartiest felicitations and sincerest congratulations on your well-deserved promotion. We have had good runs together, and we may have many more in the future. Cordial and good wishes and good luck in every respect. (signed) 'Graham, Reading.'

Fulham 2 v Tottenham Hotspur 2

Saturday 10 December 1932
Football League Division Two
Referee: W.P. Harper
Attendance: 42,111

FULHAM		TOTTENHAM H
Alf Tootill	1	Jim Nicholls
Joe Birch	2	Bill Felton
Arthur Tilford	3	Bill Whatley
Len Oliver	4	David Colquhoun
Syd Gibbons	5	Arthur Rowe
Bert Barrett	6	Tommy Meads
Bill Richards	7	Les Howe
Jim Hammond	8	Taffy O'Callaghan
Frank Newton	9	George Hunt
Johnny Price	10	George Greenfield
Jack Finch	11	Willie Evans

After winning back their Second Division status the previous May, McIntyre's Fulham put in a sustained challenge for a second promotion in 12 months, a challenge that only petered out in the closing three weeks of the season. And the club which pipped them to the second promotion place was Tottenham (no Play-offs in those days). The two clubs fought out what was Fulham's Match of the Season at the Cottage just before Christmas and it attracted a new Cottage record crowd of 42,111.

For the early part of the season, manager McIntyre kept faith with the side that had won promotion the previous year but by the autumn, he was starting to tinker with the line up. After two defeats and seven goals conceded in seven days, he bought goalkeeper Alf Tootill to replace Jake Iceton. Ever present in Wolves' Second Division Championship side the previous season, Tootill had conceded seven goals at Arsenal days before joining Fulham and this match against Spurs was his home debut. He was to be the Cottagers' custodian for the next five years, missing just four games.

Spurs came to west London that day having won eight and drawn two of their previous 10 games. The week before, a 7–0 hammering of Swansea had put them in second place in the table, while Fulham were fifth, three points behind but with a game in hand. The visitors' free-scoring forwards (51 goals in 17 games, 16 more than Fulham, the division's second highest scorers) was

remarkable for its size – all under 5ft 9in. The brains of the side were inside-forwards George Greenfield and Eugene 'Taffy' O'Callaghan. Sadly, the broken leg sustained in this match effectively ended the brilliant Greenfield's career after just 33 games. O'Callaghan was later to become a popular Fulham personality, as a player and trainer. He (and the Spurs winger that day, Willie Evans) were both signed for Fulham later in the 1930s by Jack Peart, who had managed their first club, Ebbw Vale.

The view from the Cottage of a game in 1932–33. The Fulham players are Birch, Oliver, Gibbons, goalkeeper Iceton, Barrett and Keeping.

A GOOD GAME AT FULHAM
Tottenham's Brave Effort

The Second Division match between Fulham and Tottenham Hotspur at Craven Cottage resulted in a draw, each side scoring two goals. Some 44,000 saw football that was appreciably better than that usually played by teams outside the League Championship. The game was tremendously fast and keen, much of the play was clever and it was free from those incidents common to what is popularly known as a 'local derby'.

Unfortunately the game was marred by an accident to Greenfield, the inside-left of Tottenham Hotspur, who, just after Fulham obtained their first goal, after the game had been in progress for a quarter of an hour, fell under a tackle and broke his leg. The mishap occurred when Tottenham Hotspur were attacking heavily and the chances were they would equalise: and, until the interval, with their forces so seriously depleted, they were outplayed to such an extent that it was surprising they were no more than two behind at half-time.

For the first 45 minutes, Fulham were the better team: Hammond at inside-right and Finch, on the left wing, were especially brilliant, and they were well supported by their half-backs, but at close quarters they could not get the better of Nicholls, a most efficient and daring goalkeeper. Still, when Newton scored their second goal, it seemed they were bound to win. Previously, Newton, from a penalty kick given against Rowe, did no more than shoot straight at Nicholls. His shot had such power behind it that that Nicholls was knocked out, but from this point, and as if to appreciate their luck, Tottenham Hotspur not only improved but after the change of ends put up such a fight that they not only drew level but they might have won.

The scoring began after a free kick had been given against Felton, the goal being scored by Richards who, profiting from a well-judged pass by Hammond, found it easy to beat Nicholls. After Greenfield had been injured, Finch seemed likely to score, but he was unfairly bowled over. The penalty kick was cleared but only because Newton, who took it, kicked the ball at the goalkeeper. The Fulham centre-forward, however, shortly afterwards forced the ball into the net and then Hunt shot wide of an open goal for the visitors.

After crossing over, Tottenham Hotspur almost at once took command of the game and, after 15 minutes, Hunt made the most of an opportunity created by Evans to beat Tootill. From there until the finish, Tottenham Hotspur exerted such pressure that Fulham were not only forced to concede a second goal to Hunt, but were perhaps fortunate to avoid defeat. Even so, Hammond would surely have won the match had Nicholls not saved his low and hard shot. All things considered, however, a draw was a fitting result, even if the honours were with Tottenham Hotspur, who did so well playing with one man short.

The 'Baker's Man' in 'Tales of the Cottage' in the next Fulham programme wrote: 'What a great game that was we had with

Goalkeeper Alf Tootill made his home debut in the draw with Spurs.

the Spurs, and what a classic it would have been but for the unfortunate accident to Greenfield, the young Tottenham forward. A pure accident and one for which we all, the Fulham players particularly, very much regret. Our sympathy to Greenfield in the hope he will make as speedy a return to the game as possible.

I suppose it will be argued that having a lead of two goals after 25 minutes of play against a depleted opposition, the Cottagers should have romped home to victory. In theory, this is true, but actual circumstances put a different complexion on the situation and, whatever else one may think, one has to admire the brilliant recovery of the Spurs which enabled them to draw.

We knew the North Londoners were something of a super-side, and we were prepared with a super effort by way of opposition, and for the first half certainly the brilliance of our players scintillated to best advantage. At the same time, the mishap to Greenfield must have had an adverse effect on the Spurs which was reflected in their play.

But in the second half, the tide turned. Adopting a close four forward game, the Spurs rallied surprisingly, and in many thrilling passages some grand football was witnessed on both sides. This result may be regarded as a satisfactory one.

It was particularly pleasing to hear the fine sporting comments passed on the game afterwards by leading authorities. The Spurs regarded our team as the best they have met this season and Joe Nicholls, their goalkeeper, has publicly stated that we made the Spurs realise that their upward path was not an easy one. He also added that the match proved that deadly enemies could play the game in the true spirit of sport.

Fulham 3 v Southampton 3

Saturday 3 November 1934
Football League Division Two
Referee: C.P. West
Attendance: 19,702

FULHAM		SOUTHAMPTON
Alf Tootill	1	Bert Scriven
Joe Birch	2	Bill Adams
Jimmy Hindson	3	Charlie Sillett
Bruce Clarke	4	Frank Ward
Syd Gibbons	5	Johnny McIlwaine
Bert Barrett	6	William Luckett
Jack Finch	7	Fred Tully
Jim Hammond	8	Tom Brewis
Frank Newton	9	James 'Sonny' Horton
Johnny Price	10	Arthur Holt
John Arnold	11	Laurie Fishlock

The start of the 1934–35 season marked a bold new venture for Fulham. Having surprisingly sacked James McIntyre the previous February and carried on with assistant manager Joe Edelston at the helm until the summer, the board made the remarkably imaginative appointment of Jimmy Hogan, as Manager-Coach, rather than as Secretary Manager as his predecessor had been. A former Fulham player (his final appearance was in the 1908 FA Cup semi-final), but never more than a journeyman, Hogan had become a coach, a new concept for those days, who had blazed a trail across mainland Europe for 20 years. He made his reputation particularly in Austria where the national team had come very close to beating England at Stamford Bridge 18 months earlier.

Hogan's approach was revolutionary. He got involved in tactics, diet and individual skills rather than just fitness, and worked day-to-day with the players. He disliked the defensive style of Chapman's 'stopper' centre-half and wanted to adopt the close passing 'Scottish' game of his playing days at the Cottage. The players did not respond well to his techniques and the experiment ended in tears within months, with little credit reflected on the Fulham board for their behaviour. Clearly, this was an example of a prophet being without honour in his own country.

But briefly, Hogan's ideas flourished and this game against Southampton saw one of Fulham's most dependable and popular figures of the era revel in the new freedom. Syd Gibbons was a mountain of a man, unsurprisingly nicknamed 'Carnera' after the world heavyweight boxing champion. An ex-foundry worker and one-time England junior international, the 23-year-old Gibbons was signed in May 1930 after failing to make the breakthrough at Manchester City. A rugged and uncompromising centre-half, he was the heart of the Fulham defence for over seven seasons and 318 games until injury caught up with him. But on that autumnal afternoon against the Saints, Carnera showed there was more to his game than 'stopping' and he became (and remains) the only Fulham defender to score a hat-trick, with all the goals from open play.

Gibbons (centre) leads Finch and Birch (left) and Arnold, Barrett and Oliver on a training run around the Cottage pitch.

DRAMA AT FULHAM
PERT HALF-BACKS
Gibbons Astounds With A Hat Trick

To be fair-minded all depends on the point of view and, as Mr Jimmy Hogan, the Fulham manager declared last week, all the fine arts of Soccer had their origin in keeping the ball down. Cumberworth and I paid a visit to Craven Cottage to get a demonstration. In a sequel, when a dazzling November sun was going to bed, Fulham just escaped the Irishman's rise by equalising in the last minute.

We have good cause to remember this game because five of the six goals came from half-backs. Sydney Gibbons, the warrior at the heart of the Fulham defence, actually scored three after the Saints had led by as many goals early in the second half and the centre half showed us that the so-called 'stopper' in modern football can explore other avenues when the shadow of defeat looms up as it did last Saturday.

In the opening half, the Saints played the better football, and Mr Hogan, who on the eve of the game had been extolling the defence of Fulham to a Wandsworth audience, began to feel uneasy in his scientific soul. Reward for good pressure came when Horton, the old Aldershot and Millwall player, headed through a centre from Luckett. More fat was in the fire when, during the early stages of the second half, Luckett and then McIlwaine, with a great dribble, increased the lead. Tootill was not discovered at his best at that period, particularly when he failed to hold Luckett's shot, but the Saints were now showing Fulham that mere ball manipulation in midfield was not enough.

Before the opening half closed, Ward not only hurt his leg but the head injuries to McIlwaine and Sillett demanded bandages before these worthies reappeared. Yet the Saints were nearly successful in winning their first game away from home since the Easter of 1933.

All the Fulham forwards were clever, but not clever enough as a rule to defeat McIlwaine and his able backs, Adams and Sillett. So it fell to 'Carnera', that mountainous defender, to show his forwards how it should be done. He took matters into his own hands and turned himself into an extra centre-forward, scoring three goals in 20 minutes to mark a memorable comeback. His first was a header from Arnold's centre. The other two came from headlong rushes which he led and it was his foot on both occasions which applied the touch needed to put the ball past the stubborn Scriven. Had the referee not blown for time shortly after the equalising goal, Gibbons no doubt would have finished his single-handed destruction of Southampton.

Syd Gibbons in a traditional pose attacking the ball.

One great save in the opening half by Scriven probably saved a point for his club but on the whole I thought them unlucky not to win. Fishlock, the Surrey cricketer, was seen to chief advantage in the opening half, Horton made an industrious leader and Brewis was the best inside schemer.

Fulham's defence, in which Birch, Gibbons and Clarke, a native of Johannesburg, took chief honours, was not well balanced. In attack, Hammond and Price showed enough craft to merit a better result. Arnold, himself an old Southampton player, made a greater winger, and when Newton falls into the new scheme, he, too, should be a valuable asset. Newton, however, was not allowed much rope by McIlwaine, who played great football. The receipts were just over £1,000.

In its own inimitable way, the Fulham programme for the next home game put its own spin on the match. 'Pride of place in the way of commentary must be a reference to the amazing game in the League with Southampton a fortnight ago, a game in which honours were divided equally. On the surface there is little to go into raptures over in that, but the manner in which that result was achieved will forever occupy a high niche in the annals of the club.

If the truth has to be told, and believe it or not, fabrication is not in my vocabulary when telling the Tales of Fulham, the Cottagers were prepared for the grim battle that the visitors from the south coast waged. Alas, aye and alack, things did not pan out according to plan. The Saints grabbed the whip before we could get hold of it and they lost no time in lashing it about. They leathered us good and strong and the sting took the form of three goals.

Then there was Syd Gibbons. Did he like this humiliation? Lads and lassies, he did not. Every avenue was tried in an endeavour to find where the Saints had sprung a leak, but all in vain. Our Carnera was not satisfied, and so he went up to see for himself. Net result, a glorious hat trick which saved the game. Your hat trick Sydney – our hats off to you.'

Fulham 3 v Chelsea 2

Monday 24 February 1936
FA Cup Fifth Round Replay
Referee: W.P. Harper
Attendance: 30,696

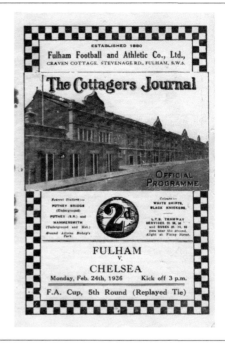

FULHAM		CHELSEA
Alf Tootill	1	Vic Woodley
Jimmy Hindson	2	George Barber
Mike Keeping	3	Tommy Law
Bert Barrett	4	Len Allum
Syd Gibbons	5	Allan Craig
Jimmy Tompkins	6	Harold Miller
Jack Finch	7	Dick Spence
Trevor Smith	8	Harry Burgess
Eddie Perry	9	Joe Bambrick
Jim Hammond	10	George Gibson
John Arnold	11	Billy Barraclough

In 1936, for the first time in a decade, the Cottagers got through to the last 16 of the FA Cup, after victories over Brighton (2–1) and Blackpool (5–2). Eddie Perry's four goals against Blackpool set a club Cup record. The reward was an away tie at Stamford Bridge, the first time the two neighbours had been paired in the Cup and the first time they had met competitively in eight years. Chelsea, comfortably placed in the top half of the First Division, had reached this stage with wins over lower-League Norwich and Plymouth.

The game, first arranged for Saturday 15th, had to be postponed because of a London fog and so took place on the following Wednesday afternoon in those pre-floodlight days. In spite of the kick-off time, and the fact Arsenal were at home to Newcastle at the same time, some 52,096 people managed to attend. They were rewarded with an entertaining but increasingly fractious and goalless encounter played on a wet pitch, which got heavier as the rain came down. Perry had the

Trevor Smith cracks Fulham's second goal past Chelsea 'keeper Woodley.

ball in the net for Fulham in the first minute, but was rightly given offside. Chelsea had Scottish inside-forward George Gibson sent off (a relatively rare occurrence in those days) shortly before the interval for a very bad foul on Jack Finch, which changed the mood of the match. Gibson received a month's suspension. Despite the attacking intentions of both sides, the defences held out and so it was to the Cottage the following Monday, kick-off 3.00pm.

The press felt the Cottagers had missed their best chance, failing to score against a Chelsea team down to 10 men and with their left-back a virtual passenger on the left wing. Each side made one change from the first game. For Chelsea, Tommy Law came in for Robert Macaulay at left-back while Fulham switched Finch to the right wing in place of Bert Worsley, with John Arnold restored to the left wing. Unlike the first meeting, this match lived up to its billing with the outcome in doubt until the final whistle.

FULHAM TRIUMPH IN CRAZIEST CUP TIE

Chelsea played to a standstill but nearly save the day

Gibbons the bulwark

The fastest, thrill-a-minute, craziest Cup tie in years put Fulham into the last eight of football's 'lucky dip' at Craven Cottage yesterday. These Fulham go-getters deserved their success. They played a luckless Chelsea team to a standstill and led them by three clear goals with a quarter of an hour to go. Chelsea at that time looked whacked, morally and physically.

Then, this dead-beat side made things crazier by netting a couple of simple goals. Barraclough bagged them both after missing the most wide open of goals at a time when a Chelsea score was most urgently needed.

What can you make of it? Here was Fulham in the first half, with dashing wings and deft, dangerous inside-forwards, sweeping down on the Chelsea goal, giving a tremendous amount of work to a commendably steady Chelsea defence in which Barber and Craig shone. Goals looked like coming every minute. They only got one. It came from a free kick headed on by Hammond to Trevor Smith.

CLASSIC AIMS

Chelsea, the while, were trying hard to play classic football. The ball simply would not run for them. That overworked football expression means to some extent that the luck is against one side. It also means that that side is not carrying out its movement with the nice precision which makes the ball run. Even so, George Gibson, as full as ever of neat touches and clever dribbles, ought to have had an equaliser. His shot actually went past Tootill and stuck in the mud on the goal line. The goalkeeper was able to turn and gather it and the situation was saved.

Bless me, if a similar thing did not happen at the start of the second half. This time, Tootill half stopped a stinger – again from Gibson. It spun out of his hands and once more stuck in the mud right on the line.

For 20 minutes in the second half, Chelsea made raid after raid, by means of highly scientific football on the hard-pressed Fulham goal. Tootill, his two semi slips apart, covered himself with glory. So did Mike Keeping and that amazingly energetic wing half, Tompkins. But the man who prevented the defence from getting flurried and completely blocked the middle was Syd Gibbons. A man of elephantine proportions, he showed the footwork of a ballet dancer and no Chelsea man seemed to want to go into a full tackle when he had possession. I have not seen Bambrick so completely blotted out of a match as he was this one.

Barraclough's miss was a terrible setback for Chelsea's hopes. The ball came to him at a time when Chelsea were throwing everything into attack – when even Law and Barber were going up into the goalmouth to get their heads to corner kicks – when a goal meant everything.

MISSED BY A YARD

He was 10 yards out and had time to steady himself and take aim. There was only Tootill to beat. His shot missed by a yard. Soon after this, Fulham broke away. Finch dashed off down the left wing and centred for Smith to score. It was here seen that Tommy Law was played out. He could not raise a gallop.

It was scarcely surprising when Finch went away again for Arnold to head through from his centre. Chelsea's defence had undoubtedly cracked badly. But before Fulham had got over their delight, Chelsea pegged them back one. Barraclough side-footed in a simple goal from Allum's cross pass. He got another with four minutes to go and it looked as if extra-time might be necessary, for plainly the Fulham defence was now wavering. It just held out to the final whistle.

Mr George Jobey brought the Derby County players, who will now meet Fulham at Craven Cottage on Saturday, to see the game. I have no doubt that they decided that they have a good chance to win and pass on to the semi-final, but this was a game from which it would be unsafe to draw conclusions. Chelsea were beaten by opponents whose teamwork was always superior. Rarely was there scheming clever enough to draw the Fulham defenders out of position and though there were enough occasions when they might have scored, they occurred in fortunate circumstances.

A few foolish spectators booed Mr W. P. Harper the referee when he entered the field, but it was notable that he was cheered when he returned after half-time. He was strict in penalising anything that looked like an infringement at the start, but this was not a match that was difficult to control.

Fulham 3 v Derby County 0

Saturday 29 February 1936
FA Cup Sixth Round
Referee: E.C. Carnwell
Attendance: 37,151

FULHAM		DERBY C
Alf Tootill	1	John Kirby
Jimmy Hindson	2	Bill Udall
Mike Keeping	3	George Collin
Bert Barrett	4	Jack Nicholas
Syd Gibbons	5	Jack Barker
Jimmy Tompkins	6	Ike Keen
Jack Finch	7	Sammy Crooks
Trevor Smith	8	Charlie Napier
Eddie Perry	9	Jack Bowers
Jim Hammond	10	Peter Ramage
John Arnold	11	Dally Duncan

There were just five days between beating Chelsea and Derby's visit to the Cottage for the Sixth Round tie. This was the Cottagers' fifth appearance in the quarter-finals and the 37,151 crowd was the biggest home Cup attendance since the visit of Manchester United in 1908. They paid £3,108 2s 6d. The team was the same as knocked out Chelsea the previous Monday and because of a colour clash, Fulham played in unfamiliar black and white hoop shirts and white shorts.

Derby travelled south hoping to improve their prospects of a League and Cup double. A First Division club since long-serving manager George Jobey had taken them to promotion in 1925, they and Sunderland were the leading contenders for the League Championship. With just one defeat in their previous 12 League and Cup games, they were also a team in form. Fulham, on the other hand, had managed just two victories in their previous eight League games. The Rams' long-established half-back line of Nicholas, Barker and Keen was the strength of the side and as good as any in the country, Jack Bowers was a prolific scorer and, in Sammy Crooks and Dally Duncan, Derby had two of the trickiest and most admired wingers in the League.

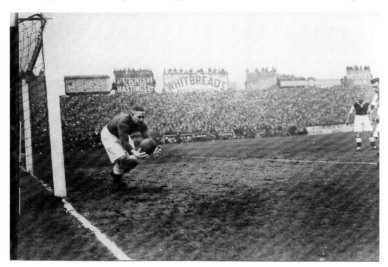

Fulham's victory was therefore as surprising as it was thoroughly deserved, and acknowledged as such by the Derby manager. The ecstatic home crowd showed their appreciation by carrying the players off shoulder high at the final whistle. If there was man of the match for Fulham, the press reports would have given it to centre-half Syd Gibbons. So in his first season as manager, Jack Peart had steered Fulham to their second FA Cup semi-final, and he had done so by using just 13 players in the five games, one of whom (Warburton) had played just once (against Brighton).

Derby 'keeper Kirby gathers the ball on a sodden Cottage pitch.

FULHAM CUP TRIUMPH

Derby Stars Failed To Dazzle

Gibbons again the hero

For this Sixth Round FA Cup tie, it was the Fulham team that beat Chelsea last Monday. Derby County had their best side out, with Bowers leading the forwards. Fulham played in the narrow black and white hoops of Queen's Park, Glasgow, while Derby turned out in Aston Villa colours.

Fulham surprised the critics, themselves and everybody in fact with a magnificent victory over Derby County. Almost from start to finish they were the better side, but in fairness to Derby, it should be mentioned that they were sadly handicapped by injuries. Ten minutes from half-time, Udall came into collision with Tompkins and hurt his shoulder so badly that for the rest of the game he played on the wing with his arm strapped. To make matters worse, Napier pulled a muscle early in the second half and hobbled about on the other wing.

But even when Derby had 11 sound men, Fulham looked the more dangerous side. Their wingers, Finch and Arnold, were every bit as effective as the famous Derby pair of Crooks and Duncan, and Trevor Smith was just about the best inside-forward on the pitch.

The man of the match, however, was Gibbons. On the other side was England's first choice for centre half, so the standard set could hardly have been higher. But Gibbons has no respect for reputations and it is no exaggeration to say that he dominated the game. Besides subduing Bowers, he advanced upfield almost impudently to set his wingers going time and time again. Keeping and Hindson tackled grimly and, as far as I can remember, Tootill only had two hard shots to save. In the first half, he tipped a piledriver from Ramage over the bar and, early in the second half, he went down full length to a grand shot from Crooks.

It is difficult to criticise Derby because for nearly half the game, nearly every forward and half-back was playing out of position. The game started at a terrific pace and both goals had narrow escapes in the opening minutes. Duncan raced half the length of the field and nearly scored with a glorious cross shot and, at the other end, Hammond was only inches wide. Fulham continued to press until half-time, and Kirby only just managed to scramble away a great header from Perry.

Five minutes after the interval, Fulham took the lead and the crowd nearly went frantic. Finch lobbed over a centre which bounced in the goalmouth and Arnold, hurling himself forward, finished up in the back of the net with the ball.

With Sammy Crooks inside to Udall and Napier at right-half and Nicholas at full-back, Derby tried desperately hard to stem the Fulham tide, but it was all unavailing, and 20 minutes later, the home team went further ahead. Swarming around the Derby goal, they forced a corner on the left. From Arnold's corner, the ball came out to Barrett and the right-half, taking it on the volley, completely beat Kirby.

FULHAM FEAR NO CUP FOE WRONG DERBY MOVES
By P. J Moss

When I say that I think Derby beat themselves by trying to play the hard game instead of their usual clever football, I am not overstating the case. As they started they finished, and fortune saved them several more goals. Watch Fulham in the semi-final, whoever they meet!

When Derby tried to play the football which belongs to their class, they found they had blunted their "keen edge."

It is the truth to say that Tootill, in the Fulham goal, did not have more than a couple of real shots to stop in the match. Indeed, the game was thirty-five minutes old before he was called upon at all. Then he tipped a great dive from Ramage over the bar.

Meanwhile, the Fulham forwards splendidly fed by a fine half back line, in which Gibbons was an outstanding figure in both attack and defense, kept on top of the Derby backs. Arnold and Hammond had both tested Kirby before Hammond missed a sitter from close in. the crowd groaned as one man.

Kirby just managed to get his fingertips to one header from Perry, and Kirby also saved from Smith and Hammond before Udall, in making a heavy charge at Tompkins, missed his man and fell heavily on his shoulder and had to leave the field

UDAL RETURNS

He – and Nicholas, who had been cautioned – had played a very heavy game against Arnold, and his absence from the defense made matters easier for Fulham's left wing. Udall soon returned-his left arm strapped to his side- only to play at outside right.

Try as they could, Fulham could not beat the defense in the first half, although they had many fine chances, and the Derby goal had some desperate escapes.

Gibbons was again in glorious form in the second half, but Derby were the first to threaten danger. Tootill got a touch to a pile-driver from Crooks, now inside right – a proper rover – before Fulham settled down to the attack again.

Nothing could stop Fulham now and two minutes later they scored again and Derby's interest in the Cup was finished. Again Arnold took a corner and this time Smith fastened on to the ball and beat Kirby from close in.

Poor Derby struggled gamely but it was all over now and the end came with Fulham still attacking. Instead of fading out in the second half as we had been led to expect, they crowded on full sail and made rings around a disorganised Derby defence. 'If you continue to play like this, no one will stop you' was Derby manager George Jobey's tribute to Fulham after the match.

An interesting criticism of the game came from four famous ex-referees who are conducting an investigation into contemporary soccer on behalf of a well-known daily newspaper. These critics came to the conclusion that Fulham played football of an excellent standard. They rose to First Division class while Derby fell to Third. Both teams were criticised for foul play, 11 fouls being given against Fulham and only five against Derby. But whereas Fulham's offences were for the most part mere vigour or use of arms, certain members of the Derby team displayed a ruthlessness which calls for strong words. Several fouls by Derby players were noticed which were not given by the referee. Arnold was roughly used and the critics were of the opinion that Nicholas and Udall were playing at Arnold rather than against him. Gibbons, the Fulham centre half, and the biggest man on the field, was also the fairest and the best. Only one foul was registered against him. He proved that weight and barging is not essential to successful defence.

Fulham 1 v Sheffield United 2

Saturday 21 March 1936
FA Cup Semi-final (at Molineux)
Referee: W. Walden
Attendance: 51,568

FULHAM		SHEFFIELD U
Alf Tootill	1	John Smith
Jimmy Hindson	2	Harry Hooper
Mike Keeping	3	Albert Cox
Bert Barrett	4	Ernie Jackson
Syd Gibbons	5	Tom Johnson
Jimmy Tompkins	6	Archie Macpherson
Bert Worsley	7	Harry Barton
Trevor Smith	8	Bob Barclay
Eddie Perry	9	Ephraim Dodds
Jim Hammond	10	John Pickering
John Arnold	11	William Bird

And so to Molineux for the semi-final three weeks later. The draw had been kind to the Cottagers. They were paired with another Second Division club, Sheffield United, while two First Division clubs, Arsenal and Grimsby, battled it out in the other tie at Leeds Road, Huddersfield. In the run up to the big day, Fulham had put seven past Bury and four past Bradford in the League, but had conceded five at Leicester. And they travelled to the Midlands knowing they had beaten the Blades 3–1 in their League meeting at the Cottage four months earlier. The tie attracted a crowd of 51,568 who paid ground record receipts of £4,766. The club organised special rail excursions at a return cost of seven shillings (35p) for the two and a half hour journey between Euston and Wolverhampton.

But Sheffield United had picked up since November. Between Christmas and the match and Molineux, the Blades had been on a 21-match unbeaten run which had taken them to the top of the Second Division and the semi-final of the Cup. Fulham were to end this long unbeaten run, but sadly not at Molineux. Ironically, the teams met in a rearranged League game five days later at Bramall Lane – and Fulham won 1–0 thanks to a Mike Keeping penalty. Some 45 years later, inside-forward Jim Hammond said he remembered those two matches against United as if they were yesterday.

Manager Peart had a selection decision to make. All the 12 players who had played in the four previous matches were fit and he decided to bring back Bert Worsley on the right wing and keep John Arnold on the left. This meant that Jack Finch, who had played in all five games and in three different positions, missed out, something he remembered bitterly late in life over 50 years later. Anyone with an opportunity to see the 'Golden Gordon' episode of Michael Palin's wonderful post-Python series, Ripping Yarns, will see brief footage from the match, with Fulham attacking the United goal.

The 1936 FA Cup squad. Jack Peart (manager), Barrett, Gibbons, Hindson, Tootill, Keeping, Tompkins, Hammond, John Dean (chairman), Tom Pearks (director), Worsley, Smith, Perry, Finch, Arnold, Doc Voisey (trainer).

FULHAM'S GREAT FIGHT
By Charles Buchan

In the last half hour of the FA Cup semi-final at Wolverhampton, Sheffield United came as near to throwing a match away as ever a team has done or will do. Leading by two goals, they concentrated on defence to an extent that Fulham were given every opportunity of forcing a replay. As it was, United can consider themselves lucky to have the clear-cut right of contesting their sixth Final.

How they could have made such a tactical mistake is beyond my comprehension. United's biggest asset is a clever attack yet they practically shelved it by falling back on defence. In the last period, ten Fulham players were in the United half, even the backs joining a furious but uncontrolled assault.

Another incident played an important part in United's victory. After 30 minutes, Arnold, robbing Hooper, provided Perry with the easiest of openings only six yards out with all the goal before him. Perry screwed the ball outside the upright, thus depriving Fulham of an equalising goal at a critical stage when they were definitely in command. An equaliser then would surely have changed the course of the game.

It was a good hard struggle even if the nervous tension of the players somewhat discounted their skill. United had the pull in this respect for I saw the real Fulham for only one period in the first half. In the main they got rid of the ball too quickly and relied too much upon long high kicking and quick dashes.

FAULTY WING HALVES

United, too, fell below their best in constructive play. Occasionally the forwards combined neatly and changed positions cleverly, but their brilliance never lasted. They were a strong, solid eleven, though not in the skilful form which has enabled them to equal a 26-year-old club record of 22 consecutive games without defeat.

As I anticipated, the Fulham wing half-backs held the key to the situation. Unfortunately for the hopes of an all-London Final, Barrett and Tompkins did not rise to the occasion. Indeed, they were so much out of position that often there were wide open spaces in the middle of the Fulham half of the field. Both United goals would have been prevented by intelligent positioning. Chief credit in the Fulham defence went to Keeping, a great general and one of the best kickers of the ball in the country, Hindson and Gibbons. The burly centre half did not entirely subdue the irrepressible Dodds, but when the centre-forward kept in the centre, Gibbons saw that he brought no serious trouble to Tootill, a reliable goalkeeper.

In attack, Smith was the livewire, for 30 minutes the complete inside-forward without a peer. In the first half, his sinuous dribbles opened out the United defence and he deserved a better reward than to see one splendid shot rebound from an upright. Fulham, however, were weak on the wings, where Worsley and Arnold could not strike their form. Each should have scored with a header directed just wide of the posts during Fulham's period of supremacy. All through, their finishing left a lot to be desired. Perry could make little of Johnson, and when he changed places with Hammond, the attack received a new lease of life. Not until the last 10 minutes did they beat down a resolute defence. Then Arnold headed through a long centre from Hindson. But they had their chances.

United's defenders were the bulwark of the side. Smith kept goal brilliantly though he could have reached the ball before Arnold when the outside left scored. Hooper, often in the wars, defended stubbornly but the big success was the 18-year-old Cox, a mere stripling taking part in his first Cup tie. He played with the assurance of a veteran, kicking and tackling with coolness and direction. His task was made harder by the slowness of McPherson, yet the youngster scarcely put a foot wrong.

STRAIGHT AT TOOTILL

Despite the poor form of McPherson, the United half-backs were superior to those of Fulham. They never attempted to be clever but their first-time methods were very effective. As a stopper who made no attempt to use the ball, Johnson was supreme while Jackson earned the praise of the best half-back afield. The United forwards disappointed. Dodds overdid the running-out-to-the-wings move and missed one glorious chance, shooting straight at Tootill from eight yards. Barclay and Pickering, delightfully neat at times, were not consistent and Barton took the honours of a line which rarely moved as a combination but made some atonement with two well taken goals.

In the 10th minute, Dodds headed the ball back to Pickering. The inside-forward sent it on to Bird whose fast, high shot left Tootill helpless. Then, 10 minutes after the interval, Gibbons headed out a centre from Barton. Pickering, collecting the ball quickly, crashed it into the net with a superb 20 yards right foot drive.

Fulham 8 v Swansea Town 1

Saturday 22 January 1938
Football League Division Two
Referee: J.M. Wiltshire
Attendance: 15,146

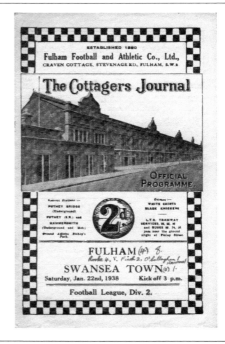

FULHAM		SWANSEA T
Hugh Turner	1	Stan Moore
Joe Bacuzzi	2	Syd Lawrence
Mike Keeping	3	Len Emanuel
Jim Evans	4	Jack Warner
Bob Dennison	5	Reuben Simons
Jimmy Tompkins	6	Joe Lloyd
Viv Woodward	7	John Foreman
Jim Hammond	8	Joe Beresford
Ronnie Rooke	9	Les Vernon
Taffy O'Callaghan	10	Tommy Olsen
Jack Finch	11	John Millington

Very little went right for Fulham in the first half of 1937–38. Friction behind the scenes spilled over into poor performances on the pitch. With just four wins from 21 games at the turn of the year, exactly halfway through the fixtures, the Cottagers were next to bottom of the table. The trouble off the field was a clash between the traditional managerial style of Jack Peart, an administrator and disciplinarian who was a bit remote from the players, and his assistant manager, Joe Edelston. A former Fulham player, Edelston had been at the Cottage since 1920 and had acted as caretaker in the months after the unexpected departures of previous managers. He was a believer in more technical coaching and a disciple of Jimmy Hogan. The poor performances of the first team, post-match demonstrations at the Cottage by unhappy supporters in the autumn, and the fact that the reserves led the Combination added to the tension. There could only be one outcome, and Edelston left abruptly.

With the outbreak of peace, the club's luck changed. After winning at Chesterfield, Fulham faced Swansea at the Cottage in their first home match of 1938 – and recorded what is still their biggest-ever win in the second tier of the League. And it sparked a revival. The Cottagers lost only three of the final 20 games, winning 12, and ended the season in eighth place, promotion form if sustained over a season.

The team was going through a period of transition and by the time Swansea came to town, it was more settled. Goalkeeper Hugh Turner, full-back Joe Bacuzzi and new signings Jim Evans and Taffy O'Callaghan were starting to make their mark. Perhaps most importantly, Ronnie Rooke rediscovered his scoring form. In the first half of the season the normally prolific marksman managed just three goals, a figure he more than doubled in 90 minutes against the Swans. There were some notable departures, including Syd Gibbons and Alf Tootill while Jim Hammond's goal in this match against Swansea was his 151st and last in a 10-year career in which he had become the first Fulham player to score 100 and 150 first-class goals for the club.

Welsh international inside-forward and a future member of the club's training staff, Taffy O'Callaghan, was in inspired form against his fellow countrymen.

SOUND SUPPORT FROM HALF-BACKS
Fulham Rout Swansea

Fulham, at home, achieved a fine performance by scoring four goals in each half. Swansea got a goal after the interval and Fulham won 8–1. Their goals came with metronomic precision, 10 minutes apart.

The biggest surprise of the day, bigger even than York City's victory over West Bromich in the Cup, was Fulham's thrashing of Swansea Town. Both teams languish at the bottom of the Second Division but no one today would have believed this of Fulham. The absence of Aenold from the Cottagers line up had little effect, Finch fitting in perfectly with O'Callaghan.

While Manager Neil Harris was out scouting for new players, his Swansea team were conceding goals at the rate of one every 10 minutes at Craven Cottage. During the first 50 minutes of this game, Fulham scored through Rooke (10 and 20 minutes.), Hammond (30 minutes), O'Callaghan (40 minutes) and Finch (50 minutes). Woodward broke this sequence when he fired wide from close range in the 60th minute, but it did not matter because there were still three more goals to come from the home team.

There is hope for Fulham after their brilliant display against Swansea, provided the new half-back line is left intact. Never before this season has the Fulham attack received such excellent support. Those through passes by Evans and Tompkins allowed Rooke, O'Callaghan and Hammond to play havoc among the non-too-safe Swansea defenders. It was refreshing to see the Fulham forwards snap up their chances and though Moore made a few mistakes, he made several masterly saves.

One could but admire this sporting Swansea team who not only fought to the last inch but displayed some clever work forward. It might have been a different story had Millington taken his chances before Fulham had scored. And Fulham had a chance before the scoring started. Very early in the game, Moore, the Welsh club's goalkeeper, took a rushing kick at the ball which struck Finch and rebounded towards the goal-line, but full-back Emmanuel just cleared in time.

Then the goals started. Fulham established a four-goal lead by the interval, and each one was nicely played for. O'Callaghan's clever back header gave Rooke the opportunity to open the scoring after 10 minutes. The second came after twenty minutes, the result of Rooke heading the ball from a corner by Finch far out of the goalkeeper's reach. Hammond took a through pass by Rooke to score number three after 30 minutes and after yet another gap of 10 minutes, the ever-consistent O'Callaghan notched number four with a great effort. He flung himself at a shot from Evans that was going out and dribbled the ball into the corner of the net.

First off the mark in the second half were the visitors. Millington, the cleverest of the Swansea forwards, scored a grand goal immediately on the resumption, only for Finch to restore Fulham's four-goal lead through Moore misjudging a centre by Woodard. This goal came on the hour, another 10 minutes after number four. Moore was at fault again when Rooke scored the sixth, for he dallied with the ball when he had time to clear. In further brilliant attacks, Rooke scored his fourth and Finch his second to leave Woodward the only Fulham forward without a goal to his credit.

As if eight goals were not enough, the Swansea goal had some narrow escapes in the closing stages, when Finch hit the crossbar and again fired across the Swansea goalmouth from an oblique angle.

Fulham 2 v Millwall 1

Saturday 8 October 1938
Football League Division Two
Referee: G. Dutton
Attendance: 49,335

FULHAM		MILLWALL
Hugh Turner	1	Harold Pearson
Joe Bacuzzi	2	Ted Smith
Mike Keeping	3	Reg Dudley
Jim Evans	4	George Lea
Ernie Hiles	5	Ted Chiverton
Jimmy Tompkins	6	Jim Forsyth
Jack Finch	7	Syd Rawlings
Bert Worsley	8	Jimmy Richardson
Ronnie Rooke	9	Bill Walsh
Viv Woodward	10	Don Barker
John Arnold	11	Reg Smith

The increasing military tension in Europe was the surreal backdrop to the 1938–39 season. As the odds on another war shortened by the day, Fulham took up in August 1938 where they had ended the previous April and made one of their most promising starts. In fact, if the League was based on a calendar year, the Cottagers would have been strong promotion contenders in 1938.

In October 1938, the club reached a new peak. Whether it was because Fulham were top of the (old) Second Division, or perhaps because it was the first home game after Prime Minister Neville Chamberlain's notorious Munich Pact with Hitler which merely delayed rather than averted war, or the attraction of an old-fashioned London Derby with fellow pace-setters Millwall, but an unprecedented 49,335 packed into the Cottage that autumnal afternoon. And the club authorities were clearly unprepared for such a huge crowd, the first time the Cottage had housed the biggest crowd of the day in the entire League, and by over 10,000. The gates were closed at 3.15, a quarter of an hour before the kick-off with thousands still locked out.

Despite the chaotic scenes, there were no serious injuries and no trouble, before, during or after the game. And the Cottagers continued their storming start to the season. Winning six and drawing two of the first nine games had put them in the top spot,

although Millwall were just two points behind having played one game fewer. For the fourth consecutive game, and the seventh time that season, manager Peart could field his strongest side, with centre-forward Rooke, scorer of seven goals in the previous three games, the man in form. The win kept Fulham in pole position and in the following weeks they attracted gates of 47,000 to White Hart Lane and Hillsborough and 64,166 to St James' Park, the largest attendance for any League game involving Fulham until the Premiership era visits to Old Trafford.

One of Archibald Leitch's turnstiles cannot take the strain of the record crowd.

MILLWALL, FULHAM PLAY FOOTBALL AT ITS BEST

If this be Second Division football, then give me more. Here was the local Derby in excelsis – fast, keen and clever. You would go a long, long way without seeing a better game of football. The only thing that was wrong with it was the score, for the balance of power swung so equally that justice would have been done had Fulham not got that second, winning goal. I don't recall such equal division all round. Even the record crowd was equally distributed.

The first half was nearly all Millwall after Forsyth had broken down the sweep of the first Fulham rush. To a roar that would have electrified an FA official, the Fulham forwards went off into a dashing attack that threatened quick goals. But this lantern-jawed, raw-boned Forsyth hurled himself into the battle with a single-minded fury that turned the tide.

Gradually Fulham began to find passes going to the feet of the big fellow and then, to the consternation of the home crowd, he found the going so pleasant that from harried defence in his own quarters, he found room to move up from defence to inter-passing attack with Barker and Richardson. These three were terrific, and maybe it was the work they put in during the first half that left them spent and unable to cope with the Fulham revival in the second.

For Fulham revived. They were a goal down at half-time and you could almost hear Charlie Hewitt tell what he would do to the Arsenal at the Den next season. This Forsyth-Barker combination did it. Forsyth broke up a Fulham attack and gave the ball to Barker at inside-left. There was no way through, and Barker took the only way – over to the right. He crossed a glorious ball to Walsh who was waiting in the goalmouth and Keeping, leaping to head it clear, deflected it into his own net.

It was hard luck on Keeping but it would probably have been a goal anyway – and Millwall deserved to be one up at the time. There was then a two-minute spell when every one of their forwards and Forsyth as well clustered round the Fulham goal and hammered away without a second's let up. The ball flashed in and out of the goal area like the point of a rapier, but it couldn't get through the magnificent Fulham entanglement of legs, heads and chests. The spell ended with JR Smith belting a low shot through and 'keeper Turner throwing himself full length to push it round the post.

Fulham might have been expected to come out for the second half a little under the weather, for they too had worked tremendously hard – though without the same finesse – in the first. This, however, would be to misunderstand completely the terrific character of this game. Fulham came out fighting and it was Millwall who showed the strain. The defence that had been on top began to waver and, as it did, Fulham forwards gained more and more confidence.

Arnold had some flashing runs on the left while Woodward, who had been a gallant trier, suddenly found the ball began to run for him. Rooke bored away as if he were just starting and, although he made one or two mistakes, he kept Chiverton busy. Their equalising goal came unexpectedly from a free kick taken at an angle by Arnold. Woodward dashed in and clinched the goal…and almost had his shirt torn off his back by his teammates.

Arnold was also involved in the winning goal. Rooke was obstructed as he was dashing through the middle and Arnold took the kick just outside the penalty box. He took a short, feinting a run that left the mass of Millwall players in doubt as to whether he was actually going to take the kick or not, and found a way through to the bottom corner of the goal. Pearson threw himself at the ball, but Evans , who was waiting around, ran up and scored.

So that was that, and although Millwall put everything they had into getting back on terms, Hiles, Bacuzzi and Keeping were giving no more presents in the shape of deflections and miskicks. Finch had a poor first half but he came away in the second. Rooke did his part but Woodward was the best forward on the field.

Millwall goalkeeper Pearson saves from John Arnold, while Jimmy Tompkins follows up.

Fulham 6 v Bury 0

Saturday 7 January 1939
FA Cup Third Round
Referee: H.N. Mee
Attendance: 11,221

FULHAM		BURY
Hugh Turner	1	George Bradshaw
Joe Bacuzzi	2	Les Hart
Mike Keeping	3	Jimmy Gemmell
Jim Evans	4	David Jones
Bob Dennison	5	George Matthewson
Jimmy Tompkins	6	Billy Whitfield
Dennis Higgins	7	Eddie Kilshaw
Bert Worsley	8	George Bargh
Ronnie Rooke	9	George Davies
Taffy O'Callaghan	10	Billy Graham
John Arnold	11	Jack Ormandy

By the turn of 1939, war was a question of when rather than if, but there was still time for a new Fulham record to be established. In January, the Cottagers were drawn at home to Bury, also of the second tier of the League, in the third round of the FA Cup. There was little that was remarkable about a 6–0 victory over a depleted side but the fact that Ronnie Rooke scored all six was significant. Although four players (Fred Harrison, Beddy Jezzard, Jimmy Hill and Steve Earle) have scored five in a League match, Rooke's double hat-trick is a club record haul in a single first-class match.

And there should be little surprise that it was Rooke who achieved it, for he was a one-man scoring machine. He started with a hat-trick on his debut against West Ham in 1936 (the first of only two Fulham players to achieve this feat), he was top scorer in each of his five seasons at the Cottage, and also hit 212 goals in 199 wartime appearances. As well as the six against Bury, he twice scored four times in a game and managed six other hat-tricks. All that for £300 from Crystal Palace reserves. Prolific barely does him justice. And then, at the age of 34, he moved to Arsenal and top-flight football for the first time. In 1947–48, he was the leading scorer in the First Division with 33 goals as the Gunners took the League title.

The reward for beating Bury was a fourth round trip to Stamford Bridge. Although beaten 3–0 by First Division Chelsea, Fulham had the consolation of playing in front of a crowd of 69,987, the biggest-ever crowd for any Fulham game up to that point. Ironically, 48 hours later, the Cottagers had a League game at home to Swansea and drew a crowd of just 3,155, the smallest Cottage attendance in the entire inter-war era. In a little over a fortnight in the closing months of an era, three pieces of Fulham history were created.

Fulham's captain in the final interwar seasons was full back Mike Keeping.

ROOKE'S COMEDY SEXTET

I don't know whether it will mean anything to poor, unfortunate Bury, but at Fulham yesterday they were beaten by Charlton. Which sounds goofy but the point is that Fulham, called upon to change colours, were supplied with two sets of red jerseys (one set for a second half change) by Charlton. What a tragedy for Bury! Midway through the second half, first Whitfield, the left-half, and soon after Gemmell, the left-back, pulled muscles and were more or less out of the game from then onwards. Gemmell went to outside left for the remainder of the first half, but Whitfield persevered in his own place. In the second half, Bury had one of the cripples on each wing, but Gemmell only remained a few minutes and went off.

Bury finished the match with three men only, Bradshaw, the goalkeeper, Hart, the right-back, and Matthewson, centre half, in their original positions. Needless to say, the game long before had become a farce.

In fairness to Fulham, they would probably have won by just as many in any case for Bury are distinctly a poor side, and this Cup defeat may be a good thing for them as it will take them all their time to keep clear of the relegation zone.

The scorer is always the hero of a match and, of course, Ronnie Rooke gets all the limelight by scoring Fulham's six goals. Long after pretty well everybody had gone home, barring the players and officials, a bunch of kids was outside the Fulham offices chanting 'We want Ronnie Rooke'. Before Rooke went home, he had been presented with the ball, which in due course will be autographed by the Fulham directors, officials and team.

The fifth of Rooke's six goals is officially credited to him in Fulham's records, which is all that matters but it was one of those goals which can be argued. It was Taffy O'Callaghan who shot, and on the way the ball hit Rooke on the chest, which deflected the ball out of range of Bradshaw, the Bury goalkeeper whom we once knew with Arsenal.

The picture I remember most was little fair-haired Ormandy, the Bury outside left who eventually went to inside-left to make way for a cripple and finally with only three forwards, he was practically the Bury forward line, showing amazing energy and craft in a hopeless cause. Bury had one scoring chance in the whole match and that was when Kilshaw, another little 'un on the other wing, made a terrific shot just outside the box which hit Keeping, the Fulham captain. Such was the force that for several minutes afterwards, Keeping was 'out on his feet'.

It seems hard on Bury to talk of the second half being a comedy, but so it was. Arnold, Fulham's outside left, should have scored a hat-trick himself. He missed in every conceivable way. He even managed to slip in the mud when he was plumb in front of the goal and it seemed as if he must score.

Bury were beaten in the first few minutes by deplorable defence work and a goalkeeping error. Rooke's first goal was almost comic. He topped a longish shot which tootled along the ground and Bradshaw went to ground to stop it with his hands at the right of the goal. Instead, the ball hit his hands, twiddled and twisted for it seemed an age, and finally trickled into the goal at the left hand side with Bradshaw still on the ground. Bury were always a beaten team after that – even when at full strength.

Fulham brought O'Callaghan in, and they can't leave him out after this. He was back to the form of his heyday with the Spurs. Rooke will be very thankful to Taffy for his help in his record-breaking goal haul.

Goals timetable

2 minutes   Rooke takes a long pass from Keeping and shoots hard and low from the edge of the penalty area. The ball slips through the goalkeeper's hands.

40 minutes   Rooke, following up, scores from close range when Bradshaw can only parry Arnold's cross.

45 minutes   From Higgins free kick, Rooke shoots on the turn past Bradshaw.

55 minutes   Rooke fastens on to Worsley's header and volleys into the net.

75 minutes   Rooke diverts O'Callaghan's shot off his chest past Bradshaw.

85 minutes   Rooke completes the scoring with a hard low drive from the edge of the box.

HAT-TRICK IN EACH HALF
BURY STRUGGLE ON WITH 10 MEN

Six goals by Rooke – and Fulham beat Bury in the cup-tie this afternoon. Bury, weakened by injuries, played with ten men in the second half.

One of the smallest crowds of the season came to Craven Cottage for the F.A. Cup-tie between Fulham and Bury.

After two minutes Fulham scored. Rooke picked up a long pass from Keeping and shot hard and low from the edge of the penalty area.

Fulham did much as they liked with the visitors in the early stages. The home forwards continually outpaced and out-maneuvered the rather slow Bury defenders.

A brilliant run by Ormandy led to a corner for Bury. Ormandy placed this across to Kilshaw, who volleyed in a terrific shot which struck Keeping full in the face. Keeping recovered after attention.

Fulham went further ahead in five minutes from the interval. Bradshaw dived forward to a catch a centre from Arnold and Rooke, following up, kicked the ball from his hands in to the net.

On the stroke of half-time Rooke got his hat-trick. Following a free-kick by Higgins he got the ball with his back to the goal, turned round, and gave Bradshaw no chance with his shot

HALF-TIME: FULHAM 3, BURY 0

When Bury lined up after the interval only Bradshaw, Matthewson, and Davies were in their original positions, injuries to Gemmell and Whitfield causing a complete change round of the players.

Gemmell hobbled along the right wing for a time and then went off.

With only ten men against them Fulham had matters pretty much their own way, and after ten minutes Rooke put them four up.

Bury battled pluckily but their weakened team could do little except try to keep the score as low as possible

Higgins hit the far post with a grand shot: then Arnold lofted the ball over the bar from five yards range.

Bradshaw later dived at Rooke's feet, grabbed the ball and cleared.

With ten minutes to play Fulham got a fifth goal.

O'Callaghan shot hard for the goal and the ball was deflected off Rooke's body into the goal.

Four minutes later Rooke scored his sixth goal with a ground shot from the edge of the penalty area.

RESULT: FULHAM 6, BURY 0

Everton 0 v Fulham 1

Saturday 14 February 1948
FA Cup Fifth Round Replay
Referee: R.J. Leafe
Attendance: 71,587

EVERTON		FULHAM
Ted Sagar	1	Ted Hinton
George Saunders	2	Harry Freeman
Gordon Dugdale	3	Joe Bacuzzi
Peter Farrell	4	Len Quested
John Humphreys	5	Jim Taylor
Tommy Watson	6	Pat Beasley
Jackie Grant	7	Sid Thomas
Stan Bentham	8	Bob Thomas
Harry Catterick	9	Arthur Stevens
Wally Fielding	10	Harry Ayres
Tommy Eglington	11	Dave Bewley

The second of Fulham's trilogy of remarkable FA Cup victories over Everton came in the second full season after World War Two. As with the other two ties, a division separated the clubs in the League, with the Toffees in the top flight, but on this occasion, the Cottagers had failed to capitalise on home advantage. Drawn at home, Fulham could only manage a draw the previous Saturday. Although having the better of the play, they had to come back from behind to earn a replay. Everton went ahead on 41 minutes when Eglington rounded off a fine passing movement between Catterick (the Toffees' future manager) and Grant. Len Quested equalised after 65 minutes with a snap shot from 20 years. Unusually, extra-time was played in the first game and both sides went close to winning the tie (Stevens for Fulham and Grant for Everton), but goalkeeper Hinton made an especially dramatic last minute save from Catterick.

A remarkable crowd of 71,587 turned up for the replay, played the following Saturday, the largest attendance for a Fulham game at a club ground until visits to Old Trafford in the Premier era. Both sides made one change (for Fulham Bewley was in for Grant and for the home side Watson for Wainwright). Everton were a mid-table side without any big stars (Lawton and Mercer had moved on the previous year) but were nevertheless favourites to finish the job on their own turf. But the result, though the Cup shock of the round, was well earned on the balance of play and in retrospect showed something was changing at Fulham.

Jim Taylor, one of the heroes of the Goodison victory.

Although Jack Peart's team was plodding along in mid-table, there had been a marked improvement in the away record. That season the Cottagers won more games away from home (nine) than they did at home (six), the first time this had happened since joining the League. This terrific win on Merseyside took Fulham into the last eight of the Cup where poor home form again let them down, Blackpool winning 2–0.

Fulham's Wounded Hero

An amazing inferiority complex on the part of Everton enabled Fulham to gain a sensational triumph by 1-0 in the Cup replay at Goodison Park. If ever a team stepped on to the football field with an air of complete lack of confidence it was Everton. That does not detract from the sheer merit of Fulham's victory which was constructed on the solidity of a mighty defence revolving around the hub of the hero of the game, Jim Taylor.

Midway through the first half, Taylor, a wing half back playing in the centre, collided with his colleague Quested and severely cut his head. For long periods, Taylor played with a sponge with which he kept mopping up blood from his face. His jersey became almost red and white. Yet he defied the might of Everton and even out-headed Catterick. Fulham had other heroes in Bacuzzi, Quested, Beasley and Thomas. They are the players who pinpointed this success on a day when Everton appeared in their poorest light of the season.

Everton's lack of confidence was reflected from the outset, when they played as if their only object was to save the game and not win it. Catterick tried hard enough, but he had neither the foot craft nor the speed to outwit a great defence off his own bat. Fulham went to the ball, whereas Everton waited for it to come to them. It was a case of Everton having three forwards and five half backs but the five were not as good as Fulham's three.

Bob Thomas won the game in the 73rd minute with a goal which Everton will always protest was unfair. Farrell was obviously fouled by Stevens before the latter beat Humphreys and slipped the ball forward for Thomas to race on to and score with a glorious shot into the corner, to which Sagar did not have time event to move. Fulham had plenty of other easy chances but they failed, even with a penalty after 79 minutes, Freeman shooting wide.

Any weakness in the Fulham side was at right back, where Freeman was too often caught on one leg; in goal, where Hinton often appeared nervous; and at outside right, where Sid Thomas too often promised so much and but failed so lamentably. Yet it was a fast, mobile Fulham who hit a particularly high standard. On this showing, they will severely test Blackpool in the sixth round. And on this display, the Londoners are justified in their quiet confidence of progressing into the semi finals.

BAND OF HEROES WON RIGHT TO PLAY BLACKPOOL

Though the result may look like it, this match does not go into the list of wither Cup surprises of flukes. Beyond all question, Fulham deserved to win. And a hearty pat on the back for all 11 of them. Typical of the team was Jim Taylor at centre half, who cut his head in the first half hour and walked off at the end with a blood stained white shirt, looking like something out of a butcher's shop.

But Taylor was only one of the Fulham heroes. Joe Bacuzzi at left back was another. He played like an international. So did Sid Thomas at outside left, most ably supported to the very end by his partner Bob Thomas, the man who got the goal. A first class goal it was, too, arriving 18 minutes from the end. Stevens, centre forward, slipped through a ground pass and Bob Thomas took it in his stride to shoot from the near the penalty spot and flash home a red-hot low ball that that beat Sagar all the way.

Fulham looked senior class and reduced Everton to third-rate status. After an all-in first half of bits and pieces, Fulham settled down to fast use of the ball and anticipation of its run. This time, Everton could not be saved by Sagar. One of his wonder leaps prevented an early Bob Thomas header flying inside the goal angle.

Against this, the admirable Joe Bacuzzi, in every shape and form the England left back, headed off the goal-line and Hinton turned a long shot against the bar and over. So far as Everton were concerned, that was all whereas the second Fulham phase promised a feast of goals.

The winning goal was scored by Bob Thomas 17 minutes from the end. He cleverly balanced himself and fastened on to a pass by Stevens to shoot fiercely past Sagar into the net. As many colleagues as could get near him mobbed Thomas and their joy was understandable. They must have been concerned their superiority would go unrewarded.

Although Mr RJ Leafe refereed finely, I cannot forgive him for taking the so-often repeated line of escape from a penalty by giving a free kick inches outside the penalty area. When Watson of Everton had so obviously lifted his arm to the ball, it was clearly well inside. Yet it did not seem a deliberate handling case when Everton's Watson, on the ground, touched the ball and Fulham were awarded a penalty from which Harry Freeman shot wide.

Fulham were a splendid mobile team of whom, on addition to Taylor and Bacuzzi, Beasley and the right wing Thomas', Sid and Bob, starred.

West Bromwich Albion 1 v Fulham 2

Saturday 5 March 1949
Football League Division Two
Referee: B.M. Griffiths
Attendance: 27,595

WEST BROMWICH A		FULHAM
Jim Sanders	1	Doug Flack
Jim Pemberton	2	Harry Freeman
Len Millard	3	Joe Bacuzzi
Ray Barlow	4	Len Quested
Jack Vernon	5	Jim Taylor
Glyn Hood	6	Pat Beasley
Billy Elliott	7	Arthur Stevens
Cyril Williams	8	Bob Thomas
Dave Walsh	9	Arthur Rowley
Jack Haines	10	Bedford Jezzard
Harry Kinsell	11	Jack McDonald

The 1948–49 season was to be Fulham's most successful in the League up to that point. It opened with manager Jack Peart at the helm, the start of his 14th year in the job. He had enjoyed a great Cup run in his first season but thereafter, it was mid-table mediocrity and seven seasons of war football. Sadly, however, as the club stood on the threshold of its best-ever League campaign, Peart died in September after a short illness, aged 59. It was a tragic start and, with just one win in the next seven games, was reflected in results. Then a successor was appointed, who stabilised the club and led it unexpectedly to the (old) Second Division Championship and into the top flight for the first time.

The 'new' man was Frank Osborne, a Fulham player in the 1920s and the first to win an England cap while at the Cottage. On retirement, he took a job with chairman John Dean's company and in the 1930s became a director. In the autumn of 1948, he was persuaded to 'step down' and take over the playing side, appointing another former player, Eddie Perry, as team manager.

Crucially, in only his third game, Fulham were beaten 2–1 at home by West Brom, the Cottagers' only home defeat of the season. Crucially, because the man who did the damage for the Baggies was their reserve striker Arthur Rowley. A couple of months later, Osborne brought Rowley to the Cottage in exchange for Ernie Shepherd. It was a masterstroke. In 22 games, Rowley scored 19 goals and was on the losing side just three times. As the season progressed, the battle for the two promotion places (no Play-offs in those days) was between West Brom, Fulham and Southampton. In March came a showdown. The first two of those clubs met for the return at the Hawthorns, and Rowley had the last word. He was as effective that day for his new club on his old ground as he had been for his former club at his current home in the autumn.

Match-winning Arthur Rowley played for both Fulham and West Brom that season.

LAST MINUTE ROWLEY GOAL BEATS THROSTLES
FULHAM WERE FLATTERED

In a game which was rendered almost farcical by reason of a continuous snowstorm, Albion lost at home to Fulham by the odd goal in three. Rowley, their former player, scored the winning goal in the last minute. Albion, in the second half, failed to make the best use of their chances, although the conditions can be blamed.

Harry Kinsell, playing his first game as an outside left, provided the spice in Albion's home game against Fulham, whose attack was led by Arthur Rowley, who was transferred to the Cottagers in December. Fine snow was falling when the teams appeared. The lines had been swept clear and about 25,000 were present when Vernon lost the toss, Albion having to face the snow and wind.

Fortunate goal

Although the visitors took the initiative at the start, nothing of any note reached Sanders in the home side's goal. Millard figured prominently in stemming some Fulham raids, and Albion were soon on the warpath.

They took the lead in 10 minutes when Williams cleverly sent Elliott away. The winger cut in and shot along the ground. Flack had the ball covered but it slipped through his hands and underneath his body into the net. A fortunate goal perhaps but it indicated the tricky conditions.

Williams prominent

The visiting defence stood up well to some warm work by the Albion forwards, among whom Williams was well to the fore. Players, however, were skidding all over the place and the unexpected so often happened, and openings went begging. A centre by Stevens was cleverly caught by Sanders, who frequently had to brush the snow from his face. There was more menace in Albion's work, and Williams was nearly through, but Taylor swept across his tracks and kicked the ball out for a corner.

Kinsell swept two hard centres across, but they were disposed of, and when Fulham hit back, Sanders had extreme difficulty in getting the ball away. Rowley was working well, and once made an opening for McDonald, whose cross shot flashed a foot wide of the bar. Each side had its spell of midfield aggressiveness, but ball control was out of the question. Elliott went through just before the interval but Bacuzzi just managed to deflect his shot in a mix-up near the post. The balance of play had been fairly even.

Half-time: WBA 1 Fulham 0

The first threat of the second half came from Albion, Elliott swinging over a centre which Walsh headed over. The fine snow was moving up the pitch almost like a cloud of steam, and it was obvious Albion were going to make full use of the elements. Again, Kinsell was a threat. He pulled back a pass to Haines whose first shot was charged down. He regained possession but shot over. McDonald, the lanky Fulham left winger, always carried a threat when he got on the goal trail and Sanders once or twice had warm handfuls.

The equaliser

On 61 minutes, Fulham unexpectedly drew level during a goal area scramble when everyone was skidding about. The ball went out to Quested who shot through a ruck of players into the net. That setback surprised Albion who made an all-out effort to regain the lead. Much of the work was falling upon Elliott, who got in two quick centres but Taylor headed both away. The Albion halves and Millard were conspicuous at times because of Fulham pressure, and it was just as well they were as the visiting forwards were quick once they got moving.

Although Albion were fighting tooth and nail, they were not having much luck. There were many who thought a Walsh shot from an Elliott centre had crossed the line before Bacuzzi turned it away. It must have been a close thing. Williams had real bad luck a short time later, and Walsh made a too-hurried header which went wide.

In the last minute, Fulham took the lead with a goal by Rowley. Millard slipped in a tackle and Rowley went on towards Sanders. The goalkeeper only partially stopped the snow-caked ball, which returned to Rowley, who promptly tapped it into an empty net.

The verdict

This was the first time Fulham had ever won at the Hawthorns and they were a trifle flattered in taking both points. The conditions were such that anything was to be expected and all the players really deserve commendation for the manner in which they tried to overcome the conditions. The visitors had the better balanced forward line and when they got on the move, the Albion defenders had to keep their wits about them. Rowley and McDonald in particular always looked threatening. In defence for Fulham, centre-half Taylor was outstanding. Individual criticism would be unfair but whatever honours were for distribution among Albion forwards would go first to Williams and then to Elliott, while the defence did well generally under trying conditions

Fulham 2 v West Ham United 0

Saturday 7 May 1949
Football League Division Two
Referee: H. Hartley
Attendance: 41,133

FULHAM		WEST HAM U
Larry Gage	1	George Taylor
Harry Freeman	2	Ernie Devlin
Joe Bacuzzi	3	Steve Forde
Len Quested	4	Norman Corbett
Jim Taylor	5	Dick Walker
Pat Beasley	6	Tommy Moroney
Arthur Stevens	7	Terry Woodgate
Bob Thomas	8	Eric Parsons
Arthur Rowley	9	Bill Robinson
Bedford Jezzard	10	Danny McGowan
Jack McDonald	11	Ken Bainbridge

There was a thrilling climax to the Second Division promotion race in the spring of 1949. At the start of April, third-placed Fulham trailed Southampton by seven points (no Play-offs and only two points for a win) with just seven games remaining. West Brom were second, a point ahead of the Cottagers and with a game in hand. But then, as Saints faltered and the Baggies wobbled, Fulham went into overdrive. They won five on the trot and a valuable point in a 1–1 draw at White Hart Lane, thanks to a late, late Bob Thomas goal, virtually assured promotion. In the final match, 41,133 went to the Cottage to celebrate and see Fulham finish as champions, one point ahead of West Brom and two more than Southampton.

On the day, Rowley was once again the key man but the season as a whole had been a wonderful team triumph. Osborne modestly gave the credit to Jack Peart, but he had made some crucial changes. Not only had he signed Rowley, but he had brought in Doug Flack in goal after Ted Hinton was held partly accountable for a run of three defeats and a draw in the autumn. And he replaced Harry Ayres at inside-forward with a young Beddy Jezzard, a man who became a pivotal figure at the Cottage for the next 16 years. For the rest, it was largely Peart's team. The half-back line of Quested, Taylor and skipper Beasley was the engine room of the side, providing energy and craft. The three were virtually ever-present, while full-backs Freeman and Bacuzzi were models of consistency. Inside-forward Bob Thomas was top scorer with 23 goals with wingers Stevens and McDonald (Peart's final signing for a club record £12,500) contributed a valuable 21 goals.

The only worry in the run-in was an Easter Monday injury to goalkeeper Flack. With Hinton also injured, Osborne had to call up third choice Larry Gage. Of his three games, two were won and one drawn, and he was blameless for the two that were conceded. These were the only matches Gage played for Fulham.

Arthur Rowley's second goal against the Hammers.

HERO WAS CARRIED AWAY
By Howard Whitten

Amid scenes of bobbysox enthusiasm, burly, curly Arthur Rowley, hero of the hour, was borne high from the field at Craven Cottage when the final whistle sounded. Two golden goals by Rowley, the best soccer buy of the season, made it a personal triumph for the 23-year-old leader whose 19 goals since he arrived from West Bromich in December have amply repaid manager Frank Osborne's faith in him.

West Ham, though never looking capable of the 3–1 win which would have meant disaster for Fulham, were in the game with a chance for the first half hour. Then Rowley broke loose from stalwart Dick Walker. He pounced on a half clearance of a Bob Thomas raid and cracked in a net-bursting drive from 30 yards. For the rest of the half, Fulham earned their lead by quick-fire attacks based on precision passing.

With 14 minutes left, Rowley for the second time found himself clear of Walker. The ball bobbed back into the goalmouth from Thomas' blocked shot and ran out to Rowley, who coolly beat Taylor from close range. West Ham, without any compelling incentive, produced spells of neat football. Fulham's Taylor played Robinson out of the game and, next to Rowley, determined the pattern. Woodgate and Parsons, fast and tricky in midfield, fell to pieces at shooting range.

Goalkeepers Larry Gage and George Taylor showed no trace of reserve status and both looked the part but West Ham's Irishmen, McGowan and Moroney, faded after some neat touches. Fulham should enjoy their success for now but realise that they need more class in three or four positions to make the grade next year.

There is an old saying, 'Don't count your chickens…' and all that sort of thing. Fulham, before beating West Ham yesterday, were scared stiffer than waxworks dummies that if they were presumptuous enough to think they had won the Second Division Championship, they would lose the prize of a lifetime. So the ban went out on any celebrations until Division One status was in the bag.

So superstitious were Fulham in fact that a couple of directors who had rustled up some champagne for the boys dare not smuggle it into the boardroom. Instead they hid the bottles in a neighbouring house from which ice was borrowed to keep it fresh. Manager Frank Osborne, according to custom, also 'disappeared' until 10 minutes before the end of the game, when broadly beaming he made a triumphant re-appearance.

Fulham really need not have worried. Team work and a rare fighting spirit have put them in the First Division. Add to that manager Osborne's inspired brainwave when he bought Arthur Rowley from West Brom and you have the West Londoners recipe for success. But also salute ex-third team goalkeeper Gage who miraculously held a screaming header from Robinson. No wonder thousands of Fulham fans poured onto the field at full time, carried Rowley off shoulder high and proudly displayed a banner emblazoned with 'Fulham Forever – Division One'.

Champions – and he sums up success in 10 words

In the deserted dressing room, empty champagne bottles lay in the litter of bandages and cotton wool and boots. It was all over now. The crowd had gone home at last. Players were along the corridor. In the boardroom. It will be quiet like this for the close season, jerseys packed away, the team all dispersed, terraces swept and clean and lifeless.

In a million homes across the country, supporters put aside their colours and rattles and look back on all the happy Saturdays our greatest game has given. I believe none will look back with more pride than those with whom I attended the last match – at Craven Cottage.

The faithful folk who have followed Fulham through all the lean years have well earned the reward of seeing the riverside club crowned champions of the Second Division. Chairman Charles Dean paid tribute to the supporters. "I know some clubs have bigger crowds but ours is undeniably the most loyal of all. Ten thousand spectators had swarmed across the pitch after the 2–0 defeat of West Ham. They stood cheering below the pavilion balcony and already there was a banner proclaiming 'Fulham For Ever In Division One'."

They called for players, directors and manager Frank Osborne without know that he had watched the game himself from the terraces. He told me, "The players look on me as a Jonah and so I said I would go to another game. Then I slipped through the gate leading from the pitch and joined the crowd."

In his triumph, Osborne remembered the disappointment of the club which for so long looked certain of winning the championship. He sent a telegram to Bill Dodgin of Southampton, "Hard luck Bill. Better luck next season." A message from Southampton said, "Congratulations and all good wishes to Fulham in the First Division."

The most superstitious manager in the League, Osborne has felt confident of promotion for eight weeks – since he saw a black swan on the Thames alongside the Cottage. "I called the players over from training and told them everything would be alright." But there has been more than luck behind Fulham's success. There has been fighting spirit – and the belief that no individual is important in himself.

When the celebration party was almost over, Larry Gage the young goalkeeper, asked to speak to the manager. He said simply, " Thanks for the square deal you've given us all, guv'nor." No need to ask now why Fulham are in the First Division. Those ten words summed it up.

Fulham 1 v Wolverhampton Wanderers 2

Saturday 20 August 1949
Football League Division One
Referee: E.S. Vickery
Attendance: 41,699

FULHAM		WOLVES
Doug Flack	1	Bert Williams
Harry Freeman	2	Lawrie Kelly
Joe Bacuzzi	3	Roy Pritchard
Len Quested	4	Billy Crook
Jim Taylor	5	Bill Shorthouse
Pat Beasley	6	Billy Wright
Arthur Stevens	7	Johnny Hancocks
Bob Thomas	8	Sammy Smyth
Arthur Rowley	9	Jessie Pye
Bedford Jezzard	10	Jimmy Dunn
Jack McDonald	11	Jimmy Mullen

Popular full-back Joe Bacuzzi scored only two goals in his long career, one of which was Fulham's first in the top flight.

There was much that was new about Fulham in their first-ever top flight season: a new manager (Bill Dodgin from promotion rivals Southampton), new kit, a new-style programme, a new band for pre-match entertainment, and new entry barriers to the Cottage. But there was something very familiar about the team. The side which took the field for the first game against Wolves (and which was unchanged for the first seven games) was the one that had captured the Second Division title, with Flack restored in goal. In fact nine of those players (Flack and McDonald were the exceptions) played in at least 34 of the 42 games in 1949–50.

The fixture list could have been kinder. Fulham's first opponents, Wolves, had won the Cup the previous April and, under Stan Cullis' management, were to become one of the dominant teams of the 1950s. The attendance of 41,699 was a foretaste of things to come for the average Craven Cottage attendance that season, of 33,030, was the highest in the club's history. It was, however, a season when attendances nationally boomed, and Fulham's average was only 88 per cent of the divisional average. In fact, in only two of the club's 21 seasons in the top flight has it come within 10 per cent of the divisional average and in the Premiership years it has been below 50 per cent.

Although it was not until the fourth game that the Cottagers managed their first win, 4–1 at home to Huddersfield, they performed creditably. Relegation was never really a threat and, despite not winning one of their last 13 games, the club finished 17th (out of 22). By the end of the season, it was apparent that changes were needed. Freeman and Thomas, as well as Flack and McDonald, were to lose their places and veteran Beasley and Rowley, who found goals hard to come by at the highest level, moved on. Wolves finished runners-up to Portsmouth missing the title on goal average. The point Fulham took away from Molineux in the return in December made the difference.

The squad at the start of the first First Division campaign. Left to right, back row: Ayres, Freeman, Quested, Flack, Kelly, Taylor, Bacuzzi, Frank Penn (trainer). Front row: Stevens, Thomas, Rowley, Bill Dodgin (manager), Jezzard, McDonald, Beasley.

In Fulham's first venture in the First Division against the Wolves, three goals were scored, the odd one going to the Midlanders: in each case the goals were the result of long shots, and all three should have been saved.

Fulham, despite this reverse, put up a good show and were by no means disgraced having by far the more play, and, at times, had the cup holders penned in their own half for long periods.

In weather more suited to Cricket, the Wolves kicked off, but Fulham were soon on the attack and their forwards were combining well, especially Stevens and Rowley, a good effort from the latter going near. McDonald had a glorious opportunity to open the account but was too hasty with his shot when he could have taken the ball close in before shooting.

During this period of Fulham ascendancy, the Wolves defence was not as cool as it should be.

TIGHT GRIP

When the Midlanders settled down it was obvious that the sting in their attack were the wingmen, Hancocks and Mullen; the inside men were well held by the Fulham halves. Taylor's grip on centre-forward Pye was especially tight. A narrow escape for Fulham occurred when Flack was only able to punch a shot from Hancocks down on to his goal-line for Taylor to kick clear with Pye ready to put the finishing touch.

Quite against the run of the play, the Wolves scored after 25 minutes. A long curling shot by left-winger Mullen was stopped by Flack: as he was rising, the ball slid over his arm into the net. No one was more surprised than Mullen.

Stevens nearly levelled matters with a great shot that missed the upright by inches, but the interval came with the Wolves lucky to be a goal up. The heat was terrific, most of the big crowd being in shirt sleeves, but the players started the second half at a great rate, and it was still Fulham that were setting the pace, the Wolves' defenders having a gruelling time.

A complete miskick by Rowley from a Stevens' centre with an open goal in front of him was atoned for a few minutes later by a cracking Rowley special taken on the turn.

In almost their first attack of the second half the Wolves scored again, this time again from about 25 yards by the other winger, Hancocks. Taking a throw-in from Wright in the centre of the field, he shot hard and low, Flack may have been unsighted by his backs, but he dived much too late, and the Wolves were two up, with two very simple goals.

LONG SHOT

Ten minutes later, a very similar long shot by full-back Bacuzzi after robbing an opponent, caught Williams in the Wolves' goal napping and, although he got his fingers to it, could not have stopped it going in the net.

A great Fulham rally followed after this and Bob Thomas banged in a grand shot only to see it tipped over the bar by the goalkeeper. This effort came to nought and, that was it except for a burst down the middle by Rowley, which resulted in him being fouled on the penalty line. From the resultant free kick taken by Freeman, the ball was deflected for a fruitless corner.

The Cottagers need have no cause for alarm on this showing as they will find few teams of the Wolves' calibre in the First Division, and they more than held their own against them. Taylor was by far the best player on the field: his colleague, Quested, at right-wing half, being the most improved player on the Fulham team: some of his passes through to his forwards were a joy to watch. Of the Fulham forwards, Stevens and Rowley were the most successful. It may seem harsh to fault Flack on this one showing after his many fine displays of last season, but the fact remains that all the goals were due to goalkeeping lapses, and all should have been saved.

Fulham 3 v Chelsea 0

Wednesday 14 February 1951
FA Cup Fifth Round Replay
Referee: H. Pearce
Attendance: 29,946

FULHAM		CHELSEA
Ian Black	1	Peter Pickering
Joe Bacuzzi	2	Danny Winter
Reg Lowe	3	Bill Hughes
Len Quested	4	Ken Armstrong
Jim Taylor	5	John Harris
Eddie Lowe	6	Bill Dickson
Arthur Stevens	7	Wally Hinshelwood
Jimmy Bowie	8	Bobby Campbell
Bobby Brennan	9	Bobby Smith
Bedford Jezzard	10	Roy Bentley
Johnny Campbell	11	Billy Gray

Fulham's record signing Bobby Brennan was the match winner against Chelsea.

For their second season in the top-flight, the board thought an investment in the team was needed and in the 1950 close season was active in the transfer market. From Southampton, came Scottish international goalkeeper Ian Black, who was to prove a stalwart for seven seasons. The Lowe brothers, England international Eddie and Reg, arrived from Aston Villa and, for a club record fee of £20,000, the skilful Irish international inside-forward Bobby Brennan was signed from Birmingham. And to succeed skipper Pat Beasley, Fulham signed the much-travelled veteran Scottish international Archie Macaulay from Arsenal.

It was hard to claim that the return in terms of points justified the outlay. Fulham finished 18th, one place lower than the previous season and rarely threatened mid-table. At the same time, they stayed clear of the danger zone for the entire season and enjoyed a run to the last eight of the FA Cup for the second time in three years and for the second time in three years, Blackpool blocked the path to Wembley. The highlight of the Cup run, and the best result of the season, was this fifth round win over Chelsea. It was third Cup meeting between the clubs, and the Cottagers' second and last success to date. The draw gave Chelsea home advantage but before a crowd of 69,434, a second-half Johnny Campbell goal equalised Roy Bentley's strike for Chelsea to take the teams back to the Cottage.

The replay kicked off at 2.30 on a Wednesday afternoon, with just under 30,000 in the ground. Although Fulham were in the bottom third of the (old) First Division, Chelsea were even lower. This was in fact the first season in which the Cottagers finished higher in the League than their neighbours. Chelsea only avoided relegation (by 0.044 of a goal) after a remarkable run in the final weeks, which included an unlikely 2–1 win at the Cottage in the penultimate game, a result which led to chants of 'Dear Old Pals' from the terraces. But in the Cup, Fulham claimed the west London bragging rights that season.

FULHAM REACH THE LAST EIGHT

Fulham and Chelsea, meeting for the right to face Blackpool in the far north on Saturday week, played the second instalment of their Fifth Round tie in the FA Cup Competition at Craven Cottage yesterday. And this time, it was Fulham, seizing their chances eagerly, who won by three goals to none, though the score itself bore little relationship to the true balance of the afternoon.

It was just not Chelsea's day. Fulham will be the first to admit it. Indeed, instead of providing a hollow-sounding victory for the home side, the match in certain circumstances might well have gone to extra time. But there it is. The side that cannot accept its chances cannot expect to survive and Chelsea will no doubt still be pondering for the next week or two their profligate waste of yesterday. But this is not to belittle Fulham's performance in a fast match full of movement, excitement and even good football. They finished properly and lasted the pace better on a heavy pitch to gain a fine victory.

Fulham clearly are a difficult side to beat at times. True they were aided on this occasion both by their opponents and by those fleeting slices of luck that are so much a part of football, but for all that they possess many solid qualities. Chelsea probably had a greater share of the ball in attack – certainly an advantage of eight to three in the matter of corner kicks – but the Fulham defence on the whole was the more impressive in times of total stress. Their half-back line, too – Lowe (E) in particular played a fine game – had a sterner note of authority about it in spite of the gallant work of Armstrong who, with Hughes, was quite the best of the Chelsea defenders.

As for the vital matter of the attack, the difference between the sides was underlined by the score. One forward line carried out its appointed task in the approved manner, the other did not. Bentley, Hinshelwood and Gray, it is true, all played well at times for Chelsea, but the finishing of the line as a whole was grotesque, and it was the partnership of Bowie and Stevens, together with the astute leadership of Brennan, that carried the greater finishing threat at the other end. Luck or no luck, it is goals that count, and in that respect, it was Chelsea who had to pay a heavy price for a wasted afternoon.

Nothing went right for Chelsea from the very beginning. At the 19th minute, a clever move between Stevens, Brennan and Bowie ended with Bowie being brought down by Dickson in the right hand corner of the penalty area and for Stevens promptly to put Fulham ahead from the penalty spot. Yet, up until that moment, it had largely been Chelsea, a phase which included a shot by Bentley merely inches wide of the target, and a great left-foot drive by Armstrong which struck an upright with Black beaten to the world. But to give Fulham their due, nothing seemed to disturb them, and once they had got their noses in front they settled down to some lively, quick attacks, with the Bowie-Stevens partnership promising match-winning possibilities. So the interval arrived with Fulham holding their slender lead.

The first ten minutes of the second half proved to be the turning point. In that period, the match was won and lost, for Chelsea might well have scored three times in a twinkling. First, Hinshelwood's clever lob, which needed but a nod from Smith, beat everyone to hit the far post. Then Smith, leaving Taylor beautifully on the turf, sent Campbell clear of all opposition. With only Black to beat from six yards range, the inside shot wide. And almost at once, Lowe (R) kicked a shot from Smith off the line with Black beaten.

But the limit had been reached and five minutes later, Fulham, turning defence into attack, were in the last eight of the Cup with a superbly taken second goal. A long clearance by Lowe (R) sent Campbell past winter and Brennan shot home to leave Chelsea open mouthed. Even then, Chelsea were given one last chance but Smith elected to shoot over rather than under the bar from almost point-blank range. And it was again left to Brennan, selling the whole Chelsea defence a clever dummy from Bowie's pass, to show them how to do things properly with a third goal. Fulham indeed finished splendidly to become the last hope of London in the Cup competition.

Fulham 3 v Manchester United 3

Wednesday 26 December 1951
Football League Division One
Referee: W.R. Barnes
Attendance: 32,671

FULHAM		MANCHESTER U
Ian Black	1	Reg Allen
Joe Bacuzzi	2	Tom McNulty
Bill Dodgin	3	Roger Byrne
Archie Macaulay	4	Allenby Chilton
Jim Taylor	5	Mark Jones
Eddie Lowe	6	Henry Cockburn
Arthur Stevens	7	Johnny Berry
Bob Thomas	8	Stan Pearson
Bedford Jezzard	9	Jack Rowley
Jeff Taylor	10	John Downie
Johnny Campbell	11	Ernie Bond

From the very first month of the season, 1951–52 had disaster stamped all over it. The first four games were lost and there was no win until the eighth match. By the end of October, Fulham were in the bottom two of the (old) First Division with Huddersfield (only two went down in those days), and these two clubs remained there for the rest of the season. The Cottagers finished bottom with just eight wins in 42 games, the fewest victories in a season at this level. The team underwent radical surgery but to no avail. Swapping the popular Len Quested for inside-forward Jeff Taylor with Huddersfield was a move for which supporters never really forgave manager Dodgin. He did, however, make two very good signings in Charlie Mitten and Jimmy Hill, but, although they were to give the club great service, both arrived too late to affect the outcome of the season.

Yet the season was not without its highpoints. In January, Middlesbrough were thrashed 6–0, the Cottagers biggest win of that three-year sojourn in the top flight with Jeff Taylor getting the only hat-trick in this period. And frustratingly, 16 of the 23 League defeats were by the odd goal, including the Christmas Day trip to Old Trafford. Matt Busby had rebuilt Manchester United in the immediate aftermath of World War Two and although they had won the FA Cup in 1948, the League title had eluded them. In five seasons, United had finished runners-up four times, but in 1951–52, they were to make no mistake.

Over Christmas 1951, lowly Fulham went to high-flying United and in front of 35,697 gave an excellent account of themselves despite losing 3–2. With 12 minutes remaining it was 1–1, and the Cottagers felt they were worth a point. The return was played 24 hours later, on Boxing Day, and was even more dramatic. The unlikely hero was Eddie Lowe, whose first goal was almost certainly the first goal ever scored at the Cottage direct from a corner. This was the outstanding game of that 1949–52 spell in the top flight.

Eddie Lowe, the unlikely hero against United.

UNITED'S HAPPY HOLIDAY HAUL

The result of the match at Fulham between the home side and Manchester United was a fair reflex on the game. The United should have won for they were two goals ahead until the last 20 minutes but Fulham fought back and drew level.

Fulham started with a rush but Lowe was brought down and went off with an injury to his knee. He came back later to play outside left and it would have much better for the United if he had not been injured for he scored two fine goals against them in spite of his injured knee. Whilst he was off, however, a brilliant move forward by Pearson and Berry left the ball at the feet of Rowley. He instantly shot and the ball went high into the net past the troubled goalkeeper. The United were without Carey and undoubtedly it was affecting their play. They were especially unconvincing in defence. Three corner kicks were given against them within almost as many minutes. Lowe, who had returned to the field, took the third corner kick. It swerved into the goal and Allen, in attempting to save, fisted it into his own net. A few minutes later, Lowe headed over the bar with Allen out of position.

With rather more brawn than skill both teams now engaged in a vigorous spell of cut, thrust and parry which was continued in the second half until the referee spoke to players on each side. The ball began to run kindly for United and Rowley, by cleverly hooking a pass in his stride flicked the ball between the backs for Pearson to shoot it past Black. Two minutes later, Bond sped as straight as an arrow through the Fulham defence and shot. Bacuzzi kicked it back and Bond swiftly hit the rebound to be beat the advancing goalkeeper. The United were now inclined to rely on defence. Without Carey, they were not too sure of themselves and they paid the penalty of over-anxiety to guard their goal instead of attacking the rather shaky defence in front of them.

When it became clear to Fulham that their opponents were on the defensive, they took heart, infused vigour and skill into their play and raided the United goal again and again. In one of the raids, the ball was bobbing up and down until Stevens crashed it into the melee and scored with a first-time volley. To complete the discomfiture of the United, Lowe flashed past Chilton and cracked in a shot which easily beat Allen. The discipline and gathering momentum of the Fulham attack was too much for the United defence. A chance came to Rowley, but he repeated his previous effort, high and over the bar, and with it, the last opportunity of victory for his side disappeared.

This draw came just 24 hours after the teams had met at Old Trafford. The outstanding feature of Manchester United's 3–2 victory was the all-round excellence of Rowley's display. It might have been a demonstration specially put on for the benefit of learners in the crowd. Another source of satisfaction to Manchester folk was the mounting confidence of Bond at outside left. Now that Mitten's shadow no longer looms over him, Bond seems freer to experiment and adventure on his own and nothing could have been better than the way he accepted the scoring chance so handsomely prepared for him by Pearson. But the choicest specimen of all from the point of view of boldness of conception and finish of execution was the last one, scored by Berry, but hammered out in the quick forge and working house of Rowley's mind.

These successes were arduously won in the teeth of much skilful and dogged opposition by Fulham for whom Macaulay (after a shaky start), Taylor (apart from his one blunder which let Rowley through) and Lowe (who used his opponents most ingeniously as arm rests) played finely. Macaulay twice imperilled his own goal but made handsome amends by rolling forward for Jezzard a scoring chance which was taken most brilliantly. Fulham's second goal by Thomas was, to say the least, exceptional. A random kick from fully 40 yards range was directed casually goalwards. To general astonishment, the ball dipped and floated in under the crossbar whither it was followed by a shame-faced goalkeeper whose painful duty it was to retrieve it.

INJURED EDDIE WAS A TWO-GOAL SCORER

Scoring goals while limping on the wing is getting to be a habit with Eddie Lowe, the Fulham left half. Twelve days ago he scored the winner at Preston. Yesterday, a recurrence of the same knee trouble forced him to move to outside left in the first few minutes of the home game with Manchester United. He scored Fulham's first goal direct from a corner kick and, in the last minute, cracked the ball into the net with his injured leg to force a 3–3 draw.

Joy tempered pain for Lowe as he left the field. That dramatic goal had enabled Fulham to salvage one point from the debris of their holiday programme. Back in the dressing room, the players joked, "Where is Charlie Mitten going to play? We've got a goal-getting outside left." Mitten is the former Manchester United outside left who will be free to play for Fulham in the New Year.

A draw was a good result. Fulham's enthusiasm balanced the craft of a United team obviously lacking the generalship of Johnny Carey. Macaulay was the brain behind most of Fulham's best movements and young Bill Dodgin showed a flair for timely interceptions.

Rowley opened the scoring for United from a Berry centre. Lowe equalised. A movement started by left back Byrne and neatly continued by Rowley enabled Pearson to score soon after the interval and Bond promptly increased the lead. Fulham struggled on and Stevens scrambled in the second goal before Lowe's match-saving effort.

Fulham 1 v Southampton 1

Friday 26 December 1952
Football League Division Two
Referee: H. Pearce
Attendance: 17,018

FULHAM		SOUTHAMPTON
Ian Black	1	John Christie
Tom Wilson	2	Bill Ellerington
Reg Lowe	3	Peter Sillett
Eddie Lowe	4	Bryn Elliott
Jim Taylor	5	Henry Horton
Jimmy Hill	6	Alex Simpson
Arthur Stevens	7	Eric Day
Bobby Robson	8	Roy Williams
Bedford Jezzard	9	Frank Dudley
Johnny Haynes	10	John Walker
Charlie Mitten	11	John Hoskins

The start of a legend, Johnny Haynes' debut.

Following relegation in May 1952, Fulham began a seven-season sojourn in the (old) Second Division that for many older supporters remains something of a golden period. What the football lacked in class, it more than made up for with excitement and goals. In the first five of those seasons, all spent in mid table, the Cottagers scored 428 goals in 210 League games, two thirds of which (2.75 per game) were scored at home. And the heart of the side were several home grown players whose talents put them right at the very top of the rankings of all-time Fulham favourites.

On Boxing Day 1952, few of the 17,018 crowd would have realised that they were witnessing the debut of one Britain's greatest players and the outstanding figure in Fulham's history. Johnny Haynes was a schoolboy prodigy who, though Edmonton born, signed for Fulham rather than Spurs or Arsenal as a 16-year-old. After working his way through the junior and reserve sides, he was called up by manager Bill Dodgin to replace the injured Bobby Brennan for the visit of Southampton. By the next month, he was the first choice inside-left and remained the dominant figure at the club for the next 18 years.

The statistics hardly do him justice. He still holds the appearances record (658 games); he set a new goalscoring record (158 goals); was capped at every level from schoolboy upwards; was only the fourth Englishman to 50 caps, and he captained both club and country. A magnificent player and inspirational leader, Haynes, or simply and justifiably, the Maestro, was as inextricably linked with Fulham for two decades as Craven Cottage. He was a midfield dictator with a superb tactical brain, and such was his supreme passing ability that his teammate Jimmy Hill believed he had eyes in the back of his head. The Maestro was a perfectionist, as demanding of himself as he was of others, and he was adored by the Cottage faithful. It all began very modestly in this mid-table fixture against Southampton and led eventually to the permanent memorial of the statue of Haynes outside the Cottage gates.

MITTEN'S COSTLY PENALTY MISS

All square at the Cottage
Fulham......1   Southampton......1

Although they played gallantly, Southampton were lucky to take a point at Craven Cottage. Not only did Fulham have a goal disallowed, but Mitten shot straight at the goalkeeper from a penalty.

Fulham made the mistake of trying to push the ball through the mud and it was not until the last ten minutes that they changed their tactics. They were unfortunate when a picture goal by Jezzard from a free-kick by Mitten was disallowed. The referee ruled that a Southampton player had been too near the ball when Mitten took the kick. Mitten's second effort was cleared.

Southampton star was centre forward Dudley. He was a one-man attack. After Stevens had given Fulham the lead nine minutes from the end, Dudley raced away and scored a magnificent goal. Mitten's penalty came four minutes from time for handling by a defender on the line.

In terms of chances, Fulham had much the better of the game, and but for bad luck and heavy mud, they would have collected both points. Although he tired towards the end, 18 year old schoolboy international Johnny Haynes did well in his first game for Fulham.

MITTEN MISSES PENALTY

It's two minutes from the end at Craven Cottage. The score is 1–1. Fulham are awarded a penalty and Charlie Mitten takes it.

Crack! The ball goes straight to Southampton goalkeeper Jack Christie's left elbow and rebounds a dozen yards beyond the penalty area.

And only just before, a free-kick goal by Mitten was disallowed because of a Southampton infringement.

Disappointing? Yes, but Fulham will be pleased with the first appearance of Mitten's young partner, Johnny Haynes. He's come to stay.

Jimmy Hill made a goal for Arthur Stevens and Frank Dudley equalized.

The irrepressible Charlie Mitten who joined Fulham from Manchester United via Bogota.

Grimsby Town 5 v Fulham 5

Saturday 9 January 1954
FA Cup Third Round
Attendance: 14,764

GRIMSBY		FULHAM
Clarence Williams	1	Ian Black
Bill Brown	2	John Chenhall
Ray Robson	3	Robin Lawler
Reg Scotson	4	Jimmy Hill
Duncan McMillan	5	Gordon Brice
Arnold Walker	6	Eddie Lowe
Derek Stroud	7	Arthur Stevens
Pat Johnston	8	Jeff Taylor
Jimmy Bloomer	9	Bedford Jezzard
Archie Wright	10	Johnny Haynes
Jimmy Madison	11	Charlie Mitten

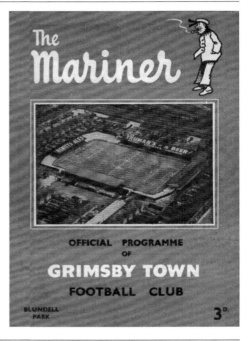

The Fulham forwards were never more prolific than in the seven seasons in the 1950s they spent in the second tier of the League. They never scored less than 76 goals in a 42-match campaign and in 1953–54 managed 98, the club's best post-war total and the highest-ever at this level. The fact they only finished eighth was due to a leaky defence which conceded 85 goals. These same habits were just as evident in the FA Cup and the third round tie at Grimsby produced Fulham's highest-ever scoring draw. Just once before, against Coventry in the Third Division South in January 1932, the Cottagers had shared ten goals, but this was the only time since 1945 and their only FA Cup tie that ended 5–5.

At the start of this season, Bill Dodgin was still the manager at the Cottage but he left in the autumn, and his departure was not even mentioned in the programme. Frank Osborne, the secretary and general manager, resumed the control of the playing side that he had relinquished on winning promotion in 1949, and things carried on much the same as before. Dodgin's legacy included a young inside-forward trio of Robson, Jezzard and Haynes, that was blossoming into one of the most envied in the country but defensive shortcomings meant kept them in mid-table.

A trip to Blundell Park to face struggling Third Division North Grimsby looked a straightforward away win. Following manager Bill Shankly's recent departure, the Mariners were sliding down the table. The Cottagers were without the injured Bobby Robson for the tie but it was his deputy, Jeff Taylor, who grabbed the headlines. He had joined Fulham a couple of years earlier from Huddersfield in a straight swap for crowd favourite Len Quested, a deal for which manager Dodgin was never forgiven. A university graduate, Taylor (brother of cricketer Ken) struggled to establish himself at Fulham but enjoyed an interesting and successful post-football career as an opera singer and academic. After the first replay was abandoned, Fulham finally beat Grimsby 3–1, only to lose to Alec Stock's Orient in round four.

Inside-forward and future opera singer Jeff Taylor was Fulham's hat-trick hero at Grimsby.

TAYLOR'S FIRST HALF HAT-TRICK

Grimsby Town gave one of their best displays of the season at Blundell Park this afternoon when they held Second Division Fulham to a draw. It was a match that can only be described as sensational and if the replay at Craven Cottage is as good, it will be worth seeing. Fulham wearing blue shirts, had Taylor playing instead of Robson who was suffering from a groin injury. The Cottagers manager Frank Osborne did not want to risk him on a heavy pitch.

Grimsby won the toss and, facing the Cleethorpes end, went straight on the attack. Scotson won the ball on the right and the Grimsby captain found Bloomer who in turn fed Stroud. The right winger crossed but Lowe was on hand to head clear. There were some lively passages of action in the Fulham goalmouth when Black, who made a bright splash of colour in his red jersey, safely fielded a header from Bloomer, who had got up to a McMillan free kick.

The Mariners supporters had been encouraged by the play at this early stage for Grimsby had done more of the pressing. Wright had seen a shot deflected while Maddison's centre dropped just behind the line. A long-range back pass by Lowe to his goalkeeper might have proved dangerous for the London club but Black was able to reach the ball before Bloomer could close in.

Fulham were not to be denied though, and took the lead in the 19th minute, Taylor heading through from a low cross by Stevens. Grimsby came back full of fight and Black must have been pleased when he turned a fierce drive from Maddison over the bar. From the resultant corner, Johnston got in a header which was easily saved by the Fulham goalkeeper. Grimsby kept up the aggression and in the 24th minute equalised through Bloomer. The centre forward pushed the ball out to Stroud, took the return pass and while the Fulham defence were standing still, drove the ball past Black from close range. And there was more. Following heavy pressure by the Mariners, Brice put the ball past his own goalkeeper in the 26th minute to give the Mariners the lead.

Grimsby were showing up well in this tough encounter. After a timely tackle, Walker put Bloomer through, he passed to Maddison, who was fouled by Chenhall. Not for the first time, however, the free kick opportunity was wasted.

But Fulham were capable of stretching the Mariners and in the 35th minute equalised. Taylor was again on the mark from another Stevens cross after the opening had been made by Mitten. Williams managed to get a hand to the ball but could not keep it out. And when Chenhall headed clear to Stevens, the right winger broke away and instead of shooting passed to Taylor who was better placed and the Fulham man completed his hat-trick in the 40th minute.

There were still five minutes of the first half left, time enough for Grimsby to force a corner on the right. Stroud crossed into the danger area and there was Scotson to ram the ball into the net for the equaliser. Right back Chenhall tried to keep the ball out with his hand but could not prevent the goal.

In the opening minutes of the second half, Jezzard, put clear by Haynes, missed a great chance from inside the six yard area. His shot hit Williams on the leg and went out for a corner. Then Williams had an anxious moment when he dropped the ball after a challenge by Haynes but retrieved it before Jezzard could take advantage. The play was end-to-end with Maddison and Johnston threatening for the home side and in the 66th minute Bloomer put them ahead for the second time, when he fastened on to yet another Stroud corner to fire past Black through a crowd of players.

This was still anyone's game and the crowd were kept on their toes as the advantage shifted constantly. The heavy conditions were proving a great leveller and helped Grimsby but the London club kept on battling. And in the 74th minute, they got their reward. Williams palmed away a Mitten cross, a Fulham player shot and the ball was deflected to Stevens who cracked in the equaliser. Then, with just 90 seconds remaining, when Hill forced his way through to add a fifth for the Cottagers, they must have thought they had won it. But there was one thrill left and in the final minute, Bloomer headed the goal which completed his hat-trick and earned Grimsby a deserved replay.

Fulham 5 v Hull City 0

Saturday 8 October 1955
Football League Division Two
Referee: J.W. Malcolm
Attendance: 21,207

FULHAM		HULL CITY
Ian Black	1	Billy Bly
John Chenhall	2	John Neal
Robin Lawler	3	Viggo Jensen
Joe Stapleton	4	Andy Davidson
Ron Greenwood	5	Tom Berry
Jimmy Hill	6	Trevor Porteous
Tony Barton	7	Ray Smith
Bobby Robson	8	Tommy Martin
Bedford Jezzard	9	Charlie Atkinson
Johnny Haynes	10	Brian Bulless
Charlie Mitten	11	Brian Crispey

During those Second Division years of the mid-1950s, Fulham's attack was as prolific as the defence was porous, a combination that made for some thrilling matches. If the craft was provided by the two young and hugely talented inside-forwards, Bobby Robson and Johnny Haynes, the power came from centre-forward Bedford Jezzard. This trio was the envy of many top-flight clubs. All three not only played for Fulham (a combined total of 1,334 games and 392 goals) but also managed the Cottagers at some point and all were full England internationals.

In many ways, Jezzard was the most under-rated of the three. Clerkenwell-born, he had joined Fulham from Watford in July 1948 and was a member of the 1948–49 Second Division Championship side. As a goalscorer, Jezzard started slowly. In 188 games in his

first four seasons, he managed just 31 goals. But on relegation in 1952, he made up for lost time, with 124 goals in the 168 games he played before injury ended his career when he was just 28. Every one of his goals came in the Football League. In those years, he was twice capped by England.

An old-fashioned English centre-forward, Beddy was always modest about his talents and achievements. But he was fast, strong, could shoot with either foot and was powerful in the air. His 39 goals in 1953–54 is second only to Bonzo Newton's Fulham record of 43 in 1931–32. He also scored four goals in a game twice and three hat-tricks but his best personal achievement was five in this match against Hull. He equalled Fred Harrison's haul in 1908, a feat that was later emulated by Jimmy Hill (1958) and Steve Earle (1969). When injury ended his career in 1956, Beddy joined the coaching staff, and his contribution from 1958 to 1964 places him in the top tier of Fulham managers. He steered them to promotion, kept them in the top flight for five seasons and got to within one bad refereeing decision of the FA Cup Final. And when he left in 1964, it was at a time of his own choosing.

Bedford Jezzard equalled the record of Fred Harrison with five goals in a League game.

HULL LOSE BLY AT FULHAM
Fulham 5, Hull 0
Evening Standard Football Reporter

Bedford Jezzard got two goals for Fulham in the first 13 minutes at Craven Cottage, where the Hull goalkeeper, Bly, was injured and carried off the field just before half-time.

The Fulham forwards were in rare form and only occasionally did Hull make any progress towards the other end.

Haynes was in Young England form- and no defense can really cope with him under these conditions.

Fulham began to slacken off and Hull came into the game a bit more. Martin was rather unfortunate when he closed in to meet a long pass from the left and smashed his shot against the junction of the stanchion and post as Black leapt desperately across the goalmouth.

TOO HIGH

A few moments later Atkinson tried a drive from outside the penalty area but this one was much too high. The Hull defence had for the moment the measure of Fulham's forward line.

Hull were unfortunate some ten minutes before half-time when they lost goalkeeper Bly. He and Davidson had both risen to meet a centre from the Fulham right and when Robson joined in the three of them crashed to the ground.

Bly was obviously hurt and was carried off. Porteous took his place in goal.

HALF-TIME: FULHAM 2   HULL 0

It was learned at half-time that Bly has sustained a chipped ankle bone and would take no further part in the match. He dressed and came out to watch how his colleagues were faring. Fulham were content that their lead was sufficient and they indulged in a great deal of tip-tap play and Porteous came when Haynes screwed a shot over the bar from just inside the penalty area.

Jezzard completed his hat-trick after 70 minutes when he beat Porteous with a not too difficult shot.

Jezzard scored Fulham's fourth goal.

Jezzard scored the fifth goal for Fulham.

FIVE GOAL JEZZARD SHOOTS FULHAM TO THE TOP
FULHAM 5........HULL CITY 0

Bedford Jezzard, Fulham's sharp-shooting centre forward, was the bright spark of an otherwise poor game at Craven Cottage on Saturday, when the home team beat Hull City 5–0.

It seems strange after watching a team win to have to criticize them, but Fulham can take little credit for this apparently big win. Bottom-of-the-table Hull had all the bad luck that was going. Their bad luck started on the journey to London when regular centre forward Patterson was taken ill. Five minutes after the game started, centre-half Berry had to leave the field for attention to his knee; it was during his absence that Jezzard opened the scoring.

The cruellest blow of all however came five minutes before half-time when goalkeeper Billy Bly was carried off with an ankle injury after a fourfold collision with colleague Henson and Fulham forwards Robson and Jezzard. Left half Porteous took over the goalkeeper's jersey for the rest of the match.

Fulham started the game as if they meant to swamp Hull and were two goals up in 13 minutes, Jezzard scoring both of them from centres from Mitten. The second goal brought protests from Hull defenders claiming that Jezzard was offside, but referee Malcolm dismissed their protests. Fulham apparently decided that two goals were enough- strange because they had almost been able to penetrate the Hull defence at will.

They allowed the City to fight back and one terrific shot by Martin struck the junction of the upright and crossbar which brought the biggest cheer of the afternoon.

It was the obvious that a straight shot at goal was going to pay Fulham dividends but it was almost half an hour after Porteous took over the goal that the Fulham forwards got around to it. They then decided to improve their goal average with further goals. Five times they got the ball into the net, but only three goals counted, three shots by the irresistible Jezzard. Robson, who got the ball into the net on the other two occasions, had the misfortune to have them both disallowed for some obscure infringements.

Hull City, who had the cards stacked against them, are to be congratulated on the fight against overwhelming odds.

This game was a personal triumph for Bedford Jezzard, his best-ever performance. He is now the leading goal-scorer in the country, with 17 goals to his credit. He has now scored more goals for Fulham than any other player in the club's history, but has still to notch the first goal in the FA Cup. Here's hoping you alter the situation in January, Bedford.

Fulham 4 v Newcastle United 5

Saturday 28 January 1956
FA Cup Fourth Round
Referee: J. Mitchell
Attendance: 39,200

FULHAM		NEWCASTLE U
Ian Black	1	Ronnie Simpson
Tom Wilson	2	Arnold Woollard
Robin Lawler	3	Alf McMichael
Norman Smith	4	Bob Stokoe
Gordon Brice	5	Bill Patterson
Eddie Lowe	6	Tommy Casey
Jimmy Hill	7	Jackie Milburn
Bobby Robson	8	Reg Davies
Bedford Jezzard	9	Vic Keeble
Johnny Haynes	10	Bill Curry
Trevor Chamberlain	11	Bobby Mitchell

For many older supporters, this was the finest game ever played at the Cottage. For excitement, controversy and romance, this match had everything and almost 50 years later it was well-enough remembered for BBC Radio to devote a half hour programme to it with half a dozen of the players from both sides. All that the tie lacked from the Fulham point of view was a happy ending but, after 90 minutes of high drama, even that did not seem to matter.

The outline of the plot was very straightforward. In the fourth round of the FA Cup, Second Division Fulham, bumping along in mid-table, were hosts to the mighty Newcastle of the First Division and the current FA Cup holders. It was a grey overcast afternoon on the banks of the Thames but the weather did not dampen the enthusiasm of the 39,200 crowd. There were also some interesting subplots. Running the line in his first Cup tie, and destined to play a crucial role in the outcome, was young Jack Taylor

Trevor Chamberlain (right, white shirt) scores one of his three in the dramatic Cup tie against Newcastle.

who, 18 years later, would referee the World Cup Final. Also involved in his first Cup tie, and destined to have an even bigger impact on the match, was Fulham's left-winger, Trevor 'Tosh' Chamberlain.

Tosh was the school friend of Haynes who, having joined Fulham earlier, persuaded the Maestro to sign for the Cottagers. Although his progress to the first team was slower, he was to make an indelible mark on the club but in a different way to his friend. It was as much for his character and sense of fun as his ability that Tosh became a legendary figure at the Cottage. His irrepressible personality tended to obscure the skill that won him Middlesex, London and England Schools honours and England Youth caps. He scored in the first minute of his debut in November 1954 but had to wait until Charlie Mitten went to manage Mansfield in 1956 before making the No. 11 shirt his own. Tosh more than anyone made this Newcastle tie an epic, and the tie was also the making of Tosh.

FULHAM K.O'D BY 'NO GOAL' IN BEST CUP-TIE I'VE EVER SEEN
By Frank Butler

Newcastle United may retain the F.A. Cup in May and so set up a Wembley record by winning soccer's most glamorous prize four times in six seasons. But Frank Osborne, Fulham's general manager, Jimmy Hill, their long-chinned skipper, Johnny Haynes, England's brilliant inside-left and Trevor Chamberlain, who scored a hat-trick in his first ever Cup-tie, will all tell you, as they told me, they were robbed of victory.

It was a remarkable match, quite most exciting Cup-tie I have seen in more than 20 years of soccer reporting. Newcastle, playing like champions, had hit up a 3–0 lead in less than half an hour, as first Jackie Milburn, then wing-halves Stokoe and Casey had banged in goals in 18, 21 and 27 minutes, to set the visiting Tynesiders off to a gay chorus as they sang the "Blaydon Races".

But this was one race in which the 200 to 1 outsider came up. Before half-time, Trevor Chamberlain, Fulham's left-winger, had sent a fine drive past Simpson, but the real excitement began 14 minutes after half-time, when Chamberlain cut round the back and scored what appeared to be the perfect goal.

Referee J. Mitchell (Lancashire) at first shared my opinion as he pointed to the centre, but then Bobby Mitchell, Newcastle's left winger ran up to him and pointed out that the linesman had flagged. Mr. Mitchell ran across the field, spoke to the linesman, and silenced the crowd by reversing his decision.

Haynes ran to the linesman and asked "why?" "I couldn't believe him when he said it was off-side" Johnny told me afterwards. "This was one of the most obvious goals I've ever seen. I would have been prepared for hands or anything else, but not offside."

My sympathies are with Fulham, because from my position in the press box, I shared the referee's first impression that it was a goal. Yet in spite of this, Fulham struck back like men of courage. Eleven minutes later, Chamberlain had responded to a piece of Haynes magic and crashed the ball in the net. This made it 3–2. In another two minutes it was all square, for Chamberlain had taken another magic pass from Johnny Haynes to make it 3–3.

And in yet another four minutes, incredible as it seemed, Fulham, the team that had been overwhelmed by Newcastle's Cup reputation in the first half, took the lead, when Hill finished off a low centre from Chamberlain which Jezzard had put his foot to.

What a turn-about. It had been caused mainly by the astonishing shooting of Chamberlain, the young man who was responsible for his school-pal Johnny Haynes joining Fulham, instead of more glamorous Arsenal or Spurs, and by the masterful touches of Haynes himself.

Yet Newcastle still fought back – and won. Two minutes later Keeble had charged an unsuspecting Black over the line to make it 4–4, and eight minutes from time the same player headed in Mitchell's centre for the winning goal.

FANTASTIC NEWCASTLE TRIUMPH AS FULHAM SCORE THREE IN FIVE MINUTES

Frenzy at Fulham…and no wonder after this fantastic, fabulous game, which was not only worthy of Wembley but had me alternately chewing my pencil in suspense or standing up in my seat roaring my tonsils out.

For Newcastle, the Cup holders, five times Wembley winners and the team which mows down oppositions with the murderous efficiency of machine guns, were themselves nearly mown down at Fulham yesterday. After trailing 0–3 to the giants of the North-east, Fulham staged one of the finest fighting comebacks I have seen, and at one stage led 4–3. But, just as it looked as if Fulham would pull of a miracle, Newcastle typically bounced back.

Just 12 minutes from the end, Newcastle wing wizard Bobby Mitchell crossed the ball. Fulham goalkeeper Black caught it but as his feet touched the ground centre forward Vic Keeble superbly charged him into the net to level the scores. The flu-ridden Keeble, who should never have played, said afterwards, "No one has ever been more relieved". Invincible, Newcastle won the match with eight minutes left. A Davies-Casey-Mitchell move gave Keeble the chance to head home the winger's cross.

But Fulham had cruel luck, especially as the referee disallowed what looked like a good goal by Trevor Chamberlain early in the second half. Fulham's mud-stained heroes were Chamberlain, who bedevilled right back Woollard and scored a hat-trick, and Johnny Haynes, whose brilliant footwork laid on Chamberlain's goals. But what a pity Fulham did not force-feed their left winger sooner.

In the first half, Newcastle toyed with Fulham, playing marvellous pin-point stuff. Their wingers, Milburn and Mitchell, were the stars of this dazzling spell. In ten blood-raising minutes, Newcastle scored three goals. In the 16th minute, Milburn smashed the ball first time into the roof of the net with his right foot from Mitchell's corner. Just four minutes later, Stokoe shot, again from Mitchell: the ball bounced off Wilson into the net. The third came five minutes after that following a mesmerizing Mitchell-Stokoe-Mitchell-Milburn movement which ended with Casey sliding through the mud and scoring with a searing left-foot drive.

Chamberlain's three left-foot goals, two from the narrowest angles, came in the 39th, 68th and 70th minutes. Hill put Fulham ahead three minutes later, again from Chamberlain, their third goal in five minutes.

Newcastle for the Cup? On this form, only a fool would bet against them.

West Ham United 2 v Fulham 3

Saturday 15 February 1958
FA Cup Fifth Round
Referee: A. Holland
Attendance: 37,500

WEST HAM U		FULHAM
Ernie Gregory	1	Tony Macedo
John Bond	2	George Cohen
Noel Cantwell	3	Jimmy Langley
Andy Malcolm	4	Roy Bentley
Ken Brown	5	Joe Stapleton
Malcolm Pyke	6	Robin Lawler
Mike Grice	7	Roy Dwight
Eddie Lewis	8	Jimmy Hill
Vic Keeble	9	Arthur Stevens
Johnny Dick	10	Johnny Haynes
Malcolm Musgrove	11	Trevor Chamberlain

Another twist on the sensational Newcastle tie was that a few weeks later, the man who had guided the Magpies to FA Cup success at Wembley in 1955, Dugald Livingstone, was appointed Fulham manager. Approaching 60 when he took over, with a long career stretching back to the 1920s as a player, coach and manager behind him, he spent little more than two years at the Cottage. But in that short time, he refashioned the team, took it agonisingly close to promotion and a Wembley Cup Final in the same season and set the club on the path to the top flight which was reached a year after his departure.

In his first few months, Livingstone had to cope with the break up of the club's prized inside-forward trio, with Robson being sold to West Brom and Jezzard's career ending with injury. He bought wisely (Langley, Bentley and Cook) and introduced promising youngsters (Macedo, Cohen, Chamberlain and Dwight), mixing both groups with the established players (Haynes, Lowe, Lawler, Hill and Stevens). By the autumn of 1957, it was starting to come together and Fulham made their first serious promotion challenge since relegation in 1952.

They also went on a Cup run. Non-League Yeovil were brushed aside in round three, but it took two games to dispose of Charlton, who, like Fulham were pushing for promotion from the (old) Second Division. Next it was to Upton Park to face another club well placed in the Second Division promotion race. Fulham and the Hammers had met in a League game at the Cottage a fortnight earlier and 42,195 had watched a thrilling 2–2 draw, a match that marked Maurice Cook's debut. Since he was Cup-tied with Watford, Stevens came back for the trip to east London. The Hammers were unchanged and at centre-forward was Vic Keeble, who two years earlier was Fulham's undoing when he was a Newcastle player in that memorable Cup tie. This tie was every bit as exciting as the earlier League encounter with West Ham at least having the consolation for losing in the Cup of gaining promotion.

Haynes is congratulated by Chamberlain on his winner against West Ham.

HAYNES CLINCHES LONDON CUP CLASH
By J. G. Orange

West Ham's see-saw Cup-tie with Fulham at Upton Park this afternoon had the crowd seething with excitement from the outset, Fulham, recovering from a 90 seconds' shock goal by Grice, replied through Dwight (12 min) and Hill (56 min) only to be pulled back to level terms by a penalty converted by Bond. Both West Ham goals resulted from errors by Langley and he must have been relieved when Johnny Haynes restored Fulham's lead 15 minutes from the end.

There was a dramatic start. Bond almost scored from a 45 yard free kick, Macedo taking the ball at the second attempt and then after 90 seconds, West Ham went ahead through Grice. His chance came unexpectedly because Langley insisted on taking an easy ball for which Macedo was better placed. Langley kicked straight to Grice who ran on a few yards and beat Macedo with a fast cross shot.

This set the crowd rocking with excitement and so did the following incidents. Hill twice went close for Fulham and Dick headed a pass from Keeble against the bar. After twelve minutes, Fulham, who had gradually recovered from their opening blow, drew level through Dwight. He ran in the middle to take a forward pass from Stevens. Two West Ham defenders, including Gregory closed in on Dwight, but he calmly lofted the ball over Gregory's head in the empty goal.

Chamberlain netted but was half a yard offside. Exchanges became a little heated when Musgrove was fouled just outside the Fulham penalty area and the referee spoke to Bentley. The drama continued. Bond shot a fierce free kick which Macedo saved brilliantly. Haynes won one of his several hard battles with Malcolm and beat two more opponents before putting in a shot which Gregory cleared only at the second attempt. For a spell the Fulham forwards abandoned their open play and began to weave. West Ham countered with a packed defense but Bentley went near with a header from a corner by Chamberlain.

West Ham were aggressive at the start of the second half. They began with two corners and Macedo made a fine save from Keeble. Keeble hurt an ankle but he soon played on. In the time of trial, Fulham's wing halves, Bentley and Lawler were strong pillars.

Fulham, who had done little pressing in this half, took the lead in their first serious attack. Hill scored taking a centre from Dwight on the volley at an acute angle. There was drama, too, about West Ham's equalizer. Grice, trying to cut in from the right, was brought down by Langley and West Ham were awarded a penalty. Bond netted, but one of his own team was in the area and the kick had to be re-taken. Bond was unperturbed and scored with his second attempt. This happened after 65 minutes.

Macedo prevented West Ham going ahead again by cutting out a fast shot from Grice. Fulham regained the lead through Haynes after 75 minutes and this proved to be the winning goal. West Ham then pressed forward, but the Fulham defense stood firm and a thrilling Cup-tie ended in success for the visitors, only the Hammers second defeat at Upton Park all season.

FULHAM'S 4 HEROES WRECK HAMMERS
By Alan Hoby

Fulham had four great heroes in this tense and serious struggle – goalkeeper Tony Macedo, a leaping, soaring figure with a rugby full-back's hands: that cunning veteran Roy Bentley, at right half: Jimmy Hill, inside right, and Johnny Haynes who, despite having right half Andy Malcolm breathing down his neck for 90 minutes, still keeping a cool enough head to score the winning goal.

But easily the greatest of these was man-of-the-match Macedo, who will be 20 on Saturday. Here, in this Gibraltar-born goalkeeper, is undoubtedly the finest prospect in the country.

The way the dark India-rubber-muscled Macedo plucked down sizzling high balls, including one amazing corkscrew save from inside left Eddie Lewis was fantastic.

West Ham were disappointing. Their "Lucky mascot" Vic Keeble, was blotted out.

Bentley took care of John Dick, at inside left. Indeed, West Ham's famous machine-gun thrusts down the middle time and again petered out against the redoubtable Fulham middle line of Bentley, Stapleton and Robin Lawler.

But West Ham cannot complain. They were given a lucky penalty in the second half and they still could not win. Their only effective forward was brilliant outside right Mike Grice.

West Ham's own famous fullbacks, Noel Cantwell and John Bond, were also unusually suspect under pressure. West Ham got what should have been the inspiration of a quick goal when Langley miskicked to Grice's feet in the second minute. The fair-haired West Ham right winger celebrated his luck with a flashing drive which left the startled Macedo helpless.

Ten minutes later Fulham equalized with a glorious, carefully planned three man goal. From centre forward Stevens a long ball reached left winger Trevor Chamberlain, who lobbed it to Roy Dwight, for the Fulham outside right to lob it over goalkeeper Ernie Gregory's head into the net.

Eleven minutes after half-time another glorious Hill-Haynes-Dwight-Hill move completely spread-eagled the West Ham defense. Going through like a guided missile, Hill screwed the ball into the net from the narrowest of angles.

After another hectic eight minutes, Langley went into a desperate late tackle in an effort to check the elusive Grice. The latter beat him, however, and then seemed to fall over Langley's legs. The referee immediately whistled for a penalty.

Bond flashed the ball home with his first kick, but Lewis had moved and he had to re-take the penalty. This time Bond made quite sure with a terrific drive.

Fulham however confirmed their mounting superiority in skill and tactics when 15 minutes from the end, Chamberlain hopelessly beat the limping Bond. From the Fulham left-winger's searching through pass Haynes, who had cleverly moved into the open space, slid the ball into the open net.

Doncaster Rovers 1 v Fulham 6

Saturday 15 March 1958
Football League Division Two
Referee: J. Kelly
Attendance: 18,189

DONCASTER R		FULHAM
Dave McIntosh	1	Tony Macedo
Brian Makepiece	2	George Cohen
Len Graham	3	Jimmy Langley
Tommy Cavanagh	4	Roy Bentley
Charlie Williams	5	Joe Stapleton
Pat Gavin	6	Robin Lawler
Peter Higham	7	Roy Dwight
Francis Callan	8	Jimmy Hill
James Fletcher	9	Maurice Cook
Anthony Reeson	10	Johnny Haynes
James Walker	11	Trevor Chamberlain

A week before the FA Cup semi-final, Fulham travelled to lowly Doncaster for a Second Division match. Well placed in the promotion race, they were the team in form and, despite this being their third game in a week with the prospect of facing Manchester United seven days later, still fielded their strongest side. In their previous four games, the Cottagers had not only disposed of Bristol Rovers in the Cup but also thrashed Grimsby 6–0 (when all five forwards scored before half-time) and beaten promotion rivals Charlton. And, just 48 hours before the trip to South Yorkshire, Fulham had defeated Leyton Orient 3–1 at Brisbane Road.

Rovers, on the other hand, were struggling in the drop zone and were eventually relegated. (A former Fulham player, Sean O'Driscoll, was Rovers' manager when they got back to this level 50 years later.) At centre-half that day for Doncaster was Charlie Williams who achieved a different sort of fame in the 1970s as a stand-up comic on the ITV series The Comedians. But for 90 minutes on that cold spring afternoon at Belle Vue, another man who was to become a major 1970s television personality took centre stage.

Jimmy Hill was one of five members of the Fulham squad (along with Black, Lowe, Lawler and Stevens) left from the first spell in the top flight. Signed from Brentford in March 1952, just months before relegation, he played in several midfield or forward positions until he settled at inside-right after Bobby Robson's transfer to West Brom. Energetic and enthusiastic rather than naturally gifted, Hill struck his best form in 1957–58. He scored 16 goals in the League and six more in the Cup, including one in every round right up to the semi-final, finishing second highest scorer, two behind Dwight. He got five of them at Doncaster, equalling the record of Fred Harrison and Beddy Jezzard but the first Fulham player to go nap away from the Cottage. A unique career as union leader, manager, television presenter, journalist and chairman lay ahead of this multi-talented individual, a footballing polymath.

A five-goal haul for Jimmy Hill at Belle Vue.

HILL IN SCORING FORM

FA Cup semi-finalists Fulham took another step towards the First Division when they crushed struggling Doncaster Rovers at Belle Vue in front of a crowd of 15,189. The man who did most of the damage was bearded inside right Jimmy Hill, although he owed much to the passes of England man Johnny Haynes and the crosses from winger Chamberlain. Although they were well beaten, Rovers never gave up and kept going to the final whistle.

Fulham took the lead after only five minutes. Macedo saved twice in early Doncaster rushes. Then Chamberlain passed to Cook who scored with a cross shot from a sharp angle, McIntosh diving too late.

Haynes and Cook harassed the Doncaster defense but the home forwards hit back and the Fulham defenders had plenty to do.

Chamberlain cut in, but McIntosh smothered his shot. After 20 minutes, Chamberlain centered and McIntosh pushed the ball out but Hill followed up and scored with close range. After 28 minutes Fulham were three up and the game was over as a contest. Hill was once again on the mark after McIntosh had partially saved from Haynes. Doncaster countered vigorously but their finishing was ragged and Macedo had only a few easy shots to save which hardly tested him.

Fulham maintained their pressure, and went looking for more goals. Hill tested McIntosh with a cross shot, which the goalkeeper held. The constant switching between Haynes, Cook and Hill caused a great deal of confusion amongst the Rovers defenders and at half-time no one could doubt that the visitors were worth their lead.

Within a minute of resuming, Fulham were four up. Stapleton played the ball out to Haynes who put it into the middle for Hill to run in and complete his first hat-trick. The fifth goal for Fulham was not long in coming. In the 52nd minute, Hill got to the ball first in a crowded penalty area to shoot in front at close range.

After this it was just a question of how many Fulham would win by, and how many Hill would score. There were just two more goals; one of course for Hill but the other was by Rovers right winger Higham, a small reward for his team's effort.

DONCASTER 1, FULHAM 6
By James Alfred

"Pull his beard" wailed a Doncaster fan as Jimmy Hill bashed in his fifth goal for Fulham. Not a very practical idea, but it was a new one and Doncaster had tried out all the others.

For most of the game the tall Fulham inside-right just strolled around spreading havoc in the Doncaster defence. His goals were all great efforts and, what's more, he hit the bar and a post and the busy Dave McIntosh pushed a header and a drive over the bar. Manchester United had better watch Mr. Hill next Saturday. They had better keep an eye too, on Trevor Chamberlain, Johnny Haynes — and, indeed, on every fellow in a white shirt, for Fulham will be no pushover.

And with their eyes on the Cup semi-final. Fulham were content to play at half speed, or the score might have made soccer history.

OUTSHONE

Fulham eased up in the last ten minutes and newcomer Peter Higham scored a consolation goal for Doncaster. But apart from that late flash, Doncaster were outclassed from the fifth minute when McIntosh pushed a Chamberlain shot out to Cook, who slammed the ball in.

The Hill goal blitz started in the 20th minute, when he flicked on a Chamberlain pass and continued after 27 minutes when he smashed home a 10 yard drive.

Two great drives and a near flick brought him three goals in 14 minutes after the interval.

MERIT MARKS (Max: 10 pts)
Doncaster 4, Fulham 9; Referee Kelly (Chorley) 8

Manchester United 2 v Fulham 2

Saturday 22 March 1958
FA Cup Semi-final (at Villa Park)
Referee: C.W. Kingston
Attendance: 69,745

OFFICIAL PROGRAMME

THE FOOTBALL ASSOCIATION
CHALLENGE CUP

SEMI-FINAL TIE

(2) **MANCHESTER UNITED** 5
v.
(2) **FULHAM** 3

VILLA PARK, BIRMINGHAM
SATURDAY, MARCH, 22nd, 1958
KICK-OFF 3-0 p.m.

PRICE - 6ᴰ. ISSUED BY ASTON VILLA F.C.

MANCHESTER U		**FULHAM**
Harry Gregg	1	Tony Macedo
Bill Foulkes	2	George Cohen
Ian Greaves	3	Jimmy Langley
Freddie Goodwin	4	Roy Bentley
Ronnie Cope	5	Joe Stapleton
Stan Crowther	6	Robin Lawler
Colin Webster	7	Roy Dwight
Ernie Taylor	8	Jimmy Hill
Alex Dawson	9	Arthur Stevens
Mark Pearson	10	Johnny Haynes
Bobby Charlton	11	Trevor Chamberlain

There can have been few more highly charged FA Cup semi-finals than Fulham's meeting with Manchester United at Villa Park. After beating West Ham, the Cottagers had defeated Bristol Rovers at home to reach the semi-final for the third time, and the first for 22 years. And they had done so without having to face higher-level opposition. Livingstone's team was managing the twin demands of a promotion challenge and a push for a first Wembley appearance remarkably well. They had won their four League fixtures and one FA Cup tie immediately prior to the semi-final, scoring 21 goals and conceding only four. The Cottagers had lost just twice in all competitions since the beginning of December, when Livingstone had revamped the side.

United, on the other hand, had experienced the appalling tragedy of the Munich air crash just weeks before the semi-final, when eight of their players were killed and many others so badly injured they would never play again. Somehow, the patched-up side under Jimmy Murphy's guidance, had battled through to the semi-final, overcoming top flight opposition in Sheffield Wednesday and West Brom (after a replay) on the way. The previous May, United had been beaten finalists, losing to Aston Villa. Now, just 10 months later, only Bill Foulkes and Bobby Charlton of the 1957 Cup Final side were playing for a place in the 1958 Final. Any uncommitted football supporter was firmly in the United camp that day even though Fulham were the underdogs.

Fulham had the luxury of their strongest side, and exactly the same team that had beaten West Ham and Bristol Rovers. The United line up included a couple of special signings, including Stan Crowther. He had played for Villa against United in the Final the previous year and was in fact already Cup tied, but United were given special dispensation. There was also the next generation of 'Busby Babes' rushed through because of the circumstances. These included inside-forward Mark Pearson, with his distinctive 'Teddy Boy' hairstyle. In 1965, he signed for Fulham.

Goalkeeper Tony Macedo beats United's Colin Webster to the ball. Joe Stapleton (No. 5) and George Cohen are in support at Villa Park.

DEPLETED FULHAM RESCUED BY MACEDO

At one point on Saturday afternoon we seemed to be heading for a new chapter in a Cup Final. Far away at crowded Maine Road in Manchester the news came that Blackburn Rovers were leading Bolton: eight minutes from half-time Fulham went ahead against Manchester United at neutral Villa Park to set every Londoner in the 70,000 crowd dancing with glee. But before the end, the ancient tradition of the Cup was preserved. There will be no all Second Division final, though Fulham may yet tread the national stage, for they are still locked in combat with Manchester United. Sharing four goals in the Midlands, the tingling battle now moves to London for its next stage. It is still anybody's match.

IMP IN RED SHIRT

Art is ordered and if properly applied it can greatly influence events. But in any fluid struggle such as this, luck can also have more than its fair say. On this occasion, United were supported by an imp who wore a Lancastrian shirt. Fulham found their forces depleted by an injury to Langley, an aggressive left back, at a critical phase. But, for another two or three minutes perhaps, Fulham might have reached Wembley Just about that time was left on the clock to the interval when Langley was suddenly felled by an accidental kick behind the knee in a tackle on Dawson. The damage was done. In the extra moments allowed for play after Langley had been examined, tendered, gathered up and carried sorrowfully away on a stretcher, the alert Charlton pulled Manchester back to 2–2 with a searing shot and the whole balance was altered. Had Fulham spanned that crisis who can say what the ending might have been? As it was, though Langley returned bravely to provide a nuisance value in the centre of their attack, Fulham were left to play an increasingly rearguard action over the final testing stages as stamina slowly oozed away.

TWO INCHES OR SO

That they survived was both wonderful and just, and due to the magnificent goalkeeping of Macedo. The United themselves would be the first to concur, though at the very end it was their same supporting imp who finally turned his face away as if ashamed of too much partiality. Just as those two fateful minutes earlier probably denied Fulham the harvest of victory, so two inches or so of woodwork at the very end kept them alive. In a flash the sprite must have moved Macedo's crossbar just that much to take the full force of another thundering drive from Charlton that all but splintered everything in sight. It would have been a goal to remember indeed, a shot at the climax of a 50-yard run that deserved to win any match. But the fates were right to level things.

Now the replay hangs delicately in the balance. Much will depend on the recovery of Langley: Taylor too, injured a hip painfully near the close, a loss Manchester could scarcely afford if he were to miss the replay, though it took a full hour before the little general got out his map and compass properly to direct the thread of attack with his Napoleonic touch of old. As it was before the balance was disturbed, Fulham looked the cooler, more thoughtful and creative side; their nerves seemed the less frayed, showing up all the pent-up tension through which their young opponents have lived this past month. This, as much as anything, may tell in the end.

There were three special warriors – Haynes and Macedo for Fulham: young Charlton for Manchester United. It was Haynes who shaped his forces and gave them authority in the first half an hour before Langley's injury. He was the puppet master, putting things and figures into motion – especially Hill, the bearded pirate – at the turn of a foot. Some of his angled through passing was superb, always probing and stretching the Manchester defence to its full. Later, after the interval, when he moved to left half with Lawler behind him, he was equally masterly as he combined effective defence against Taylor with attack. While he stands, Fulham always keep in any picture.

Macedo played his giant part as the United turned the screw powerfully over the last 20 minutes. With Goodwin and Crowther at last with a measure of control in midfield and Taylor finally adding his subtle wealth to attack, the odds seemed to lengthen every painful minute against Fulham. It was then that Macedo rose to his full height and in the last quarter of an hour alone he made three saves that seemed beyond the power of any man. He became a bird – first to fly to the top corner and flick away a header by Webster, next to turn a swift low stab from Charlton round the post, and then, floating parallel to the ground, to catch at full stretch another rocket from the same player. Even Charlton that time had to stand and applaud in astonished amazement.

Charlton himself was the dashing Prince Rupert of the battle. From beginning to end, often with little enough support from the flanks and only an occasional delicate nudge from Taylor, he alone had Fulham on tenterhooks. Inviting the tackle, he moved the ball both ways swiftly and fairly oozed past opponents with swerve and acceleration

EXPLOSIVE GOAL

And his finishing matched his approach as he showed at the 12th minute when he put Manchester ahead against the early run of play, with an explosive goal. Taking a forward touch from Taylor he hit the top corner of the Fulham net brilliantly from the edge of the penalty area. Even the acrobatic Macedo could not sniff that one.

At the start the tight pressed Villa Park crowd buzzed like a hive about to swarm. Now the roar rose and fell in waves, for in the very next minute Langley's cross pass split the United defence and Stevens, close in, smacked Fulham level. London, with Haynes the architect, gained command. Their football was controlled, patterned, and with eight minutes to half time they took their reward. Haynes and Lawler set Dwight free and there was the marauding Hill to streak through the middle and beat Gregg.

But fate was creeping up on Fulham. With half time only a stride away, and a valuable lead in their pocket, Langley fell. In a twinkling Charlton had struck once more to put Manchester level. Pearson, receiving from Taylor, saw his shot rebound off Cohen; quick as light Charlton's right foot was again the executioner.

The second half hovered like a dark cloud on the horizon for Fulham. The storm threatened and finally broke. But the scoring, it proved, was done. First, however, Gregg had to make precious saves under the United bar from Dwight and Hill yet at the end it was Macedo covered gallantly by Haynes, Bentley, Lawler and others, who held at bay a Manchester side at last playing with urgency and a sense of desire.

Manchester United 5 v Fulham 3

Wednesday 26 March 1958
FA Cup Semi-final (at Highbury)
Referee: C.W. Kingston
Attendance: 38,258

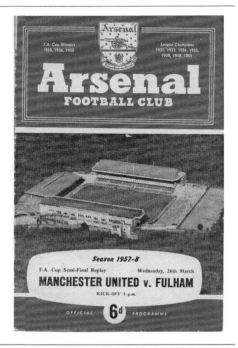

MANCHESTER U		FULHAM
Harry Gregg	1	Tony Macedo
Bill Foulkes	2	George Cohen
Ian Greaves	3	Jimmy Langley
Freddie Goodwin	4	Roy Bentley
Ronnie Cope	5	Joe Stapleton
Stan Crowther	6	Robin Lawler
Colin Webster	7	Roy Dwight
Ernie Taylor	8	Jimmy Hill
Alex Dawson	9	Arthur Stevens
Bobby Charlton	10	Johnny Haynes
Shay Brennan	11	Trevor Chamberlain

It was hard to believe that the replay could be as tense and as thrilling as the Villa Park clash. But if anything, it was more so. There were eight goals, a ninth controversially disallowed and the result in doubt until the last minutes. Played on a Wednesday afternoon (no floodlights in those days) at Highbury just four days after the first game, it was, very unusually, televised by the BBC. This was the first time ever Fulham had been shown live on television.

Langley recovered from his knock at Villa Park and so Fulham were able to field the same team. United made one change from the previous Saturday, Shay Brennan coming in on the wing, Bobby Charlton moving inside and Mark 'Pancho' Pearson making way. The reports of the game focused on two players,

The decisive fifth goal for United at Highbury.

one from each side. For United, Alec Dawson, subdued at Villa Park but a hat-trick hero at Highbury and for Fulham, Tony Macedo, who performed heroics in goal on the Saturday but had a nightmare on the Wednesday. And United, who had lost all four League games in March, scoring in just one of them, remembered their way to goal and got back on the winning habit. But there was also the personal duel in midfield between two of Britain's finest, Johnny Haynes and Bobby Charlton. The two would form an outstanding partnership for England, particularly when Haynes took over the captaincy in 1960.

After this defeat, Fulham's season disintegrated. Faced with a fixture pile up, their promotion challenge evaporated. They had to play eight games in 24 days in April, including four in a week, and two victories and three draws that month left them in fifth place, four points short. Manager Livingstone chose to go back north at the end of the season and Beddy Jezzard stepped up to the manager's job. It was a disappointing end to Fulham's best season in both League and Cup for exactly 50 years, their first in Division Two in 1907–08.

YOUNG MANCHESTER REACH WEMBLEY IN STYLE
FULHAM GOALKEEPING ERRORS ONLY PARTLY TO BLAME

Life moves in mysterious ways. Seven weeks ago Manchester United the old, the champions were torn asunder. Three, four, perhaps even five years we thought would be needed for regrouping and recovery. But here Manchester United, the new, have confounded the world. Yesterday, they beat Fulham in their FA Cup semi-final replay, making Highbury a sheath for their sword. Now, some six week hence, on May 3, they will march proudly through the gates of Wembley stadium to face Bolton Wanderers in a Cup Final of pure Lancastrian accent. The world will acclaim them. The more that was lost the more precious the little left.

Thus United continue to ride a wave of glory. They were nearly there at Villa Park last Saturday. But yesterday the throbbing struggle just tilted their way, hammered out on the pulses of a 38,000 crowd, those careless of the expected crush and preferring the real thing to the distant fireside views on television. A cup-tie, fought to the death, can be prolonged almost to eternity. At the end, one of the two must go and now the fates decreed it must be Fulham who were to be left behind in the shadows. In this there must always be sadness and if this is a truism it is none the less sad.

The heavens themselves seemed unable to remain indifferent to the outcome. Indeed, there was a strange sense of destiny in all that happened and somewhere along the winding struggle it appeared that Fulham were fated to help their foe. Fulham, in fact, in the sad person of Macedo, did very much to help United before half-time and United were in such a rapacious mood as to accept every little crumb thrown their way.

Last Saturday it was Macedo, with truly startling saves under his crossbar, who earned Fulham their replay. Yesterday he lived in a dark cavern after a beginning that threatened to cut the heart out of his opponents. In the opening 10 minutes he achieved three more flying saves of Villa Park vintage as if to show he was uncannily gifted and unbeatable. Then at the crisis in the last 20 minutes before the interval he threw two goals at Manchester's feet and that in the end swayed the delicate balance. The real sorrow of it was that these shafts of ill-fortune struck at a point when Fulham had fought themselves on top with some penetrating forward play under the masterly direction of Haynes. But these things happen: the human element is beyond calculation or explanation.

COVERED DANGER

However, Manchester United at the last won with poise and deserved honour. Apart from a gallant rally near the end, which so nearly earned Fulham a fourth goal but for the slightest of handling offenses by Haynes before Dwight shot home his pass, it was United who had the measure of the second half. Yet it was not until the last seconds were unwinding themselves that Charlton scored their last and fifth goal to brook no more further argument. Nor could any finer word have been found to close the final chapter as this dashing player flashed in his shot just under the crossbar.

On balance, Manchester United were the stronger at wing half. There, Goodwin, especially, and Crowther covered danger and fashioned their own replies with thoughts and coolness. In attack, little Taylor was the controlling genius; a goldfish in his darting dribbles. He it was, linking, jinxing, directing, who kept United playing through the smoke and thunder of the battle. At his side there lurked Charlton, an ever-present danger with his swerve, acceleration and shooting power. There were phases, true, when Charlton seemed to run out of steam. But every now and then he would turn on the tap and when that happened all the red lights winked for the Fulham defense.

Fulham themselves at times must have felt that the rub of Highbury's muddy green was against them. But in the final analysis only Langley with his constructive, aggressive defense at left-back could add any weighty supporting words to Haynes as he tried to whip a full throated answer from his forwards. For some 20 minutes, certainly, while the crisis was brewing just before half time, they began to move smoothly and dangerously.

But the luck spun wildly away from them and in the end they succumbed because Hill, their bearded poacher of goals, was blanketed by Manchester's quick thinking defense. Hill, indeed, not to put too unkind a point upon it, must have felt long before the end that he was in the barber's chair and Crowther was the man with the razor.

Yet, for an afternoon of tension and thrill it could scarcely have been surpassed. It was a struggle full of error and brilliance, of thrust and counter-thrust, of breathless escape, and of goals plentifully strung on a thread. Some were perfect, others not without a flaw. But they all counted the same. Everything seemed larger than life itself on a mild and misty afternoon in which there was a taste of rain.

HUB OF THE MATTER

All the near misses and many of the diving saves at each end must now be shelved in memory but three dives by Macedo at the very start under the Fulham crossbar as he kept out certain goals by Goodwin (twice) and Taylor all but opened the heavy skies. Then, at the quarter hour, Manchester struck home. Webster survived a lunging tackle, turned back Brennan's corner from the left, and there was Dawson diving to head in the first of three precious goals he will always remember. Bur at the 26th minute, Fulham were level as Hill the decoy let Haynes' diagonal pass reach Stevens close in. Now came those last ten minutes to half-time, the hub of the matter and Macedo's errors. First he dived late at Dawson's low cross drive from the right wing and a shot which he would normally have picked up one handed slipped disastrously under him. Yet, within minutes, Fulham, full of fight and going great guns, were level again as Langley dribbled 40 yards to give Chamberlain an open target bang in front of Gregg. 2–2.

Now again the roulette wheel spun curiously. Taylor, on a fascinating zig-zag course, offered a through pass to Brennan and Webster converging in the centre. Macedo got there first, was unseated, lost the ball and Brennan sent United with a precious 3–2 lead into the interval.

NO ANSWERING FIRE

Try as he would Haynes could later raise no answering fire from his Fulham attack and the second half rested largely in the laps of Taylor, Charlton, Goodwin and Crowther. With 25 minutes left Charlton accelerated down the left, oozed past three defenders up to the byline and Dawson once more did his duty close in. Manchester led 4–2 and it looked all over. Yet back came Fulham, their white sails catching some passing breeze. Dwight whipped home Stevens' cross, and with a quarter of an hour left it was 4–3.

Only eight minutes remained when Haynes flicked the ball back from the line and Dwight hit the United net. The excitement was mountainous. Yet it was no goal. Haynes had handled. But for a touch it could have been 4–4. But it was Charlton and Manchester who had the last word. Every clock and watch on the ground was out when he accelerated in from the right and sent a sizzling shot to the far top corner. United, like some freak rainbow on a clear and cloudless day, were at Wembley again.

BY BOB PENNINGTON

They were there – United through to Wembley. And we could still hardly credit the incredible. They had just fought their way from the ashes of Munich to football immortality.

And there were as many tears as cheers as Highbury erupted from 90 minutes of tremendous tension into a near-hysterical salute.

Jimmy Murphy, their deputy chief, stood on the touchline, his gray hair disheveled, waiting to embrace the boys who in disaster had rushed to maturity in just over six weeks.

There were tears in his eyes as he thought of the United players who might have known the sweetness of this return triumph. Everybody said they would be back after last year's Final. But after Munich, only Murphy still believed in it.

An ashen-faced boy in a green jersey brushed quickly past Murphy, racing to get away from a personal nightmare. He was Tony Macedo Fulham's brilliant young goalkeeper, who had seen all his dreams shattered in his own fumbling grasp.

Fulham will remember the bitter, despairing tears of Tony Macedo too. Destiny has been so unjustly cruel to this 20-year-old boy and his club. And the only consolation was that at least it helped balance the scales a little for United.

Now I am free to tell you of the secret fear that has haunted Fulham for the last month – the fear that Macedo might crack under the incredible strain of Fulham's fight towards Wembley and promotion.

JUST CALL IT HIS PRIVATE HELL

In the three months he has stormed his way from obscurity to challenge as England's World Cup goalkeeper. His form at Villa Park, on Saturday was world class. He was a certainty for Sweden this summer.

But in that private hell Macedo found at Highbury he made two decisive blunders that smashed his nerve and broke the heart and the hopes of Fulham.

Yet for the first 14 minutes it was still mighty Macedo. Twice he saved what seemed like certain goals from drives by Freddie Goodwin, United's match master.

The only hint of the tension he was suffering came when he dropped the ball after his first save and was fortunate to scramble it clear of the line.

I do not blame Macedo for United's 14th-minute goal. But he was left stranded as Colin Webster centered the ball for 18-year-old Alex Dawson to head into the net.

Fulham seemed overwhelmed by Murphy's master switching of Webster and Dawson, the magic of Ernie Taylor, and the drive of glorious Goodwin.

But they were back in the game with more than chance after Arthur Stevens, 37 years young, scored from a perfect through pass by Johnny Haynes.

My notes read: 27 minutes Steven's triumph… 35 minutes Macedo's despair. Despair as a speculative, soft shot from Dawson twisted out of his hands into the net.

He knelt in anguish, wondering: "Why, why didn't I catch it?"

But three minutes later Fulham were level again as bold left back Jimmy Langley surged up the wing and made a gift goal for Trevor Chamberlain.

Had Fulham remained level at half-time Macedo might have recovered. But just 60 seconds from the peace of the dressing room, Taylor rolled the ball forward in a rare poor pass.

Macedo should have cleared without difficulty. But his legs seemed leaden, his hands without power as he lost possession and Seamus Brennan pushed the ball past him to make it 3–2.

Silent sobs racked Macedo as team-manager Dugald Livingstone tried desperately during the interval to give him and Fulham the will to go out there and win.

FLURRY

Morale slumped to an all-time low when Dawson scored his third goal after a fine run by Bobby Charlton. Haynes shrugged his shoulders in resignation as all his efforts were squandered by woeful wingmen.

A flurry of fight as veteran Stevens broke away to make a simple goal for Roy Dwight (73 mins).

But though the excitement was at fever pitch and Haynes had a goal disallowed for offside, it was Charlton who scored in the last few seconds with a shot that left Macedo helpless.

Fulham 5 v Leyton Orient 2

Saturday 14 February 1959
Football League Division Two
Referee: L. Callaghan
Attendance: 20,478

FULHAM		LEYTON O
Ken Hewkins	1	Frank George
George Cohen	2	Alan Eagles
Robin Lawler	3	John Gregory
Alan Mullery	4	Mal Lucas
Roy Bentley	5	Sid Bishop
Eddie Lowe	6	Phil McKnight
Tony Barton	7	Phil White
Jimmy Hill	8	Eddie Baily
John Doherty	9	Tom Johnston
Johnny Haynes	10	Eddie Brown
Graham Leggat	11	Jimmy Andrews

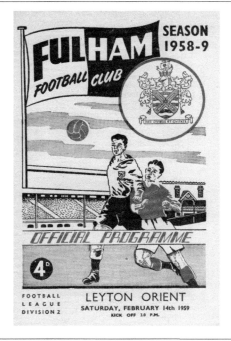

From the very first game of the 1958–59 season, a 6–1 home victory over Stoke helped by a Maurice Cook hat-trick, Fulham were promotion favourites. They won the first six on the trot, nine of the first 10 and were unbeaten until the 13th game, at home to Liverpool. It was the perfect start for new manager Beddy Jezzard (a player in the first Fulham team to win promotion to the top flight in 1949) and new signing Graham Leggat. Bought from Aberdeen for £20,000, the Scottish international winger scored in his first six games for Fulham and was to prove an outstanding acquisition.

There were some interesting results in the first half of the season. Both goals in the 2–1 home win over Charlton in December were scored by debutant left-winger Mike Johnson and against Brighton on Boxing Day, both full-backs (Cohen and Langley) were on the scoresheet in the 3–1, and both goals were from open play. The return the next day, attracted the biggest-ever crowd (36,342) to Brighton's old Goldstone Ground.

The nucleus of the team was Livingstone's from the previous season, apart from Leggat replacing Dwight. It was the season that Haynes proved himself a goal scorer as well as a goal maker. He was top scorer in this promotion campaign with 26 goals in 34 matches, a personal best for the Maestro. In this total were four hat-tricks, including one on St Valentine's Day against Leyton Orient, the third a rare header. But there was new face in the side that day that attracted the headlines, 17-year-old wing half Alan Mullery, a product of Fulham's junior sides. He kept his place thereafter until he retired and went into management in 1976, after 412 games for Fulham, 409 for Spurs and 35 for England, winning a cupboard load of honours in the process, including the MBE. Mullery's emergence meant Bentley switched to centre-half and Joe Stapleton's days in the first team were numbered.

A convincing win, a Haynes hat-trick and an outstanding debut by Alan Mullery against Orient.

TOM'S RETURN DIDN'T INSPIRE O'S ATTACK

As Leyton Orient's chirpy inside right and skipper Eddie Baily put it: "We're right out of luck at the moment. But we'll be back."

Certainly the ball did not run or bounce for Orient in this hectic, hard fought derby match with much-shuffled Fulham.

Even the dramatic re-appearance of rescue man- centre forward Tom Johnston – failed to swing fortune in their favour. Tom had only had three hours sleep before the game, and he did little but nudge the pass for each Orient game.

Fulham blended surprisingly well to achieve a decisive victory for all-round teamwork. Of course, they had their star performers. That was a fine hat-trick by inside left Johnny Haynes. Left half Eddie Lowe had a magnificent non-stop game.

But it was Scotland's outside right Graham Leggat playing at outside left who really set Fulham firmly on the road to victory with a brilliant opening goal and then within a minute, a superb through pass to "make" the second.

Considering how lively was the Fulham attack once Leggat had provided the initial boost, the Orient defense put up a good performance, with fast and effective tackling and tight marking.

Left back Jack Gregory kept a grip on Fulham outside right Tony Barton which the wing, not so well supported as Leggat, could seldom shake off.

LEGGAT WORRIES UNCERTAIN ORIENT

Graham Leggat, switched to Fulham's left-wing for the match with Leyton Orient here at Craven Cottage, gave the uncertain Orient defence an unhappy time and had a hand in all three first half goals for the home side. Orient had Tom Johnston back in their attack. He was signed from Blackburn this morning.

Leggat gave Fulham the lead in the eighth minute when he raced 40 yards to score with a right-foot shot.

A minute later, Leggat again took the ball 40 yards and slipped it through to Doherty, who beat off Bishop's challenge and hit the ball past the advancing George.

Orient could make little headway against a solid Fulham defence and in the 21st minute Leggat sparked off another goal move.

His centre was only partially cleared and Haynes slammed the ball into the net.

Leggat was going through again when he was brought down a yard outside the penalty area. Hill managed to get a foot to Haynes' free kick but could get no force behind his shot.

As Orient settled down they began to play better football, and were rewarded when Johnston headed a White centre onto Baily, who drove home a fine goal.

HALF TIME: FULHAM 3, LEYTON ORIENT 1

Fulham now eased the pace, but Leggat livened things up when he robbed Eagles and tried a shot at goal.

Then, from a corner, Haynes, tried a shot. The ball hit a defender but had enough force to roll on, hit a post and trickle into the net.

That was in the 59th minute and one minute later Andrew had hit back with a goal for Orient after three forwards had tried to reach a centre from White.

Haynes put the issue beyond reasonable doubt when he scored with a terrific header in the 66th minute. Fulham were now well on top.

There was strength, too in Orient's half-back line. In the centre, Sid Bishop was dominant, though he found that Fulham centre forward John Doherty had some clever distributional ideas.

Wing halves Malcolm Lucas and Phil McKnight followed Haynes and Jimmy Hill most faithfully. The Fulham inside men took some catching. The quick bursts of Hill and the subtleties of Haynes were always a threat. Yet Lucas and McKnight never surrendered. The Fulham defence, equally solid, had little to contend with except the astute passes of inside right Eddie Baily. He struggled hard to get the line moving but his colleagues were not moving into position with any degree of anticipation. Still, Eddie's duels with that others experienced Eddie – Lowe – were full of colour.

Seventeen-year-old Alan Mullery made an auspicious League debut, with little scope allowed to Eddy Brown at inside left for Orient.

The goals began with Leggat in the seventh minute, followed by a 30 yard Doherty piledriver a minute later. Haynes got his first, and made it 3–0, after 21 minutes and four minutes before the break, Baily reduced the arrears. It was Haynes again in the 55th minute and although Andrews got one back within sixty seconds, Haynes completed his hat trick and wrapped up the scoring with a header from Barton's corner with a quarter of an hour to play.

Fulham 6 v Sheffield Wednesday 2

Friday 27 March 1959
Football League Division Two
Referee: K. Stokes
Attendance: 39,337

FULHAM		SHEFFIELD W
Tony Macedo	1	Mike Pinner
George Cohen	2	Ron Staniforth
Jimmy Langley	3	Norman Curtis
Alan Mullery	4	Tom McAnearney
Roy Bentley	5	Peter Swan
Eddie Lowe	6	Tony Kay
Graham Leggat	7	Derek Wilkinson
Jimmy Hill	8	John Fantham
Maurice Cook	9	Roy Shiner
Johnny Haynes	10	Redfern Frogatt
Trevor Chamberlain	11	Alan Finney

The best game of an outstanding season was on Good Friday morning when the two top teams in the (old) Second Division met at Craven Cottage. Nearly 40,000 people managed to negotiate Bank Holiday public transport to arrive for an 11.15 kick-off. And their efforts were well rewarded with a fine team performance by Fulham and an individual triumph for one member of the side.

Wednesday, managed by Harry Catterick, were attempting to bounce back into the top flight at the first attempt and had matched Fulham in the promotion race stride for stride. By the time the teams met twice over Easter, the two clubs had established a comfortable margin at the top of the table. A Fulham win would put them at the top of the table, although the Owls had two games in hand. The

Cottagers were at full strength, with Mullery for Stapleton the only change from the team which had started the season. Wednesday, on the other hand, were missing their international goalkeeper, Ron Springett, for whom the amateur international Mike Pinner deputised. For 75 minutes, the game was keenly contested. Fulham led 3–2 but the outcome was in balance. This was the cue for Jimmy Hill to make his mark.

In 1957–58, Hill had an outstanding season. He had made the inside-right position his and had scored 16 League goals (the second highest behind Dwight) plus six in the FA Cup, including one in every round up to the semi-final. But in 24 games of the promotion season, he had failed to find the net. A single goal in the FA Cup defeat by Birmingham was all he had managed. Then came the final 15 minutes of this key match, and Hill delivered a hat-trick of headers. He scored three more in the remaining seven games as the Cottagers picked up 11 points from a possible 14 to finish runners-up, seven points clear of Sheffield United in third place. Promotion was clinched at Barnsley with two games to spare but Wednesday claimed the title by a margin of two points.

Hat-trick hero Jimmy Hill inspires Fulham to a decisive promotion win.

ALL SO FRIENDLY AT FULHAM

HILL HEADS OFF BOO BOYS WITH HAT-TRICK

This is the jeers to cheers story of Jimmy Hill, bearded chairman of the PFA and barracked inside right of Fulham. He crushed Sheffield Wednesday with a brilliant hat-trick of headers in the final 16 minutes of this Second Division summit meeting to put Fulham back on top of the League. He ended 11 months without a League goal and changed the cat-calls of "Go Home Hill" to roars of "Good Old Jimmy". And, above all, Hill won an honorable peace with soccer's other celebrated chairman with a chin, Tommy Trinder of Fulham. Hill said "I knew this would be one of my worst or my best games. I did not believe it could be both".

Before the match, Hill received a firm but friendly talk from Trinder in which it became apparent that, as chairman of Fulham, Tommy is anything but a comedian. Team manager Bedford Jezzard also made a peace move by restoring Hill to the first team after he had been 'dropped' in practice games.

Fulham, after 74 minutes, had proved that toughness as well as talent is needed at the top, had a 3–2 lead through Leggat (6 mins), a Langley penalty (36 mins) and Cook (63 mins), with Wednesday's goals coming from Wilkinson (20 mins) and Shiner (46 mins) Meanwhile, Hill held his head in despair. Johnny Haynes, his captain and friend turned on the Hill baiters with his demand, "Give him a break, can't you?" And with just 16 minutes left, Hill got that break from a right wing corner by outside left Tosh Chamberlain. All you could see was a black and white flash as Hill soared his head to the ball.

Hill went wild, and so did Fulham. Jimmy was hugged, thumped and buried under a crowing crowd of players while wags in front of the director's box made some impertinent gestures in the direction of chairman Trinder. But when Hill headed the fifth and sixth goals in the 78th and 88th minutes, Trinder gagged away to the crowd below, and said later "If I thought this was the formula, I'd use it every week". This was Jimmy's day. The stinker that became a blinder, the humiliation that ended in glory.

HEADS YOU WIN, JIMMY

Hat-trick kills off that vendetta

Three sky-high headers in 14 minutes gave Jimmy Hill – yes he played despite the Battle of the Long Chins with chairman Tommy Trinder! - a hilarious hat-trick and routed this skilful Sheffield Wednesday side. Hill's first League goals for 11 months put Fulham ON TOP OF THE SECOND DIVISION. The vendetta boos for 70 minutes of this fireball match suddenly changed to stupendous, if a little amazed, cheers

Hill, sleeves rolled to the armpits, beard bristling, face one perpetual grin, was gloriously mobbed at the end by hundreds of delighted school kids, let in late for this top-of-the-table thriller which caused the gates to be closed.

I shall never forget the scene in the 74th minute. The score was 3–2 and the see-saw struggle was as hectic as ever. From a right wing corner taken by left winger Trevor Chamberlain, Hill soared three feet in the air to lunge home a sensational rocket header. Every Fulham man sprinted to Hill who appeared convulsed with glee. A great wonderful white bundle ground Hill into the mud and rolled him round and round in genuine delight – AT LAST – The Beard had scored.

Inside four minutes, the head of Hill worked wonders

again, finishing off a Johnny Haynes-Maurice Cook move. Again, Hill jigged in jubilation. He finished off the magic morning with another headed goal two minutes from the end.

As Hill was mobbed, many beaming fans gave chairman Tommy Trinder friendly but animated V-signs. Trinder laughed his head off. Cracked Trinder, "If this is the formula to get Hill to score a hat-trick, we'll repeat it."

Pity Wednesday had to meet a man inspired. Until then, they were every bit as good as Fulham and had twice hit back with slick goals, had lost Alan Finney (cut eye) for ten minutes and skipper Redfern Froggatt had re-found his talented game.

Despite being a goal down to Graham Leggat in six minutes, it was no surprise when Wilkinson glanced in a header for Wednesday in 20 minutes. Right back Staniforth stopped a certain Maurice Cook goal with his hands in the 38th minute and Jim Langley put Fulham ahead from the spot. Back zoomed Wednesday with a splendid Shiner hook shot two minutes after the interval. Cook forced Fulham into the lead for the third time in the 63rd minute.

And then enter this man Hill.

Wolverhampton Wanderers 9 v Fulham 0

Wednesday 16 September 1959
Football League Division One
Referee: G.W. Pullin
Attendance: 41,692

WOLVES		FULHAM
Malcolm Finlayson	1	Tony Macedo
Eddie Stuart	2	George Cohen
Gerry Harris	3	Jimmy Langley
Ron Flowers	4	Alan Mullery
George Showell	5	Joe Stapleton
Eddie Clamp	6	Robin Lawler
Micky Lill	7	Graham Leggat
Bobby Mason	8	Jimmy Hill
Jimmy Murray	9	John Doherty
Peter Broadbent	10	Alf Stokes
Norman Deeley	11	Mike Johnson

Club records are double-edged swords. For every highest, there is a lowest, for every biggest, a smallest and so on. Each is an essential part of the club's story and any account of Fulham's last 100 years would be incomplete without some reference to the worst as well as the best. In only their second month back in the top flight, and just eight games into the 1959–60 season, the Cottagers suffered what was, and remains, their biggest-ever League defeat. It came in midweek at the hands of Stan Cullis' Wolves, a club chasing a third successive League title and one which ended that season a single point short of being the first in the 20th century to complete the elusive League and Cup double.

A fortnight earlier, the upstart Cottagers had the temerity to beat the champions in midweek at Craven Cottage. Without the injured Haynes, and with reserve striker John Doherty in inspired form, Fulham convincingly inflicted the first defeat of the season on their illustrious guests by 3–1 in front of a delighted home crowd of 32,155. Exactly seven days, it was to Molineux, a crowd of nearly 42,000 and revenge with interest for Wolves. Still without Haynes, and also deprived of Bentley and Cook (Stapleton and Hill coming in) Fulham were humiliated, and diminutive winger Norman Deeley was their tormentor in chief. The result was clearly a setback, and the Cottagers lost their next two matches. But they regained their form and then five wins on the trot which pushed them well up the table.

Inevitably, the occasion brought out some gallows humour. From the kick-off, Fulham's usual move was for the centre-forward (Doherty) to pass to the inside-left (Alf Stokes) who would then knock the ball back to right-half Alan Mullery. As they went through the routine for the 10th time that evening, Stokes apparently said to Doherty, 'You know John, I think we've got this move off to a tee now'. Very Fulhamish.

The squad for the start of the return to the top flight. Left to right, back row: Lawler, Stapleton, Cohen, Macedo, Bentley, Lowe, Langley, Mullery. Front row: Doherty, Barton, Stokes, Hill, Cook, Haynes, Chamberlain.

CRUEL CULLIS MEN MAKE IT A MASSACRE

This was a massacre without mercy, revenge without even a tinge of compassion. Fulham, brash new boys of Division 1, were not just beaten by the champs last night – they were hammered into the ground.

Never have I seen such a cold-blooded, calculated, magnificent act of revenge.

For, make no mistake, Wolves went out dedicated to a man to "cane 'em" after their 3–1 humiliation at Fulham just a week ago.

They were one up in six minutes, scored two more in the 36th minute, and got pep talk by manager Stan Cullis for leaving it at 3–0 at half-time.

The second-half was no contest – just a high-powered precision machine ruthlessly grinding the Fulham defence into a demoralised rout.

Wolves scored four more goals in one 10-minute spell of fighting fury. Still they weren't satisfied. At the end four-goal Norman Deeley and Bobby Mason were still chasing double figures.

But the sight I shall remember long after this win that takes a proud page in the Wolves record books is the Fulham team, led by Jimmy Langley, standing on the touchline to applaud their tormentors off the field.

One Excuse

Sporting Fulham had only one valid excuse – they were without their centre half, Roy Bentley, hero of their victory last week.

But no one could have held Wolves in this mean, magnificent mood.

Of the nine goals, I detail just one, the third, scored by Ron Flowers, their England wing half.

It was a goal so fantastically fast you needed a slow-motion camera to catch a trace of it.

There stood Flowers, a good 30 yards from the Fulham goal. Up went his left boot followed by a tremendous crunch of tortured leather.

All the human eye could catch was a white blur, a flashing red jersey, and Young England goal-keeper Tony

KILLER WOLVES MASSACRE FULHAM

Call it the massacre at Molineux! The killer Wolves would not be satisfied in their drive to avenge that defeat at Craven Cottage last week. Poor Fulham, sadly missing the strength of centre half Roy Bentley, did not know what hit them.

Wolves scored two goals in a minute, but that was lost by the excitement of a golden goals spell of five in 16 minutes between the 58th and 74th minutes. Even when 8–0 up, Wolves were looking for more and defending like tigers.

Jack-in-the-box Norman Deeley scored four goals, one from a penalty. He was forever the spark that started the flames. But outside left Deeley did not claim the goal of the match. Ron Flowers collected a ball in midfield, made to pass, saw the Fulham defense falling back and burst through himself. His vicious drive from 30 yards relegated Young England goalkeeper Tony Macedo to the role of spectator.

That made the score 3–0 after 37 minutes and the massacre was on. Before that, Doherty had done many clever things for Fulham without worrying the Wolves defense.

Inside left Broadbent has brought the sting back to the Wolves attack. Ask Macedo. Harold Seeger, trainer of Vorwaerts who oppose Wolves in the European Cup, called the match "Amazing", saying "Fulham were outclassed. I hope they don't strike this form when they meet us".

Macedo clawing at the air with the ball behind him, distending the white netting.

Goal Trail

Goals: six minutes, Deeley; 36 minutes, Deeley; 37 minutes, Flowers; 58 minutes, Peter Broadbent; 59 minutes, Bobby Mason; 62 minutes, Jimmy Murray; 68 minutes, Deeley (pen); 73 minutes, Eddie Clamp; 87 minutes, Deeley.

I noted only two Fulham goal attempts, the first by Alf Stokes when it was 1–0, the second by Graham Leggat when it was a mere 3–0.

Fulham team manager Bedford Jezzard said afterwards: "Wolves played some fantastic football. They were like little tigers. Few teams could have lived with them in this mood."

Fulham 1 v Tottenham Hotspur 1

Saturday 12 December 1959
Football League Division One
Referee: T.H. Cooper
Attendance: 36,772

FULHAM		TOTTENHAM H
Tony Macedo	1	Bill Brown
George Cohen	2	Peter Baker
Jimmy Langley	3	Ron Henry
Alan Mullery	4	Danny Blanchflower
Derek Lampe	5	Maurice Norman
Eddie Lowe	6	Dave Mackay
Johnny Kay	7	Terry Medwin
Jimmy Hill	8	Tommy Harmer
Graham Leggat	9	Bobby Smith
Johnny Haynes	10	John White
Trevor Chamberlain	11	Cliff Jones

During their two spells in the top flight in the 1950s and 1960s, Fulham were a club whose priority was always to avoid relegation. And they often left it very late to do so. Only once in 12 seasons did the Cottagers manage to finish in the top half of the (old) First Division - just. In 1959–60, they finished 10th out of 22 clubs and, with just a little bit of luck, it could have been higher. There was even a moment at the halfway stage of the season when the Cottagers might have gone top of the table but a serious refereeing error in this thrilling game against Spurs marked the highwater mark of the club's League achievements, until the arrival of Roy Hodgson.

Back among the elite after a seven-year interval, Fulham kept faith with the players that had won promotion. Manager Jezzard's only new signing was inside-forward Alf Stokes from Spurs, and he was unable to claim a regular first-team spot. But the Cottagers confounded the sceptics and more than held their own. They won 12 of the first 20 games, and were beaten just six times. At White Hart Lane, meanwhile, manager Nicholson had assembled the squad that would be the first in the 20th century to do the League and Cup double — the following season.

The 36,772 who went to the Cottage that murky December afternoon saw a meeting between fifth placed Fulham and Spurs, one point better off, in second place. A victory for the Cottagers that day, with a couple of other results going their way, would have put them in pole position in Division One with exactly half the season played. Fulham were without the injured Roy Bentley and Maurice Cook, for whom Derek Lampe and Johnny Key deputised, while the Spurs line-up was that which would complete the double at Wembley 18 months later, with the exception of Tommy Harmer playing instead of Les Allen. The match was drawn and Fulham's record in the second half of the season was almost the mirror image of the first.

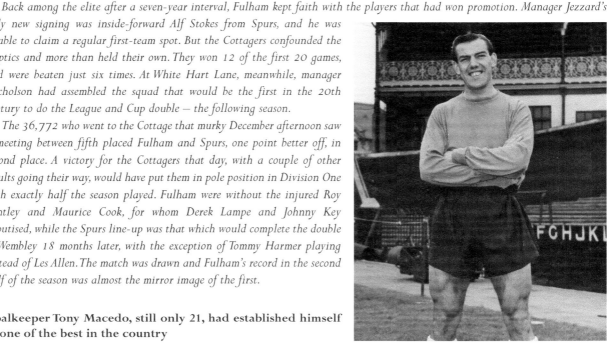

Goalkeeper Tony Macedo, still only 21, had established himself as one of the best in the country

SPURS COUNTER-PLAN FOILS HAYNES

To force a rampaging Fulham to their first draw at Craven Cottage this season was something that probably sent Tottenham Hotspur back to north London with their tails wagging on Saturday evening. No doubt in many ways they deserved a pat. But Spurs are by no means the team they were a couple of months ago and in the subtle words of the late Mr R Benchley their pats on the back were getting lower and lower.

Fulham, in fact, should have won when they dictated the whole course of the second half. But three factors combined to hold them from their prize – the failure of their wingers, Key and Chamberlain, to dot the i's in some splendid creative work by Haynes and his busy hirsute lieutenant, Hill; the tactical appreciation of Blanchflower, who lurked deep in the Spurs' defence to seal the gaps and add intelligence to the granite shield that was Norman, and, last, a single decision which seemed to deny Fulham a penalty kick.

It was a sleight of hand and it came close to the end. Delicately balanced at 1–1, the scales of the struggle were tipping as Fulham bombarded the Tottenham goal, a sudden break and flash by Hill saw Mackay in desperation divert the ball towards his own goal. Off went Brown, slightly off balance, in an effort to turn the ball over the bar. Up, too, went Baker, Tottenham's right back. Two distinct and separate arms flayed the air. One of these punched the ball to safety and some 40,000 people could have sworn that it was not swathed in the sleeve of a goalkeeper's sweater.

This sort of thing happens so quickly that the eye can easily be deceived. But had there been a referendum there would have come an overwhelming verdict. Still, as the Tottenham captain, who has the gift of aphorism, remarked later, the referee, like the customer, is always right. So Fulham, instead, received the ha'penny gift of a corner instead.

However, for all this, and the earlier award of a penalty kick which enabled Jones – the victim of Lampe's lunge – to put Spurs ahead after only five minutes, here was an exhilarating struggle. It warmed the cockles of the company, many of whom no doubt had to dodge the pressing demands of Christmas shopping.

There was a ceaseless activity, a sensitive flow and many a tingling escape. Yet in spite of all the sounds of fury, no single trainer was required to attend the battlefield, and that was as it should be: a challenging game of skill and tactics.

If any single player lit the scene it was Haynes. He has seldom played a better all-round game. But he would be the first to admit the tireless support he received from two men in particular – Hill, his bustling midfield foil, who can cleverly take the weight off him by instinctive knowledge of what to expect; and Lowe, thin on top, no doubt because he uses his brain to save his feet, a wing half who now filled in the centre gaps.

Yet Haynes was the master. He cut the field into segments and sprayed his passes fluently to each area, varying the pattern as required. After only a quarter of an hour, he gave the first signal of his mood. But for Blanchflower, who read the signs astutely to make fresh defensive depositions, it could have swept Fulham to victory.

In that moment Haynes unveiled his instinct as the ball reached him in midfield from Macedo, his goalkeeper. He must have felt rather than seen Hill streaking ahead through an avenue at the heart of Spurs' defence. In a flash, a perfect long, low pass, controlled as if on a thread, flew into Hill's galloping stride. Tottenham were split wide open and Hill, alone on the Thames waterfront, stroked his shot home to bring Fulham level.

It could have happened again, and nearly did so a number of times. However, it was Blanchflower's counter-plan, late but not too late, that largely kept Tottenham afloat. Allotting the energetic fiery, Mackay the awkward duty of hunting the elusive Haynes, Blanchflower himself assumed a covering role deep in defence.

Quick of perception, following the threads of Haynes' attacks, he virtually adopted the Italian catenaccio system of dual centre half at the side of Norman, forcing Fulham advances outwards towards the wingers who failed to make their mark. It paid Tottenham handsomely, though it might have been different had Leggat been free on the wing rather then the tight centre, to grow fat on Haynes' spoon-feeding.

Curiously, though, the two best chances of the match spun away from a Tottenham attack not really at one with itself. Twice before half-time White and Jones missed their mark miserably with the Fulham goal as wide open as a hippopotamus' mouth at feeding time. And as well, too, for the sake of justice, for after the interval, if was Fulham, under Haynes' guiding hand, who played the sounder more definitive football.

These mistakes apart, however, Spurs have some hard thinking heads in attack. The old penetration which once flowed across the whole of the line, now rested only in the swift dashes of Jones down the left flank; the old rhythm was now spasmodic because Harmer was too much off key on the soft pedal; these were merely surface irritations. Deeper down lies the seat of the trouble. Harmer and White, both clever players, are too alike, too delicate at inside forward. The need is for contrast. And Tottenham know it now.

BLANCHFLOWER BRAIN WINS A POINT

Danny Blanchflower, captain extraordinary, earned Spurs this useful championship point at Craven Cottage by the remarkable way in which he disposed his forces for the last 75 minutes.

Blanchflower saw the red light in the 15th minute when Jimmy Hill, striding on to a superlative pass from Johnny Haynes, cantered a leisurely 30 yards without challenge to make the score 1–1.

From this point, the Irishman stationed himself as a second centre-half, covering Maurice Norman and cutting off the menacing passes from Haynes before they could reach their targets.

After half-time, Blanchflower shuffled his pack again, presumably because centre-forward Bobby Smith could make no headway. Right winger Terry Medwin who has often worn the No. 9 shirt for Wales, was drafted into the middle as an auxiliary leader.

A captain blessed both with imagination and complete authority is a rare figure in modern British football. The manner in which Blanchflower controlled the strategy of this fine contest provided an extra pleasure for 37,000 spectators.

But the change in attack produced little improvement. If Spurs were destined to win this game they would have done it in the first half when the brilliant Cliff Jones – who scored from a sixth minute penalty- and White both missed chances a 14 year old would have taken.

The cure for Spurs' present goal-famine does not lie in a switching of numbers. Both Smith and Medwin are right out of form and on this day the pace of the battle was too fierce for little Tommy Harmer.

It was in defense that Blanchflower's improvisations really earned a point. Against this temporary four-back formation Fulham were able to glean precious few dangerous openings from a solid period of domination in midfield.

Indeed, Bill Brown, the Scotland goalkeeper, faced only seven shots from Fulham's forwards in the second half – and three of these were wide. It is a fact that right-back Peter Baker made the outstanding save.

STRONG, SKILFUL

Baker, I am convinced, fisted over the bar a full-blooded clearance by David Mackay which went the wrong way. Protests and roars from the terrace behind the goal earned only a corner from Bolton referee T. Cooper.

Fulham, I thought, showed themselves worth an outsider's chance in either League or Cup. Strong and fast, particularly in defence, they showed here that the skills of Haynes and Hill are sufficient to worry good sides even when Graham Leggat and John Key have poorish games.

Bristol Rovers 2 Fulham 1

Monday 26 September 1960
Football League Cup First Round
Referee: D.H. Howell
Attendance: 20,022

BRISTOL R		FULHAM
Howard Radford	1	Ken Hewkins
Doug Hillard	2	George Cohen
John Watling	3	Jimmy Langley
Peter Sampson	4	Dai Edwards
David Pyle	5	Roy Bentley
Ray Mabbutt	6	Eddie Lowe
Harold Jarman	7	Johnny Key
Alfie Biggs	8	Brian O'Connell
Geoff Bradford	9	Maurice Cook
Ted Purdon	10	Johnny Haynes
Peter Hooper	11	Trevor Chamberlain

A rare mistake by future England full back George Cohen led to Rovers winner.

Since its inception, the Football League Cup has had several titles and been through a number of different formats. Largely the brainchild of the then League Secretary, Alan Hardaker, who wanted a competition just for members of the four divisions of the League (unlike the FA Cup), it was not universally popular when it was launched in 1960. There were five top flight clubs (Arsenal, Sheffield Wednesday, Spurs, West Brom and Wolves) which declined to take part at the outset and to make the numbers work, there were more ties in the second round (32) than in the first (23). For the first seven seasons of the competition, the Final was played over two legs on a home and away basis and it was only when it was switched to Wembley in 1967 that it won general acceptance.

Fulham, however, took the competition seriously from the start and in their first-ever League Cup tie were paired with Bristol Rovers. The Cottagers travelled west on the very first night of the very first round and the fact that over 20,000 were at Eastville for the game suggests that Bristolians at least took the League Cup more seriously than some clubs and most newspapers. And Fulham manager Beddy Jezzard fielded pretty much a full first team. Missing from the side which had lost at Forest the previous Saturday were Tony Macedo, Alan Mullery and Graham Leggat but their replacements, Ken Hewkins, Dave Edwards and Tosh Chamberlain, all had plenty of first team experience. With five wins and a draw from their first nine Division One matches, the Cottagers were firm favourites to go through to meet Reading in round two.

That was not, of course, how it worked out. Despite taking an early lead through Maurice Cook, Fulham's first participation in the League Cup lasted just 90 minutes. But, because they kicked off earlier than the other ties on the first night of the new competition, and scored early in the game, Fulham's goal by Cook was the first-ever in the history of the League Cup, a small consolation for the unexpected defeat.

FULHAM KNOCKED OUT

Shock failure in first match of the new Cup

This was the opening game in the new Football League Cup competition – the West Ham v Charlton match started 15 minutes later – and what a shock it provided. Bristol's speed and skill made nonsense of their poor form in Second Division games, and for long spells they outplayed their more illustrious opponents from the First Division.

Left half Ray Mabbutt sparked off most of the Rovers attacks and Fulham goalkeeper Ken Hewkins, standing in for the injured Tony Macedo, was repeatedly in action. He made two fine saves from Geoff Bradford and three more shots were kicked off the line by full backs Jimmy Langley and George Cohen. But Rovers were over-eager near goal and their shooting was wild.

Fulham showed how simple it could be when Johnny Haynes passed to Johnny Key in the ninth minute. Key's precision centre was blasted home by Maurice Cook, well out of goalkeeper Howard Radford's reach.

Rovers equalised after 36 minutes. A shot by Alfie Biggs cannoned off the foot of the upright and new boy Harry Jarman rammed the ball home. Rovers got the winner when Cohen, harassed by Hooper, made a bad pass back. Bradford was on the ball in a flash, and drew both Roy Bentley and Hewkins before scoring from an acute angle. Haynes led his team well in a desperate rally during the last ten minutes but Rovers defence covered up superbly.

ROVERS HUMBLE FEEBLE FULHAM

Bristol Rovers treat-starved fans cheered the many great passes of England captain Johnny Haynes, tut-tutted at his tantrums and loudly loved every time he was beaten in this, the first game of the new League Cup.

Still, whatever their reasons, 5,000 more spectators than usual came to Eastville and they saw a passably clever and often exciting match. Perhaps the football didn't match the sense of occasion. Cup-fighting Fulham, lacking Macedo, Leggat and Mullery, showed their own league fault, feeble finishing. Their defence often looked lost against the full blooded sorties of the roustabout Rovers.

Fulham scored first, a casually taken side-footer by Cook after Key had unlocked the way with fine winged runs. Before that, Bentley had hooked the ball off the line, a service three times repeated by Cohen and Langley. Jarman equalized, but the goal that made Rovers the first giant killers of the season came tamely. Cohen back-passed blindly and Bradford raced in to round Hewkins and score.

The match also saw the return of South African Ted Purdon as Rovers left inside left, back from non-League limbo after being given a free transfer by Bath City. He just about shared the honours with Fulham wing half Edwards. The Bristol men rightly deserved their win. They were too bright, breezy and, despite their misses, much too full of goals for badly out-of-touch Fulham.

The 1960-61 squad. Left to right, back row: Mullery, Lampe, Macedo, Bentley, Cohen, Langley. Front row: Key, Hill, Cook, Haynes, Leggat.

HAYNES BOYS TAKE FIRST ROUND KO

The League Cup a flop? Not while it produces thrillers like this at Eastville. More than 20,000 – Rovers' second best gate of the season – turned up to watch. And Rovers, who voted against the Cup in the first place, played better than they have for years.

Fulham scored first but could not hold a team which spends each Saturday struggling near the foot of the Second Division. The reason why was clear. Rovers fought for every ball. Fulham seemed to look upon it as just another game. Johnny Haynes tried to rescue them with a late rally but not even this late glimpse of the Haynes magic could save Fulham.

Yet it was from a poor Haynes pass through which Fulham took a ninth minute lead. He screwed a pass five yards behind Johnny Key. The right winger went back for it and then set up a perfect chip so casually scooped into the net by Maurice Cook.

But the pressure was building up. Jim Langley cleared his head with a vigorous shake after heading a shot off the line. Another Rovers effort rocketed away from George Cohen's right leg. Then in the 36th minute, Alfie Biggs juggled the ball through this confused Fulham defence. His shot hit a post, spun through a thrash of legs and Harold Jarman touched it over the line, his first goal for Rovers. The winner came on the hour. Cohen's hasty back pass was seized upon by Geoff Bradford who took it round the goalkeeper. He shot from an almost impossible angle. And Roy Bentley stuck out an arm which helped the ball over the line.

Fulham 5 v Sheffield United 2

Saturday 17 March 1962
Football League Division One
Referee: A.E. Moore
Attendance: 22,709

FULHAM		SHEFFIELD U
Tony Macedo	1	Des Thompson
George Cohen	2	Cecil Coldwell
Jimmy Langley	3	Graham Shaw
Alan Mullery	4	Brian Richardson
Bill Dodgin	5	Dennis Finnigan
Eddie Lowe	6	Reg Matthewson
Graham Leggat	7	Len Allchurch
Jack Henderson	8	Keith Kettleborough
Maurice Cook	9	Derek Pace
Johnny Haynes	10	Bill Russell
Brian O'Connell	11	Barry Hartle

In 1961–62, Fulham were involved in one of the three Great Escapes from relegation in their top flight history, a fight that hardly started until this visit from Sheffield United with just 11 games to go. By then, the club's plight looked hopeless. A dreadful run had started at the beginning of November in which 13 out of 16 games were lost (including 11 on the trot) and only one was won, and the Cottagers slumped from fifth (after 15 games) to 22nd place (after 31). There was neither rhyme nor reason to the loss of form, and no injuries or transfers. In fact manager Jezzard had added to the squad with the signing of Scottish international striker Jackie Henderson from Arsenal in January. So, Fulham entered the final lap of the season six points adrift of Cardiff (just two points for a win in those days), with Chelsea occupying the other relegation place (only two down).

Yet the FA Cup had provided some cheer for the unhappy fans. Hartlepools, Walsall and Port Vale had been beaten in the first three rounds and remarkably, just three days before the visit of the Blades to the Cottage, Fulham had won a sixth round replay at First Division Blackburn to reach the semi-finals for the second time in four years. So, as spring began, Johnny Haynes and his men were chasing a double, to win a place in a Wembley Final and to avoid relegation.

This resounding victory over Sheffield United was the turning point in the League. The Blades, who had future Fulham player Reg Matthewson making his League debut, were to finish fifth that season. But they found the Cottagers in irresistible form and a revival in the League started here. They won four (including a thrilling 5–2 victory over Arsenal) and drew one of the next six and a home win over Manchester United in the penultimate game of the season ensured safety. The club survived by one point and one place, and Cardiff and Chelsea went down instead.

Fulham's effervescent full-back Jimmy Langley had an outstanding game against the Blades.

HAYNES REKINDLES HOPES AT CRAVEN COTTAGE

Haynes, the master, is almost himself again; and Fulham too.

The Craven Cottage faithfuls had been waiting since Nov. 25 for another League victory. They got it at last and loved every moment of it.

It would be incorrect to say Haynes did not put a foot wrong, but he put too many right for Sheffield United, who have thus followed 16 games without defeat with three beatings and a draw.

I have seen every one of those three defeats and thus consider myself unlikely to be appointed the Bramall Lane mascot. This latest display was no better than that at Ipswich a fortnight ago, though it must be stated at once that Sheffield were without four of their regulars, Hodgkinson, Joe Shaw, Summers and Simpson.

Their reserves, Matthewson apart, were not really adequate replacements. Once Fulham had got over a nervous first 15 minutes they took complete control.

INSPIRED COOK
Determined Langley

It must be many a long day since they played so well and it was Haynes who really made them tick. There is no player in the country more accurate with that sharp, long, arched pass out to either wing from the middle of the field. They dropped like darts in the double top and, with Leggat and O'Connell gobbling them up, United were under constant pressure.

Confidence spread from man to man. Even the lumbering Cook became inspired, scoring three goals, two of them very good ones, laying on another for Lowe and helping with Leggat's goal.

Henderson had one of his better games since moving from Highbury, Lowe was as steady as ever and always there was that indefatigable, inspiring figure of Langley, the finest defender on the field. He must have one of the longest leg-reaches in football, for he never knows when he is beaten. What a man to have in your side when you are up against relegation.

UNITED PUZZLED
Through passes galore

The ball moved sweetly from defence to attack. Sheffield became bewildered, even panic-stricken, unable to stem the tide of through passes and more often the quick pass into the penalty area and instant return into the path of some onrushing attacker.

Sheffield United are capable of better than this and in the last 15 minutes proved it with two rousing goals by Kettleborough and Matthewson. Mostly, however, they seemed a team without heart and though it was all very pleasant for Fulham I doubt whether they are quite good enough to stay in the First Division.

COOK NOW FULHAM'S HERO

Spring has come early to Craven Cottage this year, True, the trees still are bare and the late sun shines across the Thames through a shawl of mist; but the long faces have gone, the tonic prescribed for winter lethargy has been consumed in the required dosage, and the blood is coursing through tired veins like a stream in spate

The tonic, of course, was that Cup victory over Blackburn Rovers, and the man who appears to have benefitted the most from it is Cook, hero of the replay at Blackburn. Cook is not the most gracious of players, particularly seen alongside Haynes, and he has had his share of ridicule from his home crowd. But on Saturday he scored three goals to give Fulham their first League victory since the end of November.

MASTERFUL HAYNES

There is still a long way to go to escape relegation, but in this match, at least, we were treated to a carefree display of attacking football, and anyone not knowing the figures might have been pardoned for thinking the positions of the two teams in the League table to be reversed.

Sheffield United had a bad day, though it must be said that they were without several of their best defenders: the openings left by their ragged play were joyfully seized upon by Fulham, driven on by the masterful Haynes.

From a corner by Leggat, Cook charged through to head the ball hard into the back of the net and Leggat scored the second after Thompson had failed to clear a shot by Cook. A third goal before half time came when a beautifully controlled free kick from Haynes was headed back in the centre by Cook and the hardworking Lowe bounded up to head through. Cook added two more goals in the second half, one by more or less walking the ball into the net in supreme contempt for the Sheffield defence, the other tapped in after a corner.

Sheffield were seldom in the picture. They scored twice towards the end, but by that time the Fulham defenders were more concerned with whether they too could join in the goal-gathering. Kettleborough scored after a free kick, and Matthewson crowned a good first League appearance, in trying circumstances, with a goal just before the final whistle.

Fulham 1 v Burnley 1

Saturday 31 March 1962
FA Cup Semi-final (at Villa Park)
Referee: W. Clements
Attendance: 59,989

FULHAM		BURNLEY
Tony Macedo	1	Adam Blacklaw
George Cohen	2	John Angus
Jimmy Langley	3	Alex Elder
Alan Mullery	4	Jimmy Adamson
Bill Dodgin	5	Tommy Cummings
Eddie Lowe	6	Brian Miller
Graham Leggat	7	John Connelly
Jack Henderson	8	Jimmy McIlroy
Maurice Cook	9	Ray Pointer
Johnny Haynes	10	Jimmy Robson
Brian O'Connell	11	Gordon Harris

Official Programme . . .

THE FOOTBALL ASSOCIATION CHALLENGE CUP

SEMI=FINAL TIE

BURNLEY v. FULHAM

VILLA PARK, BIRMINGHAM
SATURDAY, MARCH 31st, 1962
KICK-OFF 3·0 p.m.

Price - - - - SIXPENCE
ISSUED BY ASTON VILLA F.C.

As Fulham battled to end a miserable sequence in the League, things seemed to get worse the harder they tried. In that dreadful run of losses in the winter of 1961–62, six of the seven defeats at the Cottage were by the odd goal, as were two of the away defeats. It was not hard to diagnose the problem. In 16 League games from November to the beginning of March, only 11 goals were scored, one of which was an own goal and three came in one game, a 4–3 home defeat by Chelsea.

But it was a different story in the FA Cup, albeit against lower level opposition. Hartlepools from the Fourth Division were the third round victims. Fulham won 3–1 at the Cottage, and the visitors' goal was scored by left-half Tommy Burlison. He later became Deputy General Secretary of the GMB trade union and a Labour peer. It took two games to overcome Second Division Walsall in round four, Fulham winning 2–0 at Fellows

Burnley's Adamson challenges Cook and O'Connell.

Park after a 2–2 draw at the Cottage. A controversial Jimmy Langley penalty five minutes from time was the only goal in the fifth round game at the Cottage against a Third Division side, Port Vale and it was the last eight before Fulham met another top-flight club. It was Blackburn at the Cottage in round six and late in the game, the visitors led 2–0. But a Haynes-inspired comeback earned a draw and a Maurice Cook goal won the replay at Ewood Park.

For the second time in four years it was the semi-finals and Villa Park. With holders Spurs meeting Manchester United at Hillsborough, it was two all-First Division ties and the prospect of the first-ever all-London Final. Burnley were then the League leaders, seeking a second Championship in three seasons, while third-placed Spurs had won the double the previous year. The Cottagers were bottom of the table and travelled to the Midlands with their strongest team for their fourth semi-final more in hope than expectation.

METHODLESS BURNLEY

This Cup semi-final at Villa Park began and finished under blue skies. In between, there were two snowstorms, a little rain and enough interesting, if not edifying, football to keep pace with these strange meteorological contortions. No less predictable was the form of Fulham, who came so close to providing Wembley with its first all-London final. They still have it in them to do so in the replay at Leicester, although Burnley can never surely play with so little conviction or method again.

Fulham could and should have had the afternoon sewn up by half time. They scored once – after 25 minutes when Leggat, at inside left, took Haynes' pass, swivelled and volleyed it just inside the post for a fine goal – and might easily have had two or three more. And their defence, with Langley playing the game of his life, subdued the fumbling Burnley forwards to such a degree that Macedo was kept in idleness.

Burnley, for their part, would argue that an injury to McIlroy after only 14 minutes, which reduced him to the level of other mortals, threw them off key. A valid point. But even before this, Burnley's curious and inexplicable suspicion of the big occasion was plain to see. While they pecked nervously at the ball and at the Fulham defence, their unfancied opponents, with Haynes twice the Haynes of a month ago, were taking the more direct and progressive steps that this most tense of all football occasions demands.

Certainly, with Haynes back on his throne, Fulham are in much better heart. There he was on Saturday, dark head bent studiously over the ball, left arm spread changing the point of the attack with one instinctive, incisive move and bringing out talents in Cook and O'Connell that even they must have doubted belonged to them.

Talents, incidentally, that were given generous scope by Burnley' adventurous defensive plan. This at times verged on 1–4–1–4 with the full backs advancing and often leaving that most willing warhorse, Cummings, to cover the Fulham forwards and more open space than it was fair to ask.

Burnley, however were in a quandary. With McIlroy hobbling, with Miller unable to do anything constructive, they desperately needed somebody to put the stamp of authority on their midfield fame, a task that fell exclusively to the tall and stately Adamson, a prince amongst wing-halves. And it needed all that he could give to make something of the shapeless mass around him. But somehow Adamson did help Burnley raise a less tattered flag of hope at the start of the second half. It was based primarily on Connelly's speed down the right touchline, and after only five minutes, with Langley's nose for action having drawn him five yards into the centre, the outside right took McIlroy's shrewd lateral pass to strike home a handsome equalizer. So it was that Fulham, having for a time been cast as masters, were back once more in their familiar role of underdogs. And as such they seemed to be more at home. Their first half spirit came flooding back, Cook missed a glorious chance, and 15 minutes after it, Burnley thankfully found themselves off the hook.

Goalkeeper Blacklaw saves from Leggat (partly hidden) while Cook waits to follow up.

Goalkeeper Blacklaw is beaten Graham Leggat's snap shot.

Fulham 1 v Burnley 2

Monday 9 April 1962
FA Cup Semi-final Replay (at Filbert Street)
Referee: K. Burns
Attendance: 35,000

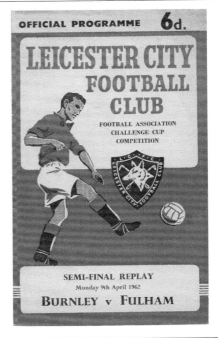

FULHAM		BURNLEY
Tony Macedo	1	Adam Blacklaw
George Cohen	2	John Angus
Jimmy Langley	3	Alex Elder
Alan Mullery	4	Jimmy Adamson
Bill Dodgin	5	Brian Miller
Eddie Lowe	6	Walter Joyce
Graham Leggat	7	John Connelly
Jack Henderson	8	Jimmy McIlroy
Maurice Cook	9	Ray Pointer
Johnny Haynes	10	Jimmy Robson
Brian O'Connell	11	Gordon Harris

The replay was arranged for nine days later, a Monday evening at Filbert Street, Leicester. Just 48 hours earlier, Fulham had lost 2–1 at Blackpool while Burnley drew a vital League game against Wolves 1–1 at Molineux. And only 48 hours after this game, the Cottagers had a crucial relegation match at home to Arsenal, and then another League fixture on the Saturday, making it four important League or Cup encounters in just seven days. Remarkably, there was only one change to the Fulham team in these four games and this at a time when no substitutes were allowed.

At Filbert Street, the unchanged Fulham side met a Burnley team which had Walter Joyce in the half-back line in place of the injured Tommy Cummings. There was also a different referee, with the renowned international Ken Aston officiating. Despite the Cottagers' impressive performance at Villa Park, the Clarets were still favourites and had already taken four points from Fulham in the League (5–3 at the Cottage and 2–1 at Turf Moor) and were still a reasonable bet for a League and Cup double. For Beddy Jezzard's men, it was 1958 all over again. As against Manchester United, they should have won this tie at the first attempt at Villa Park but in the replay, they were never as dominant.

So the Wembley Final was between the teams that finished second and third in the League. After this replay, Johnny Haynes said,

'They've all got the Final they want....but I still don't know how it happened'. Reflecting on the 1958 and 1962 semi-finals 40 years later, it was the defeat by Burnley which rankled the Maestro most. Spurs went on to retain the Cup while Fulham picked themselves up, and over the next five days walloped Arsenal 5–2 and defeated Blackburn 2–0 at the Cottage to set up a dramatic escape from relegation. They were left, however, with the unwanted record as the club which had reached most semi-finals (four) without ever making it to the Final. That hoodoo would not be lifted for another 13 years.

Despite Macedo's despairing dive, Robson opens the score for Burnley at Filbert Street

ROBSON FLATTENS FULHAM

Fulham, bravely fighting towards the strangest soccer double of all time, went out of the FA Cup after two controlled moments of Burnley brilliance in the turmoil of last night's semi final replay at Leicester.

And if the normal fortunes of football avoid Fulham as much in the second part of their "double" fight – the struggle against relegation from the First Division – as they did last night, then the magnificent Johnny Haynes and his fighters will go down.

For on the night when the neutrals in soccer won the Cup final they want to see Burnley v Spurs, it was plucky little Fulham who had everything except the breaks. And the goals.

The game was lost in the first fiery 32 minutes of a first half which seemed certain to place Fulham firmly on the proud path to Wembley and the first all-London Cup final.

Burnley were so shaken and worried by the furious flow of Fulham's football that they could not mount even one probing raid until the 25th minute, when Tony Macedo had to dive to Connelly's header.

Defeat looms

By then, Burnley goalkeeper Adam Blacklaw had already stopped half a dozen shots which should have put Fulham ahead.

But as Macedo closed his hands round that 25th-minute Connelly header, defeat was only seven minutes away for Fulham.

Right on the half hour, Eddie Lowe strode towards goal when a Burnley move broke down and sprayed a pass to Graham Leggat.

As Blacklaw's diving figure zoomed across the goal, Graham Leggat shot over from only 10 yards.

From the goal-kick Jimmy McIlroy and Jimmy Adamson managed, for once, to calm the pace down and avoid Fulham's tackling, and McIlroy stroked a pass to Ray Pointer.

The Wembley goal move was on the way.

He thrust through to the goal-line and, as Macedo waited for a split second before moving out, Jimmy Robson sped in to scoop the ball into the next.

It was Robson again who scored ten minutes from time.

But the game had really been won when Robson first whirled into the embraces of his delighted team mates.

Last gasp

Because although Fulham fought until their last gasp, they were playing like a team who believed – like the 31,000 sympathetic watchers - that they could play forever without getting a fraction of fortune near goal.

Although schemer Haynes threw himself into the thrusting role so much that he had two headers saved, and one shot in the side netting in the space of five second-half minutes, it was left-back Jimmy Langley who scored the lone Fulham goal one minute from time.

Langley, standing 25 yards out to the left of the penalty area, hit the ball first time as it flew to him from a bunch of players in the goalmouth.

It must have ricocheted from three separate players before it hit the back of the net.

Fulham 4 v Sheffield Wednesday 1

Wednesday 19 September 1962
Football League Division One
Referee: R. Aldous
Attendance: 22,625

FULHAM		SHEFFIELD W
Tony Macedo	1	Ron Springett
Barry Mealand	2	Peter Johnson
Jimmy Langley	3	Don Megson
Alan Mullery	4	Peter Eustace
Bill Dodgin	5	Peter Swan
Bobby Robson	6	Tony Kay
Johnny Key	7	Derek Wilkinson
Maurice Cook	8	Colin Dobson
Stan Brown	9	David Layne
Jack Henderson	10	John Quinn
Trevor Chamberlain	11	Edwin Holliday

FULHAM Football Club
LEAGUE DIVISION I
SEASON 1962-1963
OFFICIAL PROGRAMME
PRICE 6d
SHEFFIELD WEDNESDAY
WEDNESDAY, SEPTEMBER 19, 1962
KICK OFF 7.30 P.M.

Maurice Cook lights up the Cottage with a hat-trick

During their three spells and 20-odd years as a top-flight club, the Cottagers have usually been the poor relation to most of their divisional peers, in terms of transfers, salaries and attendances. And nowhere is this more apparent than the ground. Craven Cottage, always a ground and never a stadium, has a uniquely seductive charm but since World War One, it has never been accused of being modern or up-to-date. Not only is it much smaller than most, but as a Premier club, it was the last to become all-seater. And a generation or so earlier, it was also the last to install floodlights. Fulham fans were used to mid-winter kick-off times of 2.15pm on a Saturday, or spring / autumn midweek matches starting at 6.15pm. FA Cup replays in January or February usually had to be played on midweek afternoons.

So, there was some excitement when supporters arrived for the first match of the 1962–63 season, against Leicester, to read in the programme that the workmen had been busy at the Cottage installing floodlights, and 'the very latest in equipment'. Bad weather, however, caused some delay and the original target date of 29 August for the midweek visit of Sheffield United had to be put back. So, the opening took place three weeks later against United's Sheffield neighbours, Wednesday, and the result was much better than the 2–2 draw against the Blades.

True to their parsimonious nature, the directors did not foot the bill for the floodlights. The estimated £25,000 cost was met by the Supporters Club, which allowed the directors to spend their limited resources on bringing Bobby Robson back from West Brom. Apart from an extension to the Hammersmith End terracing, the floodlights were the first major improvement to the ground for a half a century or more. The partial covering of the Hammersmith End had to wait until 1965, the riverside stand until 1972 and the seats behind the goal were not in place until 2004. In 1962, it was still essentially Leitch's ground.

COOK'S 10-MINUTE TREBLE SHATTERS WEDNESDAY

Under their new floodlights, some of the best in the League, Fulham scored a resounding success at Craven Cottage last night, when a hat-trick by their inside-right Cook in 10 minutes play knocked the stuffing out of Sheffield Wednesday.

Fulham showed the better side of their personality – the lively, skilful one that took them to last season's F.A. Cup semi-final, not the one that so narrowly escaped relegation.

It was a performance inspired by a superb goal just on the half hour by centre-forward Brown, a first time shot on the turn at close range from Chamberlain's sharp, low centre which left England goalkeeper Springett motionless.

Up to this point there had been nothing in it, with narrow escapes at either end; Mullery clearing off his line with Macedo beaten and Springett making a couple of timely saves at the other end. Throughout, Mullery was in commanding form.

HOLLIDAY's HINT
Richards watches

Joe Richards, chairman of the selectors, was there to see discarded centre-half Swan show that he has not regained his England form and that Wednesday's outside-left Holliday, a former England international signed from Middlebrough, might be the answer in the temporary absence of Charlton.

Holliday had Mealand guessing every time he took the ball up to him and provided all Wednesday's moments of danger.

Cook coolly took his first goal from the back of the penalty area from Key's corner kick and two minutes later beat Megson on the inside and hit the ball seconds before anyone in the ground expected it, off the outside of his foot.

His third was temporarily given offside by the referee, who changed his mind (rightly, I thought) after a word with the linesman who had not signalled.

Wednesday now looked a finished team, but with some 20 minutes left, Layne put them back in the match with a stinging half-volley. Macedo dived at Holliday's feet and Fulham ended well on top again, Cook hitting the bar.

COOK LIGHTS UP FULHAM

Crackerjack Cook, ten other Fulham furies and an all-electric atmosphere made last night a night to remember at Craven Cottage. Three superb goals from hat-cookie Maurice shattered steel plated Wednesday.

Smash and grab tactics in attack and block and tackle in defence had won the match for Fulham by the 40th minute. With the light of new life shining from four magnificent pylons, Fulham struck after half an hour. Starting with a Henderson to Chamberlain move, teenage Stan Brown ran expertly into position to crash a knee-high pass from the left wing past Springett. The goal, his second of the season, was taken with the air of an Arthur Rowley.

From then on it was Maurice's match. Receiving a Key corner ten minutes later, he half-volleyed past Springett from 15 yards. Seconds later he delivered his second crashing blow. Rounding Quinn and Megson, he shot hard and low into the right hand corner of the net with the keeper groping.

Eight minutes after the re-start, he completed the hat-trick. Cutting through while Wednesday players waited for an offside decision, he shot strongly past Springett. A dispute, a consultation, a roar and it was a goal.

Wednesday managed a single goal in reply, a strike by Layne, but it was just a consolation. With marauding Maurice in the mood for goals, the visitors were not going to spoil the party.

Fulham 10 v Ipswich Town 1

Thursday 26 December 1963
Football League Division One
Referee: P. Bye
Attendance: 19,374

FULHAM		IPSWICH T
Tony Macedo	1	Roy Bailey
George Cohen	2	Joe Davin
Jimmy Langley	3	John Compton
Alan Mullery	4	Bill Baxter
Bobby Keetch	5	Jack Bolton
Bobby Robson	6	George Dougan
Johnny Key	7	Joe Broadfoot
Maurice Cook	8	Doug Moran
Graham Leggat	9	Gerry Baker
Johnny Haynes	10	Ted Phillips
Bobby Howfield	11	Bobby Blackwood

Some of Fulham's strangest games and results have occurred over the Christmas period, traditionally a very busy part of the League schedule. Boxing Day 1963 was probably the strangest of all, a record-breaking 90 minutes for the club and one individual. For the second time as a Football League club, and the first time since 1931, the Cottagers scored 10 in a game but this time it was in the top flight (the win over Torquay 32 years earlier was in Division Three South) and the opposition managed just one in reply (Torquay scored twice). The 10–1 scoreline remains the club's highest score and biggest winning margin in over a century.

And it came against a club that were League champions little more than 18 months earlier. Under Alf Ramsey's management, Ipswich had won the First Division Championship, just a year after winning the Second Division title and in their first-ever season at the highest level. Ramsey's reward for this remarkable achievement was to take over the England job in 1962, and his successor, Jackie Milburn, struggled with a team that got old all at once. They were bottom of the table by Christmas 1963, with just two wins from 23 games, scoring an average of one goal a game but conceding 2.5. Fulham were only six places better off with eight wins under their belt but scoring only two more goals than Ipswich. This was a meeting between the two lowest scoring sides in the division and the two games between the clubs in 48 hours produced 17 goals.

For Graham Leggat, Fulham's Scottish international forward, it was a personal triumph. Not only did he score four times, but his hat-trick in three minutes was and is the fastest treble in the history of the First Division/Premier. And his fourth goal completed his century of League and Cup goals for Fulham, only the fourth to pass this milestone. And he did it in 195 games, faster than anyone else in Fulham's history. Bizarrely, the Cottagers travelled to Portman Road two days later.........and lost 4–2 with exactly the same team.

Graham Leggat who scored the fastest-ever top flight hat-trick against Ipswich.

Score-a-minute Leggat sparks the big blitz

Graham Leggat equalled the First Division's fastest hat-trick record yesterday when he scored three goals in three minutes and popped poor Ipswich like a Christmas balloon.

It was misty murder in the mud, tormented by timetable to the accompaniment of clicking stop-watches and rustling record books. But it was not a match… because it takes two teams to make one.

FANS ARE HUSHED

Even the crowd remained comparatively quiet until the last minute when Fulham scored twice to make the magical 10 - for the first time in their First Division history.

It might have been 11, or 12 or any number you can think of below 20. Ipswich - Billy Baxter and Joe Broadfoot excepted - were just that bad.

Maurice Cook missed an easy goal in the 12th second, scored a difficult one by hurling himself at a cross in the 16th minute… and then the dam burst.

After the next four and a quarter minutes, by referee Peter Bye's watch, Ipswich were 4–0 down.

Fulham centre forward Leggat tapped in a rebound from the bar, spun in a second goal from a post, flashed in a third from 25 yards. Ipswich goalkeeper Roy Bailey grimaced with disgust at his defenders - but there was much worse to come.

PALMED

Bailey was just beginning the first 10 of his career… and himself made the fifth for Fulham by palming in a corner from Bobby Howfield (43 min).

Gerry Baker, played onside by Tony Macedo's hands, scored for Ipswich so close to half-time there was not even time to kick off.

Macedo was busier in Fulham's goal through the second half than Bailey was in the Ipswich goal — yet Fulham scored another five. Every other raid turned into another goal by almost non-existing marking. They mounted like this:-

Howfield (47min), Bobby Robson (62), Howfield (71), Alan Mullery and Leggat (89).

"Terrible" groaned Bailey. Ipswich manager Jackie Milburn said nothing. And even Fulham were not disposed to crow.

OLD MAN LEGGAT ZIPS TO RECORD

Crazy day at Craven Cottage ended with a record making hat-trick by four goals Graham Leggat. Three more goals by Bobby Howfield and a ten-goal spectacular that make Fulham look world beaters.

Said Leggat, after scoring the fastest ever hat-trick in first division football, three goals in three minutes: "Not bad for an old man of 26, eh?"

Said Ipswich chairman John Cobbold facetiously to mask his real feelings: "the game could have gone either way, don't you think?"

Said Fulham director Jack Walsh solemnly "we hadn't scored 10 goals for quite a time. Let me see…Last time was against Torquay in September 1932".

And the truth is Fulham scored more goals against Ipswich on this fantastic Boxing Day afternoon than they did in the first ten matches of the season.

2 OVER THE 8

Ipswich? Oh my! The sooner they're in Division II the better. I was sorry for the goalkeeper Roy Bailey, who said: "Honestly, I didn't have a drop to drink at Christmas". No, but his defense was round the bend.

The torment of Ipswich began in the 16th minute, when Maurice Cook hoisted his busted nose to head a Key centre into the net and the goal tally went like this: 16 min, Maurice Cook: 17 Graham Leggat: 43 Bobby Howfield: 44, Baker (Ipswich): 49, Howfield: 63, Robson: 71, Howfield: 88 Alan Mullery: 89, Leggat.

Spot the odd man out? The Gerry Baker goal on half time. With the score 8–1, the crowd chanted "we want ten". Mullery the Great whacked in No. 9 leaving No. 10 for Leggat.

Fulham 2 v Liverpool 0

Saturday 26 February 1966
Football League Division One
Referee: R. Aldous
Attendance: 31,616

FULHAM		LIVERPOOL
Jack McClelland	1	Tommy Lawrence
George Cohen	2	Chris Lawler
Brian Nichols	3	Gerry Byrne
Bobby Robson	4	Gordon Milne
John Dempsey	5	Ron Yeats
Stan Brown	6	Billy Stevenson
Steve Earle	7	Ian Callaghan
Graham Leggat	8	Roger Hunt
Johnny Haynes	9	Ian St John
Mark Pearson	10	Tommy Smith
Les Barrett	11	Phil Thompson
Fred Callaghan	12	Alf Arrowsmith

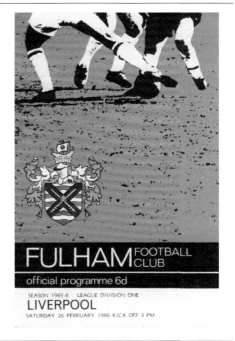

When Team Manager Beddy Jezzard decided to follow General Manager Frank Osborne into retirement in the autumn of 1964, chairman Tommy Trinder announced that he wanted to make Fulham a more professional club. From the 'hundreds' of applications received, the board selected Vic Buckingham, a man with impeccable credentials but who was remarkably ill-suited to managing Fulham. A former Spurs wing-half who had coached Pegasus and managed West Brom, Sheffield Wednesday and Ajax, he tried to change the character of the club. Not only was he a failure in personal terms but he also set the club on a downward path that took years to reverse.

It did not take Buckingham, a man unencumbered by self doubt, long to squander a relatively robust inheritance by trying to change too much too quickly. In his first full season, 1965–66, the Cottagers managed just one win in their opening 10 games. They struggled from the outset and then in November and December lost six games on the trot. The first casualty was coach Ronnie Burgess, one of Buckingham's old Spurs playing colleagues and at the turn of the year, Fulham looked doomed to relegation. Then Dave Sexton, recently displaced as manager of Leyton Orient, arrived in January 1966 to succeed Burgess.

At the time, Fulham were at the foot of the table, with just 15 points from 29 games (two for a win) and, with only 13 matches left to play, were six points short of safety. If there is such a thing as a season-changing match, this was it and against the most unlikely of opponents. Bill Shankly's Liverpool side led the table (and were eventual champions) and had won seven and drawn one of their previous eight games. Although in previous weeks against Chelsea and Spurs, there were clear signs of improvement in Fulham's play, despite losing, few of the 31,616 crowd, or the BBC Match of the Day viewers, expected Fulham to end their miserable sequence. The second 'Great Escape', and one to equal 2007–08, started here.

Match-winner Steve Earle, who was to become one of only seven players to score a century of goals for Fulham.

EARLE IS LORD OF FULHAM

Drama drenched this game right from the moment some cocky Liverpool fans stole their club's flag from among the twenty-two First Division flagpoles which adorn the back of the main Fulham terrace.

Lowering the Fulham flag to half mast was the final insult to bottom-of-the-table, luckless Fulham — who proceeded to wreck millions of football coupons with this supreme shock result.

How Liverpool, top-of-the-table aristocrats, paid for their too-smooth confidence, both on the terraces and on the field.

Fulham never played as if 20 League places and 30 points separated them from Liverpool, who are en route to Budapest for their European Cup Winners' Cup battle with Honved on Tuesday.

Liverpool ended a clean exciting game in a blaze of thoughtless indiscretion when their Scottich international forward Ian St John was ordered off by referee Bob Aldous after an incident with Mark Pearson.

It is a result which does not make sense. It was Fulham's sixth win of the season, Liverpool's sixth defeat.

Steve Earle scored both goals, and five minutes from the end the panicky right boot of Liverpool right back Chris Lawler deprived this 20-year-old of a memorable hat-trick.

How the Fulham crowd insolently twisted the tail of the perplexed Liverpool side four minutes from the end with a fierce cry of "Easy, easy, easy" — the traditional battle hymn of Anfield's famous kop.

COAXED

Perhaps it was this humiliating cry which stung St John into his indiscreet action in the eighty-seventh minute.

It was some time before St John would leave the field, and then only after the referee had accompanied him almost to the touch line.

The Fulham goals came in the eleventh and seventy-fifth minutes. The first was quite brilliant, the second was lucky.

But let's face it, Fulham have been starved of the stuff… and better the luck goes to the side on the bottom rather than the one on top.

A masterly Graham Leggat reverse pass to Johnny Haynes on the right wing let the ex-England skipper curl the most perfect of centres on to the head of Earle.

MISSED IT

Earle's tenacity for his second goal was helped by the fact that the referee appeared to miss a helping Fulham hand.

Fulham goalkeeper Jack McClelland turned in a brave and agile display, and the "old heads", Haynes, Bobby Robson, George Cohen and Pearson, slowed the pace, held the ball carefully.

Fulham's kids, left back Brian Nicholas, faultless left half Stan Brown, 18-year-old left winger Les Barrett and two goal Earle never panicked against such efficient and experienced opposition.

The Fulham flag flies high and proud again this morning.

FULHAM PIPS THE LEADERS

With a little bit of luck and bags of guts, struggling Fulham pulled off the incredible by toppling League leaders Liverpool in this explosive, incident-packed match at Craven Cottage.

Bottom-of-the-table Fulham, who before this game looked certainties to take the big drop to the Second Division, gave a magnificent display of spirit and courage.

The two goals that upset the form-book both came from right winger Steve Earle, one of the youngsters drafted into the team in Fulham's recent re-shuffle. The first was a beauty. The second — the goal 15 minutes from the end that clinched the win and eased some of the tension — should never have been allowed.

Graham Leggat, the Lion-hearted little Scot who fired the Fulham front line with menace, took a pass from winger Les Barrett and slipped the ball through to Earle. The right winger handled the ball as he stumbled through to stab home the vital goal.

The referee and linesman were unsighted but most people on the stand side must have noticed the incident. The Liverpool players protested but the goal was allowed.

It was after this goal that tempers really started to fray- on and off the field. Police had to be called to calm down the crowd behind the Fulham goal, where a large contingent of fans were gathered.

SENT OFF

The trouble on the field flared up in the dying minutes and St. John received marching orders after an incident with Mark Pearson.

Goalkeeper Jack McClelland played like a man inspired. He dived at the feet of Ian St. John to save a certain goal, stopped sizzling shots from Roger Hunt, and plucked numerous crosses out of the air.

Liverpool, perhaps finding it difficult to show their skills on a soggy pitch and hampered by a stiff wind, wasted many chances. Fulham occasionally showed flashes of brilliance — like in the ninth minute when Leggat and Haynes combined in a glorious move which ended with Earle sending a glancing header into the net for the first goal.

Northampton Town 2 v Fulham 4

Saturday 23 April 1966
Football League Division One
Referee: J.K. Taylor
Attendance: 24, 523

NORTHAMPTON T		FULHAM
Norman Coe	1	Jack McClelland
John Mackin	2	George Cohen
Mike Everitt	3	Brian Nichols
John Kurila	4	Bobby Robson
Terry Branston	5	John Dempsey
Joe Kiernan	6	Stan Brown
Harry Walden	7	Steve Earle
Graham Moore	8	Allan Clarke
George Hudson	9	Johnny Haynes
Don Martin	10	Mark Pearson
Barry Lines	11	Graham Leggat

Beating Liverpool proved to be a turning point and a battle for survival belatedly got underway. Fulham won the next four matches, scoring 13 goals and, after a blip at home to Leeds on Good Friday, went to Elland Road four days later for the return. Don Revie's muscular side were the major challengers to Liverpool for the title but, remarkably, a Mark Pearson goal gave Fulham both points. And

The legendary Bobby Robson, a hero and a villain at Northampton.

just as he had been involved in the incident against Liverpool which resulted in Ian St John's sending off, so Pearson was at the centre of the fracas that led to Billy Bremner's dismissal. It was in this match that future Leeds player, Allan Clarke, made his full Fulham debut following his club record £35,000 move from Walsall.

So the light was discernible at the end of the tunnel when Fulham made the short journey to Northampton's County Ground for what was essentially the relegation decider. Blackburn had already booked one of the two relegation places and the second was between the Cottagers and the Cobblers. Under Dave Bowen's management, Northampton had enjoyed a meteoric rise from the Fourth to the First Division, but then came up against a reality check. After a promising start (including a 4–1 League win at the Cottage), their form had slumped and they, like Fulham, were fighting for their top-flight lives. The record crowd for the club's old ground, 24,523, packed in to see it.

Sexton's vastly improved side took the honours. He had introduced young Les Barrett into the side and brought Steve Earle back who, with Leggat, spearheaded the attack. The two scored 19 of Fulham's 31 goals in 13 games during the run. The outcome of this match, and the fate of the Cobblers, hinged on one crucial incident, a disallowed Northampton 'goal' when they were 2–1 ahead. After this victory, Fulham won one and drew two of the final three games and finished two points ahead of relegated Northampton. Sadly, Sexton left in the close season, for the coaching job at Arsenal.

EARLE HITS 3 FOR FULHAM

Fulham were twice behind in the first-half of their relegation struggle at Northampton, but hit three goals in the second-half to win.

Fulham were strengthened by the return of Haynes at centre-forward.

The Fulham goal had an escape when, from a corner by Lines, Moore hit the bar with a header and Martin's shot from the rebound was cleared off the line by Nicholas.

Northampton scored in the 13th minute. Kiernan went through and shot and McClelland could only push the ball out to HUDSON, who hit it first-time into the net.

Fulham equalised six minutes later. ROBSON worked his way across to the left and from 20 yards sent in a well placed shot out of the reach of Coe high to the top of the net.

Kurila missed the ball and Leggat nipped in to shoot wide.

In the 30th minute Northampton took the lead. Walden centred and Robson tried to head away, but the ball went straight to KIERNAN, who drove it past McClelland.

Half-time: Northampton 2, Fulham 1

Fulham went into the attack straight after the interval and Clarke centred for Earle to try a header, which Coe easily saved, despite a strong challenge by Leggat. Northampton hit back and forced a corner when McClelland could only touch a swerving centre from Lines round the post.

A neat piece of interception by Robson set off a promising move for Fulham, but Leggat spoiled it by running offside. Fulham forced another corner and Leggat headed over the bar.

A fine move on the Northampton right resulted in a dangerous centre from Walden being headed away by Dempsey.

Earle scored three goals for Fulham in the second half.

Earle goals bring the glory

Two minutes to go, and the score 2–2.

It looked as if this game between the Division 1 relegation rivals was certain to be drawn.

Then, dramatically, the record-breaking crowd of 24,500 were electrified by two sensational goals by Fulham.

The first came in the 89th minute, the second actually in injury time.

Both were scored by young right-winger Stephen Earle to give him a hat-trick he will treasure for the rest of his days, and to give Fulham a wonderful chance now of staying up in the First Division.

Glorious

This victory was Fulham's eighth in their last ten games, and they have three more matches to play against the Cobblers' two.

Fulham may be accounted lucky, for it was Northampton who set the pace and seemed to hold most of the aces.

But there was no luck about Fulham's final glorious fling. Earle got his head firmly to a Graham Leggat centre for the first one.

Then, straight from the kick-off, he broke away, dribbled his way half the length of the field, rounded goalkeeper Norman Coe and crashed in the fourth goal.

The fates certainly smiled on Fulham. By comparison with the fast-thinking, quick-tackling Cobblers they look hesitant, and it was no surprise when Northampton raced into the lead in the 13th minute.

Skipper Joe Kiernan took the ball up and put so much steam behind his shot that McClelland could only beat it out.

George Hudson pounced on the rebound and slammed the ball in.

The Cottagers hit back with a very good goal by Bobby Robson in the 19th minute.

But on the half-hour the Cobblers had their fans rejoining when Kiernan flashed home a great left-foot shot from 30 yards.

It was tense, tough and exciting stuff, with Fulham unable to find the vital spark which had marked their recent great string of wins.

But they fought hard, and in the 65th minute Cohen sent the ball across for Earle, almost against the post, to squeeze the ball in.

Fulham 4 v Stoke City 1

Saturday 31 December 1966
Football League Division One
Referee: E.D. Wallis
Attendance: 24,851

FULHAM		STOKE C
Tony Macedo	1	John Farmer
Bobby Drake	2	Calvin Palmer
John Dempsey	3	Alan Bloor
Bobby Robson	4	Maurice Setters
Fred Callaghan	5	Eric Skeels
Jimmy Conway	6	Alan Philpott
Johnny Haynes	7	Gerry Bridgewod
Stan Brown	8	George Eastham
Graham Leggat	9	Peter Dobing
Allan Clarke	10	Roy Vernon
Les Barrett	11	Harry Burrows

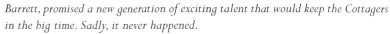

After the breathtaking escape from relegation in the spring of 1966, Fulham spent much of the following season in the comfort of mid-table. Although by the end of the campaign, they had dropped to 18th place, relegation was never a serious threat and it was the closest Buckingham came to a successful season. It was a year that marked the emergence of Allan Clarke as a striker of genuine top-flight quality. His 24 goals in 42 games remains a club record for the First Division / Premier and his partnership with Earle, Conway and Barrett, promised a new generation of exciting talent that would keep the Cottagers in the big time. Sadly, it never happened.

Over Christmas 1966, Fulham won three on the trot, and scored 10 goals, but it was one of the old guard who stole the show. In an away game at Leicester on Boxing Day, George Cohen had to go off injured and Graham Leggat came on as substitute (only one on the bench in those days). Fulham won 2–0, and Leggat kept his place for the return the following day because Earle had got a knock. At the Cottage, Fulham won 4–1 and Leggat hit a hat-trick. On New Year's Eve, Stoke visited the Cottage and Leggat scored twice in his side's 4–1 win. The next day, he was sold to Birmingham for a paltry £20,000.

In some ways, Buckingham was an unlucky manager (Cohen's injury, Robson's retirement, Haynes' ageing) but he contributed to his own misfortune with a generous helping of bad judgement. Selling Leggat, (like getting rid of Langley, Cook, Marsh, Key, O'Connell, Keetch, etc.) was a poor decision for which the club paid a heavy price. Leggat was a natural goalscorer, 134 goals (the club's fifth highest total but the only player to score a century in the top flight) in eight years, eight hat-tricks and top scorer five times, Leggat still had much to offer. He finished as he had started, among the goals in a high-scoring home win over Stoke City.

The prolific Graham Leggat signs off as he started in 1958, by scoring against Stoke.

FULHAM'S NON-STOP ONSLAUGHT DESTROYS STOKE'S POISE.

In the first half, as the sun shone with pale brilliance and a wintry wind whipped off the Thames, Stoke played with a smooth sophistication which suggested they might even win the championship.

There, on the left, lurked George Eastham, flitting like a ballet dancer over the bumpy, muddy Craven Cottage pitch. There, in the middle, swaying, swerving, nimble and fluent, sped another old-fashioned dribbling master, Roy Vernon. There, on the right, to complete this trio of magicians, floated fair-haired Peter Dobing. And when, in the 21st minute, Eastham stroked an exquisite pass through to Stoke's burly right-half, Alan Bloor, Fulham's defence was as wide open as an empty grin. Bloor swung over an outswinging cross and Vernon headed the ball into the net with the speed of a striking snake.

At this point, not even Bobby Robson, who masterminded Fulham's young defence with loving care, could steady the reeling Londoners.

Stoke, moving at half speed one moment, spurting into attack the next, twice hit the woodwork, through Dobing and right winger Gerry Bridgwood. And all the time, the dumpy Maurice Setters, who starts a 14-day suspension tomorrow, was a tower of strength at centre half.

Yet it was Setters who, when challenged by Fulham's reserve centre forward Graham Leggat, gave away the unnecessary corner which produced the equalizer. From his own flag kick, Johnny Haynes, still unequalled as a pass-maker, picked up a pass from the ever improving Les Barrett, and centered. Leggat took a fly header. The ball hit Setters and Leggat flicked the ball home, 1–1.

Then two minutes from half-time, Stoke received a sickening blow. Fulham's Fred Callaghan, who shared the match honours with that other go-go-go character Stan Brown, came counter-punching out of defence into another pounding overlapping run. From Callaghan, the ball flew to Allan Clarke who passed to Leggat. Graham slashed his shot wildly across goal but Stokes's left back Eric Skeels, haring back, crashed the ball into his own net, 2–1.

In the second half as the sun disappeared behind a purple mass of storm clouds, Stoke gradually folded up. Forced to attack, Stoke could never dam the remorseless tide of white shirts pouring into the gaps.

From a corner, another of Fulham's daring young men, centre-half Johnny Dempsey, headed to Clarke who coolly shot past goalkeeper John Farmer, 3–1. Next, Leggat and Stokes's right back Calvin Palmer were booked by the referee.

The sprinting Barrett then soloed through and although tripped by Farmer, cracked home a brilliant shot only to have the goal disallowed because the referee had already blown for a foul. The boos had hardly died when Stokes's most forceful forward, left winger Henry Burrows, fired in a tremendous drive which bounced off the bar and goalkeeper Tony Macedo into the net. Referee Challis, after consulting a linesman, disallowed the goal… for what reason he wouldn't say. It certainly looked like a good goal to me.

Finally, one minute from the end, a breathtaking Haynes centre was hammered into the net by the vigilant Leggat. Not only had cut-throat Fulham won their sixth game out of seven. They had -deservedly -completed the double over Stoke.

Fulham, the great escapers of 1966, ended the year with a spectacular wriggle from a Stoke straight-jacket.

Now they leap into 1967 fired with the confidence that comes from six wins in the last seven outings.

And Stoke's bruised championship hopes should warn everyone of the danger Fulham's former relegation strugglers now pack.

"If we go on like this we will win the lot," said Fulham's skipper-of-the-day Bobby Robson.

If they can get such convincing results from such a shaky first half position they certainly can. The Cup? Why not!

After half-an-hour Stoke looked in secure and spendid command.

Vernon goal

Roy Vernon had given them a 20th minute lead – Gerry Bridgewood and Peter Dobing had hit the bar - and Fulham's efforts against Stoke's packed defence slowed in the Craven Cottage mud.

It looked impossible for Fulham to get in four shots let alone four goals.

But Graham Leggat, who hit a hat-trick in his first-team comeback on Tuesday, started Stoke's downfall in the 32nd minute.

Stoke's defenders got in a tangle following a perfect cross from Johnny Haynes and Leggat swooped at the foot of the post to score.

Eleven minutes later Fulham had the sort of luck that helped break Stoke's stranglehold.

Allan Clarke brilliantly pushed a Fred Callaghan cross to Leggat's feet but his shot sped straight at the corner flag.

Alas, for Stoke, Eric Skeels came racing towards his goal and the ball cannoned off him into the net.

Strength counted considerably in the cloying mud and Fulham had strength aplenty in men like Callaghan, who played the role of full-back and winger without weakening an ounce.

His dashes down the left struck Stoke with blow after blow. Even Maurice Setters, who starts a two-week suspension tomorrow, could not hold his defence together.

In the 68th minute John Dempsey went up for a corner and nodded the ball back to Clarke, who swiftly brought it down to score.

Spectacular

Fulham were robbed of another after Les Barrett jinked through to score spectacularly. But referee Wallis insisted Fulham had a free-kick for a foul on Barrett at the start of his run.

Equally mysteriously, the referee disallowed a Harry Burrows goal for Stoke just afterwards.

But there was no authority in the world who could have removed Fulham's fourth goal which cannoned off Leggat's diving body after a fast low cross from Haynes.

The transformation had been completed in an exciting second half that was so different from the Stoke-dominated first 30 minutes.

Fulham's Cup price? William Hill quoted them at 25-1 last night.

Fulham 2 v Manchester United 2

Monday 27 March 1967
Football League Division One
Referee: G.D. Roper
Attendance: 47,290

FULHAM		MANCHESTER U
Tony Macedo	1	Alec Stepney
George Cohen	2	Tony Dunne
John Dempsey	3	Ronnie Noble
Bobby Robson	4	Pat Crerand
Fred Callaghan	5	Bill Foulkes
Jimmy Conway	6	Nobby Stiles
Johnny Haynes	7	George Best
Stan Brown	8	Denis Law
Mark Pearson	9	David Sadler
Allan Clarke	10	Bobby Charlton
Les Barrett	11	John Aston

Allan 'Sniffer' Clarke, Fulham's record signing, came of age in 1966–67 and scored against United.

On Easter Monday 1967, Fulham welcomed Manchester United to the Cottage. For once not involved in a relegation scrap, the Cottagers had enjoyed a moderately successful season in 1966–67. Although they had won just one of their nine League games since the turn of the year, they were in the relative comfort of 16th place. Over Easter, they had to face a United side that was pushing for (and eventually won) the First Division title twice in 24 hours. It was the second of Busby's great teams and 47,290 (the second-highest post-1945 attendance) packed into the Cottage on a spring afternoon to see the legendary Best-Law-Charlton combination in full flight. On that Easter Monday, 32,500 programmes were sold, a club record.

The huge crowd was rewarded with a spectacle to match the occasion. And just as over Christmas 1951 when lowly Fulham gave Busby's first great side (and eventual champions) a shock at the Cottage, so the Haynes-inspired team of 1967 came close to knocking the mighty United off their perch. Under new coach Gordon Jago, a more youthful Fulham team was emerging. As well as the young strike force of Earle, Clarke and Barrett (who got 44 goals between them), the likes of John Dempsey, Jimmy Conway and Fred Callaghan established themselves in the first team. In the return at Old Trafford 24 hours later, goalkeeper Ian Seymour made his debut. The future seemed to be in good hands.

But in many ways, these Easter fixtures against United were the last hurrah of those thrilling years in the top flight in the 1960s. After rare Nobby Stiles' goals denied the Cottagers a win at the Cottage and a draw the following day at Old Trafford, the club began a protracted decline. Fulham won just one more match that season and then went into two dreadful seasons when just 17 of 84 League games were won, four managers were tried and 42 different players used. The Cottagers kicked off in August 1969 in the Third Division and it was over 30 years before they were back in the top flight.

UNITED SURVIVE TOUGH COTTAGE TEST

Nobby Stiles preserved Manchester United's leadership of the First Division, perhaps decisively, with an equalizer six minutes from the end of a spectacular game.

If this point eventually proves to have won the championship then its source could scarcely be bettered. This was a game worthy of an occasion of great importance. It fell below classical limits only because of its mistakes and lulls. But it provided enough snatches of exhilarating football to stamp it as a match not to be quickly forgotten.

Fulham manager Vic Buckingham said afterwards: "Manchester United are a hell of a good side. Whenever they were in trouble, there was always someone to switch them on to the offensive. On the balance of 90 minutes I thought they deserved to win."

Fulham put United's leadership of the First Division to the sternest test.

Twice they went into the lead. The second time, in the 73rd minute, their goal was so brilliant it deserved to settle the game. United came back not only to equalize but very nearly win.

Stiles must be thanked by United not only for scoring the equalizer, but for knowing that he could.

The persistent little man insinuated himself into the attack as if certain his presence would tell. It did.

BEWILDERED

Charlton, who moved into the game only rarely, hit a low ball to the near post. Macedo had it covered, but Stiles hurled himself at it and turned the ball between the goalkeeper and the post for his second goal of the season.

It would not have been unjust had United won. They made more chances but Fulham did not deserve to lose a game they helped to make look so attractive.

In the first 15 minutes Fulham had United's defence looking bewildered and panic-stricken with a succession of clever moves that only just failed in the last pass.

Though United settled down, it was Fulham who scored first. Pearson was pushed in the back by Noble, Haynes took the free-kick and Clarke rose above Foulkes to make it 1–0 with a header.

It was Law who started the equalizer on its way. He tried to force his way through but the ball rolled to Best. Best then brilliantly swerved away from Dempsey, seemed to start to swerve the other way and suddenly but accurately stroked the ball out of Macedo's reach into the far corner of the net.

Fulham seemed to crumble. A Charlton cross caused trouble and Aston hit the crossbar. Then in the second half they suddenly took control and the seconds leading up to their second goal were the highlights of the game.

Barrett went high for a goalmouth ball, flicked it on and Cohen hit a tremendous shot against the post. The rebound flew over Cohen's head and to the feet of Aston, who hared off towards the Fulham goal with an open field before him.

Cohen sprinted after him and finally managed to harass the winger into a poor cross, then got control of the ball and pushed it back down field to Haynes.

Haynes tore off and hit the ball low to the near post. Pearson ran to it and immediately pushed in an across ball. Barrett took possession, hesitated very briefly and drove it into the roof of the net.

It is to United's credit that they were able to raise their game again. And after Stile's equalizer they could well have won the match.

Fulham 4 v Huddersfield Town 3

Saturday 23 November 1968
Football League Division Two
Referee: P.R. Walters
Attendance: 11,394

FULHAM		HUDDERSFIELD T
Ian Seymour	1	Terry Poole
Mike Pentecost	2	Alex Smith
John Dempsey	3	Billy Legg
Stan Brown	4	Jimmy Nicholson
John Ryan	5	Roy Ellam
Fred Callaghan	6	Trevor Cherry
Jimmy Conway	7	Steve Smith
Johnny Haynes	8	Jimmy Lawson
Johnny Byrne	9	Paul Aimson
Vic Halom	10	Jimmy McGill
Cliff Jones	11	Colin Dobson
Ivan Murray (for No. 11)	12	

When Fulham's fortunes turned in the late 1960s, the fall was spectacular. The club paid a very heavy price for the self-inflicted wounds of bad management and years of under-investment and when they fell, it did not stop at one division. In 1967–68, the Cottagers finished bottom of the (old) First Division, winning just 10 of 42 matches, seven points (two for a win in those days) adrift of safety. The following season was even worse. With just seven wins, they ended 1968–69 at the foot of the Second Division, the first time any club had anchored the top two divisions in successive seasons.

In calendar year terms, 1968 was the annus horriblis. Of 46 League games played, just eight were won and 27 lost, with a goal difference of −54. The year opened with a 5–0 home defeat by Leeds and closed with a 5–1 beating at Bury (relegated with Fulham that season), and in between was not much better. And, as average attendances plummeted (from 24,430 in 1966–67 to 10,259 in 1969–70), the board committed to building the riverside stand, so incurring the debt that came close to bankrupting the club and which sowed the seeds of the slide into oblivion over the next 25 years.

The turbulence was evident in the managerial merry-go-round. Buckingham departed, unlamented, when his contract expired in January 1968. Former player Bobby Robson, who had retired the previous May, returned from Canada to take up his first managerial appointment the following month, but the job was too big for someone with no experience. His sacking after just 10 months in November 1968 was, nevertheless, controversial and unjustified. The year closed with another former player, Bill Dodgin at the helm. But for a month before Dodgin arrived from Loftus Road, Johnny Haynes held the reins as player-manager. He made it clear from the start that he had no interest in taking the job on a permanent basis, a decision he was happy to confirm a few weeks into the job. But his first game in charge was the highlight of that dreadful year.

Johnny Haynes in a temporary managerial role he never coveted.

Haynes adds new zest to Fulham

If management inspires Johnny Haynes to the heights he achieved with Fulham on Saturday then the sooner he and his board decide formally to confirm his position the better.

For this was the display of a man who has been preparing all his life for the task that now faces him.

Gone were the signs of irritation, the impatient gestures and agonised criticism of colleagues that have marred the play of his declining years.

Indeed, there was no need for them. Haynes set so skilful and energetic an example that he inspired most of his team-mates to raise their own standards.

Byrne played his best game for the club, captain Callaghan emulated his manager's effort, if not his skill, and every member of the team contributed to a business-like but highly entertaining match.

As vice-chairman Chappie D'Amato said: 'There was a joy in the game that has been lacking recently. Johnny was magnificent.'

His magnificence evidently is not over-confidence, for Haynes's position at Fulham is still one of 'on approval', as much from his angle as the club's.

'We don't know at the moment,' said D'Amato 'whether Johnny will be taking up the position for good. I think he has still to make up his mind himself. As it is, he is in charge of the team and that is how we must leave it.'

It took two goals of doubtful validity to give Haynes his flying start and Fulham their first win in ten games.

All Fulham admits that Byrne handled in the goalmouth incident which gave his side the corner from which they scored their third goal. Even Byrne and a linesman admit it. Many too feel that Jones's goal, the fourth, was offside.

FIGHTING FULHAM HAD SPEED AND SPARKLE

Fighting Fulham's new player-manager, Johnny Haynes was justly beaming as his winning team were given an ovation after this Craven Cottage clash.

It was Haynes' masterly show which sent new-look Fulham surging to a rare win bonus with a display which inspired real hope to clambering from the Division Two basement.

Haynes was always in the forefront with pinpoint probing and penetration. He set a classic example for his responsive colleagues.

His performance mocked critics who have written off the Fulham master craftsman. Afterwards a delighted Haynes commented "we were shakey at the back but we made up for it by buzzing up front more than we have done all season".

But the victory which ended a dismal spell of ten games without a win was not without cost.

Left winger Cliff Jones limped away from the ground with damaged ligaments in his left ankle. "There's not much chance of Cliff playing in our re-arranged League game at Preston on Monday", said Haynes "But Les Barrett should be fit enough to come back".

The new Haynes-infused spirit was soon evident when Fulham hit back to equalize eight minutes after goalkeeper Ian Seymour's tumble was eagerly seized upon by Jim Lawson to give Huddersfield a gift second minute goal. It came when industrious John Byrne coolly accepted Haynes' immaculate prompt to score his first goal of the season.

THIS WAS JUSTICE

Another perfect pass from Haynes sent winger Jim Conway through to shoot Fulham ahead after forty-two minutes.

Dangerman Lawson snatched an unexpected leveller after fifty-seven minutes but confident Fulham were in front again within five minutes.

This time it was Vic Halom, opening his season's account, nodding in Byrne's corner. This was justice for unsighted referee Mr P. R. Walters, of Bridgewater, who was one of the few people who did not see a Huddersfield defender punch clear seconds before Poole conceded the corner.

Cliff Jones got into the scoring act with his first of the season after sixty-six minutes but ten minutes later he went off and Murray substituted.

But Fulham's uneasy start was repeated in the closing stages. They had a late shock when Alec Smith surged upfield and Paul Aimson's header brought Huddersfield a third goal.

Halifax Town 0 v Fulham 8

Tuesday 16 September 1969
Football League Division Three
Referee: D. Laing
Attendance: 5,809

HALIFAX		FULHAM
Alex Smith	1	Ian Seymour
Bob Wallace	2	Stan Brown
Andrew Burgin	3	Fred Callaghan
David Lennard	4	Stan Horne
John Pickering	5	Reg Matthewson
Lammy Robertson	6	John Richardson
Tony Flower	7	Jimmy Conway
Freddie Hill	8	Barry Lloyd
Ian Lawther	9	Steve Earle
David Shawcross	10	Johnny Haynes
Philip McCarthy	11	Les Barrett
	12	John Roberts (for No. 10)

Irishman Jimmy Conway was a pivotal member of Dodgin's team, and offered support to Earle in attack.

In a relatively short space of time, manager Bill Dodgin was able to stop the decline and set the club on a path to a very modest recovery. But he got off to a slow start. He arrived too late to change the outcome of the 1968–69 season. So deep was the malaise, that Fulham were relegation favourites by the turn of the year. And life was not much easier at the start of the club's first season in the third tier of the League for 37 years. Just three of the opening seven games were won, and three lost as the players (eight of whom had played in the top flight for Fulham) struggled to adjust to the demands of lower-level football.

Unsurprisingly, the team was changing as Dodgin tried to impose his approach on the club. Throughout his long career as a manager and coach, he believed in an open, attacking style, that worked rather better in the lower divisions. Sadly, Cohen had been forced to retire through injury, Haynes played his final game in January 1970 and Dempsey had moved on to Chelsea. In came Barry Lloyd, given the unenviable task of succeeding Haynes as No 10 and captain, Vic Halom (Bobby Robson's last signing) and goalkeeper Malcolm Webster.

During the rebuilding phase, there were signs of an improvement and none more so than this remarkable result in midweek at Halifax. Against the then unbeaten Shaymen, Dodgin's Fulham recorded the club's biggest-ever away win. The previous best was 6–1 at Doncaster in March 1958 and just as one player that day (Jimmy Hill) scored five of his side's goals, so another, Steve Earle, went nap at the Shay. He joined the exclusive band of Harrison, Jezzard and Hill who have scored five times for Fulham in a single game. The season proved to be the best of Earle's Fulham career. He finished top scorer for the first time, with an impressive 23 goals. He went on to become the sixth Fulham player to reach a century of first-class goals.

0-8!

FULHAMS BEST EVER, AWAY UP NORTH IN THE THIRD!

Incredible Fulham burst from mediocrity to astonish the Football League last night. Their 8–0 win at Halifax (all eight in the first 67 minutes) broke records in profusion.

It is the best away win ever in the reconstituted Third Division, the best in Fulham's history and equal to the best League away win since the war, Wolves 9–1 at Cardiff in 1955.

It was also Halifax's biggest home defeat. Striker Steve Earle, 24, scored five of the goals, the first after 11 minutes. He added a second midway through the half and Lloyd and Conway (penalties) made it 4-0 at the interval.

Second half goals came from Earle (46 and 61), Conway (60) and Earle (67). A Halifax team containing such experienced players as Freddie Hill and Ian Lawther were demoralized enough to miss two easy chances before the end. Relegated in successive seasons from First Division to Third, Fulham had hardly set their new station alight until last night.

FULHAM SCORE EIGHT

Steve Earle, Fulham's centre forward, last night scored five goals in his team's 8–0 win over Halifax, previously unbeaten in the League this season at the Shay.

Fulham were the speedier side, had far more ideas, and cashed in on some atrocious finishing and shocking defensive errors by Halifax.

Four of the goals resulted from long balls down the middle which Halifax's defence failed to clear, and two more came from bad defensive work by left back Andy Burgin.

There was a hint of good fortune about Fulham's opening goal after 12 minutes. Inside forward Dave Shawcross's clearance hit referee Laing and rebounded to Fulham's all-action wing half Stan Horne who crossed the ball for Earle to score the first of his five goals.

Halifax missed a glorious chance when Tony Flower blazed the ball over from five yards out and Fulham made sure of the points with two goals on the half hour by inside right Barry Lloyd and Earle.

If Halifax still had hopes of coming back after that - and they were still playing some attractive football - they had to forget them a minute before the interval when Jimmy Conway scored from the spot after Burgin had brought him down.

The fifth goal came within 60 seconds of the re-start, when Earle thundered in and steered the ball into the net with Burgin offering one of his many desperate attempts to clear. Then Barrett nipped inside and split the cover with a cross for Conway's benefit. Another firm low shot made it 6–0. Again Barrett was the architect of number seven, this time with a precise centre to the regions of the far upright, where Earle soared to head into the net.

Earle ended the scoring in the 67th minute, breaking into the penalty area from the right to endorse yet another Fulham strike, their eighth goal of the evening.

Bradford City 2 Fulham 3

Wednesday 28 April 1971
Football League Division Three
Referee: E. Jolly
Attendance: 6,430

BRADFORD C		FULHAM
Pat Liney	1	Malcolm Webster
Denis Atkins	2	Mike Pentecost
Peter McConnell	3	Fred Callaghan
Bruce Stowell	4	Stan Horne
Norman Corner	5	Reg Matthewson
Ian Cooper	6	Jimmy Dunne
John Hall	7	Jimmy Conway
Bruce Bannister	8	George Johnston
Graham Oates	9	Steve Earle
Les O'Neill	10	Barry Lloyd
John Middleton	11	Les Barrett

In their first season back in the Third Division, Fulham made a spirited but belated push for promotion. Of the last 20 games (starting with Johnny Haynes' final appearance against Stockport in January), they lost just two, which lifted them to fourth place, five points short of promoted Luton. They began the following season where they left off in April 1970, losing only two of the first 19 matches. From the start, the Cottagers were in the leading pack. A mid-winter dip saw them drop to fourth but going into the final month, Fulham and Preston led the way with Halifax and Aston Villa on their heels. There were just two games left when Bill Dodgin's men travelled to West Yorkshire knowing that a win would take them back to the (old) Second Division.

That evening at Valley Parade, Dodgin was able to field his strongest side for the fifth consecutive match. Although 21 players were used to win promotion, 12 appeared in at least half the games and nine played in 30 or more. For much of the season, the team picked itself and seven of the team that evening (Pentecost, Callaghan, Matthewson, Brown, Conway, Earle, and Barrett) were survivors of the club's First Division days. As well as promotion, Fulham had got through to the quarter-finals of the League Cup (still the furthest they have progressed) and squandered home advantage against Bristol City which would have taken them into the last four.

This victory clinched promotion and set up a title decider against Preston at the Cottage three days later. A draw would have brought the divisional Championship to west London, but Fulham fluffed their lines. The huge crowd (25,774) was in a celebratory mood but a first-half goal by Alan Spavin spoiled the party. By beating Rotherham a few days later, Preston took top spot by a single point. It was nevertheless a successful season and the 60 points won (two for a win) equalled the club record.

Left-winger Les Barrett was ever present and top scorer in the promotion year.

FULHAM BACK IN DIVISION TWO

Fulham go back to the Second Division as a result of this game. They should have had the game sewn up before half-time but the forwards tossed away some great chances. But Bradford City hit back twice to draw level.

Fulham's Steve Earle slipped through in the fifth minute but shot wide as he tried to lob the advancing goalkeeper Pat Liney. Les Barrett and Jim Conway also had narrow misses before Fulham's flowing football brought them a 32nd minute goal from George Johnston.

Almost on half-time, Bradford City got a surprise equalizer through John Hall. Johnston wasted another good chance straight after the interval but Barry Lloyd put Fulham ahead in the 55th minute with a lobbed shot. But on the hour, back came Bradford. Norman Corner headed and scored the equalizer. Johnston made amends for his earlier miss by snatching the winner in the 75th minute.

The promotion winning side was captained by Barry Lloyd.

FULHAM ROAR TO PROMOTION

Fulham are back in the Second Division. And they celebrated up in Yorkshire last night with champagne laid on by beaten Bradford City. Beamed Fulham manager Bill Dodgin, "I'm delighted. Everybody has worked hard for this. We have been under a lot of pressure. Because we have been favourites, it has been hard for us.. Tonight's game was one of our hardest and we just made it in the end."

And only just. For Fulham had to call on all their superior class to put down a fighting Bradford side which twice hit back to equalise. Now, as Fulham go for the title against Preston on Saturday, Bradford must wait until their last match to know whether they will escape relegation.

Bradford struggled badly at times last night as Fulham's fast and elusive forwards repeatedly roared into attack. But the home side would not lie down. George Johnston fired Fulham ahead after 32 minutes. Yet 12 minutes later, John Hall snapped a surprise equaliser.

Barry Lloyd put Fulham back in front after 55 minutes with a lob which keeper Pat Liney fumbled. Yet five minutes later, Norman Corner headed another equaliser.

Then Johnston headed in a centre from Les Barrett…and this time gallant Bradford could not find an answer.

And Fulham were up.

Everton 1 v Fulham 2

Saturday 15 February 1975
FA Cup Fifth Round
Referee: C. Thomas
Attendance: 45,233

EVERTON		FULHAM
Dai Davies	1	Peter Mellor
Mike Bernard	2	John Cutbush
Steve Seargeant	3	Les Strong
Dave Clements	4	Alan Mullery
Roger Kenyon	5	John Lacy
John Hurst	6	Bobby Moore
Garry Jones	7	John Dowie
Martin Dobson	8	Jimmy Conway
Mike Lyons	9	Viv Busby
Bob Latchford	10	Alan Slough
Jim Pearson	11	Les Barrett
Jim Telfer (for No. 9)	12	Barry Lloyd (for No. 7)

Although Fulham have never won a League game at Goodison Park, they have never lost a Cup tie and, of their four Cup victories over the Toffees, this was probably the most memorable. As in 1926 and 1948, the two clubs were a League division apart, with Everton topping the (old) First Division in 1975 and Fulham meandering along in the middle of the Second. The Cottagers' manager Alec Stock, who had replaced Bill Dodgin in 1972, consistently produced classic mid-table sides which averaged a point and a goal a game during his four seasons in charge. But in the Cup in 1975, his team burst into life.

It was a most unlikely FA Cup run. To get to round five, Fulham had already played seven Cup matches, taking three games to beat Hull and four to overcome Nottingham Forest, the fourth of which was played just five days before the trip to Merseyside. Both Hull and

Forest were in the Second Division and there was nothing in Fulham's League form (without a win for two months) to suggest they could take on the First Division leaders on their own turf and win. But they did, deservedly, and this game was a turning point. The manager, players and supporters all started to think the unthinkable and believe that, if they beat the mighty Everton, this could be Fulham's year.

For the press, it was the presence of the two veterans, Alan Mullery and Bobby Moore, which captured the imagination. Skipper Mullery, whose Football League career started at the Cottage in 1959, returned to his old club in 1972 after eight successful years with Spurs. The iconic Moore had signed for Fulham in 1974 for a nominal fee, and Mullery, outsmarting fierce competition from other clubs, was instrumental in persuading his old England teammate to make the journey across London when West Ham decided the former England captain could leave. These two outstanding individuals provided the inspiration on the field, lifting the performances of less naturally gifted teammates, and romance off it in Fulham's most successful Cup run.

In the run to the FA Cup Final, Fulham owed much to the idiosyncratic brilliance of goalkeeper Peter Mellor.

Busby babe up in arms

Lean as leopards after their marathon affair with Nottingham Forest, Fulham stalked Everton mercilessly for most of the game, finally going for the jugular just six minutes from the end when their stylish striker, Busby, scored a splendid second goal.

This Everton side really will not do. Once again they were exposed in front of their home fans as lacking style, cohesion, and even fire in their bellies. Second Division Fulham were often embarrassingly more skilful, intelligent and exciting, especially up front, where Busby was arrogant, little Conway like a runaway motor-mower, and Barrett an ardent supporter of both.

In mid-field, too, Mullery's range and vision was longer and sharper than any of his Everton opposite numbers, Dobson having a muted match and Clements a frustrating one. It was Mullery who had suggested that Fulham exertions over the last three weeks had sharpened rather than exhausted them.

Within 15 minutes came the proof. Barrett broke speedily down the left, centered despite Bernard snapping at him, and after a flurry of panic and terror involving Davies and Kenyon, Busby assisted an already net-bound ball over the line.

Everton's response was not to respond, at least as far as one could detect. It was Fulham who gave us the clever stuff and their happy band of followers was rapturous in appreciation of bursts of touch football with a distinctive continental flavour. Only Mellor seemed to be in any real difficulty, and that was largely self-inflicted because he insisted on challenging the brawny Lyons when the Everton striker had been blown offside. Still, flamboyant bravery is Mellor's style and he plainly relished these tussles.

In the fifty-fourth minute, Everton struck lucky. Jones, playing very well now, took a corner on the left and Kenyon managed to screw the ball down and out of Mellor's reach.

Fulham were rattled and for some time they were fighting for their lives, but Everton, who had replaced Latchford with Telfer, could not muster the fire-power to press home a definite psychological advantage. In the eighty-fourth minute, Busby came to the rescue. Conway scuttled down the left flank and centered rather too deeply, one thought for Busby to make much out of it. But he turned on the ball and clipped his shot smartly past Davies's left hand. Fulham had beaten the League leaders, and very comprehensively, too.

FANCY-FREE FULHAM GO TO EVERTON AND TAKE THE TOFFEE

"The wages of sin" read the large yellow sandwich board outside Goodison Park, "is death." If the sin was Everton's so was the demise. The fact is that, despite their current high place in the First Division, Everton are a very ordinary side both in skill and tactic. Billy Bingham has trained them in specialization: the off-side trap, the defensive ploy, the crude, physical attack, and the eternal draw. What Fulham did yesterday was merely just retribution.

Man for man, Messrs Barrett, Conway, Busby and Mullery were every inch the equals of Lyons, Latchford and other more anonymous players, while Fulham's game, economically open, and entertaining, is the dead opposite of Everton's Calvinistic stalemate.

The pattern of this full-blooded Cup tie was set early on: the first 15 minutes told us that Kenyon was uneasy, Bernard and Sergeant permeable, and that Dobson was going to have an off-day: likewise that Fulham, despite their marathon in reaching the fifth round, had come to Liverpool with their tails up. Indeed, it took just that long for Conway to make a definitive pass out to Barrett on his left, for that swift and accurate winger to centre hard and low parallel to the touch-line and three feet in, and Fulham went ahead. Davies, who had no shot to save bar the two goals he didn't, dropped to the ball, Kenyon committed the mortal sin of entwining himself with 'keeper and ball, the latter trickled goalwards and Busby was there to prod it in.

That Kenyon atoned for his earlier sin by rising well to head a cross from Jones into the narrowest of apertures, and level the score after 52 minutes was a mere aside. Everton were not playing well and they knew it.

For a while, one thought Fulham might throw the game away by mimicking Everton and settling for a draw. Fifteen minutes of this saw a lot of pressure at both ends. Three excellently unusual saves by Mellor, misses by Barrett and Busby, and some unholy mix-ups in the Fulham defense from which Everton seemed uneager to profit.

Belatedly, but with finality, Fulham rammed home an obvious superiority. Conway yet again found Bernard wanting; the middle of the Everton defence seemingly misplaced their sense of geography, and there stood Busby and Slough, unmarked, to gather in the ball Conway pulled back for them in front of goal. To a grateful Busby fell the chance: he took one step away from goal, turned with another and shot low and hard.

It was a remarkable win in which every Fulham player lived up to that cliché, the team effort. Fulham's games are usually lost in defence, on Moore's slowness of turn and abdication from 50:50 chances: through Mellor's errors of judgement and placement on high balls, and both full backs' over eagerness to commit themselves to anything but prudence; and to Fulham's saving grace, their pleasure in taking the game to the enemy. Yesterday everything worked: or rather, Everton lacked the imagination to exploit what did not.

The toast of West London last night, it is typical of Fulham's luck to be drawn away in the next round to the sheep pastures of Carlisle. Meanwhile, Everton only slightly unlucky in some of their chances, can reflect on the wages of their sins during this season. Long deadly, often boring they are now, for the Cup, very dead indeed.

Birmingham City 1 v Fulham 1

Saturday 5 April 1975
FA Cup Semi-final (at Hillsborough)
Referee: R. Matthewson
Attendance: 54,166

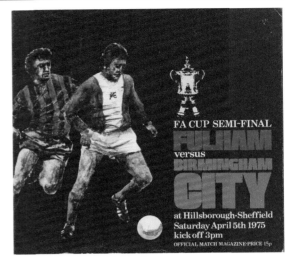

BIRMINGHAM		FULHAM
Dave Latchford	1	Peter Mellor
Malcolm Page	2	John Fraser
Gary Pendrey	3	Les Strong
Howard Kendall	4	Alan Mullery
Joe Gallagher	5	John Lacy
John Roberts	6	Bobby Moore
Alan Campbell	7	John Mitchell
Trevor Francis	8	Jimmy Conway
Kenny Burns	9	Viv Busby
Bob Hatton	10	Alan Slough
Gordon Taylor	11	Les Barrett
	12	John Dowie (for No. 8)

After Everton came Carlisle, then a top-flight club for the only season in their history.

A single Les Barrett goal divided the sides at Brunton Park and gave Fulham their fourth FA Cup win that season away from London, but it was only a superb display by goalkeeper Peter Mellor which ensured Fulham made it to through to the club's fifth FA Cup semi-final. While West Ham and Ipswich battled it out at Villa Park in the other semi-final, the Cottagers travelled to Hillsborough to meet Birmingham, their third higher division opponents in that Cup campaign. Although not an obvious glamour match, it attracted a crowd of 54,166.

It seemed that Fulham had got the easiest draw, but the Blues side had some star names, like Howard Kendall, Trevor Francis, Kenny Burns and future PFA leader Gordon Taylor. And they had FA Cup experience. This was their second semi-final in three years. In 1972, also at Hillsborough, they had been beaten by Leeds at this stage. But Birmingham's League form was at best average, having won two, drawn two and lost two of the six games between the sixth round and the trip to Sheffield. They had however won each of their previous four Cup ties at the first attempt.

For Fulham, this was their ninth FA Cup tie of the season and, despite the fixture congestion, their League form had improved. Of 11 games in February and March (on top of five Cup matches), just one had been lost and there were six League wins as well as the three Cup tie victories. In terms of injuries, the squad

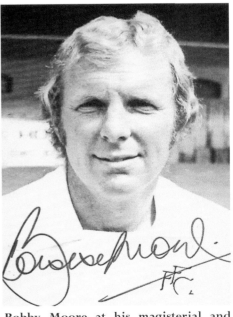

Bobby Moore at his magisterial and authoritative best.

had been very resilient. John Mitchell and Jimmy Conway were the main worries but Barry Lloyd and John Dowie had offered cover. Of Stock's preferred starting eleven, only full-back John Cutbush was missing for the meeting with Birmingham, for whom the very capable John Fraser had been deputising for several weeks.

A safety route to Maine Road

And so to Maine Road, Manchester, on Wednesday. The draw here at Hillsborough was an accurate if troublesome result of a match settled by a determination not to lose which quite overwhelmed the will to win. Though both sides eventually created their chances neither had the nerve to go for victory.

A first half between two retreating defenses quite numbed the pulse with inactivity but then, within seven minutes early in the second half, the game erupted with more vibrant and meaningful action than the entire remainder could produce.

Before the goal, and indeed afterwards, we were treated to football which at times demonstrated the frailty of the human mind and the brute strength of the body.

It is right, therefore, to start with those compelling moments. After 50 minutes Fulham completely stunned the 55,000 people who had paid more than £100,000 to see this match by taking the lead. The goal stemmed from a corner won by Barrett, whose incisive speed had throughout the first half repeatedly been nullified only by the most wilful and brutish of tackles.

The corner was never cleared and Bobby Moore, standing well behind the crowded area, demanded and got the ball. A quick pass inside found Mullery whose own pass was sent first time to Slough and on to Mitchell. Then, from the very edge of the penalty area, Mitchell delivered a shot of supreme accuracy high to Latchford's net which totally justified his selection for this match in preference to Dowie. This was the first goal Birmingham have conceded in their cautious but successful Cup run. They had nothing but praise for Mitchell's goal afterwards. "The lad would have been a real hero if that had been the only goal of the match," said Kendall, "That goal was the spur we needed to make the game more positive on our own part," commented manager Goodwin.

In another two minutes, Barrett and Busby swiftly raided inside the penalty area and Slough got in a quick shot which, luckily for Birmingham, spun high over the bar off the boot of Roberts.

There was a sudden panache and penetrating quality about Fulham, one which they as well as Birmingham had completely hidden until now. And yet there was a sudden frailty, too. After 56 minutes, a bad mistake from Mullery let Campbell in for a shot which he pulled a foot wide from only seven yards and before Fulham had settled from that, they had conceded the equalizer.

It was a scrappy affair with none of the precision of Fulham's goal. Campbell drove across from the right wing which both Moore and Lacy failed to meet, the ball dropped at the foot of Gallagher who, with his back to goal, was nevertheless given time to turn and nudge his shot low inside the far post past a surprised Mellor.

A goal for Gallagher, who had spent the week listening to his manager lauding his praises as a future England centre half, a young giant of a man who had indeed been supreme in defence throughout this match. Yet what was he doing there in the opposition penalty area at such a crucial time?

The answer had much to do with Howard Kendall, Birmingham's balding right half and skipper. With Francis showing delicate touches at times but obviously not yet match-sharp after his five months lay-off, the whole inspiration of the Midlands side came from their captain.

What a contrast this sudden frenzy was to a dull first half in which between them, the goalkeepers had been called upon to make one solitary save. That came after four minutes when Busby slipped the heavy marking of Roberts and found space to fire in a low shot which Latchford dropped on, seemed to lose and then grasped in desperation as Mitchell lunged forward.

For the rest we had to eke out our moments of pleasure from the morass of cautious and careful play. It is perhaps not original, but still indisputable, to say that Moore was his magisterial authoritative best in a defense which Birmingham until their equalizer rarely looked like punishing.

And yet for Birmingham, Kendall, a man who was denied England caps by Moore and Mullery in their day, was even more inspirational. After 34 minutes, for example, he hit an exquisite pass of 35 yards out to the right only to see it come back behind him by way of Hatton and Page, a move which redirected the play.

Who then is to win the replay? For me, Birmingham, cautious and at times cantankerous though they are, may in the end hurtfully put Fulham aside. And that judgement does not underestimate the fact that Fulham, having survived 16 ½ hours of Cup football and two defeats in 29 games, must surely be treated as fierce contenders, no longer to be regarded with amused tolerance.

If they do eventually fall to Birmingham, it is perhaps satisfying for them to reflect on the way they have matured out of recognition into a side that not even their chairman, Tommy Trinder, will be able to joke about after this season.

Birmingham City 0 v Fulham 1

Wednesday 9 April 1975
FA Cup Semi-final (at Maine Road)
Referee: W. Gow
Attendance: 35,025

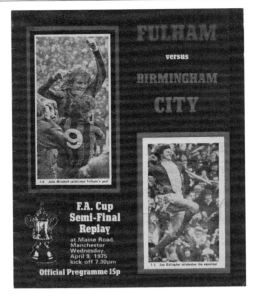

BIRMINGHAM		FULHAM
Dave Latchford	1	Peter Mellor
Malcolm Page	2	John Fraser
Steve Bryant	3	Les Strong
Howard Kendall	4	Alan Mullery
Joe Gallagher	5	John Lacy
Gary Pendrey	6	Bobby Moore
Paul Hendrie	7	John Dowie
Trevor Francis	8	John Mitchell
Kenny Burns	9	Viv Busby
Bob Hatton	10	Alan Slough
Gordon Taylor	11	Les Barrett

A more sparsely populated Maine Road, Manchester was site of the replay the following Wednesday. Coincidentally, West Ham's match with Ipswich in the other semi-final had also been drawn and was being replayed the same Wednesday evening. Among Fulham supporters, there was an understandable feeling of déjà vu. In the 1958 and 1962 semi-finals, they were the better side in the first games but were pegged back to draws, only to go down (deservedly) in the replays to Manchester United and Burnley. And in 1975, few people expected First Division Birmingham to play as badly or Second Division Fulham to play as well as they had done at Hillsborough. But Birmingham had their own ghosts. In 1945–46, they had made it to the last four where they met Derby County and, after a draw at Hillsborough, they lost the replay at... Maine Road.

The only change in the Fulham side was the enforced absence of Jimmy Conway, for whom John Dowie came in, with Barry Lloyd taking over as substitute. In the nine games from the winning match against Hull in round three to the semi-final replay, manager Alec Stock had used only 14 players. The Blues made two changes, Bryant and Hendrie replacing Roberts and Campbell. Few FA Cup semi-finals can have been decided by a goal as late and as ugly as John Mitchell's that night in Manchester. It had already been agreed that the third match would take place at Highbury when Fulham made the decisive breakthrough. And Mitchell's effort with virtually the last kick of the game was as scruffy as his strike four days earlier had been sublime.

For Fulham's matchday announcer at the Cottage, Don Durbridge, there was the satisfaction of seeing an unlikely forecast come good. Before the first home match of the season, against Cardiff, he explained that the season's fixture list in the programme was incomplete because the club did not know who they would be playing on 3 May in the Cup Final at Wembley. Now they knew it would be West Ham, the second all-London Final.

John Mitchell assured himself of Fulham immortality with his dramatic winner.

Fulham grab Wembley glory as last gasp goal ends marathon

JOHN MITCHELL scored with just two seconds of extra time to go in last night's semi-final replay at Maine Road to cap Fulham's incredible FA Cup marathon.

As Bill Gow blew the final whistle, Fulham manager Alec Stock raced on to the pitch, his arms aloft with tears in his eyes, to embrace every one of his brave Second Division players.

The first man he rushed to was Bobby Moore, who goes on to Wembley for a storybook final against his former club, West Ham.

If you believe in fairytales you had to be at Maine Road last night. Fulham, after 11 matches have got to Wembley against all odds for the first time in their history.

Stock, after 30 years in management, led his players in a victory dance all round the ground as their supporters, outnumbered and outshouted by Birmingham's fans, went berserk on the terraces.

The goal which makes history was a scrambled, untidy effort. But it was the most important in Fulham's history.

Alan Slough punted a long, hopeful centre towards the Birmingham goal as the final seconds of extra time ticked by. John Lacy headed it on and somehow Mitchell, who scored in Saturday's 1–1 draw, forced it past the diving Dave Latchford. The ball bounced once, and trickled slowly into the net.

As the tension got to breaking point Birmingham's Kenny Burns appeared to punch Moore. Burns was later booked for dissent after a foul against Mellor.

In the end Fulham deserved Mitchell's goal. They finished the stronger side and should have scored minutes earlier when Viv Busby had a free header at the far post but Latchford scrambled it away. Birmingham's players flung themselves on the ground in disbelief as Mitchell's shot trickled over the line.

At the start, Birmingham raised their game from Saturday to scare the life out of Fulham. Hendry set the tempo with three bad tackles in the first five minutes.

SIGNAL

It was the signal for Birmingham to throw everything at the Second Division defense and Mellor somehow kept out Taylor's point-blank volley. Moore somehow held Fulham together and they responded with a Busby dribble and shot which hit the post.

In the second half, Birmingham kept up the pressure and Mellor made another superb save, this time from Burns. Fulham somehow forced their way back and claimed a second corner in the 81st minute. Extra time seemed to be the signal of the end of one of football's bravest attempts at glory. But Stock's men went into the energy-sapping 30 minutes the stronger side.

Young Scot John Dowie and veteran Alan Mullery claimed the midfield back from Birmingham skipper Howard Kendall, and up front Mitchell and Busby kept running.

Then came the amazing climax.

West Ham United 2 v Fulham 0

Saturday 3 May 1975
FA Cup Final (at Wembley)
Referee: P. Partridge
Attendance: 100,000

WEST HAM U		FULHAM
Mervyn Day	1	Peter Mellor
John McDowell	2	John Cutbush
Frank Lampard	3	John Fraser
Billy Bonds	4	Alan Mullery
Tommy Taylor	5	John Lacy
Kevin Lock	6	Bobby Moore
Billy Jennings	7	John Mitchell
Graham Paddon	8	Jimmy Conway
Alan Taylor	9	Viv Busby
Trevor Brooking	10	Alan Slough
Pat Holland	11	Les Barrett

After the semi-final defeats of 1908, 1936, 1958 and 1962, being at Wembley was enough for many Fulham fans. The result was secondary to giving up the unwanted record of the most semi-final defeats without making it through to the Final. And in getting there, the Cottagers set another record, one which will now stand for all time. By taking 11 games to win five ties, they had taken the longest route to the Final ever. Each of the ties, moreover, was won away from home and none was against a club from a lower division.

For the media, the human interest stories were Bobby Moore facing his old club in what was almost certainly going to be his last Wembley appearance, as it would be for 33-year-old Alan Mullery, leading his first club to their first major Cup Final. West Ham, of course, were managed by Ron Greenwood, who in the mid 1950s was a Fulham player. There was also delight for manager Alec Stock, who showed again, as he had at Yeovil, Leyton Orient and QPR, a remarkable knack for conjuring Cup success from modest teams. For Fulham fans, the sadness was the injury to left-back Les Strong a fortnight before the Wembley game. Up to that date, he had played in all 54 of Fulham's League and Cup games that season. It meant that John Fraser and John Cutbush, who had shared the right-back role in the previous rounds, both played. With Jimmy Conway and John Mitchell both fit, Stock's only selection decision was for substitute, and Barry Lloyd got the nod over the unlucky John Dowie.

Reaching Wembley was to be something of a watershed in the club's affairs – the closing of the chapter on the FA Cup and the opening of another phase in the club's history. Apart from one brief interlude in the early 1980s, Fulham were about to start on a long downward slide, until they were rescued in 1996–97 by a team of journeymen and then powered up by the arrival Mohamed Al Fayed.

Fulham's Cup Final party at the Dorchester.

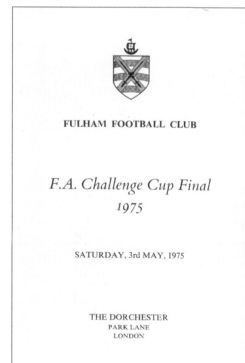

FULHAM FOOTBALL CLUB

F.A. Challenge Cup Final
1975

SATURDAY, 3rd MAY, 1975

THE DORCHESTER
PARK LANE
LONDON

FULHAM ARE BURIED WITH HONOURS

West Ham United, the favourites, beat Fulham, the choice of the sentimentalists, by two goals from Alan Taylor to none at Wembley on Saturday to lift the FA Cup for the second time in their history and so return to European competition next season.

As has happened before, Wembley again proved a goalkeeper's graveyard. It is cruel to have to say this after his many sterling performances along the way which had helped Fulham to their first Cup Final, but two mistakes by Mellor cost his side the trophy.

The first, a combination of errors and not his alone, came at the end of an hour after Fulham had made most of the running. An initial slip by Cutbush as he lost the ball to Holland, was followed by a fast low shot from Jennings which Mellor, by rights should have turned round the post.

Instead, his diving parry let the ball run loose and there was young Taylor moving in swiftly in the manner of Greaves or Law to turn it in for a precious lead. The side to score first at Wembley invariably wins.

Four minutes later came an almost exact carbon copy. This time Holland with a clever chip found Paddon moving

A ticket for the 1975 Cup Final.

intelligently into an open space down the left. Paddon's shot should have been held but again an anxious parry left the rebound free and again Taylor, who had the way of turning up like fine dust in unexpected places, was the executioner.

That first goal at last put West Ham on their way after having played second fiddle for so long. The second confirmed their sudden position with dramatic finality, though Fulham died bravely with their boots on, in effect they were blacked out, literally in the case of their boots.

Their dream of winning their first Final faded in the sunlight. But for Alan Taylor, at least the afternoon was a fairytale come true before a 100,000 Wembley crowd. He became the first player to score two goals successively in the sixth round, semi-final and final since McParland did so for Aston Villa 18 years ago.

To think that only six months ago Taylor was a fourth division player with Rochdale and about to play for them in a qualifying round against Marine Rovers before West Ham snapped him up. Such is the wheel of fortune.

If those two mistakes, one on top of the other, turned the game suddenly at one end, there were two equally important events at the other which underlined the difference one had sensed – but hoped would not be revealed – before the start. Seven minutes after the interval with Fulham calling the tune, Mitchell dummied swiftly past Lock to Mullery's throw in, cut free and shot hard inside the near post. Day however dived elastically to turn away the ball for a corner.

A quarter of an hour from the end, with Fulham throwing all their forces forward in a last act at rescue, Mitchell again broke free, this time on the left. But once more Day, advancing to narrow the angle, blocked the shot. The ball ran free to a West Ham man and Fulham at the end were thwarted. Here lay the difference: here was class goalkeeping: here was the rub of the green. So ended one of the friendliest, well mannered Cup finals for many a day. Not once was the trainer needed on the pitch nor were there any unseemly scuffles for throws in or pinching of territory at free kicks. In that sense the whole affair was a healthy advertisement for the game and an example to others. Both clubs, especially their managers, are to be congratulated.

If there was anything lacking, it was a positive end product until Taylor stole the scene – especially in the case of Fulham. Both sides played so much attractive possession football up to the penalty area, with Fulham masters for an hour, that it seemed they had forgotten the object of it all – to put the ball in the net. It was as if they were all hypnotized by their own pretty reflections in a mirror.

That apart, however, both sides were a credit as they lived up to their creative ideals. Notable for West Ham were Day, with those two vital saves, Lock, in defence, the elegant Brooking, Bonds, who grew stronger as the match unfolded, and Paddon in midfield, with the predatory Taylor proving to be the Fagin of the penalty area.

As expected, Moore's massive, calm authority and Mullery's energetic drive and far-flung passing made Fulham settle more quickly and dictate matters until the fates turned sour. Lacy, too, was a lanky tower of strength, while Busby, quick on the turn, and Mitchell had their moments.

But once West Ham took their pickings, it remained only for Moore and Mullery to stride arm in arm from the crowded stage which they have decorated so often. It was a proud sight spoiled at the end only by the invasion of the pitch by excited young East End hordes as the West Ham bubbles floated over the stadium and away in the dipping sun.

Fulham 4 v Hereford United 1

Saturday 25 September 1975
Football League Division Two
Referee: A. Robinson
Attendance: 18,935

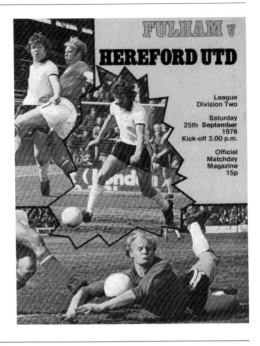

FULHAM		HEREFORD U
Peter Mellor	1	Kevin Charlton
John Cutbush	2	Dudley Tyler
Les Strong	3	Phil Burrows
Alan Slough	4	John Layton
Ernie Howe	5	John Galley
Bobby Moore	6	Jimmy Lindsay
George Best	7	Terry Paine
John Evanson	8	Peter Spring
John Mitchell	9	Steve Davey
Rodney Marsh	10	Dixie McNeil
Les Barrett	11	Roy Carter
	12	Kevin Sheedy (for No. 9)

The years immediately after the Cup Final were anti-climatic. The players thought they were good enough for promotion, but no challenge materialised and the club settled for the mid-table comfort zone. Behind the scenes, however, a storm was brewing. The debt incurred for the building of the riverside stand had not been paid and finances were starting to become a big issue. A new figure emerged as a force on the board in the summer of 1976. Ernest Clay had no previous connection with Fulham, or any involvement with any other club. His route to the Cottage came via fellow director, Eric Miller, a property man who later committed suicide when his Peachey business empire became enveloped in scandal.

In an attempt to add some glamour and excitement to Fulham, and generate publicity for the club, Clay and Miller were instrumental in bringing Rodney Marsh back to the Cottage (his career had started spectacularly with Fulham in the spring of 1963), along with George Best, who was trying to rebuild his career after his protracted departure from Old Trafford. Both were playing in the US at the time and their signings generated enormous media interest. These two gifted and individual talents helped lift attendances more than they did team performances. There was an element of showbiz about their appearances, and the two former internationals played their roles to the full.

This was never more apparent than when Hereford visited the Cottage for a Second Division match for the one and only time. With

the ITV cameras there to record the event, the large crowd was treated to scintillating display by the two showmen that was both hugely entertaining and very effective. The duo went on to establish a partnership that was to amuse fans all over the country – but on the speaking circuit rather than the football pitch. From Fulham's point of view, the pair promised more than was ever delivered and it soon petered out in the acrimony that followed Alec Stock's departure a couple of months later. Although Best stayed for a year, Marsh was gone before spring 1977.

Fulham's two high profile signings, George Best (left) and Rodney Marsh (right), turned on all their tricks against Hereford.

FULHAM PUT ON A SHOW

George Best and Rodney Marsh brought skill, flare and excitement to Craven Cottage with a dazzling display which led Fulham to a 4–1 victory over Hereford United. This was the first ever meeting between the two clubs and it attracted a large crowd of 18.935, about 10,000 up on last season. Most of these had come to see Fulham's new signings Best and Marsh. Marsh scored two excellent goals and showed plenty of tricks and Best was unlucky not to get on the score sheet with two or three exciting efforts.

Slick inter-play between Marsh and Best almost brought goals in the opening stages on Saturday. Les Barrett's low shot brought an excellent save from keeper Charlton and Best shot narrowly wide before Fulham opened the scoring.

It was Alan Slough who opened the score after 21 minutes. From inside the Fulham half he surged forward, shook off tackles in a smart one-two with John Mitchell and then hit a 20 yarder past Charlton. Evanson headed Fulham's second seven minutes later, slamming a Cutbush cross that followed a free kick when Best was upended by the veteran Terry Paine.

Dixie McNeil almost pulled a goal back when he slid in and hit the post from a centre by Dudley Tyler. However, an own goal by Ernie Howe, who headed past Mellor a routine centre from Lindsay in the 35th minute, gave Hereford a chance to draw level. They almost did so in a period of pressure after Kevin Sheedy replaced Davey in the 50th minute.

Fulham's zest did not return until the 65th minute when Best struck a post with a terrific shot from 25 yards. Five minutes later he helped Marsh to score Fulham's third. Best's centre was headed back across goal by Mitchell and Marsh scored with the simplest of headers from close range.

The final goal came in the 73rd minute when Marsh created it out of nothing more than a smart pass by Evanson. Marsh controlled it, glanced up and from 30 yards, outside the left side of the penalty box, hit a drive into the top of the net which Charlton could not reach. Barrett, Slough and Howe all went close in a matter of seconds as Fulham piled on the pressure and then Alan Slough hit the crossbar with a blockbuster from the edge of the box. The game had become one-sided by now and Best and Marsh even had time to tackle each other on the halfway line, much to the amusement of the Fulham crowd. Mitchell's shot curled just wide of the post before the referee blew for full time.

Marsh said afterwards that it was one of the most enjoyable games that he had ever played in and was especially pleased that the crowd had got behind the team.

Birmingham City 3 v Fulham 4

Saturday 18 August 1979
Football League Division Two
Referee: N.G. Peck
Attendance: 19,179

BIRMINGHAM C		FULHAM
Neil Freeman	1	Perry Digweed
Jimmy Calderwood	2	Les Strong
Mark Dennis	3	Tommy Mason
Alan Curbishley	4	Terry Bullivant
Pat Van Den Hawe	5	Richard Money
Malcolm Page	6	Tony Gale
Alan Ainscow	7	Peter Marinello
Tony Evans	8	John Beck
Keith Bertschin	9	Chris Guthrie
Archie Gemmill	10	Kevin Lock
Kevin Dillon	11	Gordon Davies

Fulham's bargain signing, Gordon Davies, kicked off the season with a hat-trick and was top scorer for the first time.

When Alec Stock left, coach Bobby Campbell stepped up to his first managerial job. A Liverpudlian, he was tough and abrasive, and a bit of an enigma. Highly rated by the players as a coach, and a very shrewd operator in the transfer market who was also good at developing young talent, his teams never fulfilled their obvious potential. The turnover among the playing squad was high and when Fulham kicked off in August 1978, there was only one player who had played in the Cup Final three years earlier – and that was Kevin Lock who was with West Ham that day. Campbell's teams promised much but his four-year tenure ended with the Cottagers dropping back into the (old) Third Division.

There was the usual pre-season optimism when Fulham travelled to St Andrews for the first game of the 1979–80 season. A team that contained the likes of Gerry Peyton in goal, defenders Richard Money and Tony Gale, Kevin Lock, John Beck and Peter Marinello in midfield and Gordon Davies and Chris Guthrie up front, was expected to do well. And for 45 minutes they did very well. Trailing 0–3 at half-time, they fought back to win 4–3 but this was virtually the high point of the season. An alarming loss of form led to a complete loss of confidence and the team finished in the relegation places, six points short of safety. As the club slipped down the table, manager Campbell appeared to be tactically very inflexible and dubiously loyal to several players who were clearly out of form. This was, nevertheless, by far the best of the seven Fulham teams to have suffered relegation between 1928 and 1994.

On the day of the game, long-term Fulham supporter Keith Castle was to become Britain's first-ever heart transplant patient. When he went under the anaesthetic, the Cottagers were 3–0 down but, when he came round after surgery, he was told they had won 4–3. 'Now you know why I am in here,' he is supposed to have quipped to the doctors.

DAVIES HAT TRICK STUNS BIRMINGHAM

Inspired by a superbly taken hat-trick from striker Gordon Davies, Fulham staged a remarkable come-back against Birmingham at St. Andrews on Saturday to take both points.

Three nil down at half time and looking set for another five goal drubbing by the Archie Gemmill inspired Midlands outfit, Fulham fought like tigers to win their way back into the game and with the lethal front-line partnership of Marinello, Guthrie and Davies firing on all cylinders they ran out winners.

For the first thirty minutes of the match things were evenly balanced with both sides feeling each other out, then the goal rush began. Gemmill launched the attack with a superb pass to full-back Mark Dennis on the left flank and he ran through to place in a fine cross which Evans sent past Digweed with a strong header.

Birmingham went further ahead when Dillon controlled a cross from the right and sent a low shot under the diving Digweed. Bertshin made it three when he headed in after Dillon had picked up a great ball from Gemmill and sent in another good cross from the left.

HALF TIME 3-0

When Fulham came back out for the second half the feeling around the press box was how many more would Birmingham get? Six minutes into the half Fulham opened their account with a neat goal. Winning a corner on the right, Lock floated in the kick, Money headed it on and Gordon Davies popped up in the penalty area to send a fine header over Freeman in the Birmingham goal. The large noisy crowd were stunned into silence by the slickness of the goal and they were to be silenced even more before the end.

On the hour, Fulham were celebrating another headed goal, this time by Chris Guthrie, jumping and twisting in the air he sent the header past helpless Freeman.

Fulham were on level terms in the 75th minute when Marinello again left his man for dead and sent a good cross which Davies touched across the goal-line and two defenders although appearing to put the ball in themselves were just too late as it had crossed the line, and Davies although winded in the hustle for the ball was able to celebrate his second goal.

Davies completed his first-ever League hat-trick when he scored what was to be Fulham's winner. The little Welsh striker held off a strong challenge from Page and placed the ball under the body of the advancing Freeman and into the net to send the small band of Fulham supporters, who made the trip to St. Andrews, wild with joy.

Indeed, but for some desperate defending by Birmingham in the last ten minutes of the match, Fulham might have had five, but they had won and what a victory it was! The character and fight in the Fulham side left me both stunned and pleased, for this was one of the most memorable matches I have seen for years.

No wonder the Birmingham officials looked shell-shocked after the game. I was still in a state of shock myself! This is what is needed not only to bring the crowds back, but it is form and fight like this that will win the Second Division promotion race this year. For Fulham, my man of the match had to be Gordon Davies. Without doubt, this young Welsh striker is one of the most exciting goal-snatchers I have seen for years and he must be the bargain buy and find of last season. Bobby Campbell was proved right in his gamble on Davies and now he can sit back and watch as Gordon scores the goals that could win Fulham promotion. The little man's partnership with Guthrie and Peter Marinello is worth its weight in gold and can only improve as the seasons go on.

In support of Davies I thought John Beck had a superb game and Kevin Lock, Peter Marinello, Richard Money and Chris Guthrie all did well.

Fulham 1 v Lincoln City 1

Wednesday 18 May 1982
Football League Division Three
Referee: E. Read
Attendance: 20,398

FULHAM		LINCOLN C
Gerry Peyton	1	David Felgate
Jeff Hopkins	2	David Carr
Les Strong	3	Phil Neale
Sean O'Driscoll	4	Glenn Cockerill
Roger Brown	5	Trevor Peake
Tony Gale	6	Steve Thompson
Gordon Davies	7	George Shipley
Robert Wilson	8	Phil Turner
Dean Coney	9	Gordon Hobson
Peter O'Sullivan	10	Tony Cunningham
Ray Lewington	11	Stuart Hibberd
Dale Tempest (for No. 3)	12	David Gilbert (for No. 11)

FULHAM v LINCOLN CITY
Tuesday 18th May, 1982

FOOTBALL LEAGUE DIVISION THREE

	P	W	D	L	F	A	W	D	L	F	A	P
Burnley	46	13	6	3	36	19	8	10	5	29	25	79
Fulham	45	12	8	2	43	21	9	6	9	33	29	77
Carlisle	45	17	4	2	44	21	5	7	10	20	29	77
Lincoln	45	13	7	3	40	16	6	6	8	25	23	76
Oxford	46	10	8	5	28	18	9	6	6	35	31	71

Tonight is the night when the outcome of our quest for promotion, which began some nine and a half months ago, will be decided. Thus the marathon race will end in a sprint finish. As the top of the table shows, a win for either Lincoln or ourselves tonight will ensure promotion and Second Division football next season: for the losers, there will only be the frustration and disappointment of a near miss and fourth place.

This is therefore the most important night in our history for many years: in its long-term implications, it is probably more important than our 1975 Cup run. In view of the significance of the occasion, we decided to prepare this insert to the programme prepared for the original date for the visit of the Imps, January 9th. This was of course postponed because of the snow, but not until after the programmes had been printed. The costs are such that we cannot afford to discard these magazines, but we hope that this insert is an acceptable compromise.

Malcolm Macdonald has written a script every bit as gripping as our rugby league director Colin Welland's Chariots of Fire. By 9.15 tonight, Les Strong will know whether he will become the fifth Fulham captain to lead a side to promotion. It was exactly 50 years ago that Len Oliver led us out of Division Three South. Subsequently, Pat Beasley and Johnny Haynes captained the teams which won promotion to the First Division, in 1949 and 1959, whilst in 1971 Barry Lloyd was skipper when we last went up from Division Three. For Les, it could be the start of one of the most memorable weeks of his career for on Friday we play the England team for his testimonial match.

This is the first opportunity we have had of welcoming Lincoln to Fulham for almost 24 years, since September 1958. We won 4-2 on that occasion, with Johnny Haynes scoring all four of our goals in a season which ended with us winning promotion. These historical parallels will count for nothing after 7.30, as the Imps battle to get the points that will secure their promotion for the second successive season. Neither side could have a greater incentive.

Whatever the outcome, this has been an eventful and enjoyable season at the Cottage. It is abundantly clear that we have turned the corner, and that the future is very bright indeed. When we return after the summer break, there will be a new-look Fulham team in the literal sense of the word. We are about to sign a two year sponsorship deal, the details of which will be announced on Friday. Don't forget also the shop in Fulham High Road, the ground improvements and new playing surface, all of which indicates we are prepared to meet the challenges of the future.

We feel certain there is no need to ask for your full backing tonight. Equally, the players will give everything they have. The scene is set for a great drama, a piece of pure theatre. But win, lose or draw, next season will be upon us before we know it. We hope you will be here to share it with us, but until then, thank you for your support this season, and we hope you enjoy the summer break.

Manager Bobby Campbell did not long survive relegation in 1980. His replacement was a surprise, the board turning to the club's Commercial Director Malcolm Macdonald. A former Fulham player who had gone on to become 'Super Mac' at Newcastle and Arsenal, his career had been cut short by injury before he was 30. Brash, outspoken and supremely self-confident, Macdonald had never managed or coached and his appointment was a gamble. But he was a revelation. With a management style that took the fear away from players, he used top quality coaches and his teams not only won but played with a flair that was admired by neutrals. His brief period in office was the one bright spot in Fulham's long decline from the Cup Final in 1975 until the Micky Adams' promotion in 1997.

In 1981–82, Macdonald's first full season, the team was among the divisional pacesetters all season. All the players he used, moreover, with the exception of free transfer Peter O'Sullivan, were at the club when it was relegated two years earlier, but Macdonald and coaches Ray Harford and George

Manager Macdonald and goalscorer Roger Brown celebrate promotion after the draw against Lincoln.

Armstrong seemed able to get more out of them. At the back, the classy Tony Gale and the inspirational Roger Brown kept things tight, while Gordon Davies and Dean Coney were on fire up front, and the team played with a style and self belief that delighted the critics.

But the outcome of the 46-match promotion campaign came down to the final 90 minutes. There were four teams competing for three places and, as luck would have it, two of them met on the last day in midweek at the Cottage. Because of a Boxing Day postponement, Fulham took on Lincoln knowing that a draw was enough to win back Second Division status while Lincoln needed a win to be sure of going up instead of Fulham. The Cottagers got the point they needed in front of a bumper crowd north of 20,000, but it was a dramatic and tense finale.

20,000 FANS GO WILD AT CRAVEN COTTAGE

Fulham are back in the Second Division – and there was singing all the way at Craven Cottage. Malcolm Macdonald – goal-scoring hero of so many sides in his playing days – has proved everybody wrong by making the transition and winning promotion in his first year as a manager.

Supermac was told by Chairman Ernie Clay he would be "crazy" to take over as Fulham boss.

HAPPY FOR CLAY

But oh how silly that seemed last night as the Fulham faithful danced for joy and headed off for a celebration pint.

But even super confident Macdonald admitted he was a bit worried by promotion rivals Lincoln. "Lincoln went off like a steam train and didn't let us settle down", he said.

Lincoln manager Colin Murphy said "Good luck to Fulham but it was a tremendous performance from my country bumpkins. Most of them are only earning about £7,000 a year".

Having outplayed and outsmarted Fulham in the first half, Lincoln were dealt two hammer blows in the 57th minute.

Their hard tackling defender Steve Thompson was sent off for bringing down Dean Coney. He had already been booked in the first half. Head bowed and sobbing, Thompson slowly trudged to the touchline where within seconds he was horrified to see further evidence of his own misdemeanors. From the ensuing free kick taken at the edge of the box by Tony Gale, Fulham took a lead they didn't deserve with a header from Roger Brown.

But there was a happy ending to Lincoln's nightmare when Dave Carr scrambled an equalizer off a Phil Turner corner in the 72nd minute.

This heart-stopping match was climaxed with thousands of delighted Fulham fans swarming on to the pitch calling for Macdonald and his men.

Now brave Lincoln must wait for the result of Carlisle's match at Chester tonight. If Carlisle lose then Lincoln go up on goal difference – but victory for Carlisle means they go up instead. And if Carlisle manage the impossible and win by eight goals, they will go up as champions ahead of Burnley who drew 1–1 at home to Chesterfield last night.

In an edgy last 10 minutes Sean O'Driscoll cleared off Fulham's line from Tony Cunningham.

BOOKINGS

Referee Eric Read booked four players before half-time – Fulham's Robert Wilson and Jeff Hopkins, and Lincoln's Trevor Peake and Thompson.

Lincoln's Gordon Hobson found his way into Read's notebook for a foul in the second half.

Macdonald added later: "I am the first to admit we did not play much football tonight.

"But we produced the goods throughout a 46-game programme playing with a style I am sure will stand us in good stead in the Second Division.

"We are basically a young side and now my players have got to work during the summer and show me that they are good enough to complete at a higher level.

"The brightest thing about tonight was a gate of more than 20,000. That is really amazing when you consider we haven't topped 10,000 this season.

"That kind of support gives us all here at Craven Cottage a lot of heart to build for the future."

Fulham returned to the Second Division last night. They gained the point they needed for promotion in a taut nervy contest at Craven Cottage in which Steve Thompson, the Lincoln defender, was sent off in the 58th minute.

Thompson, who had been booked in the first half for following through on Peyton, the Fulham keeper, brought down Coney just outside the penalty area and Eric Read, the referee had no alternative but to dismiss him.

From the free-kick, Gale lobbed the ball into the goal-mouth and Roger Brown headed home off the underside of the crossbar. So in a few decisive seconds Lincoln's own promotion hopes all but disappeared. Yet they could still go up if Carlisle lose at Chester tonight.

FURTHER PRESSURE

Lincoln competed bravely throughout even after being down to 10 men. They put further pressure on Fulham's nerves with an equalizer in the 72nd minute through Carr.

Hard as they tried, Lincoln could not again pierce Fulham's defence, although most of the 20,398 crowd suffered agonies before the final whistle. That was the signal for thousands of fans to flood on the pitch and call for their heroes to make an appearance on the balcony.

Lincoln often troubled Fulham's defence through the thrust of Cunningham their tall, coloured striker, and Shipley's dominance in midfield.

Fulham's promising young forwards, Davies and Coney, were too tightly marked to threaten often and in the end the Londoners had to be grateful for outstanding defensive play by Hopkins, Brown and Gale.

This became even more important when Strong, their experienced captain, who is in his testimonial year, had to go off with a back injury in the 37th minute but young Tempest came on to do a capable job as his replacement.

Newcastle United 1 v Fulham 4

Saturday 14 October 1982
Football League Division Two
Referee: A. Robinson
Attendance: 29,490

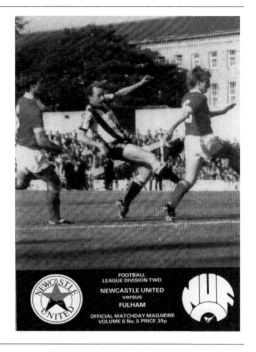

NEWCASTLE U		FULHAM
Kevin Carr	1	Gerry Peyton
John Anderson	2	Jeff Hopkins
Wes Saunders	3	Kevin Lock
Mick Martin	4	Sean O'Driscoll
Jeff Clarke	5	Roger Brown
Steve Carney	6	Tony Gale
Kevin Keegan	7	Gordon Davies
Kevin Todd	8	Robert Wilson
Imre Vradi	9	Dean Coney
Terry McDermott	10	Ray Houghton
David McCreery	11	Ray Lewington
Ken Wharton (for No. 8)	12	Dale Tempest (for No. 3)

When promotion was won, Malcolm Macdonald banned the use of the word 'consolidation' from Craven Cottage. Far from wanting just to re-establish Fulham's credentials in the second tier of the League after a two-year interval, he wanted to go for a second promotion in 12 months. He kept faith with the players that had served him so well the previous season, adding only Ray Houghton, a free transfer signing from West Ham, to replace the veteran Peter O'Sullivan. Behind the scenes, George Armstrong left the club in the summer leaving Ray Harford in charge of the coaching duties.

In the opening months of 1982–83, Macdonald's young side played with a verve and vitality that took the division by storm. With 10 wins and three draws from the first 16 games, the manager's claims seemed justified. Away from home, they were especially effective, winning five and drawing one of the first eight on the road, scoring 21 goals, including four in a game three times. The outstanding performance in this sequence was the trip to Newcastle, Macdonald's first back as a manager to the club where he had become a folk hero wearing the symbolic No. 9 shirt.

Stability was the key to Fulham's form. Remarkably, only 12 players had been used to start the first 10 games of the season. The third match was the last of skipper Les Strong's 424 appearances for the club and Kevin Lock took over the left-back slot. In the Magpies line up was the former England star and future Fulham manager Kevin Keegan, who had moved to Tyneside from Southampton that summer. The BBC cameras were there to record Macdonald's triumphant return to St James' and Fulham's brilliant performance. And two of Fulham's goals that day, Gordon Davies' first and Ray Houghton's superb chip made it to the last three of Match of the Day's Goal of the Season competition, a unique achievement for a second division club. A sour note emerged at the final whistle when Macdonald wondered about the legitimacy of the two penalties 'won' by Keegan, only one of which was converted.

Ray Houghton produced a stunning chip for Fulham's third goal.

Mac back in style to blast Tyneside

Newcastle welcomed Malcolm Macdonald back to Tyneside with open arms. The prodigal son, who made himself a legend during his great goal-scoring days at St. James Park, re-paid their warm generosity with a smack between the eyes.

Supermac returned to the old stamping ground as boss of comfy, lovable Fulham. But he had a nasty surprise in store for Kevin Keegan and company.

Fulham, newly promoted and transformed by Macdonald's boundless enthusiasm, turned on the heat to blast Newcastle out of sight. Gordon Davies, much in his manager's mould, hit two goals in a 4–1 thrashing.

Before the game, Macdonald agreed: "There is nowhere in the world like Newcastle to play football. They live the game here. I can understand why Kevin decided it was the only place to go". But if Newcastle thought Macdonald's men were going to be a soft touch, they were very much mistaken.

EMPHATIC

Afterwards the Fulham manager said: "This was an unforgettable day for me. Everything we did was emphatic. We did it in style, the only way to play. We wanted a bright start and that's exactly what happened. My lads are full of confidence and after this performance we have a very reasonable chance of being up in the promotion race at the end of the season."

The only black marks on an otherwise great day were Newcastle's two penalties. "They were suspect", said Macdonald. " Any team three goals down will try to win these awards."

Both decisions involved challenges on Keegan . The former England captain scored with his first spot-kick but goalkeeper Gerry Peyton, caught up in Fulham's euphoria, dived full length to save the second. Fulham were soon into top gear. Davies hit goal number one with a first time effort after only ten minutes. Dean Coney made it two and Ray Houghton got the third in the 37th minute when he lobbed goalkeeper Carr from 25 yards.

Keegan's first debatable penalty gave Newcastle a glimmer of hope, but Carr failed to hold a fierce shot from Coney and Davies reacted quicker than everyone to pop the ball over the line.

Newcastle manager Arthur Cox admitted: "We just didn't play in the first half. We were too arrogant, in fact our players thought Fulham should not have been in the same field."

Kevin Keegan, one of football's greatest ambassadors, was criticized by former England team-mate Malcolm Macdonald after Fulham's impressive win.

The Craven Cottage manager and director said it was "sad to see someone of such calibre, who achieved so much in the game, doing things like that".

Macdonald, the one-time Supermac hero of Tyneside, was referring to the way in which Keegan earned the first of his two penalties. "Tony Gale didn't do a thing to him" he said. "Keegan ran into him, bounced off him and then went down."

Fulham goalkeeper Gerry Peyton, outstanding in the second half which produced both penalties for alleged offences on Keegan, claimed: "Both were harsh. And that's an understatement." Peyton, in fact, saved Keegan's second.

The former England captain agreed that the penalties were 'a bit harsh. Particularly the first'.

Most of the 29,490 crowd had to keep looking at their programmes to identify Fulham's players. But they will not forget the names of creative midfield men Ray Houghton and Sean O'Driscoll or two-goal striker Gordon Davies.

Derby County 1 v Fulham 0

Saturday 14 May 1983
Football League Division Two
Referee: R. Chadwick
Attendance: 21,124

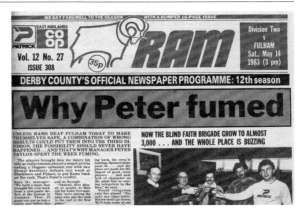

DERBY C		FULHAM
Steve Cherry	1	Gerry Peyton
John Barton	2	Jeff Hopkins
Kenny Burns	3	Kevin Lock
Archie Gemmill	4	Sean O'Driscoll
George Foster	5	Roger Brown
Paul Futcher	6	Tony Gale
Mike Brolly	7	Gordon Davies
Bobby Davidson	8	Robert Wilson
Kevin Wilson	9	Dean Coney
Paul Hooks	10	Ray Houghton
Paul Emson	11	Ray Lewington
John McAlle (for No. 4)	12	John Reeves (for No. 4)

To be pipped at the promotion post after leading for much of the season was disappointing enough. But to be cheated out of it at the last moment by crowd violence and spineless authorities was not only a huge blow to Fulham's fortunes but also an insult to fair play and decency. By allowing this result to stand, Graham Kelly and his timid administrators ignored the evidence from the television cameras and referees, condoned criminal behaviour and encouraged hooliganism.

Fulham travelled to the East Midlands for the final game of 1982–83 knowing that nothing less than victory would give them any chance of winning a second promotion in 12 months. After a superb start to their Second Division campaign, Malcolm Macdonald's young side had stumbled in the new year, allowing Leicester to close the gap in the chase for the third promotion place. At the same time, Derby were desperate for the points to avoid relegation and there was a tense atmosphere at the packed Baseball Ground. With minutes remaining, the Rams led 1–0 but the crowd had spilled over on to the pitch and formed the touchlines. Several Fulham players were assaulted by Derby 'supporters' and in the 88th minute, the referee took the teams back to the dressing rooms. He later said in his report that he had abandoned the game.

To the amazement of much of the football world, after a League inquiry days later, the result was allowed to stand, even though the game had not been completed. The appalling Kelly offered a fatuous explanation of not being able to recreate the conditions (several clubs were in the promotion mix) of the final Saturday. In effect, he underwrote the cheque to hooligans. While promotion was technically lost that day, and Fulham's return to the top flight delayed for another 18 years, Macdonald probably looked back ruefully to the visit to Oakdale in October. His side led Barnsley 3–0 at the interval but contrived to lose 4–3, three points squandered which would have ensured third place.

The closing minutes at the Baseball Ground when encroaching supporters led to abandonment of the game. But the result stood.

Double-edged win

Derby, by scoring a magnificent goal late in the second half, not only saved their own Second Division status but condemned Fulham to another season in the same company. It was a great occasion for Derby's best League crowd of the season, and marked a sensational recovery from the disastrous position which Peter Taylor inherited when he came to the Baseball Ground in November.

A header by Coney put Davies through down the middle but he could not get the ball under control and managed only a weak shot. Lewington managed a better one a minute later, but Cherry was perfectly positioned to deal with the situation. It was Derby who came nearest to scoring, when Emson, one of two players on the Derby side not being retained for next season, found Brolly whose header caught Peyton off his line and hit the underside of the bar. Peyton was relieved and a little lucky to collect the ball as it rebounded. Cherry saved Derby with a fine save at the far post from Coney's header after a long spell of Fulham pressure, and a clever cross by Robert Wilson found Derby in disarray.

In the second half, the tension started to tell and the football deteriorated in consequence. Emson made a good run, when Lewington gave the ball away to him. Gemmill, always in the action, shot over the top when the ensuing corner was only half cleared and then raced back into defence to get in a good tackle on O'Driscoll. Again Brolly came nearest to scoring. Kevin Wilson set him up well on the right side of the penalty area; Brolly's shot beat Peyton but hit the angle of the post.

By now, something out of the ordinary was needed to settle the issue, and Derby's goal was well worthy of the occasion. Emson passed the ball to Brolly on the far wing; Brolly headed it back and there was Davison in the middle to hammer home a superb volley into the roof of the net. Gemmill went off, his job done, and Derby, with a superb late save by Cherry from Houghton, were safely home.

AUTHORITY FACING DIFFICULT DECISIONS

The pitch invasion at Derby County's Baseball Ground on Saturday means that the very backbone of the football authorities will be questioned, not once but twice in the following week. The first test takes place in the High Court in the case brought by Steve Foster, of Brighton, against the Football Association over his suspension from the FA Cup Final; the second at Lytham St Anne's today when the Football League Commission meets to discuss the encroachment of Derby supporters during the closing stages of the important Second Division match against Fulham.

The League are in a predicament. Whatever they decide, they will not be considered right by everyone. But whether they are fined or not, Derby would, as their manager, Peter Taylor, was quick to point out be only too happy to stage "two or even three replays with Fulham". Derby are now safe from relegation, even if Saturday's three points be deducted from their total.

Fulham, who have to win any rematch to deny Leicester promotion, seem to have a case since the touchlines disappeared for the last seven or eight minutes underneath the intruders: Wilson, their midfield player, was clearly kicked by a spectator while the ball was in play, and Hopkins, their fullback, was reported by the Fulham manager, Malcolm Macdonald, to have been assaulted and was left in a state of shock as the teams left the field.

Had the referee insisted on playing the 78 seconds that remained, Macdonald would not have been able to send out a full team, having used his substitute and been deprived of at least one player due to the hostilities. Nor, as Macdonald pointed out, were any of the trespassers from Fulham. They were all from Derby, celebrating the fact that their team had stayed up, which was certainly quite a feat, bearing in mind that they had once been so far adrift.

Fulham 1 v Liverpool 1

Tuesday 8 November 1983
Milk Cup Third Round
Referee: K.W. Baker
Attendance: 20,142

FULHAM		LIVERPOOL
Jim Stannard	1	Bruce Grobbelaar
Jeff Hopkins	2	Phil Neal
Kevin Lock	3	Alan Kennedy
Cliff Carr	4	Mark Lawrenson
Paul Parker	5	Steve Nichol
Tony Gale	6	Alan Hansen
Gordon Davies	7	Kenny Dalglish
Robert Wilson	8	Sammy Lee
John Marshall	9	Ian Rush
Ray Houghton	10	Mike Robinson
Ray Lewington	11	Graham Souness

Following the disappointment of the previous season, Fulham made a very slow start to 1983–84.With just three wins in the first half of the season, they looked like serious relegation candidates.Yet the team was virtually the same as the one that had gone so close to promotion, and the squad was strengthened with youngsters like Jim Stannard, John Marshall and Peter Scott all staking claims to a place. But it took a series of memorable League (Milk) Cup ties to show that the quality was still there and start to turn the season around.

After Doncaster were brushed aside in round two, the Cottagers were handed a plum draw, a home tie against the all-conquering team of the 1980s, Bob Paisley's Liverpool, holders of the trophy, Division One leaders and reigning League champions,The tie ran to three matches and showed that the young side Macdonald and Harford had built could hold its own with a team that included the likes of Dalglish, Hansen, Rush and Souness. For the first game, centre-half and captain Roger Brown was left out and, shortly afterwards, he was on his way back to Bournemouth. First Jeff Hopkins and then Paul Parker were given the task of keeping the best strike force in the country quiet and both emerged with their reputations enhanced.

In the first meeting at the Cottage, Fulham raised their game and, with more clinical finishing, might well have won. A fortnight later, at Anfield, the Cottagers showed remarkable resilience and came back from a Dalglish goal early in the second half to equalise with five minutes left, again with an immaculate Kevin Lock penalty.The third game at the Cottage went to extra-time and was settled by a mishit Souness shot.This was effectively the last hurrah of the brief Macdonald era. He went in the spring, to be succeeded by Harford, at which point the chairman, Ernie Clay, began selling the best players. Just two years later, Fulham were relegated and the drift down to the basement of the Football League was underway.

Kevin Lock's immaculate penalty which earned Fulham a deserved draw against Liverpool.

Rush to the rescue

Liverpool might have reached the quarter-finals of the European Cup and resumed their place at the top of the First Division but last night their hold on the Milk Cup often looked extremely tenuous. Fulham severely disturbed Liverpool's equilibrium in an exhilarating third-round tie at Craven Cottage at the end of which the League champions were relieved to escape with a 1–1 draw and a replay on November 22.

The Milk Cup has become Liverpool's insurance for a place in Europe should all else fail. They have won the competition for the last three years and their initial approach to last night's match suggested that the thought of being knocked out had never crossed their minds.

If so, they were swiftly dis-illusioned by a Fulham side whose energetic, inventive football utterly belied their low position in the Second Division. Fulham refused to allow their opponents to impose the soporific rhythm on the match which had so bemused Bilbao the previous week and they wrestled the game from Liverpool between the penalty areas in a manner which had proved beyond Everton two days earlier.

Carr, Houghton and Lewington challenged tenaciously for possession in midfield and space near goal, helped by the initial number of occasions on which Liverpool gave the ball away, and several times Wilson or Gale opened up gaps in the Liverpool defence with imaginative passes.

However, Fulham's best player proved to be Parker, their stocky supporting centre-back, whose consistently well-timed tackles, intelligent covering and composure in bringing the ball out of defence gave their movements solid backing throughout.

Given similar composure at the other end, Fulham would surely have won. Just past the half-hour, in an attack heavy with undertones of Anfield, Wilson pushed the ball inside Neal and Carr, catching the defence square with a late run, found himself with only Grobbelaar to beat. However, he was thwarted by the Liverpool goalkeeper's speed off his line, Grobbelaar blocking an attempted lob.

At the start of the second half Gale released Davies on the right. A year ago, the Welshman might have scored without hesitation but now he turned inside Hansen and after Grobbelaar had pushed out his shot, Carr shot into the goalkeeper's hands.

When Fulham did take the lead, their visions of glory were fleeting. In the 62nd minute Lawrenson cannoned into Davies and Liverpool seemed a mite put out to find a penalty awarded against them instead of an indirect free-kick. Lock duly sent Grobbelaar the wrong way.

Still celebrating, Fulham lost their concentration for a few seconds and after Robinson's centre had been flicked on by Lee, Rush prodded the ball past Stannard, his 14th goal of the season and his eighth in four games. However, Liverpool's survivial owed as much to the excellent covering of Lawrenson and Fulham's missed opportunities.

The slip that cost Fulham the scalp of the champions

Liverpool, who have not been beaten in a Milk or League Cup tie since losing a semi final to Nottingham forest four seasons ago, are still in this year's competition, but only just. One moment of inexperience cost Fulham the scalp of the League champions in last night's Third Round match at Craven Cottage. After taking the lead midway through the second half, Malcolm Macdonald's young team made the mistake of briefly losing their composure. Against some sides you can afford to do that but not against Liverpool who forced a replay by equalising within a minute.

Yet Fulham can take great pride in their performance which was based on the constant hustling of the Liverpool midfield and on a willingness to take on their opponents defenders around the penalty area. Their goal moreover was the first Liverpool have conceded in seven matches and helped bring to an end Liverpool's run of five successive victories. In scoring, Fulham succeeded where, among others, Athletico Bilbao, Everton, Luton Town and Queen's Park Rangers have all failed in recent weeks.

Most of Liverpool's early attacks were directed through Nichol whose speed on the left wing created several openings. But Fulham's willingness to contest every ball and deny Liverpool space in midfield soon took effect and Souness in particular began to put passes astray. It took Fulham time to work out how to beat Liverpool's offside trap but when the finally did so after 31 minutes, only Grobbelaar's speed of thought and stride prevented a goal. Wilson's through ball left Carr with only the Liverpool goalkeeper to beat but Grobbelaar raced out of his penalty area and with typical inventiveness chested Carr's shot to safety.

Four minutes later, Carr went close again. Lock's pass found the Fulham midfield player unmarked at the edge of the penalty area and his rasping drive flew inches over the crossbar.

If Liverpool had discussed the fallibility of their offside trap during half time, it was hardly evident. Within three minutes, Gale beat it with a perfectly timed 40 yards pass down the right wing to Davies who rounded Lawrenson but should have done better than shoot straight at Grobbelaar. After 63 minutes, however, Fulham finally got the goal their endeavour and persistence deserved. Davies, on the edge of the box and with his back to goal and apparently posing no danger, was tripped by Lawrenson whose protests to the referee were in vain. Lock, who at that moment appeared the calmest person in the ground, drove the penalty high into the corner of the net.

It seemed cruel that Fulham's lead should last just one minute but for once their defence, until then admirably organized, were caught hopelessly out of position. Neal was given room to measure his cross from the right and after Lee had flicked it on, Rush's outstretched leg from five yards did the rest. Fulham had had their chance and it will take a mighty effort for them to salvage anything from the replay at Anfield.

Portsmouth 4 v Fulham 4

Tuesday 1 January 1985
Football League Division Two
Referee: B. Stevens/J. Carter
Attendance: 17,636

PORTSMOUTH		FULHAM
Alan Knight	1	Jim Stannard
Gary Stanley	2	Paul Parker
Mick Tait	3	Cliff Carr
Kevin Dillon	4	John Marshall
Noel Blake	5	Jeff Hopkins
Malcolm Waldron	6	Kevin Lock
Bobby Doyle	7	Leroy Rosenior
Mick Kennedy	8	Robert Wilson
Neil Webb	9	Dean Coney
Alan Biley	10	Ray Houghton
Vince Hilaire	11	Ray Lewington
	12	Gary Barnett (for No. 8)

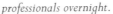

As a coach, Ray Harford was among the very best, as his post-Fulham career showed. And as a person, he was terrific company, the possessor of a very droll sense of humour. None of this was, however, apparent to the Fulham fans. After Macdonald, who was never short of something to say and was his own best PR man, Harford appeared to be dour and withdrawn. He disliked the showbiz side of management and thought football was a private business between the coaches and the players. He made little effort to endear himself to supporters but the players thought he was top class. And he inherited the job at a very difficult time, when the chairman was selling off the best players, like Gale, Davies, Houghton, Wilson and Lewington and expecting Harford to turn the juniors into seasoned professionals overnight.

Looking back, it was remarkable that he held it together so well for as long as he did. In his first full season in charge, 1984–85, Fulham finished a very respectable ninth (out of 22), just three wins short of the third promotion place. And there were some remarkable games, none more so than the visit to Fratton Park on New Year's Day. Exactly 12 months earlier, on New Year's Eve 1983, the Cottagers had made precisely the same journey and returned after a stunning 4–1 win, their first away victory of the season and the game which kick started the League season.

This game was, if anything, even more dramatic, and it had longer-term consequences. Retrieving a point after trailing 4–0 at the interval was probably a bigger achievement than winning 4–3 at Birmingham in 1973 having been 3–0 down at the interval. To call this the ultimate game of two halves would be an understatement and once again it was the unflappable Kevin Lock who clinched the draw in the final minute. For Pompey, it mattered, because at the end of the season, they finished in fourth place on the same number of points as promoted Manchester City. That 90th minute penalty changed the outcome of their season.

Dean Coney started Fulham's amazing comeback at Fratton Park.

IT'S THE GREAT POMPEY PANTO

The King's Theatre provided the ball at Fratton Park yesterday and Pompey responded by producing a New Year's Day pantomime of their own. But while the audience may leave the Kings laughing at 'Mother Goose', no one at Fratton Park was laughing as they watched Alan Ball's side toss away a four-goal lead and end up with a single point.

Pompey had gone off to a standing ovation from a crowd of almost 18,000 at half time, luxuriating in the largest lead Pompey have known in a first half for 17 years. But at the close, the chant of 'what a load of rubbish' swirled around their bowed heads as they trudged to the dressing room seconds after Fulham had completed their dramatic recovery with a 90th minute penalty.

It was stunning, inexplicable. In the first half they had punished a series of ghastly defensive errors by hitting the biggest score of the season and then proceeded to produce their own string of New Year gifts for the visitors in the second.

At the start, everything seemed set fair for Pompey as they settled quickly to the task of examining an ill-at-ease defence. By the time they bounced into the lead in the 16th minute, Fulham had already lost influential midfield man Robert Wilson with damaged ankle ligaments and had seen a goal by Noel Blake disallowed for one of a string of offside decisions which disrupted the action,

The visiting goalkeeper Jim Stannard's nightmare began. He sprawled to cover Mick Kennedy's free kick, the ball bounced off his chest and Malcolm Waldron tapped in a formal first goal for the club. Within two minutes, it was two. Webb's looping header from Dillon's corner sailed over Stannard's flapping arms came back off the bar and Biley hurled himself forward to head his way into the double figures for the season. Fulham's

problems were far from over and in the 23rd minute the unhappy Stannard and Jeff Hopkins confused each other as they went for a huge clearance by Alan Knight and Webb nipped between them to chip into the far corner from the edge of the penalty area.

Pompey's fourth goal in the 39th minute was another curiosity. Biley flicked on a long cross by Stanley, Hopkins's clearance smashed against Biley's face and looped over the stranded goalkeeper.

General complacency was punctured just two minutes into the second half. Ray Lewington, who had a magnificent match as Fulham's midfield inspiration, swirled a long cross in from the left, Blake was beaten by its flight and Dean Coney lunged in at the far post to make it 4-1.

Suddenly the escape route opened for Fulham with two goals in three minutes. First Tait tried to head the ball down to a teammate but found only Leroy Roisenior who clipped a shot over Knight. And then a cross from busy fullback Cliff Carr found substitute Gary Barnett unmarked to score a close range header.

So Pompey had 13 minutes in which to survive and take the prize which had seemed a formality. Five minutes had ticked away when Dillon was caught in possession by Coney. Knight could only push away the cross but Carr squeezed his shot just wide. Pompey bounced to the other end and Hopkins's wretched afternoon took another nose dive as he headed Dillon's free kick into his own net only to be reprieved by the referee ordering a retake.

And so the final minute arrived with Pompey's tenuous lead intact. Carr surged forward once more, this time Blake cut him down, and Lock's nerve held as he drilled in the penalty with Knight going the wrong way.

Fulham 0 v Chelsea 1

Wednesday 6 November 1985
Milk Cup Third Round
Referee: A. Seville
Attendance: 20,190

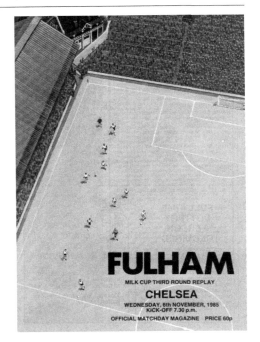

FULHAM		CHELSEA
Gerry Peyton	1	Eddie Niedzwiecki
Brian Cottington	2	Darren Wood
Cliff Carr	3	Keith Dublin
Peter Scott	4	Colin Pates
Jeff Hopkins	5	Robert Isaac
Paul Parker	6	Joey Jones
John Marshall	7	Pat Nevin
Kenny Achampong	8	Nigel Spackman
Dean Coney	9	Kerry Dixon
Chris Pike	10	David Speedie
Gary Barnett	11	Kevin McAllister
	12	Paul Canoville (for No. 11)

In 1985–86, the roof fell in on Fulham. After winning two of the first three games, they won only three of the next 39 and finished bottom of the table, a massive 13 points short of safety. The 26 defeats that season is the highest in the Cottagers' League history at any level. With his best players being sold from under him, Harford was forced to the short-term expedient of loans but the challenge of achieving safety was beyond even his considerable coaching skills.

Yet there was one highlight, a rare moment to savour, which could have been even better but for a missed penalty. In the League (Milk) Cup, Fulham drew neighbours Chelsea in the third round after overcoming Notts County in the Second. It was the first time the clubs had met in this competition and the first time in a Cup competition since the FA Cup nearly 35 years earlier. The Blues, then in the (old) First Division, had home advantage and a relatively small crowd of 19,669 were at the Bridge for the game. Managed by John Hollins, Chelsea were a top three side and when Micky Hazard gave them the lead in the second half, it looked all over. But Fulham played their best football of the season that night. When Gary Barnett was fouled in the penalty area in the final minute and Cliff Carr slotted home the penalty, the draw was well deserved.

For the replay, Harford picked the same side and the tie attracted the first 20,000 crowd at the Cottage for two years and the last for 16. On the night, Fulham played even better than at the Bridge but failed to make the most of their chances. The most glaring miss was by skipper Carr who failed from 12 yards after Spackman had tripped Achampong. In fairness, it was yet another outstanding save by Chelsea goalkeeper Eddie Niedzwiecki who was unbeatable on the night. In 2010, of course, the Welsh international came to the Cottage as part of Mark Hughes' coaching team.

Cliff Carr, penalty hero at the Bridge, villain at the Cottage.

Chelsea can thank Niedzwiecki

Chelsea are back in the last 16 of the Milk Cup. They beat Fulham in a fast and entertaining third round replay at Craven Cottage last night with Kerry Dixon's 11th goal of the season, but it took some out-standing goalkeeping by Eddie Niedzwiecki to keep them in the competition. The Second Division side dominated long periods of the match with imaginative attacking football and hit the bar early in the second half.

Fulham, who had forced a 1-1 draw at Stamford Bridge with a late penalty from Carr, thought they had saved the tie again nine minutes from the end when Achampong, having beaten Spackman once, was brought down by the Chelsea player when he attempted to do so a second time. Up stepped Carr once more to take the penalty, but this time Niedzwiecki stopped the ball with his legs and so Chelsea moved on to meet Everton at home in the fourth round.

Not surprisingly, the large contingent of Chelsea followers among a crowd of just over 20,000 chanted their goalkeeper's name - christian name that is - as the players left the field. It had been a remarkable display of anticipation, agility and courage by Niedzwiecki, whose speed off his goal line and determination in going down at opponents' feet thwarted Fulham time and again.

Even then Fulham came off rueing a number of scoring chances that might have been accepted given a fraction more composure. Much of their football lacked nothing in thought or vision. Scott and the rest of the midfield often controlled the game between the penalty areas and always made sure that the front runners had instant, urgent support.

However, Barnett's miss in the opening minute, when he shot off balance and sent a good chance high and wide, proved prophetic as far as Fulham were concerned. They were playing neat, astute football in the strong wind which blustered off the Thames, and Chelsea were under siege.

But natural goalscorers like Dixon are made for this sort of situation. In the 18th minute he met Wood's long high ball from the right with a firm header, and when this was blocked, he volleyed in the rebound.

Until they began catching Fulham on the break towards the end, Chelsea seldom looked like winners and have rarely looked so ineffective.

After falling behind, Fulham resumed their attacks with even greater intensity. In the space of two minutes Coney shot just wide of one post, Niedzwiecki pushed a shot from Marshall round the other and following the corner, Cottington and Hopkins had successive shots charged down by defenders.

Ten minutes into the second half, Coney nodded on a corner from Barnett on the left and Hopkins headed against the Chelsea bar. Soon after the penalty had been saved, the luckless Barnett seemed certain to take advantage of another mistake by the Chelsea defence, but almost as soon as he shot there was Niedzwiecki flinging himself sideways to grab the ball.

Fulham's supporters must have felt they had gone through all this before. A few years back they had seen their team dominate a protracted Cup tie against Liverpool only to finish the losers. Last night's game was of a similar pattern.

DIXON STRIKES AND PUTS PAID TO FULHAM

Kerry Dixon's 18th minute goal pointed Chelsea's towards the last 16 of the Milk Cup, yet it was the inspired goal-keeping of Eddie Niedzwiecki which denied Fulham constantly in an exhilarating third-round reply.

It was quite like old times down by the Thames, with a 20,000 crowd reminiscent of Fulham's First Division days of 20 years ago, swelling Craven Cottage with three times their usual gathering for a Second Division fixture.

They saw Fulham carve out six clear chances, including a penalty. Niedzwiecki superbly saved five times, including Cliff Carr's penalty, with the woodwork denying Fulham on the other occasion.

If Dixon's 11th goal of the season advanced his claims for England selection next week, then Niedzwiecki, born in Bangor of Polish extraction, more than proved he is ready for a first Welsh cap, if Neville Southall, the goal-keeper of Everton, Chelsea's opponents in the next round, is ever unavailable for his country. As John Hollins, Chelsea's relieved manager exclaimed afterwards: "I have never seen a goal-keeping display like that. It seemed as if Eddie had had an extra-arm transplant. Without him, it could have been about 5–3 for Fulham."

Chelsea had opted for two wingers, and this left them short in midfield against the four men Fulham designated for that area. The home side frequently burst through from midfield, with Marshall outstanding.

Marshall drew the first agile save from Niedzwiecki after 22 minutes, but by then Dixon had shown Fulham precisely what top class finishing is all about.

Dixon signaled to Wood to provide a long centre, and won it in the air. When his header bounced back off Hopkins, Dixon struck the ball home with nonchalant accuracy.

Then Niedzwiecki's inspired saves continued before half-time to punish Barnett's hesitancy by closing in on him and saving with his legs — and later twisting sideways to frustrate Pike.

Hopkins's close-range header hit Chelsea's crossbar early in the second half, and with 10 minutes left, Fulham's penalty arrived after Spackman tripped Achampong. Carr, whose penalty last week forced a replay, shot too chose to Niedzwiecki, who saved with his legs.

Still Fulham were not finished, and Barnett burst through two tackles to close in on Chelsea's hero. Again Niedzwiecki's anticipation and agility were superb as he spun sideways to save yet again.

Liverpool 10 v Fulham 0

Tuesday 23 September 1986
Littlewoods Cup Second Round First Leg
Referee: J.W. Lloyd
Attendance: 13,498

LIVERPOOL		FULHAM
Bruce Grobbelaar	1	John Vaughan
Gary Gillespie	2	John Marshall
Jim Beglin	3	Brian Cottington
Mark Lawrenson	4	Peter Scott
Ronnie Whelan	5	Kevin Hoddy
Alan Hansen	6	Paul Parker
Kenny Dalglish	7	Gary Barnett
Steve Nichol	8	Kenny Achampong
Ian Rush	9	Dean Coney
John Wark	10	Wayne Kerrins
Steve McMahon	11	Ray Lewington

Ray Lewington, a key figure at Fulham from 1986 up to the present day, was just weeks into his managerial career when the cottagers went to Anfield.

For many Fulham supporters, the years from 1986 to 1997 formed a lost decade. Both on and off the pitch, the club's fortunes sank to previously unplumbed depths and reached the point that the Cottagers' continued existence was seriously doubted. Both the start date and the end date of this traumatic period are easy to pinpoint. In the summer of 1986, shortly after relegation to the (old) Third Division, the deeply unpopular Ernie Clay sold the club and the ground at a substantial profit to himself to people who were to become even more unpopular than him – David Bulstrode and Robert Noonan, the two men in charge of Marler Estates, the company that owned Stamford Bridge.

At first, the new owners made placatory noises to allay supporters' suspicions about their true motives. The immensely popular Ray Lewington returned from a season with Sheffield United to become player-manager in succession to the departed Harford. It was his first managerial appointment, but it was a poisoned chalice. Any illusions he might have had about the size of the task he faced must have evaporated in the second month in the job. Just three years after the epic encounters with Liverpool in the same competition (now renamed the Littlewoods Cup), Fulham went to Anfield for a second round tie.

While Fulham had slipped into the obscurity of the (old) Third Division, the Reds had gone from strength to strength, and had completed the League and Cup double the previous season. Ray Lew had played in the memorable matches in the Macdonald era, as had Coney, Marshall and Parker, but there was never any chance of Fulham pulling off a surprise. Dalglish's Liverpool were merciless that night and inflicted on the Cottagers their biggest-ever first class defeat, a humiliating experience for all involved but at least it was against the best team in Europe at the height of their powers. The second leg was a more respectable 3–2 defeat at home for Fulham but the 180 minutes highlighted the gulf that had emerged in a relatively short space of time. And there was worse to come.

Kenny's Red Destroyers Leave Fulham Reeling

Kenny Dalgish recalled Bruce Grobbelaar for last night's Littlewoods Cup tie at Anfield in place of unfortunate deputy Mike Hooper, but the colourful goalkeeper might as well have stayed in Zimbabwe.

Apart from a couple of spectacular catches, he could do little but watch and admire the men in front of him, as they destroyed a Fulham side lacking half a dozen regulars. It was three years since Fulham forced two draws with Liverpool in the same competition, before going down to a late winner from Graeme Souness, and an awful lot happened in the interim,

They have sacked Malcolm Macdonald as manager, sold most of their best players to First Division sides, and now look only a shadow of a once formidable team. Although two of the survivors, central defender Paul Parker and striker Dean Coney, showed occasional flashes of class, they were completely overrun and could well have conceded more than the ten goals which have virtually guaranteed their elimination.

Four of these came in a one-sided first half, and the other six during an 18-minute spell in the second half when Liverpool seemed likely to score every time they had possession.

Had not Steve McMahon missed a penalty, Ian Rush twice hit a post and several players missed from less than 10 yards, the final score would have soared past the club record of 11 by which they thrashed the Norwegians of Stromsgodset in the Cup Winners Cup of 1974.

Liverpool's quickness to the ball, the accuracy of their passing and their commendable refusal to ease up after taking a commanding lead were just too much for opponents who seemed capable of doing little more than standing and watching a superb exhibition.

If Rush was much too sharp for Fulham's central defenders, and though happy to score twice and take his seasonal total to nine, he must be wondering how he failed to double his collection, after hitting both the goalkeeper and an upright within a matter of seconds.

John Wark, making his first appearance of the season in place of Jan Molby, also scored twice while Steve Nichol and Ronnie Whelan got one each. The undoubted star of the night was Steve McMahon, who atoned for his penalty miss by grabbing four excellent goals, three of them in the space of ten minutes midway through the second half.

That was surely a record for a Liverpool midfielder, to set alongside Fulham's record defeat in any event. As the goals piled up in the second half, the Kop gave the hapless John Vaughan in the Fulham goal a terrible time, but earlier they had been clearly out-shouted by the contingent from Fulham who would not have been there at all if Liverpool had followed Luton's example by banning them.

Paul Parker found his visit to Anfield in 1986 very different from 1983.

Fulham 2 v Walsall 2

Saturday 28 February 1987
Football League Division Three
Referee: M.J. Bodenham
Attendance: 5,944

FULHAM		WALSALL
John Vaughan	1	Fred Barber
Wayne Kerrins	2	Andy Dornan
Jim Hicks	3	Bob Taylor
Leo Donnellan	4	Craig Shakespeare
Kenny Achampong	5	Phil Hawker
Brian Cottington	6	Peter Hart
Gary Barnett	7	Mark Rees
Chris Pike	8	Nicky Cross
Gordon Davies	9	David Kelly
Cliff Carr	10	Trevor Christie
Gary Elkins	11	Bobby Hutchinson

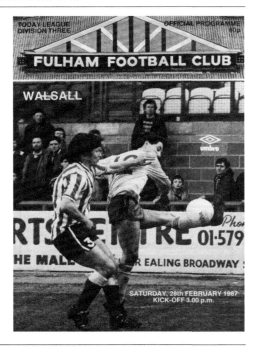

It was not long before Fulham's new owners revealed their hand. Within days of buying QPR and Loftus Road from Jim Gregory to add to their football portfolio, Bulstrode announced proposals to merge Fulham with Rangers (Fulham Park Rangers), play at Loftus Road and turn the more lucrative Craven Cottage site into a housing development. Unsurprisingly, there was a massive public outcry and in retrospect it is possible that Marler never intended to merge the two clubs at all. It was instead just a negotiating ploy. If a buyer could be found for the football club, they would sell very cheaply on condition Fulham voluntarily vacated the Cottage. It was a cheaper and cleaner route to achieve their objectives but in February 1987, everyone took the threat of merger at face value.

Walsall were the first visitors to Fulham after the announcement was made, and it was clear there would be a demonstration against the board, even though the directors' box was predictably empty. The supporters expressed their feelings that day with a mixture of sadness and dignity and never once did the emotions threaten to spill over into violence. The visiting Walsall players and officials played their part, showing where their sympathies lay, although ironically they were to have their own problems with a corrupt chairman. On the day, a draw was a fair result.

The groundswell of hostility to the developers that was evident that day was not a token gesture. A bandwagon started to roll which culminated in a group headed by Jimmy Hill and bankrolled by Bill Muddyman buying the football club from Marler (for the price of Paul Parker and Dean Coney moving to QPR), but not the ground. Fulham remained tenants while the owners of the football club and the landlords sorted out the next steps. This solved one problem but created another which was not resolved for another 10 years. And for all the media sympathy for Fulham that week, the attendance at the Walsall game was just 5,944.

Gary Barnett rescued a point for Fulham on a highly charged day.

Walsall had two goals disallowed for offside as they sought to take their Cup-form into the Third Division at doomed Craven Cottage today.

David Kelly and Nicky Cross both had strikes ruled out but Fulham, cheered on by a bigger than usual crowd, also had their chances.

Fred Barber managed to beat out one shot with his legs but seconds from half-time Nicky Cross missed a great chance for the Saddlers.

With the crowd right behind them, Fulham surged forward from the kick-off and after an attempted clearance by Doran had been intercepted by Carr, Kerrins fired high over the bar.

The Saddlers had a goal disallowed in their first real attack.

Hart's free kick was headed down by Hutchinson and in the scramble that followed Kelly stroked the ball into the net but it was ruled offside.

There was another controversial incident in the 13th minute when Achampon cleverly beat two men bursting into the penalty box and, with Dornan alongside, he dived full length hoping for a penalty.

All he got was a thump from one of his own players for wasting a possible scoring chance.

Walsall again had the ball in the net through Cross but it was again ruled offside.

Walsall, looking for their first win in five League games, were holding their own comfortably though not yet producing much sparkle from midfield.

Walsall were beginning to settle down and in the 30th minute another knock-down from Christie saw Rees turn inside before hitting a scorching left-foot drive which Vaughan brilliantly saved.

Fulham suddenly stepped up the pace and should have taken the lead in the 34th minute.

Pike beat the offside trap and coolly pulled the ball back from the goal line in to the path of Barnett who tried to place his shot but Barber somehow managed to deflect it with his feet.

At the other end, Rees combined well with Kelly to put the home defence under pressure and Shakespeare's drive on the turn was tipped over the bar by Vaughan.

On the stroke of half-time, Cross missed a sitter for Walsall, shooting straight at Vaughan after being sent clean through by Shakespeare.

During half-time, the pitch was invaded by over one thousand Fulham fans demonstrating against the merger that could kill off their club.

They waved banners and chanted and at one stage stood in front of the terracing where about 600 Walsall supporters were standing.

The rival fans applauded each other warmly, Walsall people remembering only too well what a fight they had to prevent the Saddlers merging with Birmingham City at the end of last season.

When the teams took to the field, five minutes after the second half should have started, they were engulfed by the fans who stayed on the pitch despite several appeals over the public address system saying: "We have every sympathy with you in your fight but please leave the playing surface so that the match can resume, there are still three points at stake."

"You have done your job, now let the players do theirs."

A small group of supporters sat down in the centre circle ignoring police requests to leave the pitch but eventually they went back into the terraces and the second half started 18 minutes late.

Walsall were awarded a free kick for a foul on Hawker by Pike and when Taylor floated the ball into the area Hart was up there to head wide.

There was a close call for the Saddlers, however, in the 48th minute, Achampong heading on a long throw from Cottingham but Davies failed to meet it cleanly on the volley and the ball rolled gently into the hands of Barber.

So far Hutchinson had made a disappointing debut, failing to get into the thick of the action, and the Saddlers badly needed him to take hold of things in the middle of the park.

Fulham, looking for the win that would boost their campaign for survivial forced two successive corners, but Walsall managed to survive.

Walsall broke the deadlock in the 65th minute through a Christie penalty and then went further ahead three minutes later through Cross.

Fulham pulled one back through Donnellan in the 74th minute from the penalty spot.

Barnett's late equaliser at least gave the fans the consolation of a point.

In an emotion-charged atmosphere, the fans and players of both clubs provided a committed, but dignified response to those who would see them as unwanted tribes in a rebuilt urban landscape.

Before their highest League gate this season, Fulham came on to a tremendous ovation. Unfortunately sickness and injuries meant it was a patched up side that struggled against Walsall who, perhaps in view of the occasion, and their on going Cup epic with Watford, didn't capitalize fully on Fulham's weaknesses.

The first half was mainly enlivened by fierce terrace debates on the merits of various schemes and actions, over a soundtrack of abuse of all things Bulstrode and Ramsden.

There then followed a friendly pitch invasion in the true Fulham fashion, given official thanks over the loud speakers. The players returned to mingle with the crowd, waves of affection rolling over the ground as supporters chanted for each other's club. The demo finally dispersed in an arrest free manner, one fan taking another crying from the tactful arms of the police. Fulham then continued in tradition by going two down, followed by Leo Donnellan's penalty and a deserved equalizer when Pike's low cross was swooped on by Barnett at the far post like an avenging Valkryie. The crowd roared their support to the very end and long afterwards, the PA blasting out in defiant irony their 1975 Cup Final song 'Viva la Fulham'.

Before unaccustomed ranks of tape recorders and national press, Ray Lewington praised his players, many facing uncertain futures. "They're the poor sods I feel sorry for, and the fans, especially the ones that turned up against Rotherham."

Then an unscripted bonus, as a small child appeared at Dad's side for a few gap-toothed smiles and comments. It was time to go, before hardened lips began to quiver.

Wolverhampton Wanderers 5 v Fulham 2

Saturday 11 February 1989
Football League Division Three
Referee: I.S. Hemley
Attendance: 15,621

WOLVES		FULHAM
Mark Kendall	1	Jim Stannard
Andy Thompson	2	Gary Elkins
Floyd Streete	3	John Marshall
Gary Bellamy	4	Doug Rougvie
Mark Venus	5	Glen Thomas
Bob Dennison	6	Gary Barnett
Mick Gooding	7	Peter Scott
Nigel Vaughan	8	Robert Wilson
Keith Downing	9	Michael Cole
Steve Bull	10	Gordon Davies
Andy Mutch	11	Clive Walker
Phil Robinson (for No. 11)	12	
Bob Kelly (for No. 8)	14	

This was a very odd game, one in which Fulham were well beaten but which turned the season around for the better and saw a major club record established. For much of 1988–89, the Cottagers were bumping along in mid-table in the (old) Third Division, when they travelled to divisional leaders Wolves. At Molineux, they were well beaten, suffering their third straight defeat and finishing the game with only 10 men, Clive Walker seeing red. But, on the plus side, new signing, Doug Rougvie, scored on his debut, despite feeling under the weather. A Scottish international central defender who had previously played for Aberdeen and Chelsea, Rougvie was signed from Shrewsbury and he had an immediate impact.

He was made captain, and his physical presence and experience immediately lifted the team. After the Molineux defeat, Fulham went on a run of 11 wins and three draws in the next 17 games, finishing in fourth place and the Play-offs. This was, however, as far as they got because Bristol Rovers won both legs of the semi-final, by an aggregate of 5–0. At the end of the season, Rougvie was gone, back to Scotland after just 20 appearances. And it was another eight years before the Cottagers were again to come as close to promotion.

Gordon Davies scored the other Fulham goal that day, his 159th first class goal for the club. This was one more than Johnny Haynes' record (which he had equalled three weeks earlier against Mansfield) and there was still more to come from the Welsh international. By the time he left the Cottage in 1991, Ivor had taken his total to 178 in 418+32 appearances, made up of a club record 159 in the League, eight in the FA Cup and 11 in the League Cup. He is the most recent of the seven Fulham players to score a century of goals for the club and, had he not spent two years between 1984 and 1986 at Chelsea and Manchester, he might well have got to 200.

Gordon Davies who scored his record breaking goal at Molineux.

DAVIES BEATS GOALSCORING RECORD

Despite a 5–2 defeat for Fulham, Gordon Davies, their veteran striker, had something to celebrate. His goal meant that he had beaten Johnny Haynes' record of 157 goals for the Cottagers. He said afterwards that he was not aware that he had beaten the record but was happy that he had.

Fulham were given a torrid time by Wolves star striker Steve Bull who hit the Cottagers with a hat-trick. The goalkeeping of Jim Stannard prevented a rout. Fulham were without the injured Jeff Eckhardt and had Doug Rougvie making his debut in a re-shuffled defence.

Wolves took an early lead following a corner. Dennison's cross was miscued by Wilson and Mutch's close range shot was blocked, but the ball ran loose to the unmarked Bull, who scored from close-range. Wolves were two up by the 14th minute and it was Bull again who scored. Rougvie misjudged a centre from Thompson and Bull pivoted and hit a dive past Stannard in the Fulham goal. Jim Stannard then made an excellent save to deny Bull another goal.

Gordon Davies scored his record breaking goal after 21 minutes after a fun run down the flank by Clive Walker whose cross evaded keeper Kendall and Davies drove the ball into the roof of the net. Fulham's comeback was short-lived as Glen Thomas headed into his own net with Bull breathing down his neck. Wolves were 4–1 up after 31 minutes from the penalty spot. Peter Scott brought down Downing and Thompson gave Jim Stannard no chance with the spot kick.

Fulham looked as though they were about to get a hiding but steadied the ship after the break. After Dennison and Vaughan had gone close to adding to Wolves' score, Steve Bull completed his hat-trick. Stannard did well to get a hand to Bull's close range shot but the power of his shot took the ball over the line. Gordon Davies then headed wide just as Fulham made a comeback. A minute from time, Walker gained a corner and his kick found Rougvie whose well-placed header went inside Kendall's right hand post. Although the scoring was now complete, there was still time for Walker to be sent off for retaliation.

Fulham were just unable to cope with the goal scoring power of Steve Bull, who must be one of the best forwards outside the First Division and on this form looks as though he may soon feature in an England line-up. After the match, debutant Doug Rougvie complained of flu and had seemed under the weather in a lethargic performance. Fulham's reshuffled defence will not meet many better teams this season than the Wolves.

Swansea City 2 v Fulham 1

Saturday 7 May 1994
Football League Division Two
Referee: P. Danson
Attendance: 4,355

SWANSEA C		FULHAM
Roger Freestone	1	Jim Stannard
Steve Jenkins	2	Simon Morgan
Mark Clode	3	Martin Pike
Mike Basham	4	Jeff Eckhardt
Mark Harris	5	Robbie Herrera
Kwame Ampadu	6	Glen Thomas
Jason Bowen	7	Julian Hails
Dave Penney	8	Ara Bedrossian
Andy McFarlane	9	Martin Farrell
John Cornforth	10	Gary Brazil
John Hodge	11	John Marshall
Steve Torpey (for No. 7)	12	Robert Haworth (for No. 8)
Darren Perrett (for No. 3)	14	Martin Ferney (for No. 3)

Gary Brazil's goal at Swansea was too little too late.

After the brief flirtation with promotion and the Play-offs in 1989, Fulham's attentions in the next few years were generally focused on the other end of the table. There was an especially narrow escape from the drop in 1989–90 and again the following season when they avoided relegation only because three rather than four clubs went down. Ray Lew reverted to coach and two managers came and went, Alan Dicks and Don Mackay. In what would be a very crowded field, both would have strong claims to being the worst manager in Fulham's history. Fulham's Dark Age was at its darkest in the 1990s.

Even so, Fulham went into 1993–94 in a reasonably upbeat mood. They had finished in the comfort of mid-table the previous season and with the likes of Simon Morgan, Jim Stannard, Gary Brazil, Jeff Eckhardt and John Marshall, there were some good players with experience of higher level football. But with just two wins in the first 16 games, the club was on the back foot from the earliest weeks. A modest recovery in the winter months lifted the Cottagers into mid-table before a spring slump saw them drift downwards. On a Sunday in March at Brisbane Road, manager Don Mackay was effectively sacked at half-time with the team trailing 1–0.

With nine games remaining, the thankless task of trying to keep the club up fell to Ray Lew. A couple of wins and three draws gave Fulham a chance but a home defeat by fellow strugglers Exeter was terribly damaging. Nevertheless, the Cottagers travelled west for the final game against Swansea knowing that a win would keep them up, but they failed to rise to the occasion. In a sense they were unlucky to have been relegated with 52 points (only three clubs had gone down before from this division with as many or more points) but in truth the League basement had been beckoning for several years. The only consolation was that because of the establishment of the Premiership, it was no longer called the Fourth Division.

Despair for Fulham as relegation hits

Fulham fans, players and acting manager Ray Lewington were left in despair on Saturday after the club were relegated to Division 3 for the first time in their history.

Supporters stood motionless on the terraces at Swansea City long after the final whistle had condemned their club to demotion.

No-one could quite believe that one of the country's most historic clubs, having seemingly won their fight for Craven Cottage, could now have lost their battle for Division 2 survival.

It was a tragic moment in the club's history, and now everyone involved with Fulham must come to terms with what is likely to be a very difficult future – both on and off the pitch.

More than 2,000 Fulham fans made the trip to the Vetch Field on Saturday, knowing victory would guarantee survival.

But in the end, the team were simply not good enough to hold on to their Division 2 status.

As news came through that relegation rivals Blackpool had beaten Leyton Orient 4–1, Fulham succumbed to the inevitable.

On a depressing afternoon there had been very little for the faithful away fans to cheer – although they shouted themselves hoarse all afternoon. Unfortunately, the players were not so admirable in their efforts.

They certainly put in enough effort, but it needed goalkeeper Jim Stannard to keep them afloat and Swansea (who have only lost twice at home all season) always looked the better team.

FULHAM GO DOWN

Fulham were finally relegated from Division Two after this spirited performance- but spirit alone does not win matches, writes Mark Caswell.

Relegation to the Football League's basement division for the first time in the club's long history was anticipated by many of the honest supporters at the club. This team was simply not good enough to survive and it was a surprise to many that they did not avoid the drop until the last game of the season.

The new manager will certainly have a job on his hands but if Fulham can keep hold of seven of the more experienced players and blood some of the excellent youth players an automatic return to Division Two cannot be ruled out.

For the record Jason Bowen, who caused plenty of problems for Fulham throughout the afternoon, and Darren Perratt scored for Swansea, with Gary Brazil's 19th goal for the season replying for Fulham.

Fulham: Stannard (7). Marshall (5). Thomas (5). Morgan (6). Pike (5). Hails (7). Eckhardt (5). Bedrossian (6). Herera (5). Brazil (8). Farrell (5). Subs: Ferney (5), Haworth, Harrison

Martin Pike left the field after just 15 minutes with a thigh injury and the Swans, after exerting intense pressure, went ahead after 34 when Jason Bowen fired home.

Jeff Eckhardt had a glorious chance to equalise, but when his header sailed over the bar it summed up Fulham's day.

Swansea also missed an open goal just after the break and Eckhardt ballooned over again before it was 2–0.

Stannard did superbly to save a close-range shot, but the rebound was tucked home by Perrett.

Fulham, roared on by the desperate away fans, hit back when Sean Farrell had an effort saved and then Gary Brazil found the net in injury time. But it was all too late.

Fulham 7 v Swansea City 0

Saturday 11 November 1995
FA Cup First Round
Referee: P. Rejer
Attendance: 4,798

FULHAM		SWANSEA C
Tony Lange	1	Roger Freestone
Duncan Jupp	2	David Barnhouse
Robbie Herrera	3	Andy Cook
Lee Barkus	4	Michael Basham
Kevin Moore	5	Christian Edwards
Terry Angus	6	Colin Pascoe
Martin Thomas	7	John Hodge
Simon Morgan	8	Carl Heggs
Gary Brazil	9	Steve Torpey
Mike Conroy	10	Shaun Chapple
Nick Cusack	11	Jonathan Coates
Rory Hamill (for No. 10)	12	Darren Perrett (for No. 4)
Danny Bolt (for No. 9)	13	
Paul Brooker (for No. 4)	14	

The board's choice as manager was the former Reading and Southampton manager, Ian Branfoot. He had endured a torrid time at The Dell and Fulham supporters (and there was an average crowd of just over 4,000 in his first season) were not slow to voice their disapproval at the appointment. Branfoot did little to endear himself to the fans but the players who worked under him compared him very favourably with his predecessors. He added some much needed discipline and fought for the players with the club administration. Among his signings, as player coach, was Micky Adams, who was Branfoot's successor and led Fulham to promotion in 1997. Yet several of the key players date Branfoot's tenure as the turning point.

It was true, nevertheless, that there was a more physical edge to the Cottagers' game in the League basement division and it was reflected in the signings he made. Terry Hurlock, in fact, received a record number of bookings in 1994–95. Results were disappointing and Fulham rarely aspired to much above mid-table. By Christmas, with just six wins in 20 games, it was clear an early return to the (new) Second Division would have to be put on hold. It got worse in 1995–96, with only five wins in the first half of the season (23 games) and an air of despondency hung over the Cottage.

Remarkably, however, Fulham made history in the FA Cup. In 1995–96, they drew Second Division Swansea in the first round at home, the club which had pushed them

The introduction of substitute Paul Brooker was the turning point in the game.

down 18 months earlier. Revenge of a sort was achieved when the Cottagers won 7–0, which is the biggest win ever recorded over a side from a higher division in the history of the FA Cup. It was a result which, but for an early injury and substitution, might not have happened. But it brought welcome relief to the Cottage and is one of four FA Cup records the club holds. This win remains Fulham's biggest winning margin in an FA Cup tie (although beating Luton 8–3 in January 1908 is the biggest score).

SEVEN GOAL SENSATION

Fulham fans may feel aggrieved the Match Of The Day 'comprehensive' coverage of The Road To Wembley ignored one of the day's more remarkable results, but manager Ian Branfoot probably couldn't care less.

He might well have had 'vindicated' on his forehead as he basked in the glory of Fulham's record FA Cup

Paul's Ryan mighty

Fulham boss Ian Branfoot has unearthed a Ryan Giggs in the making.

Sub Paul Brooker, 18, scored a wonder goal to cap a majestic performance that gave Fulham their biggest-ever FA Cup victory and ended a run of 14 games without a win.

Branfoot said: "The lad is very exciting. He has so much potential and can go all the way."

Brooker, yet to make his full debut, was discarded by Chelsea. But they will regret it if the magic he produced here after coming on in the 18th minute for the injured Lee Barkus is anything to go by.

Within seconds, he was set free down the right to attack Swansea full-back Andy Cook.

A split second later, Cook had been turned twice and left in a dazed heap on the ground as the whizkid winger sped by.

He followed that with another mazy run into the Swan's area, beating four defenders in the process. And he capped his breathtaking performance with a rasping 78th minute volley.

Weights

Fulham skipper Simon Morgan declared "He is something special. We can all see that.

"He is very level headed and, if he keeps progressing, there is no telling where he can end up.

"He is only 5ft 7in and looks like he weighs nothing. He reminds me as much off Pat Nevin as Ryan Giggs and has a mature footballing brain."

Swansea, behind from the third minute, were slaughtered. Boss Bobby Smith admitted: "We were a disgrace. That performance hurt me deeply.

"What we need are footballers at this club, not that lot."

A hat-trick from Mike Conroy and further strikes from Duncan Jupp, Nick Cusack and Martin Thomas completed the scoring.

win. Branfoot said this performance had been coming for a few weeks, but nobody could have envisaged this.

The carnage began after two minutes, ironically after Tony Lange denied Swansea's Steve Torpey. The Fulham keeper promptly kicked up field, Nick Cusack headed on and Mike Conroy beat Swansea keeper Roger Freestone with ease.

Conroy's second came 16 minutes later when Freestone failed to hold on to a Martin Thomas shot from 20 yards out. The ball fell invitingly to Conroy for a simple tap-in. After 28 minutes Fulham were three up. Simon Morgan mistimed his jump to meet a Brazil corner, and when Christian Edwards failed to clear, Duncan Jupp scored from eight yards.

Fulham's only concern at this stage was the withdrawal of Lee Barkus after 19 minutes but the introduction of Paul Brooker gave Fulham even more impetus. After Lange made a superb double save on the half hour to deny Torpey, the second half saw Brooker opening up the Swansea defence at will.

Torpey could have made a game of it after 54 minutes when he screwed his effort wide, but Conroy's hat-trick, completed on the hour, sealed Swansea's fate. Again it was a Cusack flick at the near post which caused the panic in the Swansea ranks and Conroy bundled the ball home.

Cussack then got in on the act, placing a low drive past the hapless Freestone before Brooker got his reward for a fine individual display. A cross from substitute Danny Bolt after 80 minutes found Brooker at the far post to blast the ball home but that merely preceded the best of the magnificent seven.

It came five minutes from time, courtesy of a rasping drive from Thomas when he met a cross from Robbie Herrera.

Torquay United 2 v Fulham 1

Saturday 3 February 1996
Football League Division Three
Referee: G. Singh
Attendance: 2,594

TORQUAY U		FULHAM
Ray Newland	1	Martin Lange
Steve Winter	2	Duncan Jupp
Scott Stamps	3	Robbie Herrera
Ian Gore	4	Nick Cusack
Alex Watson	5	Kevin Moore
Paul Ramsey	6	Mark Blake
Lee Barrow	7	Martin Thomas
Charlie Oatway	8	Rod McAree
Paul Baker	9	Mike Conroy
Simon Garner	10	Rob Scott
Ian Hathaway	11	Phil Barber
Mark Hall (for No. 4)	12	Rory Hamill (for No. 7)
Richard Hancox (for No. 11)	14	John Marshall (for No. 10)

Football clubs are quick to celebrate and remember their biggest achievements, and for the likes of Fulham there has often been a long wait for trophies and honours. But where there are highs, there are also lows and it is remembering the worst of times that makes the best of times so enjoyable. Fortunately for the Cottagers, the low point was followed very quickly by a big revival in their fortunes, although in February 1996, most supporters would have said the Conference was a more likely destination for Fulham in the next five years than the Premiership.

If the darkest hour really is just before the dawn, then for the Cottage faithful it was the last week of January and the first of February that year. With half the season gone (23 games), Branfoot's team had recorded just five wins and they were plummeting down the table. And then it got worse. In that fortnight, there were three matches, and all were lost, the first at Mansfield and the second in midweek at home to Scunthorpe. On a freezing cold night, this game attracted just 2,176 people to the Cottage, the lowest-ever official attendance for a first class game at the Cottage.

Only Torquay separated three clubs, Fulham among them, on 26 points from the 92nd place in the Football League. And as luck would have it, the Cottagers travelled to Plainmoor in February for a vital game. When they returned from Devon on the wrong end of a 2–1 scoreline, the table showed Fulham next to bottom of the fourth tier of the League, the lowest placing since joining in 1907. It was clear that time was running out for Branfoot. When, the following week, the club had to settle for a draw at home to Hartlepool having led 2–0, the change was made. Coach Micky Adams stepped up to his first managerial job, while Branfoot became General Manager. The switch worked, and Adams steered his charges to enough points to finish 17th, still the lowest ever, but welcome relief after the winter darkness.

Manager Ian Branfoot came under enormous pressure after this result.

Garner thunderbolt leaves Fulham in lowest ever position

All at sea...

FULHAM'S season reached a new nadir on Saturday when Ian Branfoot's side were not only defeated by the League's bottom club but sent to their lowest ever League position - 91st.

A team already creating unwelcome history for the club are now finding the realisation of playing football in the Vauxhall Conference next season an alarming possibility.

Fulham were never short of effort in the most important game of their season so far, but how they could use the type of quality conjured up by Simon Garner eight minutes from the end of this contest which snatched the points for the Gulls.

In fact the match was barely a minute old when Torquay found the necessary penetration to puncture the visitors' defence.

Ian Hathaway sent in a low cross which allowed Paul Barker to sweep the ball past Tony Lange in the Fulham goal.

With Fulham already at sixes and sevens, Baker nearly doubled his tally after five minutes and it took Fulham a full 20 minutes to find the shape to create an opening.

Nick Cusack, switched to the midfield role he played against Brighton in the FA Cup Second Round replay, exchanged a neat one-two with Phil Barber but his long-range shot went well wide.

However, Fulham's efforts to get back into the match paid dividends on the half hour.

A long throw by Rob Scott found Rod McAree whose shot was pushed away by Torquay 'keeper Ray Newland. The resulting corner by Martin Thomas was flicked on by Kevin Moore and Mike Conroy scored at the near post.

Just before the interval, a Cusack cross was met athletically by Thomas but his header lacked the power to produce anything more than a comfortable save from Newland.

Fulham were beginning to take the upper hand but were unable to completely dominate.

Torquay winger Mark Hall remained a constant menace for Fulham full-back Robbie Herrera, while Mark Blake and Kevin Moore never found the composure to do more than boot the ball out of defence at the earliest opportunity.

The influential Cusack was yet again involved in Fulham's first serious attack of the second half.

His nod down set up Conroy but the striker saw his shot beat Newland only for the Torquay defence to clear the danger.

Soon after Fulham may feel they were unlucky not to win a penalty when Newland's indesision allowed Scott to steal in only for the Fulham striker to be felled inside the area.

However referee Gurnam Singh was having none of it and simply waved play on.

With Branfoot sensing that three points and their first away win were up for grabs, he brought on Rory Hamill for Thomas and was subsequently forced into a second substitution when John Marshall replaced the injured Scott.

Yet to everyone's surprise, Torquay delivered the sucker punch on 82 minutes.

A deep cross by Steve Winter was volleyed back across goal by Richard Hancock for Simon Garner, on-loan from Wycombe, to volley emphatically past Lange.

This was an improved performance from Fulham but as the prospect of relegation looms larger, results, and results alone, are all that matters now.

FULHAM HIT ROCK BOTTOM – ALMOST

Fulham slumped to the second bottom in Divison Three, the lowest position in their long history, after a rock-bottom performance at Torquay United on Saturday.

Torquay are now the only team between Fulham and the Vauxhall Conference, and the Devon club are just six points behind the Whites after this vital victory.

The table makes miserable reading for Fulham and although manager Ian Branfoot insists they do not deserve to be so low, it is little consolation for the club's long-suffering fans.

Ironically, Fulham did more than enough to clinch three points in Plainmoor on Saturday. They dominated for long periods, particularly in the first half, and wasted several very presentable chances. But their cause was not helped by conceding a goal in the very first minute by Paul Baker. Mike Conroy did equalize for the visitors, when he pounced from close range after Kevin Moore had flicked on a 30th minute corner. But Fulham wasted the other chances that came their way. First, Martin Thomas saw his shot saved and Conroy failed to reach the rebound.

And then Phil Barber failed to make the most of a one-on-one minutes later. Inevitably, Torquay took heart and grabbed victory when veteran striker Simon Garner (on loan from Wycombe) lashed home a 82nd minute winner. "I thought we at least deserved a draw" groaned manager Branfoot. "Tony Lange didn't have a shot to save apart from the two goals. The problem is we aren't converting our chances. We created more chances in the last three games than in the previous ten. But we haven't scored from them." Striker Conroy, who moved into double figures for the season with his strike, also produced some fighting talk. He said: "We are bitterly disappointed. We were caught cold early on but I thought we rallied well and we were unfortunate not to get a share of the spoils. But if we carry on performing like we have in the last three games, there is no reason why we can't move up the table."

Fulham 3 v Doncaster Rovers 1

Saturday 12 October 1996
Football League Division Three
Referee: G.R. Pooley
Attendance: 5,516

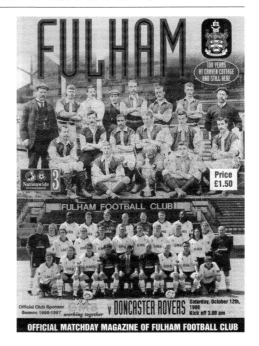

FULHAM		DONCASTER R
Mark Walton	1	Dean Williams
Paul Watson	2	Jamie Murphy
Robbie Herrera	3	Tim Ryan
Nick Cusack	4	Darren Moore
Terry Angus	5	Ian Gore
Mark Blake	6	Ian Clark
Rob Scott	7	John Schofield
Richard Carpenter	8	Martin McDonald
Mike Conroy	9	Scott Colcombe
Simon Morgan	10	Colin Cramb
Darren Freeman	11	Paul Birch
Micky Adams (for No. 7)	12	Steve Pearce (for No. 3)
	13	Jack Lester (for No. 6)

Striker Micky Conroy who had a purple patch in the first half the 1996–97 promotion season.

With six wins in their first seven games, Fulham were surprisingly among the pacesetters in the Third Division. Manager Micky Adams had made some cheap and shrewd signings (Paul Watson, Danny Cullip, Glenn Cockerill and Darren Freeman) while striker Mike Conroy enjoyed a purple patch, scoring 17 League goals by Boxing Day. The Cottagers were never out of the promotion pack and their away form was remarkable. The six straight away wins recorded between August and October is a club record.

Off the pitch, it started to come right as well. This match against Doncaster reminded supporters that the future of the Cottage was still undecided. The day of the Rovers game was the closest date to the 100th anniversary of the first match on the ground, against Minerva in the Middlesex Senior Cup in October 1896, a game Fulham won 4–0. Few clubs in Britain were so closely associated with their home ground, the ownership of which had been a threat to Fulham's existence since 1987. Behind the scenes, a divided board of directors struggled to find a solution. Clay had sold out to Marler Estates in 1987, who in turn had sold to Cabra Estates. This company, run by John Duggan, fell victim to the early 1990s recession and, after a compulsory purchase order by the local council was rejected at an inquiry, the title reverted to the Royal Bank of Scotland. Director and former player, Tom Wilson, a senior figure in the property industry in the City, was on the threshold of agreeing a deal to buy Craven Cottage for the club, the first time Fulham would have owned their own home.

Since the Leitch redevelopment of 1905, the only major change had been the building of the Riverside Stand, agreed when the club was in the top flight but completed when it was in the (old) Third Division. The outstanding debt to McAlpines the builders had created an opportunity for several businessmen to exploit for their own advantage and at the club's expense. This, like the slide down the divisions, was about to come to an end.

Scott beams up

Rob helps Fulham celebrate centenary in spectacular fashion

The home hoodoo was not only laid to rest but buried by two of the finest goals Craven Cottage witnessed in its 100 year history on Saturday. The stars of the past were paraded in its centenary programme, but forget Johnny Haynes and George Cohen. It was Rob Scott and Richard Carpenter who made the fans gasp on Saturday.

Scott admitted that his 30 yard thunderbolt in the 64th minute was "the best strike of my career." The forward added: "I didn't bother to look. I was already running back to the centre celebrating." Skipper Simon Morgan made light of media reports which stated Robbie Herrera had scored the goal. He said: "At least your paper will get it right – how can you mistake a Colombian drug dealer for a pretty boy!" The ball cannoned off the underside of the bar and struck the back of keeper Dean Williams, but it still deserved to win the game single handedly.

Six minutes later Carpenter did his best to better his team-mate's effort. A one-two played with Nick Cusack found Micky Adams' latest signing striding on to the return pass and he unleashed a 20 yard effort which neither hit Williams' back, or any other part of his anatomy, as it smashed into the back of the net.

Both followed Mike Conroy's 10th goal of the season which wasn't spectacular but underlined the confidence of a team seriously beginning to believe in itself.

In the 51st minute, a Scott howitzer throw-in caused panic in the Doncaster penalty area. The ball fell to Simon Morgan who shaped to blast but instead played a clever chip to the right to find an unmarked Conroy to head home.

Any latecomers who missed the first 45 minutes were lucky. The best action before then was before the game when Conroy's wife Sarah and daughter Megan released thousands of black and white balloons to mark the ground's landmark.

Rovers had started the more lively and forced three corners in the opening minutes. It was fitting that they had the last word in the game through veteran Paul Birch who wall passed with substitute Jack Lester before rifling a low right foot drive past Mark Walton in the 82nd minute.

Doncaster striker Colin Cramb, a team-mate of Adams at Southampton, got his marching orders in the 58th minute after he went for defender Terry Angus. His manager, Kerry Dixon, said: "He will be fined. Until then it was finely balanced but his red card handed Fulham the game."

FULHAM CELEBRATE 100 YEARS IN STYLE

Fulham celebrated 100 years at Craven Cottage by going top of Division 3 on Saturday. The Whites scored three classy goals to see off Doncaster and move into pole position ahead of Cambridge. It was a game of landmarks for Mickey Adams men because the game also saw Mickey Conroy move into double figures for the season and Rob Scott scores his first League goal of the campaign. Fulham found it tough going early on but they held out well against a lively Doncaster side, managed by former Chelsea favourite Kerry Dixon.

Having kept the score at 0–0 at half time (thanks in part to a goal line clearance from Conroy), Fulham stepped up a gear after the break.

Conroy made it 1–0 when he headed home a back-post cross from skipper Simon Morgan in the 51st minute. It was his 10th goal of the season and the veteran striker was delighted. He said: "It's nice to hit double figures and to do it a month or two before Christmas is a bonus. It was a difficult one to finish because I had to gamble with the sun, it is very bright at the end of the pitch. But I got my head to the ball and it ended up in the net. It's a big boost for us to go top of the League and we're ready to take on all-comers."

Conroy certainly impressed Doncaster's Kerry Dixon, who had a special message for him after the match. He said "I was impressed with Fulham, especially the three up front. I have to say that Mick Conroy is the best striker we've come across this year." Rob Scott made it 2–0 Fulham when his 30-yard thunderbolt crashed off the bar and in the net. And new boy Richard Carpenter repeated the trick with another long-range effort in the 70th minute.

Afterwards Scott said the teams were delighted with the result: "We were a bit shaky at first, but we ground it out until half-time and then moved a little.

"We played well as a unit, including the guys at the back and we are always confident about scoring goals. I'll certainly be shooting from anywhere from now on."

Carlisle United 1 v Fulham 2

Saturday 5 April 1997
Football League Division Three
Referee: E.K. Wolstenholme
Attendance: 9,171

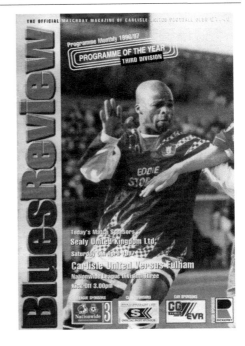

CARLISLE U		FULHAM
Tony Caig	1	Mark Walton
Tony Hopper	2	Matt Lawrence
Owen Archdeacon	3	Danny Cullip
Dean Walling	4	Nick Cusack
Will Varty	5	Terry Angus
Stephane Pounewatchy	6	Paul Watson
Lee Peacock	7	Rod McAree
Matt Jansen	8	Glenn Cockerill
Rory Delap	9	Simon Morgan
Steve Hayward	10	Christer Warren
Warren Aspinall	11	Mike Conroy
Rod Thomas (for No. 7)	12	Rob Scott (for No. 11)
Allan Smart (for No. 8)	13	Martin Thomas (for No. 10)

If the start date of Fulham's slide towards oblivion can be identified as the 10–0 hammering at Anfield in 1986, so can the day on which the tide finally turned be pinpointed with equal certainty. Winning at Brunton Park made promotion from the Third Division (or the fourth tier of the League) a virtual certainty, and it was the first success of any sort the club had enjoyed for 15 years. It was a remarkable personal triumph for Micky Adams in his first full season as a manager, moulding a squad of veterans, journeyman, cheap signings and promising youngsters into a promotion winning unit when the previous season the team was threatened with non-League football.

Although the Cottagers made an impressive start to the campaign, there was a bit of a wobble in the winter months when four of five matches were lost. A dramatic late win over Swansea (the team that had sent them down), thanks to a Paul Brooker goal, stopped the rot. Just one of the remaining 14 games was lost. This was a home defeat to Northampton days after promotion was mathematically clinched at Mansfield. The celebrations had taken their toll but the unexpected defeat cost the club the divisional title. In the next four years, they would win the Championships of Divisions Two and One, and this defeat cost the club a third in five seasons.

There were three teams running neck and neck most of the season, Carlisle and Fulham, together with Wigan. So the trip to Cumbria was vital and the victory every bit as thrilling as the Cup win 22 years earlier. It meant just one more point was needed to be certain and that came days later in midweek at Field Mill. After 46 games, Wigan finished top and Fulham second on the same number of points. Carlisle were third. That summer, the purchase of the ground was completed and Mohamed Al Fayed bought the club. A new era was about to start and Adams' reward for promotion was to be replaced by Kevin Keegan.

Promotion was a personal triumph for skipper Simon Morgan.

McAree puts Fulham on course for promotion

If he never hits another goal like it Rod McAree will treasure his wonder strike which set up Fulham's first promotion party for 15 years.

The Irish midfielder playing his first game since September 21 caught the ball in the sweet spot after Simon Morgan and Christer Warren had combined to set him up in the 55th minute. Carlisle keeper Tony Craig might have seen it coming but could nothing to stop the 25-yard rocket which flew past his right hand.

The 2,000 Fulham fans went wild when only six minutes earlier it looked as if their 680-mile round trip had all been in vain as Fulham went a goal down.

Fulham trailed by a 20th minute header from Rory Delap after an even opening had swung Carlisle's way. McAree then played a leading part in the equaliser four minutes earlier. His far post cross was met by Danny Cullip who headed back across goal for Mike Conroy to out-jump two defenders on the line. Boss Micky Adams had been dealt a treble body-blow when injuries to Richard Carpenter and Darren Freemen forced them on to the sidelines alongside suspended Mark Blake.

Having lost the spine of his team, the manager opted to attack and drafted McAree and Glenn Cockerill into the team. It proved an inspired choice.

Cockerill, who made a surprise recovery from a calf injury, was the one Fulham player who put his foot on the ball and set up the few half chances that fell to McAree.

At the other end, Mark Walton made the save of his life from a one-on-one with Warren Aspinall after 14 minutes. Walton then tipped over a Steve Hayward free-kick as referee Eddie Wolstenholme took a leading role in the action. By half time, he had booked five players and at the end had filled up his yellow card with five more – 6- 4 in Fulham's disfavour.

Even though the fussy official frequently halted the play he couldn't stop the heart-stopping action in the second half.

With Fulham ahead, Carlisle woke up and the unlucky Aspinall hit the underside of the bar before Nick Cusack mis-scooped against his own post before Wolstenholme mercifully brought the proceedings to an end.

Rod McAree

Aston Villa 0 v Fulham 2

Saturday 23 January 1999
FA Cup Round Four
Referee: D. Elleray
Attendance: 35,260

ASTON VILLA		FULHAM
Michael Oakes	1	Maik Taylor
Ugo Ehiogu	2	Wayne Collins
Gareth Southgate	3	Rufus Brevett
Gareth Barry	4	Simon Morgan
Steve Watson	5	Chris Coleman
Riccardo Scimeca	6	Kit Symons
Ian Taylor	7	Steve Hayward
Lee Hendrie	8	Paul Bracewell
Alan Wright	9	Geoff Horsfield
Julian Joachim	10	Paul Peschisolido
Paul Merson	11	Steve Finnan
Darius Vassell (for No. 9)	12	Neil Smith (for No. 10)

The Fayed Revolution kicked off in September 1997, and started with a flurry of activity. Kevin Keegan was enticed out of 'retirement' to be Chief Operating Officer and he brought in Ray Wilkins as team manager. Players were signed for unheard of sums, Ian Selly for £500,000 followed weeks later by Fulham's first £1 million fee (Paul Peschisolido) and then Chris Coleman for close on £2 million – all in the first three months. This influx of expensive talent, however, did not lead to an improvement in results immediately. Although Fulham made the Play-offs in May 1998, they lost out to Grimsby.

It was the following season that the Cottagers clicked into top gear. Wilkins went and Keegan took over responsibility for the team. Not only was 1998–99 a record-breaking season in the League for the club but there were also some impressive Cup results which suggested Fulham were well equipped to play at a higher level. Premier side Southampton were beaten in both the League (Worthington) Cup and FA Cup, even though the draw had given Saints home advantage. But the most impressive performance was the fourth round FA Cup win at Villa Park, the first Cup meeting of the two clubs since Fulham were thrashed in the non-League era of 1905. It was the first time since joining the League in 1907 that Fulham had beaten a team two divisions higher in the Cup.

Keegan's team travelled to meet the side that was then leading the Premier table. But the day started badly for the hosts when Dion Dublin was ruled out by injury and Stan Collymore was sent home by manager John Gregory for refusing to be a substitute. The Fulham goals were scored by a Birmingham City supporter (Simon Morgan) and an ex-Villa's junior (Steve Hayward). In the end it was a comfortable and convincing victory, the reward for which was a trip to Old Trafford in round five. Despite fielding a much-depleted team, Fulham gave United a scare. Although they lost 1–0, they were just a John Salako toenail away from snatching a draw.

One of the scorers against Villa, Simon Morgan.

HAYWARD THE HAPPY VILLA SUPPORTER

Steve Hayward's footballing pedigree is hardly unique. He was born, for instance, in the same year as Stan Collymore, brought up in a neighbouring part of the Midlands and may well have rubbed shoulders with the £7m enigma on the Holte End. On Saturday night, however, Hayward was probably the only Aston Villa supporter out celebrating the club's demise in the FA Cup.

With speculation raging about the extent to which Collymore's no-show had affected the Premiership title contenders, there was no doubt about Hayward's contribution to the defeat of his boyhood heroes. As the driving force of Fulham's midfield, he created the first goal for Birmingham City supporting Simon Morgan and claimed the second himself after his free kick took a deflection off Paul Peschisolido.

It was, said Hayward with great understatement, his greatest day since arriving at Fulham from Carlisle shortly before the advent of Mohammed Al Fayed and Kevin Keegan late in 1997. As a boy he had watched Villa and trained with them before committing himself to Derby, while last week his spare time had been eaten up by the problem of acquiring more than 50 tickets for his extended family.

Whatever they cost, it was worth the outlay. Once the goal bridge-head to the last 16 had been established, the control exerted by the Second Division promotion favourites was so complete that beating the side who have led the Premiership virtually all season never really felt like a giant killer.

Hayward, who also scored at Southampton in the third round, reasoned that teams from the top flight are not accustomed to being "hustled and hassled" the way Fulham snapped at Villa's heels. They also allowed opponents "more room to play", which was surely an indictment of John Greggory's side on the day rather than the Premiership as a whole.

The scorer of the second goal against Villa, Steve Hayward.

Kevin Keegan, still working under the nonsensical title of chief operating officer, was equally effusive. Apart from Liverpool's Wembley triumph 25 years ago, the Cup had not been kind to Fulham's managers, but it now offers them a welcome respite from their role as the Manchester United, the moneybags, of the lowest Leagues.

"We were totally relaxed" said Keegan. "It was the exact opposite of what we experienced in the League every week. The boot was on the other foot. But what really pleased me was the way we played. We weren't scrambling around, but playing properly. The better the quality of the opposition, the better we play".

That much was perhaps to be expected, given that Keegan has lavished some £10m on upgrading the Craven Cottage squad. Like Hayward's ticket-scrounging, it looked like money well spent, with no one more impressive than the £2.1m captain, Chris Coleman, at the heart of an unflappable three-man defensive unit.

Fulham 3 v Preston North End 0

Saturday 7 May 1999
Football League Division Two
Referee: P.S. Dawson
Attendance: 17,176

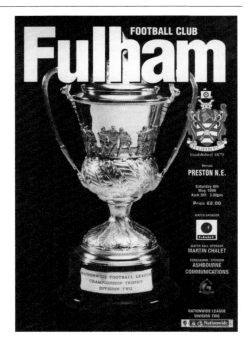

FULHAM		PRESTON NE
Maik Taylor	1	David Lucas
Jamie Smith	2	Graham Alexander
Rufus Brevett	3	Ryan Kidd
Simon Morgan	4	Colin Murdock
Chris Coleman	5	Michael Jackson
Kit Symons	6	Sean Gregan
Steve Hayward	7	Paul McKenna
Neil Smith	8	Mark Rankine
Dirk Lehmann	9	Jonathan Macken
Wayne Collins	10	Jason Harris
Barry Hayles	11	Michael Appleton
Gus Unlenbeek (for No. 8)	12	Julian Darby (for No. 8)
Steve McAnespie (for No. 2)	13	Steve Basham (for No. 10)
Paul Moody (for No. 9)	14	

Phase One of the Fayed Revolution was completed in a little under two years. Exactly 50 years all but a day since they had first won the Second Division title, the Cottagers were again presented with the divisional trophy (now the third tier), the club's first piece of silverware since 1949. Promotion had been clinched against Gillingham with six games to spare and the title the following week against Millwall with four games still to go. With Keegan in sole charge, Fulham swept all before them, setting a new points total record for the division (101) and finishing 14 points clear of second-placed Walsall. They were also the highest scorers in Division Two and had the best defensive record.

Against Preston, they signed off in style, and against a club (managed by David Moyes) that had made the Play-offs and had won 10 away games. But the visitors were not going to spoil the party or put a damper on the carefully orchestrated, Harrods-inspired celebrations that took place after the final whistle. The largest League crowd of the season (and the best for 16 years) saw Fulham record their 19th home win in that memorable campaign. But while it was clear that Keegan had assembled an expensive squad that could compete at a higher level, it was one of the old stagers who stole show. Paul Moody had been one of Micky Adams' last signings but his time at the Cottage was dogged by injury and then he fell out of favour. This was his final Fulham appearance.

There was just one discordant note at the party. A few weeks earlier, manager Keegan had decided to take over the England job following Glenn Hoddle's resignation. What had upset the club and supporters were the mixed signals Keegan had been sending out about the job, sometimes saying he wanted to stay at the Cottage or sometimes that he could do both jobs before deciding to go, and announcing it on television. Viewed in retrospect, it was not untypical behaviour and perhaps the final decision was one that he and many others ultimately regretted.

A hat-trick in his finale, Paul Moody got all three against Preston.

Moody farewell

Kevin Keegan made an emotional farewell to Fulham yesterday with some fans calling him "Judas" and others giving him a standing ovation.

But substitute Moody hit a remarkable second-half hat-trick in 12 minutes to make sure Fulham's championship celebrations went with a bang.

It was a triumph for the striker who was playing only his second game since breaking a leg eight months ago. Yet for Keegan this was more of a bitter farewell than a fond return.

After the match he explained that he was told to stay away from the game because there were fears for his own safety.

Keegan said : "I was advised by Neil Rodford our MD not to come today for my own safetly. He had seen the reaction of fans on the internet following my announcement that I was leaving the club to become full-time England coach.

"But I wasn't going to hide. The fans had a go at me today yet I have no regrets.

"It would have been wrong not to have been here to accept the criticism."

Keegan, Fulham's departing chief operating officer, denied that there had been a bust up between him and chairman Mohamed Al Fayed at the training ground on Friday.

He insisted: "I did not speak to the chairman when he came to the training ground.

"Our relationship is just as good as when I started and he is perfectly entitled to talk about compensation from the FA."

Keegan added: "Tonight's party at Harrods is me finished with Fulham. Now it is up to a new man to take them into the Premier League.

"Perhaps sometime in the future people will give the staff the credit they deserve for what we have achieved in winning the Division Two championship.

"We finished with 101 points and that is only one point short of the record.

"And we have gained the first piece of silverware to go in the Cottage trophy cabinet for 50 years."

If there was any ill-feeling between Fulham and Keegan it did not show in the on-pitch championship celebrations as Al Fayed welcomed him on to the presentation platform.

But Keegan refused to take a medal and gave it to his assistant Frank Sibley who, together with coach Paul Bracewell, is waiting anxiously to find out if they will figure in the plans of the new boss.

That will probably be Ruud Gullit or Italian Fabio Capello.

Preston finished with a terrible run of only one win in their last nine games and so blew their chance of automatic promotion.

But manager David Moyes said: "It's an achievement to get into the play-offs and we can still go up."

Defences dominated the first half but Keegan changed everything with a masterly substitution in replacing Lehmann with Moody for the second half.

Moody put Fulham ahead within 19 minutes by heading home a left wing cross from Brevett.

The substitute striker then converted a 74th minute penalty after Hayles burst through, only to be brought down by Alexander.

Moody completed his hat-trick two minutes later, heading in Hayward's free kick to send the 17,176 crowd wild with delight.

Preston skipper Sean Gregan, a target for Villa, Leicester, West Ham and Wimbledon, set up chances for Rankine and on-loan substitute Basham but they were foiled by keeper Taylor. And Fulham's party took off.

Kevin Keegan donned a tin helmet and defied furious Fulham fans to wave an emotional goodbye to the club he is quitting.

Keegan ignored managing director Neil Rodford's pleas for him not to attend the match for his own safety after supporters left angry messages on the internet. But the former Newcastle manager, now ready to take up the England job full time, insisted that only a death threat would have prevented him from taking up his position in the dugout for the last time at Craven Cottage.

Fulham's players gave him the perfect send-off with a hat-trick from Paul Moody helping the champions burst through the 100-point barrier. But Keegan had to endure the anger of fans who thought he had let them down. They yelled "Judas" at him as he walked onto the pitch both before and after the game. Yet Keegan was adamant that nothing would prevent him from enjoying the last day of an incredible season along with his players and Chairman Mohamed Al Fayed.

Keegan joined the players for their medal ceremony at the end, climbing on to the podium for photographs. When Fayed presented him with a medal, Keegan gave it to his right-hand man Frank Sibley. He also joined the party laid on for the promotional heroes at Harrods. Clearly drained at the end of an extremely difficult day, Keegan said: "These fans are entitled to their opinions. They pay their money and have every right to air their views. But I'm not going to let what a few people think of me ruin this occasion. I'm bigger and stronger than that. Neil Rodford had read out a few things fans have said on the internet. But I've never been one to look at the internet or let that bother me. I had a hostile reception when I signed and something of a hostile one now I've left. But I enjoyed the bit in the middle very much. I still believe I've done things in the right way. I have no regrets. There is no easy way of leaving. There is no split between myself and Mr. Fayed. I leave on terms as good as when I first arrived. I would love nothing more than to see Fulham promoted to the Premiership. I firmly believe they can do that."

Asked why he gave his medal to Sibley, Keegan said: "It just wasn't the real McCoy. Just one made up for the presentation. We get the real ones tonight at the party."

While emotions ran high on the pitch, Moody enjoyed his own party on it with a glorious comeback hat-trick.

Moody, making his first appearance for eight months due to a broken leg, came on in the second half and left Preston begging for mercy with two headers and a penalty.

Fulham 3 v Tottenham Hotspur 1

Wednesday 1 December 1999
Worthington Cup Fourth Round
Referee: D. Gallagher
Attendance: 18,134

FULHAM		TOTTENHAM H
Maik Taylor	1	Ian Walker
Gus Uhlenbeek	2	Justin Edinburgh
Rufus Brevett	3	Mauricio Taricco
Andy Melville	4	Steffen Freund
Chris Coleman	5	Sol Campbell
Kit Symons	6	Chris Perry
Wayne Collins	7	David Ginola
Lee Clark	8	Tim Sherwood
Geoff Horsfield	9	Chris Armstrong
Barry Hayles	10	Steffen Iverson
Steve Hayward	11	Oyvind Leonhardson
Paul Trollope (for No. 7)	12	Luke Young (for No. 2)
	13	Ramon Vega (for No. 6)
	14	Jose Dominguez (for No. 9)

Geoff Horsfield ran the Spurs' defence ragged and inspred Fulham's win.

After Keegan's departure, the club promoted Paul Bracewell to his first managerial job. A player for Keegan at Newcastle before both signed for Fulham, he was an unknown quantity as a manager but offered the advantage of continuity. His early forays into the transfer market were promising, getting Stan Collymore from Villa and Stephen Hughes from Arsenal on loan with the possibility of buying, and also paying a club record £3 million to his old club Sunderland for Lee Clark. Of the three, Clark proved excellent value but the other two went back at the end of the loan period.

Bracewell, however, had one huge disadvantage compared with Keegan – he was boring, very very boring. After the Cavalier football of Keegan, this was very much the turn of the Roundheads. Even though Fulham were playing at a higher level, their first back in the second tier for 13 years, the fans (and the chairman) expected more than four consecutive goalless draws and a 2–0 - defeat, the outcome of five League fixtures in December. In fact, only four times in Bracewell's 39 League games at the helm did Fulham score at least three in a game and 15 times they failed to find the net at all. The manager's lease on the job was brought to an abrupt end at the end of March and for the remaining seven games, the German World Cup player, Karlheinz Reidle acted as caretaker.

But there were moments of cheer and none more so than this victory over Spurs in the League (Worthington) Cup. This was only the fifth Cup meeting of the two London clubs in 90 years (three in the FA Cup and now two in the League Cup), and it was Fulham's first win. And the manner of the victory showed that when the side played without the caution so obvious in the League, it could beat the best. George Graham's Spurs were a top six Premiership side but that night, they were made to look very ordinary, and their defence had no answer to a rampant Geoff Horsfield.

Spurs Have No Answer To Horsfield

Mohamed Al Fayed has never been to Wembley with Fulham – even though he is rich enough to buy it – but this could be his season.

As Tottenham's custody of the Worthington Cup came to a desultory end at Craven Cottage last night, Fulham's owner became the richest cheerleader in the history of cup upsets.

Al Fayed's heroes played with the kind of panache you expect to find in his Harrods food hall.

But Spurs – hopeless, hapless and complacent beyond belief – defended with all the savvy of refugees from a greasy spoon cafe.

WORST

Their goose was cooked when Geoff Horsfield sprang Tottenham's offside trap 13 minutes from time to seal the worst night of George Graham's reign.

Fulham had served notice on the Premiership's big guns that they were not to be taken lightly when knocking Southampton and Aston Villa out of last season's FA Cup.

Those triumphs masterminded by Kevin Keegan, brought Al Fayed swaying into the dressing room to distribute chocolate bars the shape of gold bullion to his players.

And the confectionary stall will take another pounding after this memorable evening by the Thames.

Just 18 months ago, Horsfield was a part-time centre-forward with homely Halifax and had to work as a hod carrier to make ends meet. He would often return from trips to the unglamorous backwaters of Welling, Woking or Yeovil at 3am and be back among the bricks and mortar of the building site three hours later. Even when Keegan shelled out £300,000 of Al Fayed's petty cash to bring Horsfield to Fulham 14 months ago, people who had never seen him play laughed when Keegan spoke of him as a potential England striker.

But look at him now. Leicester have already had a £2.5 million bid rejected and the way Horsfield roughed up Sol Campbell has probably added another nought to his market value.

Spurs? They were hopeless. Normally you have to wait until the Varsity Boat Race to see clueless twits shambling along the Thames near Putney Bridge. They got precisely what they deserved – nothing – and, in the end, their defence of the Worthington Cup was no more spirited than Manchester United's desertion of the FA Cup.

No wonder the fans who trekked across the capital to watch this languid garbage gave them such an earful as they shuffled off at the final whistle.

Fulham had subjected their supporters to a loyalty quiz, when they put tickets on general sale for this turn-up, fearing they may fall into eager North London hands.

Their starter for ten last night was: Who were the imposters Premiership side? Answers on a postcard, please.

And for a bonus point, can anyone tell me who clocked Marico Taricco in the fifth minute melee which set the tone for Tottenham's miserable display and proved they did not have the stomach for a fight.

The shoving match followed Chris Coleman's gratuitous body-check on David Ginola Certainly there was no conferring between referee Dermot Gallagher and his linesman and, once Taricco had dusted himself down, Steve Hayward was the only player booked.

REFLEX

Within seconds, Fulham keeper Maik Taylor had pulled off a fabulous reflex save to thwart Chris Perry's header from Ginola's left-wing cross.

The holders were still trying to work out how Taylor kept Perry's efforts out when they fell behind after nine minutes. Graham will be holding a steward's enquiry into the marking shambles which allowed Wayne Collins two stabs at Horsfield's near-post centre without a defender in sight.

Although Ian Walker managed to hold the fort for a while, he had no time to phone a friend for help and Barry Hayles buried the rebound from five yards. Down in the dugout, Graham looked baffled by Fulham's tenacity. And on the pitch, his players were none the wiser, bemused from the moment an excitable interloper in a baseball cap cantered across the pitch during their pre-match kick-in, waving a Fulham scarf like a matador's red rag.

Any other exhibitionist would have been thrown out – but this was the proprietor of an incomparable corner shop in Knightsbridge who had lavished £30 million of his petty cash on the fixtures and fittings at Craven Cottage.

And Al Fayed loved it as his First Division upstarts set about Graham's swaggering millionaires with old-fashioned gusto. Ginola, spared the defensive chores of playing left-wing, was given license to roam by Graham. But he made little headway and it took a ghastly blunder by Taylor to gift Spurs an equaliser they barely deserved a minute before the break.

The Fulham keeper's clearance only reached Steffen Iversen, who skipped clear to pick his spot from 15 yards, his 10th goal of the season and surely the easiest.

TRIVIAL

Yet while Iverson's aim was true, this was otherwise a night on which Tottenham were incapable of completing even the most trivial tasks. And their incompetence was so rampant that they could not even hold out for the remaining 60 seconds to the interval. Hayles and Lee Clark brushed aside challenges so feeble they belonged in the same class as some of the heavyweight stiffs once fed to Frank Bruno, and Collins drilled a right-footer past Walker to restore Fulham's advantage.

Graham responded to the ineptitude of his defence during those torrid opening 45 minutes by replacing both centre-back Chris Perry and full-back Justin Edinburgh at the break.

On came Ramon Vega and Luke Young to slot into the back-four. Tottenham did at least display some more urgency, without creating clear-cut chances. With 25 minutes left, Graham's last throw of the dice was to introduce his final substitute, Jose Dominguez, for Armstrong.

Leicester City 3 v Fulham 3

(Leicester win 3–0 on penalties)
Wednesday 12 January 2000
Worthington Cup Fifth Round
Referee: M. Reed
Attendance: 13,576

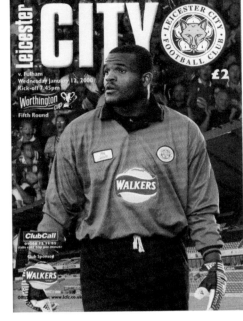

FULHAM		LEICESTER C
Maik Taylor	1	Pegguy Arphexad
Andy Melville	2	Frank Sinclair
Chris Coleman	3	Gerry Taggart
Kit Symons	4	Steve Walsh
Steve Finnan	5	Matt Elliott
Paul Trollope	6	Andy Impey
Simon Morgan	7	Robbie Savage
Wayne Collins	8	Stefan Oakes
Steve Hayward	9	Theo Zagorakis
Geoff Horsfield	10	Emile Heskey
Paul Peschisolido	11	Ian Marshall
Rufus Brevett (for No. 11)	12	Amar Gunnlaugsson (for No. 6)
	13	Phil Gilchrist (for No. 9)
	14	Graham Fenton (for No. 8)

Paul Peschisolido, Fulham's first £1 million signing, opened the scoring at Filbert Street.

Since its inception in 1960, Fulham have achieved very little in the League Cup in all its various incarnations and formats. It is a competition they have taken seriously from the very first, but have had little to show for their efforts. In 1967–68, they reached the last eight when, as a top flight club, they squandered home advantage to Second Division Huddersfield. They made it to the quarter-finals once more in 1970–71, but this time went out to Bristol City, again after having home advantage. And that was it, until 1999–2000 when victories over Northampton, Norwich, West Brom and Spurs put the Cottagers in the last eight with the prospect of a trip to Leicester, then in the top half of the Premiership, managed by Martin O'Neill and still playing at Filbert Street.

It was a meeting between out-of-form teams. Leicester had lost four and drawn one of their previous five League games and had managed three goals in 450 minutes of football. Similarly, Fulham had drawn four and won one of their previous six games, but scored just once in 540 minutes of League football, and that was an own goal by Tranmere's Roberts. A high-scoring match did not appear to be on the agenda. Fulham went into the game with several enforced changes. Lee Clark and Barry Hayles were both suspended and Paul Trollope and Paul Peschisolido came in as replacements. Simon Morgan, playing just in front of the back three, was up against his former club for the first time.

If ever Fulham had a match in which they snatched defeat from the jaws of victory, this was it. They led 2–0 with five minutes remaining and then 3–2 in extra-time. And the penalty shoot-out was just an embarrassment. This was pretty much the last moment of cheer in Bracewell's short reign. In most circumstances, mid-table would be a reasonable achievement for a club playing its first season at a higher level. Fayed's Fulham was different. The standards were higher and more challenging. How things should be done became apparent under the next manager.

LEICESTER BACK FROM THE BRINK

A pulsating Worthington Cup quarter-final was decided in the most unsatisfactory of ways when Fulham, who led 2–0 after 85 minutes, missed all their penalties in the shoot-out.

Leicester had never been ahead in the 120 minutes but they advance to the semi-finals where they will meet Aston Villa. This was Leicester's second successive Worthington Cup shoot-out victory; they beat Leeds in this manner in the last round. Yet there was no hint of the drama and excitement to come after a sterile first half. Neither was there any hint that Leicester would reach their third League Cup semi-final in four years as they trailed by two goals against a Fulham team who were withstanding everything the homeside's giant forward line, supplemented again by Matt Elliott, could throw them.

It is difficult not to feel sympathy for Fulham, who lost their nerve when it came to the crunch. The First Division club have claimed five Premiership scalps in the last 18 months and Leicester were odds-on to be number 6.

Chris Coleman and Paul Trollope put their penalties high and wide while Pegguy Arphexas saved Geoff Horsfield's effort.

Arnar Gunnlaugsson, Robbie Savage and Graham Fenton scored and Leicester were able to celebrate a victory that had looked beyond them as normal time was coming to an end. No Leicester player was more relieved than Steve Walsh who was responsible for Fulham's first two goals. Walsh lost possession on the right and after excellent work by Horsfield, Paul Peschisolido scored with a side-foot shot from near the penalty spot.

Fulham went further ahead in the 75th minute when Walsh inexplicably gave the ball to Peschisolido. Gerry Taggart got in a tackle but the ball fell to Horsfield and, with Arphexad stranded, the Fulham striker slotted the ball into an empty net.

Fulham were holding on until the 85th minute when Stephan Oakes's centre was helped by Walsh for Ian Marshall tried to score with an acrobatic bicycle kick.

Leicester were far from full strength, yet Martin O'Neill has instilled a spirit that can compensate for any lack of personnel.

Two minutes later Marshall turned provider and Walsh made amends for his earlier mistakes to score with an unstoppable half-volley.

Fulham were now on the ropes, but three minutes into extra-time they took the lead again when Coleman rose to head Steve Finnan's left-wing corner high into the net.

Just when it seemed Fulham would reach their first League Cup semi-final Marshall made it 3–3 after the visitor's defence had reacted slowly when Elliott gained possession in the penalty area. The Scot laid the ball off to Marshall who claimed his second goal.

O'Neill said afterwards: "Villa manager John Gregory was here. I think he went home with 10 minutes to go. He probably thinks they're playing Fulham."

Fulham 5 v Barnsley 1

Sunday 10 September 2000
Football League Division One
Referee: A.R. Hall
Attendance: 10,437

FULHAM		BARNSLEY
Maik Taylor	1	Kevin Miller
Steve Finnan	2	Carl Regan
Rufus Brevett	3	Chris Morgan
Andy Melville	4	Brian O'Callaghan
Chris Coleman	5	Meteo Corbo
Sean Davis	6	Mitch Ward
Bjarnie Goldbaek	7	Matty Appleby
Lee Clark	8	Darren Barnard
Louis Saha	9	Robbie Van Der Laan
Fabrice Fernandes	10	Neil Shipperley
Barry Hayles	11	Mike Sheron
Eddie Lewis (for No. 8)	12	Adrian Moses (for No. 3)
Steve Hayward (for No. 7)	13	Scott Jones (for No. 10)
Luis Boa Morte (for No. 11)	14	Alex Neil (for No. 5)

Appointing Jean Tigana to succeed Bracewell as Fulham manager was a huge surprise but proved to be an inspired choice. A brilliant midfield player in the French side that was cheated out of a place in the 1982 World Cup Final by Germany but which won the UEFA European Championship in 1984, he had achieved managerial success with Lyon and Monaco. He revolutionised affairs on his arrival at the Cottage, from diet, to training, to playing. And his opening months saw what was probably the best football ever played by a Fulham team at Craven Cottage. Opponents were simply brushed aside as Fulham marched imperiously to the First Division title and back into the top flight.

From the start, the records tumbled and none was more impressive than winning the first 11 games of the season, and winning them convincingly. This was a club record and it equalled the divisional record but fell two short of the Football League record. And although

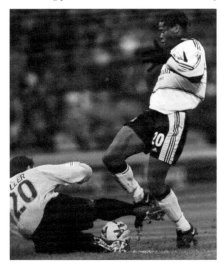

he was later to spend big in the transfer market, Tigana's initial outlays were relatively modest. His breathtaking brand of football was played by a team comprised largely of the squad he inherited. His significant early acquisitions were Louis Saha (from Metz), Luis Boa Morte (on loan from Southampton) and John Collins. Signed from Everton, Scottish international midfield player Collins was with Tigana at Monaco and at the Cottage did the manager's bidding on the pitch.

Barnsley were the visitors to the Cottage for the fifth game of the season, a match that was played on a Sunday and televised. This was the most impressive of the opening 11-game winning sequence, the ruthless and clinical destruction of a reasonable mid-table side by playing high tempo possession football, out-passing and out-running the opposition. The run came to an end in the 12th game, a goalless draw at Molineux, and the undefeated run a week later at Deepdale. This proved to be a minor blip and the 33 points from the first 11 games was the springboard for another momentous season.

Louis Saha first gave British fans an idea of what he could do with a hat-trick against Barnsley.

KING LOUIS III

TIGANA ALL SMILES
AS SAHA HITS HAT-TRICK

Life is going swimmingly for Jean Tigana. Top of Division One, a 100 per cent record and one manager of the month award already in his bag.

Tigana also seemed to have unearthed a real gem in striker Louis Saha. The £2.1 million signing from Metz scored a brilliant first-half hat trick to end Watford's brief stay at the top of the table and has now grabbed five goals in his first three matches. Saha, so good, you could say.

Strikes from Barry Hayles and sub Luis Boa Morte completed an awesome performance by the banks of the Thames — before Tigana carted them off to a local swimming pool. The French boss believed the water of the West London baths would soothe his men's muscles after the game. Although it is hardly as if they had to work too hard yesterday.

Barnsley had no answer to a super-slick team which will regard anything other than promotion as failure.

HONEST

Goal hero Saha, 22, said, "We are all going for a swim – the whole team. We have a home game against Burnley on Tuesday which does not give us much time to prepare. The water will help our recovery. But after a match like that, the whole team is delighted. Personally, it was also a big day. I came here to improve my game and did not expect such a good start. Hopefully we can continue this."

Barnsley boss Dave Bassett believes Mike Sheron had a perfectly good goal disallowed in the first period but was still honest enough to admit his side were outclassed. He said, "I don't think Tigana will be ringing me up to buy any of my players. Sheron's goal was not offside, as TV has proved. But we just weren't in it. After the third goal, Fulham got out their cigars and deckchairs."

What will delight Tigana is the way his team are mixing it. A couple of weeks ago, they had to roll up their sleeves and scrap for a 1–0 win against Norwich.

But yesterday they swapped the dour stuff for the delightful.

At times, the Barnsley defence did not know what the hell had hit them as Fulham played quick, intelligent football with a killer finish to match. Such showpiece performances are a bit rare down in this division. Another of Tigana's signings was equally as impressive – midfielder Fabrice Fernandes, who is on loan from Rennes. He delivered the seventh minute free-kick which saw Fulham edge ahead. Saha timing his run perfectly to glance in a header.

Striker Hayles and Lee Clark both missed good chances before Fulham got their second in the 31st minute.

Hayles' shot was blocked by keeper Kevin Miller. Saha seized on the loose ball and drilled it from the edge of the box. The Frenchman completed his first hat-trick in English football in the first-half stoppage time. Bjarne Goldbaek was flipped over by Miller and Saha drilled in the spot-kick. Saha then had a second-half effort hit the post before he set up Hayles for the fourth.

The Frenchman found space on the right in the 58th minute before delivering a low cross turned in from close range by Hayles.

Following the eventual and bizarre dismissal of Mitch Ward, Barnsley pulled one back through Matt Appleby, who rounded Maik Taylor in the 72nd minute.

But Fulham, although having stepped off the gas had the final say in injury-time. Defender Brian O'Callaghan crazily tried to walk the ball out of defence and was robbed by Boa Morte, who scored from a tight angle.

It completed Fulham's best performance under Tigana, although it is just a shame the local public have yet to wake up and realise there's a decent little team on their doorstep.

Only 10,437 turned up, although when Fulham reach the top-flight – and it is **WHEN** – plenty more will probably come out of the woodwork.

Blackburn Rovers 1 v Fulham 2

Wednesday 11 April 2001
Football League Division One
Referee: C. Wilkes
Attendance: 21,578

BLACKBURN R		FULHAM
Brad Freidal	1	Maik Taylor
John Curtis	2	Steve Finnan
Craig Short	3	Rufus Brevett
Henning Berg	4	Andy Melville
Damien Duff	5	Kit Symons
David Dunn	6	Sean Davis
Alan Mahon	7	Bjarnie Goldbaek
Garry Flitcroft	8	Lee Clark
Keith Gillespie	9	Louis Saha
Marcus Bent	10	John Collins
Matt Jansen	11	Barry Hayles
Stig Bjornebye (for No. 5)	12	Alan Neilson (for No. 11)
Craig Hignett (for No. 9)	13	
Eyal Berkovic (for No. 3)	14	

Sean Davis' last minute winner virtually assured the Cottagers of the Championship title.

By the end of March, there was very little doubt that Jean Tigana's Fulham were going to reclaim the place in the top flight that Bobby Robson's Fulham had lost 33 years earlier. Challengers to the club's place at the top of the table all fell by the wayside. Watford, for example, clung on to the Cottagers' coat tails until Christmas and then, despite brave words from manager Graham Taylor, were swept aside 5–0 on Boxing Day (with a help of a Barry Hayles hat-trick) and then given a lesson on their own ground a few weeks later. No club seemed likely to stay the pace. Then it was Bolton and West Brom, but neither club beat Fulham and the Cottagers took eight points from a possible 12 in the four games.

In the run in, Blackburn made a surge that looked likely to get them a promotion spot, but manager Graeme Souness had the temerity to suggest that they were the division's form side and could take the title. His comments provided the backdrop for the top of the table clash at Ewood Park with just seven games of the season to go. For Fulham, a win virtually assured promotion and the title, and for Blackburn, a victory was the last chance to stop the Tigana juggernaut. Not surprisingly, this midweek fixture was televised live and attracted a crowd of nearly 22,000. The viewing audience was well rewarded.

The team was pretty settled most of the season with one major exception. Chris Coleman, a commanding figure at the heart of the defence and an inspirational captain, was so badly injured in a road accident in January that he never played again. And two years later, when he made a dramatic reappearance as manager, the effects of the crash were still apparent. Tigana brought in Alain Goma from Newcastle for £4 million to replace him but, for the trip to Blackburn, Kit Symons partnered Andy Melville at the back. The normally impassive Tigana's jig down the touchline on the final whistle showed just how much this game mattered.

FULHAM ON THE BRINK OF GLORY

LAST-DITCH DAVIS GIVES 10 MEN POINTS

Fulham are just three points from the Premiership after snatching a dramatic injury time win with 10 men at Ewood Park last night.

Victory over Huddersfield on Saturday would be enough for Jean Tigana's side after they dug deep to turn potential calamity into an unlikely triumph against their nearest rivals.

Already trailing to Matt Jansen's 20th goal of the season after six minutes, there seemed no way back when defender Rufus Brevett was sent off for lashing out at Blackburn midfielder Garry Flitcroft in the 41st minute.

But they equalised through Louis Saha in first-half injury time and moved within touching distance of a return to the top flight after 33 years when Sean Davis rammed home the winner two minutes into added time.

If that was a moment to savour for the runaway leaders, it was celebrated with even greater relish following Blackburn manager Graeme Souness' bold pre-match claim about the First Division's true order of merit.

Midfield Lee Clark picked up on Souness' declaration that Blackburn had the edge over their promotion rivals by saying: "I thought we did brilliantly in the second half when you consider we were down to 10 men and up against the best team in the league. There was always going to be a bit of hype but we just tried to do our talking where it mattered, out in the middle. Let's just say we showed Blackburn a bit more respect than they showed us. People have wondered whether we have got the bottle and heart to go with the class, and we surely answered that tonight."

Fulham were up against it when Keith Gillespie floated a cross to the far post where the unmarked Jansen planted a header past Maik Taylor.

Worse followed in the 41st minute when Brevett fell under a challenge from Flitcroft and recklessly kicked out at the midfielder in full view of referee Clive Wilkes, who instantly produced a red card.

Yet, just as Fulham appeared destined for a rare defeat, they were handed a reprieve in the 45th minute when Brad Friedel claimed Steve Finnan's cross with ease, only to spill it at the feet of Saha after clattering into Henning Berg.

Saha could barely believe his luck and prodded the loose ball into an unguarded net.

Jansen led a second-half charge that had Fulham at full stretch and was desperately unlucky with an 85th minute shot on the turn that flew agonisingly wide with Taylor beaten.

Flitcroft blazed over from 15 yards but Fulham had the final word with Davis perfectly placed to cash in after Clark's drive had been deflected into his path.

Souness said: "It simply wasn't our night. It had been Fulham's season and they are going to win the Championship, let alone go up. Good luck to them."

Manchester United 3 v Fulham 2

Sunday 19 August 2001
FA Premiership
Referee: P. Jones
Attendance: 67,534

MANCHESTER U		**FULHAM**
Fabien Barthez	1	Edwin Van der Sar
Denis Irwin	2	Steve Finnan
Mikael Silvestre	3	John Harley
Gary Neville	4	Andy Melville
Phil Neville	5	Alain Goma
Jaap Stam	6	Sean Davis
David Beckham	7	Bjarnie Goldbaek
Paul Scholes	8	John Collins
Ruud Van Nistelrooy	9	Louis Saha
Juan Veron	10	Barry Hayles
Ryan Giggs	11	Steed Malbranque
Andy Cole (for No. 5)	12	Andres Stolcers (for No. 7)
Luke Chadwick (for No. 9)	13	Kevin Betsy (for No. 10)
Wes Brown (for No. 10)	14	Abdes Ouaddou (for No. 11)

Playing in the top flight for the first time since May 1968, and five years (all but two days) since kicking off against Hereford in the fourth tier, Fulham were given just about the toughest fixture possible for openers. They travelled to reigning Premiership champions Manchester United for a Sunday afternoon televised match, which attracted a crowd of 67,534, the largest crowd up to that time for a League match involving Fulham. For the Hereford game in 1996, the attendance was 5,277. The transformation in the club's fortunes had been breathtaking but surviving among the elite was the biggest challenge of the Fayed era.

For Tigana, it was the first trip to Old Trafford since his Monaco team had dumped United out of the European Cup three years earlier. Although he kept faith with most of the players who had won the First Division in such style the previous season, he strengthened the squad with a couple of key signings and raised the club's transfer record in the process. Dutch international goalkeeper Edwin Van der Sar was signed from Juventus for £7 million. Already rated as one of the best goalkeepers in Europe, he spent four seasons at the Cottage before moving on — to Manchester United. Also making his debut that day was Steed Malbranque. Virtually unknown on his arrival, the 21-year-old French Under-21 midfield player was an outstanding success in his five seasons at the Cottage but strangely failed to fulfil his apparent potential subsequently at Spurs and Sunderland.

Despite losing, and United needed a controversial free-kick converted by Beckham to get back on terms, Fulham acquitted themselves with great credit. They scored in the first minute of each half, both by Louis Saha, who in January 2004 moved to Old Trafford for a Fulham record fee of £11.5 million. Days later, at home to Sunderland, the Cottagers recorded their first victory in the Premiership and held their own for the rest of the season, never going lower than 15th in the table. It was a promising debut.

Fulham's most expensive signing up to then, Edwin Van der Sar, made his debut in the Cottagers first Premiership game at Old Trafford and later moved to United.

Fulham so close to the Perfect Return

It was gripping and ground-breaking, but ultimately for Fulham their first match in the Premiership end in grief.

The most exciting newcomers to the top flight for a decade served notice that they are a burgeoning force to be reckoned with, but they were undone by another Premiership new boy in the form of Ruud Van Nistelrooy.

The £19 million Dutchman scored twice in two minutes on his debut to secure a winning start for Sir Alex Ferguson in his last season as manager of Manchester United.

His strikes and one from David Beckham – direct from a free- kick, it hardly needs to be said – snuffed out two goals of exceptional quality from Fulham's brightest young star Louis Saha.

The result, however, showed just how far Fulham have come in a short space of time. Three years ago, the Cottagers opened their league campaign in the less than glamorous surroundings of Macclesfield's Moss Rose ground.

That their first fixture of the 2001-2 season should have been 15 miles further away at Old Trafford shows just what the deep coffers of chairman Mohamed Al Fayed and managerial skills of Jean Tigana have achieved.

This is just the first rung on the Premiership ladder, but just to be facing the likes of Juan Sebastian Veron and Van Nistelrooy must be a delight to the fans of a club which had played their last game in the top flight 31 years ago.

Fulham's sense of disbelief must have turned to incredulity when they took the lead four minutes into a game which was thrilling from the first whistle to the last.

Sean Davis, the promising 21-year-old midfielder who has now played for Fulham in all four divisions, lofted an accurate, but hopeful long pass which picked out Saha's run through the defence.

Saha, scorer of 32 goals last season, held off Gary Neville and brought down the ball with exquisite skill before deftly lobbing the stranded Fabien Barthez.

Beckham, confined to the right wing again despite Roy Keane's absence due to suspension – Phil Neville was assigned the holding role in midfield by Ferguson – struck the wall from a free-kick before Jaap Stam did enough to put off Saha when he seemed certain to score again.

Dutch keeper Edwin Van der Sar, signed from Juventus for £7 million in the summer, brilliantly kept out Beckham's curling effort from long range in the 14th minute, and had the woodwork to thank shortly afterwards.

Giggs' dazzling run saw the Welshman surge past their full-blooded attempts to stop him and from his cross United should have scored.

Van Nistelrooy swung at the ball and missed and then Paul Scholes hammered a first time effort against the bar.

But it was not all United and Barthez was forced into a diving save after 25 minutes to parry Saha's forceful header from Steve Finnan's cross.

After less than 35 minutes, Ferguson effectively conceded that his policy of playing Scholes as a support striker to Van Nistelrooy was not working when he brought on Andy Cole in place of Phil Neville.

Within seconds, United had equalised, though that had nothing to do with the substitution and everything to do with a controversial refereeing decision and Beckham's brilliance at set-pieces.

Another weaving Giggs run was ended by Finnan 25 yards out, with an apparently exceptional tackle. Referee Peter Jones, however thought otherwise and awarded United a free-kick, much to the chagrin of the Fulham players.

Beckham waited for Cole and Neville to exchange places and then curled in a free kick which rattled the underside of the crossbar on its way into the net.

Fulham had another glorious chance to take the lead again when Hayles raced through onto Saha's pass, but Barthez blocked his shot with his feet.

United too had a near miss, when Scholes, back in customary position in central midfield, hammered in a drive which Van der Sar saw late and was perhaps fortunate to deflect wide with his body.

Less than three minutes into the second half and Saha stunned Old Trafford for the second time.

The long-legged 22-year-old Frenchman possesses frightening pace and when he burst onto Steed Malbranque's through-ball – once more leaving Neville trailing – the outcome seemed inevitable.

And so it was as Saha slotted the ball to Barthez's right. United then completely changed the course of the match, with Van Nistelrooy pouncing to score two poachers' goals in the 52nd and 54th minutes.

Ferguson's side had looked far more threatening with Cole playing alongside the Dutchman, and it was the substitute who manufactured the first, Nistelrooy reaching his pass a second before his compatriot Van der Sar to flick the ball in.

In United's next attack the striker seized on some dithering in defence by Bjarnie Goldbaek to put the home side ahead from close range.

With 19 minutes remaining, Cole spurned a chance when, unmarked he headed Beckham's cross wide.

Ferguson then shut up shop, replacing Van Nistelrooy with Luke Chadwick and Wes Brown for Veron, the £28.1 million Argentinean midfielder who in his own way had had as effective a game as the Dutchman.

Chelsea 1 v Fulham 0

Sunday 14 April 2002
FA Cup Semi-final (at Villa Park)
Referee: G. Poll
Attendance: 36,147

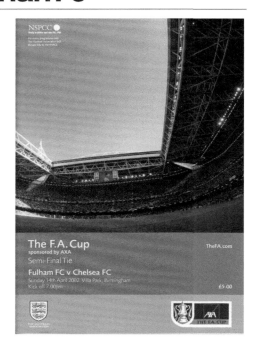

CHELSEA		FULHAM
Carlo Cudicini	1	Edwin Van der Sar
Mario Melchiot	2	Steve Finnan
Marcel Desailly	3	Rufus Brevett
John Terry	4	Andy Melville
Graham Le Saux	5	Alain Goma
Frank Lampard	6	Sean Davis
Emmanuel Petit	7	Sylvain Legwinski
Jesper Gronkjaer	8	John Collins
Mario Stanic	9	Louis Saha
Eider Gudjohnsen	10	Steve Marlet
Jimmy Floyd Hasselbaink	11	Steed Malbranque
Albert Ferrer (for No. 5)	12	Luis Boa Morte (for No. 8)
Boudewijn Zenden (for No. 9)	13	Barry Hayles (for No. 7)
Slavisa Jokanavic (for No. 11)	14	

Besides consolidating their position in the big time, Tigana's Fulham enjoyed an extended FA Cup run in 2002. It ended at the penultimate round but it has to be said that the run to the last four was the most straightforward of the six trips Fulham have made to the semi-finals. Although drawn away every time, their opponents in the four earlier rounds were all from lower divisions, Wycombe Wanderers (managed by Lawrie Sanchez) from the third tier, York from the fourth, and then Walsall and West Brom from the second. York City were in serious financial trouble at the time and in a typically generous gesture, Mohamed Al Fayed suggested that they keep Fulham's 40 per cent share of the gate receipts.

In the semi-finals, Arsenal took on Middlesbrough while Fulham were drawn against neighbours Chelsea. As if to underline the contempt football authorities have for club supporters, those who pay out of their own pocket to watch, the tie between two west London clubs was arranged for Villa Park, Birmingham, on a Sunday, kicking off at 7.00pm. The final whistle went after the last train for

London had departed New Street Station and so thousands of fans whose teams were at either end of the Fulham Road had to travel 100 miles or more up motorways and then be guaranteed congestion on the way back. The FA in its wisdom was telling supporters that the interests of those who do not pay to watch live football but only bother when it is on television are far more important than those who follow their clubs week in week out. Television was calling the shots.

By April, when the semi-final was played, Tigana had made more signings. The experienced Sylvain Legwinski, who had played for Tigana at Monaco, cost over £3 million in August 2001 but his versatility in midfield served Fulham well. Far more controversial was the club record £11.5 million paid to Lyon the following month for Steve Marlet, a deal that effectively cost the manager his job and ended in court proceedings. Both played against Chelsea.

Fulham's midfield mastermind John Collins could not find a way through the Chelsea defence.

Chelsea win through over local rivals

Chelsea centre-back John Terry scrambled the ball home to leave Claudio Ranieri's men just 45 minutes from the FA Cup final at Villa Park tonight.

Terry squeezed the ball under Fulham goalkeeper Edwin Van der Sar and into the net via the boot of Louis Saha almost on half-time.

The west London rivals kicked off tonight's FA Cup semi-final showdown at Villa Park just 90 minutes from a guaranteed place in next season's UEFA Cup.

Arsenal's 1–0 success against Middlesbrough in the other last-four showdown means the Gunners' FA Cup final opponents will – barring Champions League qualification – take the competition's UEFA Cup spot, as Arsene Wenger's men have already clinched a Champions League berth in the League.

The Blues were boosted by the return of Graeme Le Saux and Jesper Gronkjaer from injury.

Manager Claudio Ranieri, who signed a new five year contract on Friday, left Albert Ferrer and Gianfranco Zola on the bench, while Celestine Babayaro missed out with a thigh strain. For Fulham, who were unable to sell 3,000 of their 19,000 ticket allocation for tonight's game, boss Jean Tigana started with Steve Marlet and Louis Saha up front.

A heavy pre-match shower had soaked the Villa Park pitch – but had done nothing to dampen the enthusiasm of the crowd, who created a deafening roar as the teams warmed up.

Chelsea's hopes took a blow after just three minutes when left-back Le Saux, returning from an injury to his left calf, appeared to strain the muscle again when jogging under no pressure. After two minutes treatment he was stretchered off to be replaced by Ferrer.

Despite the injury, the Blues settled into their rhythm better than their capital opponents – although Cottagers frontman Marlet enjoyed a promising start to his duel with Chelsea centre-back John Terry.

After 10 minutes, the Chelsea man had to be alert to hook away a Sylvain Legwinski cross as the French striker seemed poised to pounce. However, the opening goal almost arrived at the other end three minutes later. Fulham skipper Andy Melville half-cleared a corner and Terry, who scored Chelsea's winner in the forth-round clash with West Ham, connected with a sweet volley which Edward Van de Sar brilliantly clawed round the post.

Emmanuel Petit wasted a great crossing opportunity at the halfway point in the first period.

He aimed for the Premiership's top scorer Jimmy Floyd Hasselbaink, but sliced his delivery into Van der Sar's grasp.

Ranieri's men were definitely enjoying the upper hand, with Van der Sar needing to acrobatically whack the ball clear as Eidur Gudjohnsen's mis-hit cross bobbled towards the lively Frank Lampard.

Ferrer was the first name in referee Graham Poll's notebook, after bringing down Marlet who had just beaten him in midfield.

Fulham finally added some impetus to their forward forays when midfielder Legwinski masterminded a stirring counter-attack on the half hour.

He raced to the edge of the Chelsea penalty area, played a neat one-two with Marlet, and forced Carlo Cudicini to make a smart diving save. Van der Sar unconvincingly tipped a looping Hasselbaink header over his crossbar, before the Dutch forward failed to react when Mario Stanic nodded Gronkjaer's cross back across goal.

Despite the half chances – occurring mainly in the Fulham goalmouth – this semi-final clash was failing to live up to its billing as a thrilling battle between two London rivals.

The goal the game needed finally arrived in the 41st minute, from a goalmouth scramble in the Fulham six-yard box after a Hasselbaink left wing corner.

Mario Melchot was unable to react in time – but he deflected the ball into the path of Terry, who shot from a tight angle.

His side foot effort squeezed under Van der Sar and hit the unfortunate boot of Cottagers forward Saha on its way into the net.

Fulham opened the second half in determined fashion, with Marlet in particular lively up front. Chelsea's fans in the 36,147 crowd were in good voice, although their hearts were in their mouth three times as Fulham rallied.

First Saha fended off Petit and raced towards goal, before Marcel Desailly poked the ball clear. Then John Collins almost danced through the heart of the Blues back line – and from the follow-up shot Malbranque fired a foot over the bar.

Chelsea came back strongly as the atmosphere finally reached the feverish level expected before kick-off. Gudjohnsen set up Petit to send a 20-yarder flashing wide – and the Icelander rejected another easy lay-off to brilliantly curl a precise angled shot over Van der Sar but against the face of the far post.

The ball rebounded into the Cottagers' goalmouth and was scrambled away to safety. The game was far more like the spectacle thousands of fans had driven 150 miles up to M40 to witness.

With time rapidly running out, Fulham, who had already replaced Collins with the attack-minded Luis Boa Morte, threw more men forward to support Marlet and Saha.

A clever diagonal through ball from Boa Morte – after his one-two with Malbranque – almost picked out Saha inside the Chelsea box, but Cudicini sprinted from his goal to gather. Referee Poll had to be alert to prevent the match boiling over as it entered the last 10 minutes.

Petit theatrically tumbled to the ground and claimed he had been elbowed by Davis who was keen to remonstrate with the Frenchman.

While Poll was dealing with that incident, Hasselbaink and Fulham defender Alain Goma were involved in a spate of handbags- and immediately afterwards, Gronkjaer was booked for pulling down Brevett.

When the game resumed, Gudjohnsen, who had been in red-hot goalscoring form this season, missed two wonderful chances as full-time neared.

Latching onto two Gronkjaer crosses, he skied one shot and scuffed the other well wide.

Fulham 3 v Bologna 1

Tuesday 27 August 2002
Inter Toto Cup Final Second Leg
Referee: M. Busacca
Attendance: 13,756

FULHAM		BOLOGNA
Edwin Van der Sar	1	Gianluca Pagliuca
Steve Finnan	2	Michele Paramatti
Rufus Brevett	3	Giulio Falcone
Zat Knight	4	Marcello Castellini
Alain Goma	5	Carlo Nervo
Sean Davis	6	Renato Olive
Sylvain Legwinski	7	Leonardo Colucci
Junichi Inamoto	8	Christian Zaccardo
Steve Marlet	9	Tomas Locatelli
Fecundo Sava	10	Julio Cruz
Luis Boa Morte	11	Giuseppe Signori
Louis Saha (for No. 9)	12	Cladio Belucci (for No. 11)
Steed Malbranque (for No. 8)	13	Vlado Smit (for No. 2)
John Collins (for No. 6)	14	Alessando Frara (for No. 9)

Fulham's first real foray in Europe (the Anglo-Italian Cup in the early 1970s does not really count) was in the Inter Toto Cup in 2002. Defined as EUFA's summer club competition, the format was as incomprehensible as most things that are Euro badged. There were five rounds, but staggered entry and three Finals, with no outright winner. But the three winners gained a place in the UEFA Cup, a predecessor of today's Europa League. The whole tournament had to be settled by the end of August. This meant that Fulham's 2002–03 season began in the first week of July (before the Wimbledon tournament had been completed) and by the time the League campaign got underway, the Cottagers had already played seven competitive games.

Perhaps Tigana's men surprised themselves with the progress they made. Entering in the second round, they beat Finnish club FC Haka and then Egaleo of Greece over two legs to reach the semi-finals. There, an impressive 3–0 aggregate win over French First

Division side FC Sochaux led to a Final with Italian Serie A side Bologna, a club with an impressive pedigree and with a number of experienced internationals in their squad. In the first leg in Italy, Fulham emerged with an impressive 2–2 draw. Home for the next two seasons was now Loftus Road, as the club decided on where its long-term home should be, an all-seater Craven Cottage or perhaps a brand new ground. Whatever the merits of the competition, beating Bologna 3–1 in the Inter Toto Final was a memorable result and an exciting occasion, which was Japan's Junichi Inamoto's finest hour in a Fulham shirt.

The European trail had further to run. Victories over Hajduk Split and Dinamo Zagreb took the Cottagers into the third round of the EUFA Cup where they lost 2–1 away to Hertha Berlin but were held to a goalless draw in the second leg at Shepherd's Bush. In this 14-match run, Fulham had lost just one game and emerged unscathed from very intimidating atmospheres in Croatia which showed the progress the squad had made under Tigana.

Fulham's first Japanese player, Junichi Inamoto, secured a thrilling victory with a hat-trick.

Fulham's Thrilling Euro Success

EDWIN VAN DER SAR cannot believe that his new Fulham team-mate Junichi Inamoto was allowed to spend a year at Arsenal without being given a proper chance.

The Holland goalkeeper watched the 22-year-old score a hat-trick as they took their club into the UEFA Cup for the first time last night by winning the InterToto Cup and then questioned the judgement of Arsenal manager Arsene Wenger.

The Gunners released Inamoto in the summer after taking him on loan for a year and granting him just 149 minutes of first-team football and not one second in the Premier League.

Fulham snapped him up last month on another temporary transfer from J-League side Gamba Osaka and last night he showed why.

His treble gave Jean Tigana's side a second-leg 3—1 win over their final opponents Bologna at Loftus Road and a 5—3 aggregate victory.

He also scored an eye-catching goal in the 2—2 first leg draw and sandwiched between the two games became the first Japanese player to play in the Premiership.

Van der Sar said: "I am surprised Arsenal did not hold on to him. I know they have a lot more quality than us, but I cannot believe he did not play one Premiership match.

"He has some good qualities as a player and he showed that against Bologna and at the World Cup with Japan."

The Dutchman may not have the proven talent-spotting skills of Wenger, but he has a point.

Despite the exceptional midfield players Arsenal have, if they sign someone for a year it would make sense to try them out properly before letting them go.

Perhaps Inamoto lacked confidence in training as he was compared with stars such as Patrick Vieria and Robert Pires, but if so he recovered quickly to star at the World Cup finals for Japan and scored twice.

Former Ajax and Juventus keeper Van der Sar added: "We are happy with the signing. I think it is Fulham's good fortune and so far so good."

Inamoto seems pleased too. He said: "I would like to stay here and am going to try my best to make any transfer a permanent one. The environment and atmosphere is really good and I hope I stay longer."

Off the pitch, the midfielder refuses to rub Wenger's nose in his apparent mistake, but on it last night he produced more than a gentle reminder to him.

Inamoto, making his first start for Fulham, scored his first goal of the night after just 12 minutes when he combined well with striker Facundo Sava and slotted home neatly from the edge of the penalty area. A Tomas Locatelli effort from 15 yards, which deflected off defender Zak Knight on 34 minutes cancelled that out but Inamoto, who impressed with his movement and work-rate, came back for more.

Two minutes into the second half, a cross for striker Steve Marlet was half-cleared by a defender and, as it bounced in his path, Inamoto produced a fantastic volley which flew beyond former Italian goalkeeper Gianluca Pagliuca and into the net.

Inamoto's third goal - and his first professional hat-trick - was completed on 50 minutes when he latched on to a Marlet pass and scored at the second attempt after bursting into the box and having his first shot parried by Pagliuca.

The Japanese star received a standing ovation when he was replaced by Steed Malbranque 18 minutes from time with the contest - which started as a blood and thunder cup tie and was spoilt only by some niggly fouls and theatrical behaviour - effectively over.

Fortunately for Fulham, they do not have to rush to sign Inamoto permanently as they have an option to buy him at the end of his loan, but Tigana said: "I think the chairman (Mohamed Al Fayed) will want to keep him, although I haven't spoken to him."

Fulham showed great spirit and fluid movement throughout the team and scored goals, which were so badly lacking last season.

They deserved more than the pathetically small InterToto Cup trophy they were presented with after the game, but the real prize is being in Friday's UEFA Cup first round draw and getting the chance to compete against other entrants such as Lazio, Chelsea, Leeds, Rangers, Palma and Panathinaikos.

Until then they can revel in an historic achievement for the club - and make sure that the deal which gives them first refusal on buying Inamoto next summer is water-tight.

INAMOTO MAKES CONTEST HIS OWN

Fulham could be forgiven for asking UEFA to rename their least-popular competition the Inamoto Cup after Japan's rising son delivered the club into the UEFA Cup for the first time in their history,

Unwanted at Highbury, Junichi Inamoto is fast proving that even Arsene Wenger sometimes gets it wrong and he claimed an outstanding hat-trick on his first full Fulham appearance, at Loftus Road last night.

Mohamed Al Fayed, the club's owner and chairman, has long claimed that Fulham are the Manchester United of the south; now, having secured the back-door route into the UEFA Cup — in only their second season in the Premiership — by winning the Intertoto Cup, they will be offered the chance to prove it.

The standing ovation that Inamoto received must have been heard across London, at Highbury, and few could deny Fulham the right to set off on a lap of honour with a trophy that resembles an outsized golden egg cup.

Bologna, held to a 2—2 draw at the Stadio Renato Dall'ara a fortnight earlier, allowed themselves to become rattled; Fulham remained disciplined, produced several impressive individual performances, and will look forward with relish to Friday's first round draw.

Inamoto claimed his first goal after 12 minutes when he exchanged passes with the exceptional Facundo Sava before beating former Italian international goalkeeper Gianluca Pagliuca.

Fulham's aspirations suffered a set-back in the 34th minute when Bologna restored aggregate parity, with Tomas Locatelli beating Edwin Van der Sar with a deflected shot.

Unsettled by Bologna's last first-half response, Fulham were stung into action and within 75 seconds of the restart, Inamoto scored again, delivering a stunning right-foot volley from 20 yards.

He completed a memorable night when, in the 50th minute, he claimed his hat-trick, following up after Pagliuca had saved his initial shot.

Fulham 3 v Tottenham Hotspur 2

Wednesday 11 September 2002
FA Premiership
Referee: M. Halsey
Attendance: 16,757

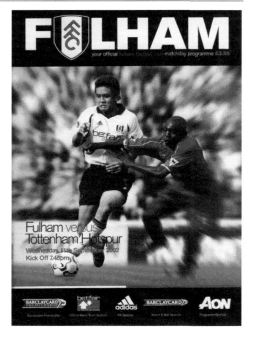

FULHAM		TOTTENHAM H
Edwin Van der Sar	1	Kasey Keller
Steve Finnan	2	Chris Perry
Pierre Wome	3	Dean Richards
Zat Knight	4	Anthony Gardner
Alain Goma	5	Ben Thatcher
Sean Davis	6	Goran Bunjevcevic
Sylvain Legwinski	7	Simon Davies
Junichi Inamoto	8	Milenko Acimovic
Louis Saha	9	Matthew Etherington
Fecundo Sava	10	Teddy Sheringham
Luis Boa Morte	11	Les Ferdinand
Barry Hayles (for No. 9)	12	Steffen Iverson (for No. 9)
Steed Malbranque (for No. 11)	13	Christian Ziege (for No. 8)
John Collins (for No. 3)	14	Gary Doherty (for No. 2)

Influential midfielder player Sylvain Legwinski sealed a brilliant Fulham comeback with a winner at the death.

Fulham's final home game of 2001–02, a goalless draw against Leicester, was thought at the time to be the last League match at Craven Cottage. The old ground was clearly unfit for the demands of Premiership football, both in terms of capacity and facilities. The club had been given special dispensation to play for one more season at the Cottage, despite the fact that the Putney and Hammersmith Ends were still standing areas. Fulham's long-term home was again the number one item on the agenda. The choice was between trying to bring the Cottage up to speed with Premiership requirements or build a new stadium, perhaps sharing with QPR. Until a definitive decision was made, the club moved out of the Cottage and ground shared with Rangers at Loftus Road, and began their homeless existence in August 2002 with a 4–1 'home' win over Bolton.

Over the next two seasons, Fulham played 38 League games at Shepherd's Bush, winning 20 and losing 11, a reasonable record. There were also 14 ties in four Cup competitions of which nine were won and the other five all drawn. This was a very reasonable record. Of all 52 games that Fulham played there, the most exciting was this win over Tottenham. Of all Fulham's London rivals, matches against Tottenham appear most frequently in the rankings of outstanding matches. This was a thrilling match, the outcome of which was determined by Tigana making a shrewder use of substitutes than Hoddle.

Managed by Glenn Hoddle, the Spurs side included goalkeeper Kasey Keller, who performed so well for Fulham in the dramatic battle against relegation in 2008, and Simon Davies, who joined Fulham just over four years later after a spell at Everton. Tigana's major close season acquisitions had been Argentinian striker Fecundo Sava, robust French international defender Martin Djetou from Italian club Parma, Japanese star Junichi Inamoto and Cameroon's international defender Pierre Wome, who had been playing in Italy. Only Sava (whose occasional goals were marked by a bizarre celebration involving a mask) and Inamoto began against Spurs.

LAST MINUTE LOFTUS ROAD DRAMA

New signing Robbie Keane kicked his heels in frustration on the Tottenham bench as Fulham transformed a two-goal deficit into a memorable 3-2 victory with a stirring second-half revival.

Having spent all summer desperately trawling Europe for a striker, Glenn Hoddle bizarrely chose to leave Keane in the dug-out as his side tamely capitulated at Loftus Road.

Even when Hoddle made his last throw of the dice, it was to Steffen Iversen that he turned as Les Ferdinand and Teddy Sheringham remained on the pitch.

Then again, he had rather more defensive worries on his mind by that time as his side, who had powered into a 2-0 half-time lead through Dean Richards and Sheringham, were under constant Fulham pressure.

Inspired by half-time substitute Steed Malbranque and driven forward remorselessly by the effervescent Sean Davis, Jean Tigana's side simply refused to give up.

Junichi Inamoto pulled a goal back with 22 minutes remaining and then Malbranque struck a penalty equaliser and Sylvain Legwinski scored a late winner.

While it was expected that Keane would start, Hoddle had evidently decided that Les Ferdinand and Sheringham deserved to keep their places up front after the club's promising start to the season.

Initially, his faith looked to be misguided as Ferdinand struck his first half chance wide of the far post, headed the next over the bar and was then dispossessed in front of goal by Alain Goma.

However, the home side's early lack of cutting edge, with Louis Saha limping off, was matched by their defensive disarray in the absence of captain Andy Melville.

Tottenham duly took full advantage as Richards rose above Zat Knight to powerfully head home Acimovic's corner on 35 minutes.

Fulham's defence remained worryingly suspect thereafter and it was not long before Spurs' lead doubled with Fulham again only having themselves to blame following a weak clearance.

The ball was quickly returned to Ferdinand, who controlled it into the path of Matthew Etherington and his neat touch found Sheringham, who swept a shot home from 12 yards out.

As the game wore on the Fulham pressure was gradually increasing and Inamoto managed to haul the home side back into contention with 22 minutes left.

Davis was the catalyst behind the move and when his shot was weakly blocked by Chris Perry, the Japanese international delivered a stinging shot back into the far corner.

That was the inspiration which Fulham desperately needed and while Finnan clipped the bar, Gardner tangled with Hayles inside the area.

Although referee Mark Halsey did not immediately point to the spot, he consulted his assistant before awarding a penalty with six minutes left. Malbranque calmly planted his spot-kick to the right of Keller's desperate dive.

Tottenham were by now hanging on desperately for a point as Keller produced superb saves from Finnan and then Malbranque.

However, they were undone again in injury-time as Legwinski burst through the centre of their slipshod defence to beat Keller and claim a memorable victory.

Fulham 3 v West Bromwich Albion 0

Wednesday 19 February 2003
FA Premiership
Referee: U. Rennie
Attendance: 15,799

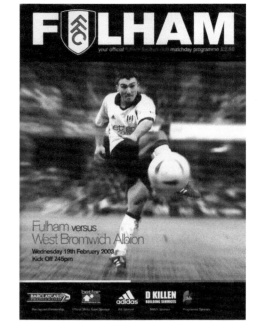

FULHAM		WEST BROMWICH A
Maik Taylor	1	Russell Hoult
Steve Finnan	2	Sean Gregan
Pierre Wome	3	Darren Moore
Andy Melville	4	Phil Gilchrist
Alain Goma	5	Adam Chambers
Martin Djetou	6	Derek McInnes
Steve Marlet	7	Ronnie Wallwork
Junichi Inamoto	8	Jason Koumas
Louis Saha	9	Neil Clement
Fecundo Sava	10	Lee Hughes
Steed Malbranque	11	Danny Dichio
Abdes Ouaddou (for No. 5)	12	Scott Dobie (for No. 10)
Andres Stolcers (for No. 11)	13	Ifeanyi Udeze (for No. 9)
	14	Jordao (for No. 11)

With the arrival of Mohamed Al Fayed as chairman and the Cottagers' rapid rise through the divisions, Fulham 'caught up' with developments in English football that mattered less in the lower reaches of the League. In particular, the influx of foreign players into the English game had by-passed Craven Cottage until the arrival of Keegan. Even then, the foreign influence was modest, and usually involved overseas players who were already at other British clubs. It was only really under Jean Tigana that the foreign contingent at Fulham started to rise quickly, and most of these players he brought to the club were signed from overseas clubs.

This French Revolution reached a climax on a freezing cold Wednesday evening at Loftus Road when struggling West Brom visited Loftus Road. It was a match Fulham won convincingly with three goals in five minutes. But the real story was the starting 11. It comprised two Irish internationals (Maik Taylor of Northern Ireland) and Steve Finnan (the Republic), a Welsh international (Andy Melville), five Frenchmen (Alain Goma, Steed Malbranque, Louis Saha, Martin Djetou and Steve Marlet), and players from the Cameroon (Pierre Wome), Japan (Junichi Inamoto) and Argentina (Fecundo Sava). The two substitutes were from Latvia (Andres Stolcers) and Morocco (Abdes Ouaddou). Not a single Englishman played for Fulham that evening, the first time that had ever happened.

No sooner was the revolution completed but it ended. After the exit from the EUFA Cup, League form was rather erratic and Tigana

seemed to lose enthusiasm. A series of lacklustre displays culminating in a 2–0 defeat at Anfield which was far more emphatic than the scoreline implied led to the manager's departure. It was an unhappy ending to a bold and successful experiment. In his place, on a temporary basis, came Chris Coleman, the effects of his car accident still evident. He stepped up from a backroom role, steered the club to three wins and a draw in the last five games and decided he wanted the job permanently. Given his contribution to the club, it was hard to refuse him, despite his youth and lack of experience.

Steed Malbranque, one of Jean tigana's best signings, was at his very best as Fulham's foreign legion beat Albion.

Malbranque to the fore as Fulham fire three

Three goals in four minutes by Louis Saha, Pierre Wome and Steed Malbranque edged Fulham nearer Premiership survival, after a game that seemed destined for a goalless draw suddenly sprang into life with a quarter of an hour remaining.

Fulham moved into 14th place, 12 points above the survival line which West Bromwich remain below – Albion's chances of a second season among the elite are increasingly in doubt.

This was Fulham's third consecutive home league win and their 46th match of the season – more than any other Premiership club – yet there was no sign of tiredness as the home side punished defensive mistakes by the visitors.

Malbranque was by far the game's outstanding player, yet the sponsors' man-of-the-match award incredibly went to Saha – one can only presume the yardstick for the bottle of bubbly was whoever scored the first goal.

"He improves game after game," said Fulham's assistant manager, Christian Damiano, of Malbranque, "He has a great talent. He's more aggressive and is involved in the game more now."

The West Bromwich manager, Gary Megson, had said the next five days would be a significant bearing on Albion's chances of staying up. Sunday's relegation show-down with West Ham is what he called "the first of 11 big ones for us".

Megson did not hide his dissapointment at his team's dreadful defending. He said: "You can't defend how we did for a five-minute spell like that, it had to be seen to be believed.

"We'd coped with everything – then we decided not to clear the cross for the first goal. That was a bad performance from us.

"But there are still points to play for. If it comes down to battling, spirit and enthusiasm we're as good as anyone but you have to take chances and defend better as a unit. If we defend as we did tonight we won't win any of those 11."

Fulham, on the other hand, can breathe more easily with 33 points and another five would almost certainly be enough to ensure safety.

The home side were a little flattered by the scoreline even though they had the better of the match.

To their credit, Albion did not come to defend, but Lee Hughes and Danny Dichio were an ineffective strike force with Hughes having a particularly frustrating night.

Still searching for his first Premiership goal, Hughes was through one-on-one in the 44th minute and should have scored. Hughes, who had also seen a half-volley saved by goalkeeper Maik Taylor, was then fortunate to escape without a caution for a theatrical dive in an effort to win a penalty when challenged by Abdeslam Ouaddou,

Phil Gilchrist had cleared off the line from Saha and Fulham – and Malbranque in particular – seemed the more likely to break the deadlock. They did and it was through Saha, in the 73rd minute, after Gilchrist failed to track the Fulham striker as he headed home Malbranque's centre.

A minute later Malbranque touched a free-kick to Wome who opened his Fulham account in some style with a thumping 25-yard shot.

"We knew Saha and Malbranque would be a goal threat," said Megson. "But we didn't figure on Wome, too."

A needless push by Neil Clement on Saha in the 76th minute gave Malbranque the chance to score his eighth goal in six games from the resulting penalty.

"This was a big win for us." said Damiano. Fulham also had the bonus of Junichi Inamoto, returning from injury, completing his first 90 minutes since September.

Fulham's squad will be tested to the full with two games in three days next week – at home to Tottenham in the Premiership on Monday and then away to Burnley in an FA Cup fourth-round replay on Wednesday.

Manchester United 1 v Fulham 3

Saturday 25 October 2003
FA Premiership
Referee: P. Jones
Attendance: 67,727

MANCHESTER U		FULHAM
Tim Howard	1	Edwin Van der Sar
Gary Neville	2	Moritz Volz
Rio Ferdinand	3	Jerome Bonnissel
John O'Shea	4	Zat Knight
Michel Silvestre	5	Alain Goma
Christiano Ronaldo	6	Lee Clark
Nicky Butt	7	Sylvain Legwinski
Eric Djemba-Djemba	8	Steed Malbranque
Ryan Giggs	9	Louis Saha
Ruud Van Nistelrooy	10	Luis Boa Morte
Diego Forlan	11	Mark Pembridge
Quinton Fortune (for No. 5)	12	Junichi Inamoto (for No. 11)
Paul Scholes (for No. 6)	13	Martin Djetou (for No. 3)
David Bellion (for No. 8)	14	Barry Hayles (for No. 10)

During the 2003 close season, Fulham considered a number of candidates to succeed Jean Tigana and plumped for former captain Chris Coleman. It was something of a gamble. He became the youngest manager in the Premiership and he had no previous management experience whatsoever. His tactical knowledge and coaching skills were unknown and he brought in coach Steve Kean as his assistant manager. But, as a player, Coleman was a natural leader noted for his passion and commitment and it was these qualities that would serve him well as a manager.

After the big spending of the Tigana years, budgets were more constrained. The dependable Finnan left for Liverpool and goalkeeper Taylor, fed up with playing second fiddle to Van der Sar, went off to Birmingham. And, after just one match in 2003–04, record signing Steve Marlet went off to France and was never seen at Fulham again. In came two free transfers, full-backs Moritz Volz and Jerome Bonnisel, veteran midfield player Mark Pembridge and the much-travelled Mark Crossley as back-up goalkeeper. This was pretty much the story of Coleman years. Most of Keegan's and Tigana's expensive signings got older or left the club, to be replaced (with the odd exception) by cheaper alternatives. Predictably, the football became more direct, and the surprise of Coleman's years at the helm is not that Fulham failed to win anything but that they managed to stay in the top flight relatively comfortably.

In his first season, the team made an average start and were in mid-table when they travelled to face defending champions Manchester United at Old Trafford. Days earlier, Fulham had lost at home to Newcastle, while United had won four and drawn one of their five previous matches. Although United left out Scholes and Keane, it was still a formidable line up and few gave Fulham much of a chance. But the victory, the club's first at Old Trafford for 40 years, was thoroughly deserved. The star was Steed Malbranque, who scored one and set up the other two and it was a victory that helped establish Coleman's credibility as a manager.

Lee Clark set Fulham on the road to a sensational win with a goal in the early minutes.

Champions Humbled By Bold Fulham

Super Steed Malbranque starred in Fulham's amazing smash-and-grab raid on Old Trafford.

The Frenchman ran the champions ragged as Chris Coleman's buoyant Londoners stormed to their first win over United for 39 years.

Fulham deserved to win by more on an afternoon where the home side's defensive frailties surfaced again and left boss Sir Alex Ferguson — starting his two-match touchline ban — seething in the stand.

Lee Clark set Fulham on their way with his third minute strike and United were hugely fortunate to go in level at the break from Diego Forlan's injury-time strike.

But the brilliant Malbranque ran the show in the second half, firing Fulham's second in the 66th minute and providing the through-ball for Junichi Inamoto to wrap up a wonderful victory 11 minutes from time.

Louis Saha and Luis Boa Morte each could have grabbed a brace while United were only left to rue a missed Forlan effort early in the second period which could have changed the course of the game.

Fulham immediately began to over-run a United midfield bearing no resemblance to that which had battled out a midweek win at Ibrox.

How Ferguson must have wished he had not rested Roy Keane and dropped Paul Scholes to the bench as Chris Coleman's confident side took control.

Malbranque set up the opener with three minutes on the clock when he caught Mikael Silvestre and John O'Shea sleeping down the right and crossed to give the unmarked captain Clark the simplest of chances.

The visitors maintained their early momentum and but for wayward finishing would have had a first-half hatful.

Saha's header was held by Tim Howard in the United goal while his counterpart Edwin Van der Sar was only called into action once in the early stages when he saved well from O'Shea.

Fulham were entirely swayed by their famous surroundings and continued to look the more likely to grab the game's second goal.

They came agonisingly close in the 18th minute when Volz cut the ball back from the right and Mark Pembridge hammered a rising 20 yard effort which clattered the crossbar before bouncing down onto the goal-line and away to safety.

Then Boa Morte almost connected with a header in front of goal as Fulham completely dominated.

Ruud Van Nistelrooy was being shackled so well by Volz and the towering Zat Knight while Ryan Giggs swapped flanks with the unimpressive Ronaldo.

Forlan shot across the face of the goal but whenever United began to exert pressure they were undone by the fluidity of Fulham's sweeping counter-attacks.

Howard was called upon to deny Saha again in the 28th minute after he had swivelled between Ferdinand and Silvestre and fired a left-foot shot which the United keeper parried.

Giggs shot across the face of goal for United and Ronaldo resorted to a long-range effort which careered over the bar.

But Fulham were still given acres of space and Saha was inches wide with a free header from Clark's right-wing cross.

Forlan grabbed an undeserved equaliser deep into first half stoppage time when he raced onto a Giggs through-ball and shot home to Van der Sar's right.

Quinton Fortune replaced Silvestre at the re-start — but was immediately booked by referee Riley for his bench not signalling the change in the required fashion.

And although United began the second period with much more purpose, their defensive frailties were soon to resurface.

Forlan should have scored his second in the 54th minute when he sprang the Fulham offside trap only to shoot horribly wide to Van der Sar's right.

But Fulham were not to be denied. O'Shea's brilliant challenge denied Saha a clear run on goal in the 63rd minute.

Three minutes later Fulham were back in front when Ferdinand failed to clear Boa Morte's left-wing cross and Fortune deflected the ball into the path of Malbranque, who drove home low past Howard.

Ferguson flung on Scholes in a desperate bid to turn the tide but only succeeded in giving the rampant Londoners more space to exploit.

Again it was the sensational Malbranque who did the damage, knocking an inch-perfect through-ball in the 79th minute which Inamoto swept majestically over Howard to seal their wonderful win.

United came close to reducing the deficit but substitute David Bellion's close-range effort hit Van der Sar's legs.

Fulham 1 v Chelsea 0

Sunday 19 March 2006
FA Premiership
Referee: M. Dean
Attendance: 22,486

FULHAM		CHELSEA
Mark Crossley	1	Petr Cech
Moritz Volz	2	Paulo Ferreira
Liam Rosenior	3	William Gallas
Zat Knight	4	Claude Makelele
Ian Pearce	5	John Terry
Steed Malbranque	6	Robert Huth
Mark Pembridge	7	Shaun Wright-Phillips
Michael Brown	8	Frank Lampard
Luis Boa Morte	9	Hernan Crespo
Collins John	10	Michael Essien
Brian McBride	11	Joe Cole
Heidar Helguson (for No. 10)	12	Damien Duff (for No. 11)
Philippe Christanval (for No. 6)	13	Didier Drogba (for No. 7)
	14	Ricardo Carvalho (for No. 6)

A controversial win was settled by Luis Boa Morte's early goal.

When Fulham kicked off at home to Birmingham in August 2005, Coleman's third full season in office, the team was his and barely recognisable from the Tigana era. Only Malbranque, Boa Morte and an increasingly injury-prone Goma remained from those free-spending days. The team had a 'make do and mend' look about it but it nevertheless continued to punch above its weight. And the club went back in 2004 to where it belonged, Craven Cottage. Plans for a new stadium near the White City did not materialise and so the terraced areas at the Hammersmith and Putney ends were converted into seats and in a style that blended in perfectly with the character of the old ground. Craven Cottage was a Premiership arena but it retained its unique charm, a ground but never a stadium.

When Chelsea visited the Cottage in March 2006, the match mattered to both sides as the season entered the home straight. The Blues, defending champions and League leaders, did not want to give the chasing pack any encouragement while Fulham, just two places above the relegation places, did not want to get sucked into the relegation scrap. The biggest crowd at the Cottage for 23 years (when Chelsea were again the visitors) came to see this Sunday afternoon game, even though it was televised live. Fulham had not beaten their neighbours at the Cottage for 29 years. In a characteristic 'Coleman' performance, the home side upset their high-flying and more skilful guests with commitment, energy and dogged perseverance. And a decision by referee Dean was crucial – unquestionably the right decision, as Jose Mourinho admitted, but not necessarily for the right reasons.

It was not always pretty, but it was effective, which was how the Coleman teams survived. With four wins from the last five games, they finished a respectable 12th. And winning their penultimate away game at Manchester City meant they avoided going an entire season without a victory on the road. But just one win in 19 games equalled the club's worst record in a season and was to be a recurring theme in subsequent seasons.

CHELSEA BEATEN AS REF RILES MOURINHO

Jose Mourinho will have better days than this. Forced to deflect rumours about a move to Italy beforehand, he spent the game trying to shore up a battered, bewildered team.

This may have been only Chelsea's third defeat of a season in which they have dominated the English game, but it was indicative of the wear and tear of a long and hard campaign.

Fulham fighting for their Premiership lives were desperate for the points. Chelsea's patchy form over the past month or so finally caught up with them.

While Mourinho himself was dignity personified later, his players were not. William Gallas's sending off in the last minute for stamping on Heidar Helguson showed all too clearly their irritation. Chelsea still have a 12 point lead over Manchester United and will probably still win their second successive title. But Chris Coleman's Fulham showed that football can never be taken for granted.

Coleman went into yesterday's game under the most intense pressure of his three-year career as Fulham manager.

With two board members sacked the week before last, the word was that the young Welshman's time was limited, his team's dismal run having plunged them back into a relegation tussle.

Coleman had said his side needed three wins from their remaining eight games. This deserved victory, which came courtesy of Luis Boa Morte's fortunate goal, eased that pressure.

The Fulham manager set out his side to frustrate and contain Chelsea and it was a tactic that paid off. The hosts could and should have had a penalty inside the first six minutes, as full-back Moritz Volz charged down the right and was felled by a scything challenge from John Terry but referee Mike Dean thought otherwise.

It did not matter. Barely 11 minutes later, Coleman's side were ahead and it was no more than they deserved, even if it was a lucky goal.

Boa Morte found Steed Malbranque on the edge of the area. The Frenchman's shot took a deflection off Terry and flew through Robert Huth's legs. As Boa Morte moved in on the ball at the far post, Paulo Ferreira tried to clear, but it came off the Portuguese striker, past Petr Cech and into the net. The 'Special One' is not one for hanging about when it comes to changing things. Off came Joe Cole and Shawn Wright-Phillips and on went Didier Drogba and Damien Duff. Inter Milan take note. This guy is decisive.

But Fulham could have made it worse. Frank Lampard carelessly gave the ball away in midfield and Mark Pembridge sent Collins John clean through with an astute pass.

The young Dutchman shot straight at Cech as the Chelsea keeper raced out. He knew he should have done better. Lampard then had a tussle with the tigerish Michael Brown as Chelsea's frustration showed and though Duff saw his shot well saved by Mark Crossley, Mourinho's side had made worryingly little impact. Fulham were creating the better chances. When Michael Essien gave away a free-kick on the edge of the area, Pembridge's low shot shaved the outside of the post as Cech stood helpless. But Coleman's team soon had an escape of their own when Drogba chased and won the ball in a race with Zat Knight but clearly controlled it with his hand before beating Crossley,, who had made a mad dash from goal.

Fulham's players protested furiously as referee Dean ran across to consult his linesman. The ruling was in Fulham's favour – relief for Crossley, fury from Mourinho. The pressure began to mount. Drogba whipped a free-kick just over the bar and hit the woodwork with a header, Boa Morte headed off the line and Lampard lashed a shot over. Just before the whistle Chelsea's rage boiled over with Gallas's lunge at Helguson. A melee ensued, but Gallas (red) and Claude Makelele (yellow) were the only ones shown cards.

Gallas showed a thumbs down to Fulham fans as he walked off. It could have been the verdict on his team.

Fulham 2 v Arsenal 1

Wednesday 29 November 2006
FA Premiership
Referee: H. Webb
Attendance: 24,510

FULHAM		ARSENAL
Antti Niemi	1	Jens Lehmann
Moritz Volz	2	Justin Hoyte
Liam Rosenior	3	Mathieu Flamini
Zat Knight	4	Gilberto Silva
Philippe Christanval	5	Kolo Toure
Papa Bouba Diop	6	Philippe Senderos
Michael Brown	7	Alexander Hleb
Tomasz Radzinski	8	Alex Song
Brian McBride	9	Robin Van Persie
Claus Jensen	10	Thierry Henry
Luis Boa Morte	11	Tomas Rosicky
Heider Helguson (for No. 9)	12	Johan Djourou (for No. 11)
Wayne Routledge (for No. 8)	13	Cec Fabregas (for No. 8)
	14	Theo Walcott (for No. 7)

Brian McBride, a hugely popular figure at the Cottage, opened the scoring with a trademark header.

Although Fulham got off to the worst possible start in 2006–07, few would have predicted the turbulence that lay ahead in the second half of the season. With the season just 20 minutes old, Fulham trailed Manchester United 4–0 at Old Trafford in front of 75,115 (a new record for a Fulham League game) and a huge television audience. But the Cottagers bounced back, lifted by new signing Jimmy Bullard who came in as crowd favourite Malbranque left for Spurs. Bullard, however, was so seriously injured in the fourth game at Newcastle that he was out for almost 18 months, a big blow to the club. But the team was lying comfortably in 12th place when sixth placed Arsenal visited the Cottage for a midweek League game in November.

Since their return to the top flight in 2001, Fulham had managed just one draw in 10 meetings with the Gunners, and had lost all five meetings at home. It was in fact over 40 years since the Cottagers had last beaten Arsenal. For captain Luis Boa Morte and full-back Moritz Volz, both former Gunners, there was an extra edge to the game and the Portuguese international had one of his best games in a Fulham shirt. The crowd was Fulham's best up to that point in the Premier (24, 510) and the atmosphere was electric.

For Coleman, the win completed the set, victories as Fulham manager over the Big Four, Arsenal, Chelsea, Liverpool and Manchester United, but not all in the same season. After this success, it all started to unravel. A run of one win in 15 games saw the Cottagers plunge perilously close to the drop zone and with five games to go, Coleman left after four years in the job. The overall verdict is largely positive because he did not have the same resources as his predecessors and successors, and there was an exodus of high quality players. He was not a great success in his transfer dealings but despite this, he kept Fulham in the top flight.

Old Boy Boa Stuns Gunners

Arrogant Arsenal suffered carnage at the Cottage as Arsene Wenger paid the ultimate price for his lack of respect.

The Gunners boss had described this match as the beginning of Arsenal's "moment of truth" after slipping further adrift of Premiership leaders Manchester United at the weekend.

Yet he still reckoned he could afford to rest Cesc Fabregas, Freddie Ljungberg and full-backs Emmanuel Eboue and Gael Clichy for the tougher tests ahead.

And that proved a reckless miscalculation by an increasingly desperate manager as his team suffered their first loss to Fulham since January 1966.

Now they are a massive 16 points behind United and even Wenger can no longer kid himself that Arsenal are still in the title race.

Their position is even worse than at this stage last season when they eventually limped home 24 points adrift of Chelsea. And this time, Wenger could have no excuses as his team were out-fought and out-played by a side sick of being Arsenal's whipping boys.

The visitors were a beaten team long before Philippe Senderos' 66th minute dismissal for a second booking. Howard Webb was forced to show 11 yellows and one red card as he struggled to keep control of a fiercely-contested match which always teetered on the brink of anarchy. Yet every booking was merited as Arsenal lost their way – and then their heads. Behind after six minutes, the Gunners' rookie defence was never able to cope with Fulham's blistering pace down the flanks.

The home side were in control from the moment Claus Jensen's inswinging corner was met by a firm near-post header from Brian McBride. It was the 12th time this season Arsenal had conceded the first goal.

Maybe it was Wenger's team selection or the memory of two four-goal batterings last season which was motivating Fulham.

Skipper Luis Boa Morte was tearing poor Justin Hoyle to pieces down the flank and plunged the visitors deeper into trouble in the 19th minute.

Off-loaded by Arsenal seven years ago, the unpredictable Portugese international rarely replicates his talent consistently. But he showed Wenger just what he was missing as he flicked the ball over Hoyle's head and then through Alex Song's legs before delivering a wicked low cross into the area. Tomasz Radzinski, arriving at the back post, hurled himself ahead of Mathieu Flamini to turn the ball home at the expense of a nasty collision with the advertising hoardings. Arsenal were a shambles at the back and even the return of skipper Thierry Henry from injury was not enough.

The Frenchman has been out of sorts of late and, on this showing it is hard to argue with the judges who left his name off the shortlist for the World Player of the Year. He rarely troubled Coleman's makeshift defence last night. Instead Robin Van Persie launched the fight back with a sensational 30-yard free-kick into the top corner on 36 minutes. But even that goal could not halt the onslaught and Jensen curled a free-kick wide before Jens Lehmann saved from McBride at the end of a breathless first 45 minutes.

Fabregas replaced the hapless Song at the break as Arsenal looked to claw their way back. Fulham were grateful to an eagle-eyed linesman who spotted Henry was inches offside before turning in Alexander Hleb's 51st minute pass.

And any chance of a comeback was crushed when Senderos brought down Boa Morte and received a second booking.

Boa Morte hit the bar with the free-kick, while sub Theo Walcott had a low shot touched on to a post by Antti Niemi.

With their title hopes gone, Wenger should consider resting stars for Saturday's derby with Spurs ahead of next week's Champions League decider in Porto. Somehow, I do not think he will make the same mistake.

Fulham 1 v Liverpool 0

Saturday 5 May 2007
FA Premiership
Referee: S. Bennett
Attendance: 24,554

FULHAM		LIVERPOOL
Antti Niemi	1	Jose Reine
Liam Rosenior	2	Alvaro Arbeloa
Zat Knight	3	Emiliano Insua
Philippe Christanval	4	Xabi Alonso
Carlos Bocanegra	5	Gabriel Paletta
Tomasz Radzinski	6	Sami Hypia
Michael Brown	7	Jermaine Pennant
Papa Bouba Diop	8	Mohamed Sissoko
Simon Davies	9	Robbie Fowler
Vincenzo Montella	10	Craig Bellamy
Brian McBride	11	Mark Gonzalez
Clint Dempsey (for No. 10)	12	Steve Finnan (for No. 3)
Heidar Helguson (for No. 11)	13	Nabil El Zhar (for No. 7)
Moritz Volz (for No. 6)	14	Harry Kewell (for No11)

A dreadful run of one win in 15 games from Christmas through to the spring saw Fulham plunge down the table and after a lacklustre display at home to Manchester City, who were easy 3–1 winners, Coleman went. The board surprisingly turned to Northern Ireland manager Lawrie Sanchez to see the Cottagers through the final five crucial games. It was a surprising choice but the task was simple. At least one win was needed to preserve top flight status. Sanchez started with a defeat at Reading and a home draw against Blackburn. Of the final three games, two were away (at Arsenal and Middlesbrough) and one at home, to Liverpool. Given Fulham's dreadful away record, just one win at the start of the season at Newcastle, the visit of Liverpool to the Cottage was crunch time.

There was the usual congestion at the bottom of the table, and three from Watford (already doomed), Charlton, Sheffield United, Wigan, Fulham and West Ham were the candidates. The Hammers had hit top form at the right time, helped, unfairly it was claimed, by the signing of Carlos Tevez. But Fulham knew three points against the Reds would secure another season in the Premiership and they received unexpected help from their opponents which led to protests from other clubs in the danger area.

With nothing to play for in the League, Liverpool's minds were focused on Athens, and the Champions League Final against AC Milan. Rafa Benitez's starting line up against Fulham included just three of those who kicked off against the Italian champions a couple of weeks later, Reina, Alonso and Pennant. Although it might be argued that a team that also included Hypia, Fowler, Bellamy and Arbeloa was not exactly weak, and that these players were playing for a place in the forthcoming Final, many believed that Fulham were not up against Liverpool's strongest side. The crowd of 24,554 was a new Cottage Premiership record and they saw safety secured by Clint Dempsey's first goal for the club in his ninth appearance as substitute.

Clint Dempsey's first goal for Fulham ensured Premiership survival.

CLINT STRIKE TAKES SANCHEZ TO BRINK OF SAFETY

It is 19 years since Lawrie Sanchez's glanced header catapulted him and Wimbledon to fame by beating Liverpool in the FA Cup Final.

Yesterday Sanchez inspired another 1—0 win against the Merseysiders – and it could turn out to be just as crucial.

For Fulham's victory against the Reds should be enough to keep them in the Premiership.

"For some reason me and Liverpool seem to have some connection," said Sanchez. "But this wasn't about me. It was about the players and they proved they were good enough."

It was the Northern Ireland coach's first win for the Cottagers – but the Premiership strugglers still owe a big debt to Chris Coleman, the man Sanchez replaced last month. It was one of the Welshman's last signings, Clint Dempsey, who scored the goal that effectively closed the trap-door.

Supersub Dempsey, a £1.5 million buy from New England Revolution in January, struck a winner to rival Sanchez's header for the Crazy Gang all those years ago.

The American played a one-two with Liam Rosenior and whipped the ball first time past José Reina.

Charlton must now win their two final games – and Fulham lose at Middlesbrough – for Sanchez's boys to drop down into the Championship. And even then it will be down to goal difference.

It was a great way for Mohamed Al Fayed to celebrate his 10 years as chairman – and the Egyptian might now consider extending his caretaker manager's stay at the club.

"He came in to congratulate me afterwards," said Sanchez, who had Papa Bouba Diop sent off late on after two bookings. "It's his decision who becomes manager; whoever takes over will have a good team. It's still mathematically possible that we'll go down, but we've taken a big step towards safety."

Zat Knight said in the programme he wanted a Cup Final atmosphere at Craven Cottage – and the giant defender certainly got it. The home crowd's passion whipped up at one point by the inspirational Rosenior, helped Fulham shake off a torpor which has afflicted them for their previous 10 games during which they had taken just a measly four points.

This was a must-win game – and Sanchez, with a little help from Rafa Benitez, delivered. Benitez rested nine players from the side that overcame Chelsea to reach the Champions League Final. Only Reina and Jermaine Pennant survived.

Charlton, West Ham and Sheffield United will not be reassured by Benitez's explanation. "We took the game seriously", he insisted. "We attacked and played to win. In fact we missed five clear chances. We rested players but if those teams complaining were in our position they would probably do the same."

Craig Bellamy had two early chances, released first by Pennant and then by Robbie Fowler. But Antti Niemi twice came to Fulham's rescue with fine saves.

On another five occasions, Fowler's intelligent use of the ball split the home defence wide open. But, as Rafa implied, the finishing left a great deal to be desired. Fowler himself was guilty of the miss of the match when Pennant drove the ball in from the right and the Kop legend miskicked from only a few yards out.

Fulham created very little. But Vincenzo Montella was desperately unlucky not to score when his spectacular overhead kick, after Knight had headed Radzinski's free-kick across the goal, deflected off Xabi Alonso on to the post.

While the Cottagers are all but safe, Liverpool have a little date in Athens on their minds. The Champions League Final might still be two-and-a-half weeks away, but Benitez felt it important to leave out stars like Jamie Carragher, Steven Gerrard, Dirk Kuyt, John Arne Riise and Peter Crouch.

The Spaniard was incensed with referee Steve Bennett for failing to spot a headbutt by Michael Brown on Alonso. The Liverpool boss said: "Brown clearly headbutted Alonso and it changed the game. The FA will take action I am sure. I don't know how any of the officials failed to spot it. It's unbelievable."

Manchester City 2 v Fulham 3

Saturday 26 April 2008
FA Premiership
Referee: M. Dean
Attendance: 44,504

MANCHESTER C		FULHAM
Joe Hart	1	Kasey Keller
Elano	2	Paul Stalteri
Michael Ball	3	Aaron Hughes
Vedran Corluka	4	Brede Hangeland
Sun Jihai	5	Paul Konchesky
Darius Vassell	6	Simon Davies
Gelson Fernandez	7	Danny Murphy
Michael Johnson	8	Jimmy Bullard
Martin Petrov	9	Clint Dempsey
Stephen Ireland	10	David Healy
Benjani Mwaruwari	11	Brian McBride
Geovanni (for No. 10)	12	Diomansy Kamara (for No. 10)
Felipe Caicedo (for No. 6)	13	Eric Nevland (for No. 11)

For reasons that were hard to fathom, Lawrie Sanchez was offered the job on a permanent basis. There was nothing in his brief spell in charge of Fulham at the end of 2006–07 to commend him (one win and three defeats in five games) and his time as Wycombe Wanderers manager hardly seemed to be an adequate apprenticeship for top-flight football. And it was a disastrous appointment. He was right to move on a number of players who were short of Premier quality and signed some very good (as well as some less good) players, but the team performed poorly. Sanchez did not last long. After two wins in 17 games he was gone, and Fulham were floundering. Ray Lewington again stepped in temporarily until Roy Hodgson arrived just after Christmas.

Almost the forgotten man of English football, Hodgson had worked successfully in Europe before and after his brief stint in charge of Blackburn in 1997–98. Avuncular and professorial in his approach, he was one of Fulham's most significant appointments. But he had no magic wand and his impact was not immediate. It was his sixth game before his first win and even then the slide continued for another two months. With just five games remaining, the Cottagers were next to bottom, six points adrift and to all intents and purposes, down.

But, strengthened by the return from injury of Bullard and McBride, the signing of central defender Hangeland and a revitalised Murphy, Fulham went to fellow strugglers Reading and won 2–0, their first away win of the season. But this seemed not to matter when Liverpool had an easy win at the Cottage. And so came the trip to Eastlands, a strange and defining game which has few equals in Fulham's history. At half-time, trailing 2–0 and with Birmingham beating Liverpool, Fulham were statistically relegated. But after 45 pulsating second half minutes, and Joe Kamara's finest hour, there was still hope, albeit very slim. The greatest of the Cottagers' three Great Escapes was still on.

Joe Kamara wheels away after the dramatic winner against Manchester City.

Amazing Fulham Cling To Premiership Life

Fulham had the first good chance of the game after six minutes, and City had Joe Hart to thank for keeping the game at 0–0. Davies' cross was met with a sweet volley from Dempsey, and City's keeper made a superb save low to his left to push the ball wide of the post.

But we did not have to wait too long for a goal, and when it came it was something special. Petrov took advantage when Stalteri dithered on the edge of his own area, he then backheeled to Stephen Ireland who curled a wonderful shot beyond the despairing Keller into the top left hand corner.

It could have been even worse for Fulham on 14 minutes when Keller slipped on the edge of the area, but Benjani could not drag the ball back from the by-line with the American stranded.

Bullard forced Hart into another save with a low, long range shot, and Vassell could not quite get on top of a Petrov cross. Then on 21 minutes, the former Villa man set up City's second goal.

Elano fed Vassell on the right, the ball was pulled back into the box to Benjani who made no mistake from around 10 yards out – and this time the Zimbabwean treated the City fans to his trademarked finger-pointing goal celebration!

Dempsey went into the book for elbowing Elano in the face, the Brazilian staying down for several minutes for treatment before carrying on. The playmaker-turned-right back was enjoying his new role, spraying passes across to Petrov, who was just short of putting Ireland in again on the half hour.

Hart was to the rescue again on 30 minutes, the England Under 21 making a wonderful one-handed save from David Healy's point-blank range header.

Petrov was just inches away in stoppage time, Keller plucking a through ball off the top of the Bulgarian's head on the very edge of the box.

Vassell went close just two minutes into the second half, Keller doing well to push the striker's shot from a tight angle away from danger. A minute later the American stopper made another good save, blocking Benjani after he had found space on the edge of the six yard box.

The game went quiet, livening up when Geovanni replaced Ireland on 56 minutes, the Brazilian still a folk hero after his derby-winning exploits back in August. Just afterwards, Benjani rose to meet a Petrov corner but his header flew a long way over the bar.

It was all City now, with Petrov shooting wide on the hour mark when a pass to Vassell would surely have brought goal number three.

Fulham had hardly got out of first gear, but Bullard had a chance on 63 minutes, whipping a free kick just past Hart's left hand post.

And the visitors threw themselves a Premier League lifeline on 69 minutes, Diomansy Kamara eluding Corluka to drive home a low shot off Hart's right ankle, the visiting fans finally having something to cheer after looking resigned to their fate.

They came close to levelling the game two minutes later, Joe Hart pulling off another great save, this time diving to his right to push a Bullard free kick away. A game that City should have been winning with ease looked to be in the balance.

The plucky west London side then drew level in dramatic circumstances. Sun Jihai was adjudged to have pulled down Nevland in the area. Danny Murphy stepped up and saw Joe Hart save the spot kick low to his right – only for the ball to rebound back to Murphy, who drove the ball in to make it 2–2 with 12 minutes to go!

Both sets of fans were stunned, and three minutes later Bullard's rasping drive was just fractionally wide of Hart's left post. The City stopper was called on again seconds later, flying to his right to save a Dempsey header.

Then City nearly retook the lead, Geovanni finding the side netting with half of the ground thinking he had scored. With three minutes to go, Elano crossed all the way over to Petrov, whose volley flew wide. Seconds later, Benjani and Caicedo were enable to combine when a goal seemed certain, and then the Ecuadorian shot wide after finding space in the area.

The drama was still not over, Petrov going on a great run before shooting, only to see Keller make a great save with the rebound fortunately not falling to anyone.

And in the dying seconds Fulham completed an amazing comeback, Diomansy Kamara breaking into the box and drilling the ball past Hart to the astonishment of everyone in the ground. There was barely time to restart, the away fans acclaimed their side and City's supporters could only scratch their heads at what they had just seen.

Portsmouth 0 v Fulham 1

Saturday 11 May 2008
FA Premiership
Referee: M. Clattenburg
Attendance: 20,532

PORTSMOUTH		FULHAM
Jamie Ashdown	1	Kasey Keller
Glen Johnson	2	Paul Stalteri
Lassana Diara	3	Aaron Hughes
Herman Hreidarssn	4	Brede Hangeland
Jermain Defoe	5	Paul Konchesky
Sylvain Distin	6	Simon Davies
Noe Pamarot	7	Danny Murphy
John Utaka	8	Jimmy Bullard
Nico Kranjcar	9	Clint Dempsey
Kanu	10	Diomansy Kamara
Pedro Mendes	11	Brian McBride
Sean Davis (for No. 11)	12	Leon Adreasen (for No. 10)
Sulley Muntari (for No. 3)	13	Eric Nevland (for No. 9)
Milan Baros (for No. 10)	14	

If Fulham left it late to beat the drop in 2007, they left it even later the next year. It was the penultimate game the previous season but in 2007–08, they scored the all-important goal with just 14 minutes of the season left. And it was the climax of a thrilling escape masterminded by Roy Hodgson. After the win at Eastlands, Fulham took on fellow strugglers Birmingham at a packed Craven Cottage and goals from McBride and Nevland earned them a 2–0 win. This win meant their fate was in their own hands. With Derby already relegated, the other two places were between Fulham, Reading, Birmingham and Bolton.

And with Birmingham thrashing Blackburn 4–1, Reading winning 4–0 at Derby and Bolton getting the point that guaranteed them safety at Chelsea, nothing less than a win would do. So, Fratton Park was the venue for the Cottagers' biggest game as a Premiership club. Just as 12 months earlier, Liverpool had the Champions League Final to look

Danny Murphy's goal at Fratton Park which kept Fulham up.

forward to, so Pompey were a week away from the FA Cup Final. Although Harry Redknapp fielded almost his strongest line up (only James, Campbell and Muntari were missing from the Cup Final starting side), thoughts of Wembley may have been on their minds.

Over the season, the Fulham team had changed substantially. There were only five survivors from Sanchez' first match (Konchesky, Davies, McBride, Dempsey and Kamara). By the end of the season, Hangeland had become a towering presence in midfield, Hughes his dependable partner, Murphy was inspirational in midfield and Bullard an impish presence who confused his colleagues as much as the opposition. For all that was at stake, however, nobody was calmer then Hodgson, and his team played in the same measured and controlled way. And on the final whistle, there was no triumphalism from the manager, just a dignified interview expressing his sympathy for Steve Coppell and Alex McLeish, the two relegated managers. This historic win was also a fitting way for captain Brian McBride, who had contributed so much, to sign off from British football.

Fulham complete amazing escape act

Danny Murphy's 76th-minute header proved enough to secure Fulham's Premier League status as they beat Portsmouth, despite a nervy display.

Fulham were heading for relegation, with rivals Reading and Birmingham winning, until Murphy's strike.

The Cottagers created little else in the match, but when Murphy rose to power in Jimmy Bullard's free-kick, their travelling fans celebrated wildly.

Fulham had never before won three Premier League away matches in a row.

And for long long spells it had seemed to be an impossible mission. Fulham started the day knowing that their future was in their own hands – a win would see them escape relegation regardless of what Reading and Birmingham did in their matches, barring Reading scoring an improbable number of goals against Derby.

It should have seen them play with drive, determination and desire, but instead they seemed paralysed by nerves. They were faced by Portmouth players who had two incentives – to arrest a run of three consecutive defeats and to stake their claim for a starting place in the FA Cup Final line up.

But the hosts appeared unwilling to break to a sweat, which should have played into Fulham's hands, yet they could find no rhythm or penetration. Bullard attempted to spray the ball around, but with little movement from his team-mates it was not proving easy.

In the Portsmouth midfield, Pedro Mendes – making his return to the starting line-up – was struggling to assert himself, despite being informed he was playing for a Wembley spot.

Simon Davies' early shot was the only effort on goal that Fulham managed in the first half, even though they must have realised results elsewhere were not going their way.

At that point, their relegation rivals were winning their matches and the Cottagers were staring the Championship in the face.

And it might have been worse for them had Kanu been up with play to turn a John Utaka cross mid-way through the first half, or if Jermain Defoe had kept his stabbed shot under the bar after being played in by Glen Johnson.

Soon after the break, Fulham got their second sight of goal but Murphy's header was comfortably saved. But the visitors knew that if they continued to defend well they had a lifeline. However, their toothless attack was a cause for concern.

And as Fulham continued to look jittery, Bullard tried a speculative long-range shot which left boss Roy Hodgson clearly displeased by his player's decision and the execution. And as the visitors tried to build up momentum there was a passage of head tennis after a corner but Pompey managed to clear.

Another set of corners saw Portsmouth scrambling to get the ball away, but again Fulham could not break through.

And then it came. A free kick from the right was superbly delivered by Bullard and an unmarked Murphy nodded the ball into the corner. It sparked scenes of jubilation in the stands, although Hodgson looked unmoved. The Fulham boss must have been concerned about the 14 minutes his side needed to hold on.

But he need not have worried as his side kept Pompey out, and kept themselves in the top flight with an historic victory – and their first at Fratton Park.

Danny Murphy and Jimmy Bullard celebrate beating the drop.

Fulham 2 v Manchester United 0

Saturday 21 March 2009
FA Premiership
Referee: P. Dowd
Attendance: 25,622

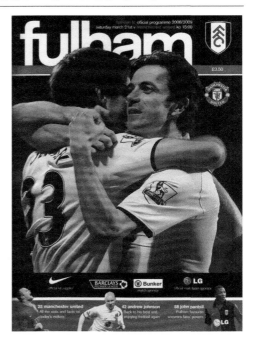

FULHAM		MANCHESTER U
Mark Schwarzer	1	Edwin Van Der Sar
John Pantsil	2	John O'Shea
Paul Konchesky	3	Rio Ferdinand
Aaron Hughes	4	John Evans
Brede Hangeland	5	Patrice Evra
Simon Davies	6	Darren Fletcher
Danny Murphy	7	Ryan Giggs
Dickson Etuhu	8	Paul Scholes
Clint Dempsey	9	Ji-Sung Park
Bobby Zamora	10	Christiano Ronaldo
Andrew Johnson	11	Dimitar Berbatov
Zoltan Gera (for No. 9)	12	Wayne Rooney (for No. 11)
Diomansy Kamara (for No. 10)	13	Carlos Tevez (for No. 2)
Olivier Dacourt (for No. 7)	14	

After the breath-taking escape from relegation, Hodgson went on to take Fulham to heights previously unimagined. In his first full season in charge, the club finished in seventh place, their highest-ever position and, through the Fair Play League, qualified for the newly-created Europa League. He did it with only a modest amount of spending (£10 million for Andrew Johnson was his one big buy) and by relying on the same group of players week in, week out. In fact, the back five of Schwarzer, Pantsil, Hughes, Hangeland and Koncheskey played in 36 of the 38 games. Hodgson did not avoid controversy. Selling Jimmy Bullard in mid season upset some supporters but proved to the right decision in playing and financial terms.

Yet it was not always obvious that this was the best Fulham team ever. Progress was slow and in the autumn the club was in the bottom six. But they learnt first to stop losing (six draws in seven games in the run up to Christmas) and then to start winning. The away record was still a problem. Without a win in 14 away games, seven draws (six of them goalless) was the best they could manage, it all changed with a trip to Bolton, and a surprise 3–1 win. They won two and drew one of the last four away games and three of the last four home games, which took the Cottagers to the dizzy heights of seventh.

The first of those home wins was a sparkling display against champions-elect Manchester United. Fulham had lost 3–0 at Old Trafford a month earlier in the League and just a fortnight before were thrashed 4–0 at home by United in the FA Cup. Another full house saw a thrilling game, with a penalty, two sendings off and the result in doubt until a brilliant goal three minutes from time. Hodgson's Fulham had arrived. Few of his team would have got into the United side, but on the day were the better side. The whole was greater than the sum of the parts, the secret of good management.

The inspirational Danny Murphy set up this marvellous win with a penalty and maintained the jinx he seemed to have over United.

FANTASTIC FULHAM BURST MANCHESTER UNITED'S BUBBLE

Unreal, quite unreal. It was supposed to be a gentle afternoon in the sunshine by the Thames for Manchester United, ready to prove their defeat by Liverpool was just a blip on their inexorable march to the title.

Instead, it ended in rare and unexpected darkness for Alex Ferguson's men, what with a resounding defeat by a magnificent Fulham side, just nine men left on the pitch and serious question marks over both his side's temperament and ability to stop the blip turning into a full-blown crisis.

You would loved to have known what Ferguson was thinking as he chewed impassively after Zoltan Gera had finished off United in the dying seconds, hooking in Fulham's second goal acrobatically.

His side had lost Paul Scholes and Wayne Rooney to sendings off, they had taken a first half hammering which few of his sides have ever experienced and tomorrow Liverpool have a chance of reducing their lead at the top to just one point.

And will he blame himself? The game changed after the interval once he had brought on Rooney for the totally ineffective Berbatov, but, by that point, they were struggling desperately after the double whammy moment in the 17th minute when Paul Scholes was sent off for handball on the line, allowing Danny Murphy to convert the penalty.

Ferguson ended the afternoon having to shepherd his players away from complaining at referee Phil Dowd, who late on incurred their wrath when he gave Rooney a second yellow for petulance in throwing the ball away.

Yet he will know they had no-one to blame but themselves. He had called for a stirring response after the Liverpool debacle and, apart from a major rally in the last half-hour when only the brilliance of Mark Schwarzer repeatedly kept a 10-man United at bay, he got only incoherence.

Indeed, United could probably count themselves lucky that they aren't losing Cristiano Ronaldo for a couple of games because, on a day when he too lost the plot with his posturing and moaning, he could easily have been sent off himself just before the end.

It was bizarre; amid laughs and chants of outrage, Ronaldo kept showing off the top of his thigh to Dowd to suggest that he had been assaulted by Fulham's defenders. If it had been one of his female admirers, it might have been different; the official was so unimpressed he gave Ronaldo, who had already been booked, a final warning.

Ferguson had threatened to attack any complacency and five changes from the Liverpool shambles proved his assertion. Dropping Rooney was calamitous, though.

United were curiously lethargic from the off as Fulham repeatedly bore down on them with the zest of a team which clearly felt a measure of release after their first away win of the season at Bolton the previous week, United were ragged and absent-minded.

Calamity befell them as Simon Davies slung the ball across from a corner; Bobby Zamora had one close range header clawed away by Van der Sar but, from the rebound, the striker nodded towards the top corner only for Scholes to instantly raise his hands to keep the ball out. He knew he was off.

Murphy's subsequent clinical finish from the spot was merely the signal for Fulham to batter United, Zamora keeping Van der Sar busy with shots from all ranges.

United were so under the cosh that the dismal Berbatov had to be sacrificed at half-time.

At least, Ferguson could have no complaint with the second half spirit as United, even with 10 men, finally began to make their class tell.

Ronaldo though was so frustrated after being the victim of one assault on his Achilles that he lunged in almost knee high at Murphy. If he had connected he would have been off; Dowd settled for the yellow.

Yet Ronaldo's wildness at least energised him and United. He forced one brilliant save from Schwarzer from a header before the Australian made an amazing double stop to keep out Park and Rooney.

Rooney's self-control deserted him as the clock ticked down, and he chucked the ball away in disgust, leaving Dowd no option but to send him off a few minutes after he'd been yellow carded for a foul on Olivier Dacourt. It put the seal on United's most wretched day of the season.

FC Basel 1893 2 v Fulham 3

Wednesday 16 December 2009
Europa League Quarter-final Second Leg
Referee: S. Johannesson
Attendance: 20,063

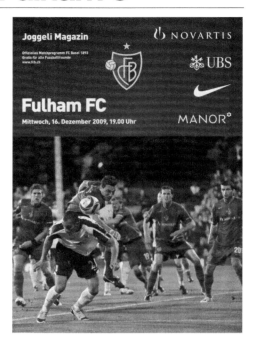

FC BASEL		FULHAM
Massimo Colomba	1	Mark Schwarzer
Samuel Inkoom	2	John Pantsil
David Abraham	3	Chris Smalling
Cagdas Atan	4	Aaron Hughes
Behrang Safari	5	Stephen Kelly
Carlitos	6	Bjorn Helge Riise
Cabral	7	Danny Murphy
Benjamin Huggel	8	Dickson Etuhu
Valentin Stocker	9	Jonathan Greening
Alexander Frei	10	Zoltan Gera
Marco Streller	11	Bobby Zamora
Xherdan Shaqiri (for No. 5)	12	Clint Dempsey (for No. 9)
Pascal Schurpf (for No. 6)	13	Damien Duff (for No. 11)
Frederico Almerares (for No. 7)	14	

In the Europa League campaign, Bobby Zamora emerged as a striker of real quality.

Remarkably for a club that just 13 years earlier was in 91st place in the Football League and which 15 months before was staring over the precipice of relegation, Fulham kicked off their 2009–10 campaign in a major European competition. Admittedly the Europa League was the Champions League's poor relation, and it would take 19 games to win the trophy (half a Premiership season), but the Cottagers had qualified in their own right and could well come up against some of the biggest names in Europe. The fixtures would unquestionably put a strain on playing resources and financially, it was not really worthwhile until the knock out stages. But the competition put Fulham in the big time and Roy Hodgson in territory with which he was very familiar.

It all started in the Lithuanian capital of Vilnuis in July, and one month and four qualifying games later, Fulham had won through to the group stage, at the cost of a serious injury to Andrew Johnson. In Group E, they were up against CSKA Sofia, FC Basel 1893 and AS Roma. The first five games produced eight points and the Cottagers went to freezing St Jakob Park in Basel just before Christmas knowing that only a win in the last match would save them from elimination. It looked a tall order. In their two group away games, Fulham had lost (controversially) in Rome and drawn in Sofia and in the decider were up against a Swiss side that had won all five of its previous Europa home games by two goals or more.

But a superb performance in which Hodgson's weakened team showed maturity, resilience and flair, saw Fulham edge through to the knock out stages. With 11 points, they finished runners up to Roma (13 points) and two ahead of Basel. And when the knock out stages of the competition started in February, Fulham would be joined by eight clubs which dropped out of the Champions League, including Liverpool, three of which the Cottagers were to meet. The real test was about to start.

Fulham stun Basel in the snow

Fulham withstood a second-half comeback to qualify for the last 32 of the Europa League with victory over Basel.

The superb Bobby Zamora met Bjorn Helge Riise's cross with an assured finish to open the scoring.

Zamora doubled the lead by heading in another Riise centre but Alexander Frei pulled one back from the spot after Chris Smalling handled.

Zoltan Gera slotted Fulham's third before Marco Streller nodded home a late corner to ensure a tense finish.

The result sees Fulham progress from Group E alongside Roma, who won 3–0 at CSKA Sofia to finish top of the pool.

In the first knockout round, Roy Hodgson's men will avoid fellow English clubs Liverpool and Everton but could face the like of Juventus, Marseille, Ajax, or Benfica.

Hodgson admitted before the match that he was more concerned about Saturday's visit of Manchester United in the Premier League, but he will surely be delighted with this win.

Basel had won all five of their previous European home games this season by two goals or more and Fulham were yet to win on their travels in the group stage.

But the Cottagers, whose line-up featured six changes from the one that started at Burnley last weekend, were worthy victors.

They got off to a bright start in snowy conditions at St. Jakob-Park and might have opened the scoring inside a minute when Basel failed to clear Riise's right-wing cross and Jonathan Greening came close to poking home.

Fulham's 4–4–1–1 formation denied Basel the chance to settle on the ball in attacking areas while their three-pronged central midfield of Murphy, Greening and Dickson Etuhu dominated possession and dictated the game's tempo.

Murphy saw a half-volley well-saved before Frei stepped inside Stephen Kelly but a poor touch enabled Mark Schwarzer to foil the Swiss striker.

That was Basel's only clear-cut chance in a one-sided first half and Fulham were rewarded for their superiority when Riise curled in a delightful cross from the right, which an unmarked Zamora met with a clinical finish at the back post.

Basel were furious that referee Stefan Johannesson waved away appeals for a free kick in the build-up to the goal but there was no excuse for their woeful marking.

Zamora, who had already seen a goal disallowed after collecting Riise's chip and slotting in the bottom corner, was causing the home defence no shortage of problems and deservedly doubled his side's lead three minutes later.

The 28-year-old diverted Schwarzer's long kick forward to Riise and the Norwegian stood up an inviting cross which Zamora met with a towering header for his ninth goal of the season.

With his side needing only a draw to progress, Basel coach Thorsten Fink introduced striker Frederico Almerares and the attack-minded Xherdan Shaqiri at the interval.

And, despite Zamora testing home goalkeeper Massino Columba with a deflected free-kick early in the second half, the changes initially had the desired effect.

Cheered on heartily by their boisterous supporters, Basel were suddenly enjoying the lion's share of possession and got themselves back into the match.

Smalling handled an Almerares cross and, after some confusion over whether Johannesson had pointed for a corner or a penalty, Frei lashed his spot-kick into the top left-hand corner.

With Fulham showing minimal attacking intent, it looked as though a full-scale comeback was inevitable.

But the goal merely proved a wake-up call for Fulham, who reasserted control over proceedings and then stretched their lead as a 15-pass move ended up with Gera applying a first-time finish to Kelly's cutback.

Basel continued to fight for their lives and Frei drilled a shot against the bar before Streller angled Valentin Stocker's corner past Schwarzer.

But Fulham held out and could even have grabbed a fourth when an unmarked Dempsey headed Riise's cross straight at Colomba.

Fulham manager Roy Hodgson: "Bobby Zamora carried on from where he left off in the Premier League. I thought he was very unlucky to have a first goal ruled out for offside, and he was a real thorn in the flesh of the Basel defence.

"I took him off as a precaution, he had a slight problem with his back. But he's got to be delighted with his performance.

"Bobby is one of our more popular players, he has a chant of his own and the fans seem to appreciate and like him.

"The one criticism is he hasn't scored enough goals but nine goals is a pretty good return for any forward. We were pretty good value tonight for the goals we scored and we could have scored more."

Fulham 4 v Juventus 1

Thursday 18 March 2010
Europa League Round of 16 Second Leg
Referee: B. Kuipers
Attendance: 23,458

FULHAM		JUVENTUS
Mark Schwarzer	1	Antonio Chimenti
Stephen Kelly	2	Fabio Cannavaro
Paul Konchesky	3	Fabio Grosso
Chris Baird	4	Jonathan Zebina
Aaron Hughes	5	Felipe Melo
Brede Hangeland	6	Hasan Salihamidzic
Damian Duff	7	Mauro Camoranesi
Dickson Etuhu	8	Mohamed Sissoko
Zoltan Gera	9	Antonio Candreva
Bobby Zamora	10	Diego
Simon Davies	11	David Trezeguet
Clint Dempsey (for No. 2)	12	Alex Del Piero (for No. 3)
Bjorn Helge Riise (for No. 9)	13	Paulo De Ceglie (for No7)
	14	Zdenek Grygere (for No. 9)

In the Round of 32, Fulham were paired with Shakhtar Donetsk the holders of the UEFA Cup (the Europa League's predecessor), with the first leg at home. Among the favourites for a second successive European title, the Ukrainian side (backed by oligarch Rinat Akhmetov) combined East European strength and determination with Brazilian flair. After a thrilling 2–1 win at the Cottage, Fulham put up a magnificent defensive performance in freezing conditions to come away with a draw and a 3–2 aggregate win. They had to travel 1,500 miles to meet a team that won the Ukranian Championship that season and were unbeaten at home.

Far from putting a strain on the players, several blossomed in this competition. Bobby Zamora and Zoltan Gera were outstanding, scoring spectacular goals but also contributing fully to the team effort. Hangeland looked immense when the pressure was on and Schwarzer was consistently brave, agile and dominating. In the Round of 16, Fulham achieved the most unlikely victory on a night of tension, drama and romance rarely equalled at Craven Cottage. For older fans, to see the Cottagers up against Juventus, among the aristocrats of European football (27 times Italian champions and twice European Cup winners) was a thrill in itself. To see Fulham players take on the likes of World Cup winning captain Cannavaro, and established internationals with impeccable pedigrees like David Trezeguet, Alex Del Piero and Fabio Grosso was something few ever thought possible.

But Fulham made it hard for themselves. Without the suspended Murphy, they lost 3–1 in Turin. All the goals came in the first half, with Juve leading 2–0 before Dickson Etuhu's away goal, a fortunate deflection, offered a lifeline. A goal from Trezeguet on the stroke of half-time, however, appeared to put the game beyond Fulham's reach. And within two minutes of the start of the home leg it got even worse, Trezeguet's snap shot making the aggregate score 4–1 to the Italian giants with 88 minutes remaining. What followed had the 23,458 crowd spellbound and the climax came in the 82nd, described by Patrick Barclay as 'a goal of ethereal beauty'.

In the European run, Simon Davies scored some crucial and brilliant goals, none more so than against Juventus.

Dempsey seals Fulham's amazing comeback

He had talked the talk and, on Thursday night, gloriously, irrepressibly, he walked the walk. Bobby Zamora led Fulham to an exhilarating, improbable, fabulous victory in the Europa League, trouncing and traumatising a shell-shocked Juventus. At Craven Cottage the Old Lady had an attack of the vapours.

Zamora had spoken of how he was going to give Fabio Cannavaro a hard time. It wasn't an empty threat. He did just that. Except then the veteran Italian international got himself sent off, a straight red card, perhaps harshly, perhaps a moment when his cynical play finally caught up on him, for bundling over Zoltan Gera with an hour to go. That lit the touch-paper on an already raucous response from Fulham.

At the final whistle, having over-hauled a deficit that, at one stage stood 4–1 in favour of the Italians after their first-leg 3–1 victory, and who were eventually reduced to nine men, Jonathan Zebina's injury-time dismissal for kicking out at Damien Duff, the disbelieving Fulham players went on an exhausted lap of honour. Alessandro Del Piero tried to escape but Simon Davies caught him to swap shirts — and who could blame him?

This was, probably, surely, the greatest night in Fulham's history and everyone who was here, except for the shell-shocked, silenced Juve supporters, will recall it time and time again.

They will recall the way in which Zamora, the much-maligned, much-criticised, and, at times, lumbering striker out-muscled the canny Cannavaro — using some of the defender's own dark arts to create space — to chest down and volley past 39-year-old, third-choice goalkeeper Antonio Chimenti who went on to have an horrific evening.

They will recall two goals from Zoltan Gera and they will recall, above all, the way in which Clint Dempsey shimmied along the edge of the penalty area to drift the most exquisite of right-foot chips up and over Chimenti and into the top corner of the net.

As the ball arced through the air, it was unerring. It was almost as if time stood still for the breathless Fulham supporters and how their team deserved such a brilliant goal to win a brilliant match and cap a brilliant performance, a brilliant comeback.

They march on into the quarter-finals of this competition, with the draw on Friday, but it's almost immaterial. An adventure that started last July in Lithuania and appeared to have died last week in Turin goes on and on.

Exhausted limbs are being dragged from match to match and this will be a season to remember. Juventus may be a pale-shadow of the side which once dominated Europe, twice wwinning the European Cup, but they are still studded with big names.

This was a big scalp with Fulham having already knocked out the holders, Shakhtar Donetsk and they did it without a dozen or so injured or suspended players.

None of the clubs left in the competition will want to play them such is the spirit, the organisation, the belief, instilled by manager Roy Hodgson whose reputation grows and grows. He was exuberant, disbelieving himself but when he looks back over what just happened he will know it was a match in which he out-coached Alberto Zaccheroni and his team out-played their much-vaunted opponents.

And to think, Juve had gone ahead after precisely 90 seconds with the kind of goal that crushes spirits. But not for Fulham. When Stephen Kelly and Brede Hangeland made a hash of clearing a routine cross, the ball broke to David Trezeguet and he swept it into the net. Silence.

And then a response. Despite the goal, fulham sensed an vulnerability. Juve creaked in defence and Chimenti, playing only his second game in two years, having conceded three goals at the weekend, looked shaky. So when Paul Konchesky crossed, Cannavaro went to ground and Zamora, in front of England manager — and former Juve coach — Fabio Capello scored. The striker then spun in the centre-circle to slide a pass to Gera who, as he collected the ball, and through on goal, was bundled into by Cannavaro.

Red card number one from referee Bjorn Kuipers. It looked harsh and the Italians were furious while Chimenti clawed away Zamora's free-kick. Fulham won another. This time Simon Davies lofted it against the cross-bar and the rebound struck Zamora and was scrambled away. From the corner, Dickson Etuhu smacked a header against the outside of the post. But Fulham were relentless and in the move of the match Konchesky played the ball into Zamora who cleverly flicked the ball up to Davies who squared it low for Ger to stab it in at the near post.

Fulham sensed something special and soon after the re-start Gera hared down the right, back-heeling a pass into the path of Duff whose cross struck Diego's hand. Unintentional but unmistakeably so and Kuipers pointed to the spot. Gera, calmly, side-footed home the penalty. Little wonder the Hungarian pointed to the heavens.

Having levelled up the tie Fulham, inevitably, lost a little momentum. It had taken some effort to get this far but, finally, they went again. Chimenti beat out a snap-shot from Davies, Dempsey, on as a substitute, had a header pushed away before the goalkeeper repelled Gera's shot.

As improbable as it seemed at kick-off, extra-time loomed. But not so. There was Dempsey's wonderful intervention after Etuhu rolled the ball into his feet and the Juve defenders, suicidally, stood off. What a goal, what a tie, what a night.

Fulham 2 v Hamburg SV 1

Thursday 29 April 2010
Europa League Semi-final Second Leg
Referee: C. Cakir
Attendance: 23,705

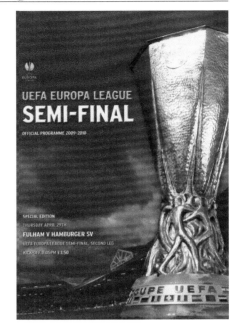

FULHAM		HAMBURG SV
Mark Schwarzer	1	Frank Rost
John Pantsil	2	Joris Mathijsen
Paul Konchesky	3	Dennis Aogo
Danny Murphy	4	Jerome Boateng
Aaron Hughes	5	Guy Demel
Brede Hangeland	6	Ze Roberto
Danian Duff	7	Robert Tesche
Dickson Etuhu	8	David Jarolim
Zoltan Gera	9	Jonathan Pitroipa
Bobby Zamora	10	Mladen Petric
Simon Davies	11	Ruud Van Nistelrooy
Eric Nevland (for No. 2)	12	Tomas Rincon (for No. 7)
Clint Dempsey (for No. 10)	13	Jose Paolo Guerrero (for No. 12)
	14	David Rozehnal (for No. 8)

Another player who rose to the occasion in Europe was Zoltan Gera, and his goal put Fulham in the final.

Like Juventus, Wolfsburg, Fulham's opponents in the quarter-final, found their way to the Europa League via the Champions League. The club, founded by carmaker Volkswagen, were reigning champions of Germany but had finished third in Manchester United's group. They had the dangerous Edin Dzeko upfront, who was later to join Manchester City. It was Zamora and Duff who scored for Fulham in the home leg, although a late German strike could have been expensive. But in Wolfsburg, Bobby Zamora's first minute goal settled Fulham's nerves and left the hosts in need of three goals to progress. They rarely threatened and so, after 16 games, Fulham found themselves in the last four of the Europa League, with Liverpool.

If ever a team had an incentive to win a semi-final it was Hamburg, the Cottagers' next opponents. The Final was to be played on their home ground. The German side had knocked out Eindhoven, Aderlecht and Standard Liege, all seasoned European campaigners on the way to the semi-final and held the distinction of never having been relegated from the Bundesliga since its formation in 1963. The previous season they were managed by Martin Jol who was then replaced by Bruno Labbadia. But days before the second leg at the Cottage, the manager and the club parted company and coach Ricardo Moniz was his temporary replacement. They were on a bad run and all was not well behind the scenes.

Volcanic ash meant Fulham had to make the 600 mile, 27-hour trip to Hamburg for the first leg by road rather than by air but this did not hinder the performance. Even with Ruud van Nistlerooy, who had scored nine times in 10 appearances against Fulham in their attack, the home side could not break down a solid Fulham defence in which Schwarzer and Hughes were outstanding. Gera and Dempsey might even have won it for Fulham but they returned to the Cottage knowing the Final was within their grasp. The ground was full to its 25,700 capacity and they were treated to another memorable evening of high drama.

FULHAM DO IT AGAIN TO DENY HAMBURG HOME FINAL

A critical away goal down, appearing spent, their talisman Bobby Zamora having limped off injured and exhausted, Fulham turned it around with two astonishing second-half strikes in seven crazy minutes to propel themselves in the final of the Europa League against Athletico Madrid on May 12.

Just when the history men appeared to be history, they did it. They had to win and they did. As ever, their manager Roy Hodgson held his nerve amid the din and delirium, a magnificently impassive figure at times but one imbued with a studied belief, a quality he has consistently transmitted to these players who were determined to succeed. And they did just that. How this old stadium rocked. How they blinked in utter, pinch-me disbelief.

This odyssey will now return to Hamburg, making one more trip, where next month's final will be hosted, having criss-crossed the continent since last July, starting in Lithuania against the obscure minnows of FK Vetra in a qualifying round, defeating the holders Shakhtar Donetsk, Juventus, Wolfsburg and now, another formidable Bundesliga club along the way.

The name of Hodgson and the players are written large for Fulham and in the club's folklore Simon Davies' breathtaking equalising goal, when all seemed over, will now take its place alongside Clint Dempsey's dink that did for Juve. It wasn't quite an evening as unforgettable as that victory over the Italians but it came mightily close and, in significance, surpassed it.

"You never give up man," Dempsey said last night and it's been the motto of this season. The t-shirts are probably being printed right now, with that as the slogan, and, at the final whistle, the players, to be honest, didn't quite know what to do. They caroused around, hugged and then stood motionless — while John Pantsil sprinted round on two, not just one, one-man laps of honour. Mohamed Al Fayed, also, was on the pitch, but, by then, Hodgson had simply disappeared. His night's work done.

Finally the heavens opened but the Gods had been smiling and Fulham deserved their indulgence. Such effort, such discipline, such organisation, such courage deserves its reward and the plaudits, too, will rain in just as they have increased throughout the last few months as Hodgson's heroes have held their own. And then some.

Players had been rested and recalled but this has been a trying campaign.

Mental effort, having to play catch up in the Premier League one after the other European tie, was catching up on a modest squad. The fact that Fulham so comfortably avoided any threat of relegation this season was almost as impressive as their cup deeds.

For this tie, the manager had feared the away goal, following the goalless affair of last week, and after Zamora, given a clear strike on just two minutes, with a clever exchange of passes with Zoltan Gera, was denied by goalkeeper Frank Rost, Hamburg rapidly took control.

They had shed their coach Bruno Labbadia earlier this week, having been hammered at the weekend at Hoffenheim, and they were galvanised into action, providing glimpses as to how they had qualified for the Champions League last season.

And no one more so than Mladen Petric. When Ze Roberto was brought down by Danny Murphy, a full 30 yards out, up stepped the dangerous Croat striker to loop a deceptive, left-footed free-kick which caught out Mark Schwarzer. The goalkeeper appeared to be at fault, for sure, losing the flight of the ball and the goal was like a punch to the solar plexus.

Prior to that it had been raucous, raw. Fulham were certainly dazed. Zamora, his fitness a problem, conceding too many fouls, was shackled by the powerful Jerome Boateng, who will join Manchester City for £11 million this summer, while the quicksilver Jonathan Pitroipa was an elusive threat for Hamburg and slammed a low shot narrowly wide while also being pulled up for offside as he threatened to double the advantage. It was knife-edge stuff with Petric threatening to twist the blade. The Germans had a grip and Fulham didn't appear likely to loosen it.

Zamora, in front of England manager Fabio Capello, and despite the urging of his name had to go. He was limping badly, the effects of the painkilling injection he had on his troublesome Achilles wearing off, and the introduction of Dempsey re-energised the home side. Damien Duff, who had probed and harried, squirted a shot across goal, after Dempsey was fouled and Paul Konchesky took a quick free-kick, while Schwarzer palmed up David Jarolim's lofted effort following more fine work from Petric.

And, then, from almost nothing, the breakthrough. Davies was at the heart of it, laying the ball off, with it eventually being ferried to Murphy, who picked out his fellow midfielder. Davies had by now arrived in the penalty area and flicked the floated pass up with his right foot, then deftly beat Guy Demel with another touch before, seamlessly, stabbing the ball into the net with his left foot before he was clattered.

Suddenly it was game on. Davies — Digger as he is known — had dug deep having appeared to be likely to be replaced. He now was limping back for the re-start but Fulham were up and running again. One more goal. Surely not? But how the impetus on such occasions can shift. Hamburg's confidence was fragile and was quickly smashed. Demel was again the fall guy. Fulham had kept their shape — Hodgson's mantra — and it was reaping its rewards.

They wore them down, this time the Hamburg defender failed to clear a corner, won by the hard-running Davies, and the ball broke to Gera who swivelled and steered his shot beyond Rost as the visitors froze, getting in the way of their own goalkeeper. It had been some turnaround.

Now it was Hamburg who were desperate, throwing players forward to try and rescue their own season. There was, agonisingly, plenty of minutes to go.

Fulham threw their bodies on the line, Aaron Hughes in particular aided by Brede Hangeland, but a chance finally fell to Ruud Van Nistelrooy inside the area. It was set up for the cruellest of turns but the veteran, dead-eyed assassin miscued and Fulham were through. Alive and kicking and strutting their stuff back to Germany. "Stand up if you still believe," the supporters had sang as their team trailed. They stood tall last night, and the still believe. The feel-good story of the season has a final chapter, in the final.

Fulham 1 v Athletico Madrid 2

Wednesday 12 May 2010
Europa League Final (in Hamburg)
Referee: N. Rizzoli
Attendance: 49,000

FULHAM		ATHLETICO MADRID
Mark Schwarzer	1	David De Gea
Chris Baird	2	Tomas Ujfalusi
Paul Konchesky	3	Luis Perea
Danny Murphy	4	Alvaro Dominguez
Aaron Hughes	5	Antonio Lopez
Brede Hangeland	6	Jose Antonio Reyes
Damian Duff	7	Paulo Assuncao
Dickson Etuhu	8	Raul Garcia
Zoltan Gera	9	Simao
Bobby Zamora	10	Diego Forlan
Simon Davies	11	Sergio Aguero
Clint Dempsey (for No. 10)	12	Eduardo Salvio (for No. 6)
Eric Nevland (for No. 7)	13	Jose Manuel Jurado (for No. 9)
Jonathan Greening (for No. 4)	14	Juan Valera (for No. 11)

And so to Hamburg, Fulham's second major Final, the first for 35 years, and their first in Europe. It was also their 19th Europa Cup tie and the 63rd first class game of the season, the most in the club's history. Schwarzer and Gera led the way, with 18 appearances each in the Europa, with Hughes (16+1), Zamora (16+1) and Hangeland (15) not far behind. In all 21 different players had made a start for Fulham in the competition. Goalkeeper Mark Schwarzer also played in 37 League games and five FA Cup ties in 2009–10, a total of 60 appearances, beating the previous best of 57 in a season by Peter Mellor and Alan Mullery in 1974–75.

In the Final, Fulham met Liverpool's conquerors, Athletico Madrid. They had finished fourth in the Spanish League the previous season and were knocked out of Chelsea's group in the Champions League. As well as Liverpool, Athletico had accounted for Turkish club Galatasaray, Sporting of Portugal and Valencia of Spain, three times going through on the away goals rule. In Diego Forlan, once of Manchester United, the Spanish club had the holder of Europe's Golden Shoe who averaged two goals every three games. Another familiar figure was Jose Antonio Reyes, who had scored for Arsenal against Fulham in 2004.

Fulham's entire allocation of tickets was sold out and there was a celebratory mood in the stadium. Manager Hodgson had injury-related selection problems with which to wrestle. Baird was preferred to Pantsil, who had suffered a cruciate ligament injury over Christmas and was left on the bench, while a less than 100% fit Zamora started with Dempsey as substitute. The game was decided in the 118th minute, with just two minutes of extra-time remaining. Heartbreaking as it was, it was better won properly than with penalties. And the game was a climax in more ways than one. For Roy Hodgson, the overwhelming choice of his peers as Manager of the Year, it was his last game in charge of Fulham. A memorable and record breaking period in the club's history came to an end.

Nobody achieved as much as a manager in so short a space of time as Roy hodgson, who transformed the club's fortunes in less than three seasons.

Brave Fulham fail at the death

Fulham had dealt with everything thrown at them in Europe this season, from the black-and-white shirted offspring of the Old Lady of Turin to Mother Nature's volcanic eruptions, but they were finally undone when Lady Luck decided to be a Spanish hussy for the night, shamelessly smiling on Atletico Madrid.

How cruel, how utterly unfair this defeat was on Roy Hodgson's relentlessly purposeful side, who lost to two suspect goals from Diego Forlan, the Manchester United discard who once again embarrassed English opposition. There's only one F in Forlan.

Fulham had 11 impressive men. Atletico only two: Forlan and Sergio Aguero. Fulham had reacted well to adversity, fighting back from Forlan's controversial opener to equalise brilliantly through Simon Davies. Fulham had dealt with the loss of Bobby Zamora and then Damien Duff, departing early as their injuries caught up with them.

The moment that made a mockery of sporting justice arrived deep into extra-time. When Aguero crossed, Forlan flicked the ball goalwards, his effort clipping Brede Hangeland to beat Mark Schwarzer and break Fulham's hearts. Nobody, just nobody, connected to Fulham Football Club deserved this iniquity.

Not Fulham's fans, who sang their hearts out for two hours, frequently chanting, "Stand up if you still believe," making a whole stand rise in salute to Hodgson's industrious players. The supporters' flags said it all: "England Expects, Fulham Believes." And they did.

The Fulham family had come from far and wide for this, from Dubai and Australia as well as south-west London, and they were not going to fall quite simply because a United reject had scored.

They lifted the volume when Forlan struck his first and particularly rallied when the Uruguayan added his second, attempting to console Hodgson's stricken players from afar. As Hodgson embraced his coaching staff at the final whistle, as Atletico's bench poured on to the pitch, Fulham's players slumped to the sodden turf.

Davies sunk to his haunches, shaking his head, unable to absorb what had befallen Fulham. Gera finally stopped moving, sitting still on the grass, emotionally and physically drained. Dickson Etuhu, who had grown in influence after half-time, lay there, his shirt draped over his face as if unwilling to face up to this disappointment. None of them deserved this most brutal of late blows.

None of Etuhu and Gera, Davies and the rest deserved to bow out like this after giving everything for so long, this game reflecting an extended season that had begun against FK Vetra in July. They merited something from this marathon, from running through the wall with such a small squad. They can reflect that Atletico's strike-force was worth more than £60 million, while their leading light, Zamora, could offer only 55 minutes before his Achilles gave way.

Hodgson will find little consolation but he can take pride in his team's performance. All of Fulham's qualities had been on display in the first half, particularly the resilience to recover from Forlan's goal after 32 minutes.

Fulham fans waved a banner proclaiming "Roy for Prime Minister" but the No 10 they needed to focus on was Aguero. Forlan took the goal but Aguero caught the eye.

The stocky, spinning top of an Argentine striker shimmered with menace in the first period, seizing on a rare poor piece of control by Murphy, darting down the inside-left channel before releasing Forlan. The Uruguayan tamed the ball with his left and then swept a low shot from left to right, clipping a post. This seasoned scourge of English defences was merely setting his sights.

Jose Antonio Reyes began the move for Forlan's goal, racing down the right with trademark pace before cutting inside and sweeping a crossfield pass to Simao. Atletico's left-winger knocked the ball back inside to Aguero, who flicked it up before scuffing a shot that appeared to be heading harmlessly through to Schwarzer. Desperately for Fulham, Forlan diverted it at speed into the goal.

Frustration briefly bit into Fulham, who must have suspected Forlan was offside, but all the officials signalled a goal, arguing that Hangeland played the Atletico forward on. Yet there is strength of character to Fulham under Hodgson, a belief in their ability to overcome adversity, as witnessed so thrillingly against Juventus and Hamburg in earlier rounds.

Fulham fans increased their volume, singing their hearts out for Hodgson's lads. Feeding on the supporters' energy, Murphy stepped up a gear, driving his team forward. Zamora, demanding one more shift from his creaking Achilles, suddenly stormed into life, cutting in from the left, overrunning the ball but nudging it on to Duff near the penalty spot.

The Irishman transferred it neatly to Gera, who lifted the ball towards the six-yard box. With Zamora lurking, Paulo Assuncao had to intervene, the Brazilian leaping up to head the ball away from Zamora but on to Davies, whose response was utterly mesmerising.

The Welshman's volleying technique had already been seen: the head still, the ball leathered, the save made by David de Gea, Atletico's highly-regarded young keeper. The Spanish teenager had no chance this time, Davies connecting so sweetly with the ball that it disappeared in a blur into the net. Davies' celebration matched the quality of the goal, almost emulating Marco Tardelli with his wild-eyed, fist-pumping slalom run.

As the tension of the second half mounted, Davies' ability to strike a dropping ball continues to alarm Atletico. But then, deep into extra-time, came Forlan. Lady Luck should be ashamed of herself.

ND - #0359 - 270225 - C0 - 275/195/14 - PB - 9781780912950 - Gloss Lamination